MILIEU

MILIEU

A Creaturely Theory of the Contemporary Novel

ELISHA COHN

STANFORD UNIVERSITY PRESS
Stanford, California

Stanford University Press
Stanford, California

©2025 by Elisha Cohn. All rights reserved.

Published with the support of the Hull Memorial Publication Fund of Cornell University.

No part of this book may be reproduced or transmitted in any form or by any means, electronic or mechanical, including photocopying and recording, or in any information storage or retrieval system, without the prior written permission of Stanford University Press.

Library of Congress Cataloging-in-Publication Data
Names: Cohn, Elisha, author.
Title: Milieu : a creaturely theory of the contemporary novel / Elisha Cohn.
Description: Stanford : Stanford University Press, 2025. | Includes bibliographical references and index.
Identifiers: LCCN 2024036673 (print) | LCCN 2024036674 (ebook)
  | ISBN 9781503641761 (cloth) | ISBN 9781503642379 (paperback) |
  ISBN 9781503642362 (ebook)
Subjects: LCSH: Fiction—History and criticism—Theory, etc. | Animals in literature.
Classification: LCC PN3331 .C64 2025 (print) | LCC PN3331 (ebook) |
  DDC 809.3—dc23/eng/20240813
LC record available at https://lccn.loc.gov/2024036673
LC ebook record available at https://lccn.loc.gov/2024036674

Cover design: Daniel Benneworth-Gray
Cover photograph: © Matthew Maran / naturepl.com

CONTENTS

	Acknowledgments	vii
	Introduction	1
ONE	Breaking the Zoo	35
TWO	Speaking Otherwise	62
THREE	Dog Friends	93
FOUR	Cat Kin	130
FIVE	Wilder Things	166
	Coda	200
	Notes	205
	Bibliography	245
	Index	265

ACKNOWLEDGMENTS

In completing this book, I benefited from considerable institutional support, including opportunities for collaboration sponsored by the Brett de Barry/Mellon Interdisciplinary Writing Group in 2014 with Antoine Traisnel, Samantha Zacher, and Peter Gilgen, and later the Society for the Humanities Writing Retreat in 2023. I am deeply indebted to many colleagues in the Cornell Literatures in English Department for their support, especially Shirley Samuels, Caroline Levine, Laura Brown, Masha Raskolnikov, Emily Fridlund, and Elizabeth Anker. I also enjoyed learning about texts and scholarship new to me from conversations with colleagues past and present: Amanda Jo Goldstein, Jenny Mann, Carol Warrior, and Juliana Hu Pegues. I want to acknowledge, as well, the work of *many* others at Cornell whose work I read in the course of researching this book; I am delighted to be able to cite so many of my own colleagues and dazzled by the range of fascinating projects happening all around me.

I am grateful to the Dean's Office in Cornell's College of Arts and Sciences for their sponsorship of a manuscript workshop, which afforded me the chance to discuss this project with scholars I greatly admire—Rita Felski, Kari Weil, Bénédicte Boisseron, and John Marx. To John, too, I am also grateful for editing and publishing my article "Paperback Tigers" in *Contemporary Literature* and soliciting an essay for the *Oxford Research Encyclopedia of Literature* that led me to read much more widely in the field and solidified my sense of the scope of this book. In writing a book in a new-to-me field, I also continued to benefit from the guidance of colleagues in Victorian studies, particularly Ivan Kreilkamp and Andrew H. Miller, who offered feedback and support. I benefited, too, from opportunities to present some of this work at the Birkbeck Centre for Nineteenth-Century Studies, as well as on panels at MLA and ASLE.

Working with graduate students has sustained this book in many ways. A seminar on affect theory in 2021 and 2023 gave me the opportunity to test some of my readings through conversation. Moreover, this project was often propelled by discussions with wonderful now-former students; working with them has immeasurably enriched my thinking about fictional form, embodied life, ecological crisis, and contemporary narrative. Kristie Schlauraff's work on sound in nineteenth-century gothic fiction prompted me to rethink sensory relationships in narrative. Christina Fogarasi's work on alternatives to the trauma model of first-person narration led me to new angles on contemporary fiction's resistance to individualism. Aaron Rosenberg and Molly MacVeagh, each in different ways, illuminated the evolution of realism in a period of climate crisis from the end of the Victorian period to the present. I have learned so much not only from sustained dialogue with each of them about individual novels but also from their published work—I am thrilled to cite their innovative scholarship.

In developing this manuscript, I am indebted to the expertise of Michelle Nieman and Kali Handelman, each of whom I consulted at pivotal points. I would also like to thank Mint Damrongpiwat for research assistance and Hunter Phillips for his scrupulous eye in helping me prepare this manuscript (as well as our new conversations about animal studies).

The care of friends made both direct and indirect impacts on this book. A profoundly supportive Facebook space for academic mamas of children born in 2018 played a unique role, not least because it spawned an online working group in which much of this book was drafted. Special recognition to Christina Marea and Mariah Schug for showing up week after week as we got things done despite all the chaos around us—perhaps someday we'll meet in real life. And my love and gratitude: to Irina Mikhalevich, for (among other things) the enduring convergence of interests that attuned me to perspectives in the philosophy of cognition; to Julia Chang, for being such a sharp and supportive listener; to Liz Anker, for endless advice, including transformative suggestions about the title of this book; to Ben Parris, for generously reading my work and offering biopolitics guidance over many years; and to Kasia Bartoszyńska, for lucid and galvanizing comments on drafts and enthusiasm for the project when I really needed it.

With so much love to my family, who offered me infinite encouragement and patience as I saw this through: my parents, my sisters, Theo, Miles, Elliott, and the cats who occupied my lap—Minna, Sylvie, and Pepito. This book is for Miles, who once coined the phrase "first-dog narrator," and Elliott, who wanted to know "how aminals make words."

MILIEU

Introduction

In Rachel Cusk's *Outline* (2014), creative-writing students resist when assigned to "write a story involving an animal." Finding it difficult to include an animal in their fiction, they argue that the instructor "intended . . . to present [them] with an obstruction."[1] Their complaint assumes that human characters are not animals, nor are animals an integral or ordinary part of the common life represented in fiction. But contemporary world literature suggests otherwise. Its animals are not obstructions but rather prompt formal innovations when they appear as companions, as populations in peril, and often both.[2] Precisely because animals have long been denied the capacity for subjectivity in the post-Enlightenment philosophical tradition, they are pivotal to contemporary fiction's interest in an alternative to individual character: world itself.

In this book, I show how contemporary fiction's animals prompt a distinctive reimagining of experiential *worlds* as *milieus*, where that center we often call self, subject, or character is inextricable from its context as a responsive organism. In novels by a range of global writers, this framework animates a rivalry between individual consciousness and the situated relations of the milieu that emerge through styles of perception. These narratives are interested in being in the "middle," or, as Georges Canguilhem puts it, "between two centers."[3] Theorizing milieu by narrating it, these novels evoke the embedded, processual,

1

sensory, and affective relations through which thinking emerges within an environment to create a perceptual world.[4]

Milieu's deep structure is profoundly at odds with individualism. Although the ancient Greek *ethos*, or character, also meant "habitat" or "milieu," character and environment have diverged because critics have focused on the critique of Enlightenment ideals that make individuality a disciplinary category.[5] For Kyla Schuller, in the nineteenth century the concept of milieu became a biopolitical tool for allocating and racializing the human as against animalized others: "biopower works by situating individuals in dynamic relation and calculating and regulating how their bodies affect one another within a milieu. It governs through a pervasive anomaly hierarchy that unevenly apportions the capacities of plasticity and determinism among a population."[6] Contemporary animal novels turn to milieu in a less deterministic way, without reinvesting in characters as autonomous, plastic individuals pitted against the supervening and deterministic systems that manipulate them. Their rendering of sentience also resists the logic of the "simultaneous modernization of the individual and maturation of the novel," in Nancy Armstrong's words.[7] In that influential view, the novel participates in a broader cultural consolidation of a speciated conception of human individuals as separate, interiorized selves, differentiated from the social and national backdrops against which they appear. In many contemporary novels that center animals, however, individual subjectivity and "character" are substantially reframed—still significant but also newly secondary, emerging out of distributive sensory processes that are reflected in narrative voice.[8] Narrative voice, in these texts, constitutes a dynamic and responsive environment for sentience.[9] Not only does the concept of milieu illuminate the central role of animals in contemporary fiction, but the new centrality of animals highlights how narrative style revises consciousness into a more capacious model of sentience, suggesting that the representation of animals should matter to any reader invested in the novel as a form.

The relationship between character and environment is an enduring issue in the history of the novel, and I would argue that nineteenth-century realism sets in play more recent possibilities of experiment. Gillian Beer shows that Victorian writers struggled with "the problem of finding a scale for the human . . . a scale that will be neither unrealistically grandiose, nor debilitatingly reductive, which will accept evanescence and the autonomy of systems not serving the human, but which will still call upon Darwin's often-repeated assertion: 'the relation of organism to organism is the most important of all relations.'" For Beer, the "moment-to-moment fulness" of evolutionary narratives highlights multispecies environments.[10] Such a moment comes in George Eliot's *Middlemarch* (1874–1875), concerned with representing the existential texture and possibilities of moral growth within a particular "middle." Certainly, when the narrator announces that "there is no creature whose inward being is so strong that it is not greatly determined by what lies outside it," the "creatures" the novel is most interested in are human. And yet one of its best-known passages—a quotation that operates as a little world unto itself—offers a relevant provocation. The narrator breaks from depicting a young woman's misery about her marriage to comment on the constraints of perception. The passage's tone mounts from authoritative, pseudo-statistical informativeness to wondering sublimity:

> That element of tragedy which lies in the very fact of frequency, has not yet wrought itself into the coarse emotion of mankind; and perhaps our frames could hardly bear much of it. If we had a keen vision and feeling of all ordinary human life, it would be like hearing the grass grow and the squirrel's heart beat, and we should die of that roar which lies on the other side of silence. As it is, the quickest of us walk about well wadded with stupidity.[11]

Turning away from the representation of the character's inward struggle, this passage offers the representation of an animal's life—its "palpitating life," as Eliot puts it later, as a reorientation of the human sensorium that might be possible in the evolutionary future of our own species. "Not *yet* wrought": what is for now a sublime distraction from the urgency of attending to the suffering of a human other is also a suggestion that narrative realism can enhance evolutionarily received modes of sense-perception. Eliot's claim is rooted in an understanding of percipience as shared with other animals but also different from the "coarseness" and fragility that marks ordinary human consciousness. While the passage claims to represent by negation what is not sensible, it proposes the use of other-than-currently-human perceptual faculties, suggesting the malleability of sensory orientations toward the world.[12] This attention to the milieus in which animals live adjusts human character space temporarily, but Eliot returns after this moment to investigating the complex and ordinary otherness of *human* thought and feeling.[13]

Contemporary fiction, though, often listens to the squirrel's heartbeat. And it does so with more sustained consequences for the fate of individual character.[14] For instance, Jon McGregor's *Reservoir 13* (2017) reshapes individuals' perceptions as sentience, subverting expectations around another conventional narrative of a young woman's tragedy. Written in the third person, it begins as detective fiction that would unravel the mysterious truth of a charismatic teen girl's disappearance from an English village. But this deeply anticlimactic novel ultimately focuses on a multispecies milieu rather than the fate of individuals. Increasingly untethered to its ostensible focus on a mysterious character's fate, *Reservoir 13* highlights multiple, proximate habitats and networks of care without ultimately landing on a character-driven solution to the murder. The prevalence of environmental description, interspersed with reflections on individuated characters, suggests so strong an investment in "setting" as a context for human life as to reframe the village space as a responsive milieu for multispecies habitation. Readers may be initially seduced by wanting to solve the young girl's disappearance, but the novel makes clear that such a rationale for the representation of this place is a pretext.

If in *Middlemarch* "ordinary life" is mostly human, in *Reservoir 13* long, seasonally oriented passages describing animal communities are everywhere interspersed with the registration of human habits of living among the reticent inhabitants of a Derbyshire village. The narrative voice flattens distinctions, moving in long paragraphs among thoughts, which are reported through free indirect discourse; conversations unmarked by quotation marks; and passive-voice depictions of human actions, landscapes, and animal behavior.[15] McGregor at once highlights a sense that any character might exemplify a larger population's modes of being, feeling, and doing but also rejects it. *Reservoir 13* holds individuality and population in tension. But it also deflects its focus from the revelation of human inwardness toward creaturely ongoingness. As a representative sample, the following passage emphasizes the village as a dynamic environment:

> Les Thompson walked his fields in the evening while the sun was still warm on the grass. In the beech wood the fox cubs were taken away from their dens and taught to find food for themselves. A white hooded top was found in a clough on the top of the moor.... The make and design were confirmed as a match by the missing girl's mother. The forensic tests took weeks and were inconclusive. (86)

A declarative, poignant style often structured by the passive voice allows small pleasures and seasonal rhythms to predominate over a character center. What would, in another novel, look like disorientation thanks to the relentless metalepsis, here accrues a sense of careful attention to lateral relations that depend on enmeshment in a shared environment.[16] The novel's attitude toward character profoundly affects the impact of the formal device. In Jean Genette's foundational account, metalepsis is a "a shifting and sacred frontier between two worlds": the borders between levels in this case reflect distinctions in how different species perceive, evoking networks that share space but often do not interact directly.[17] For instance, when McGregor's narrator comments on a group of young fox cubs, "The edges of the territory were understood," the narrative traverses internal boundaries in order to evoke a convergent sense of place.[18] People move in and out of the village, which is far more porous than its rural locale would suggest; but while the dead girl and her family are outsiders, destabilizing the village milieu, over the course of the novel it returns to a tentative stasis, achieved through its aesthetic of distributive attention that seems to model the low-key inhabitation it reports. The modulation of narrative voice is key to its substitution of milieu for character, and creature for human.

McGregor's novel offers a particularly distilled example of current narrative practices for highlighting the dynamics of multispecies interconnections, and conversely, suggests the consequences of attunement to multispecies relationships for narrative form.[19] In this book, I show that a transnational group of contemporary novels, read along with theory from a range of disciplines, especially comparative cognition, Black studies, and Indigenous studies, converge around concepts of milieu as a site and a theory of aesthetic value. Each chapter foregrounds formal resonances in texts from the mid 1990s through the present, including work by Yann Martel, Haruki Murakami, Téa Obreht, Yoko Tawada, NoViolet Bulawayo, Sigrid Nunez, Jesmyn Ward, Linda Hogan, Lucy Ellmann, Amitav Ghosh, and Aminatta Forna. Their negotiation of narrative voice affords less individualistic assumptions about perception to affirm that humans too are an animal species. These readings challenge scholarly approaches that understand animal narratives as biopolitical allegories of citizenship and population. Drawing on accounts of milieu from Jacob von Uexküll, George Canguilhem, and Sylvia Wynter in particular, I show how fiction redresses what has become a firmly entrenched, mutual reinforcement of literary form and biopolitical capture. Animal allegories can be extremely effective narrative forms for biopolitical diagnosis: they present animal lives as politically pointed models of human abjection. Moreover, critical reading that turns on allegory is often subtended, however unintentionally, by a liberal humanist sensorium that valorizes the epistemic labor of arriving at an abstract, disembodied knowledge of systems.[20] In *Milieu*, I argue that recent animal novels show a diminished reliance on allegorical figuration, oscillating between abstraction and resonance to evoke what biopolitical allegories demonstrate has already been devalued or excluded, and invite a less allegorical method of critical interpretation.[21] This view emerges from a critical middle ground—between allegory-as-critique and the postcritical—to show how animal narratives contribute to literary knowledge production.

The explosion of animal fictions in recent decades tracks with two cultural shifts since the 1990s: the evolution of pet culture and the widespread awareness of ecological catastrophe.[22] Ecological activism and biopolitical suspicion have been mainstream throughout most of these writers' lives and educations. One might argue that, under these ever more urgent circumstances, animal fictions—especially those that fixate on an individual human's response to an individual pet—constitute a contained or depoliticized response to environmental threats to a distinctively human existence. However, what the inclusion of animals often truly means for the novel form complicates that sentimental frame. The novels I discuss use the formal affordances of narrative favored by postcritical methods—mood, tone, pace, voice—to evoke non- and less anthropocentric modes of world-making. These stylistic modes, even when used in allegorical frameworks that put other-than-human animal lives to human purposes, center the material dimensions of perception that are often difficult to put to immediate political use. In avoiding, deferring, or complicating modes of figuration—and critical interpretation—that confirm human privilege, the novels I examine depart from the framework of the individual and turn to milieu. At the same time, they propose the relevance of a distinctively literary epistemology to conceptualizing the present-day peril of living in a multispecies world.

1. THEORIZING MILIEU

This book highlights the enduring theoretical significance of milieu to show how theory of the novel and animal studies share a commitment to form as world-making. The concept of milieu presents the structure of perceptual worlds as inherently formal. The term comes first from Jean-Baptiste Lamarck's *Zoological Philosophy* (1809), where it refers to the circumstances that enable and constrain an organism's development; for Lamarck, the concept is neither wholly deterministic (development is absolutely determined by environment) nor strongly agential (organisms form through relations to their physical and social environments).[23] Auguste Comte's *Course on Positive Philosophy* (1830–1842) would soon go on to apply the term to human culture.[24] Twentieth-century uses of the term increasingly justify claims for the common deep structure of sentience across species lines. Georges Canguilhem develops the term in his essay "The Living and Its Milieu," where he theorizes it as an extension of the turn-of-the-century German ethologist Jacob von Uexküll's concept of *Umwelt*. For von Uexküll, *Umwelt* means the production of an organism's perceptual world as actively created, a process shaped by that organism's perceptual orientations. *Umwelt* was and remains an influential term in comparative cognition because it accounts for the common conditions of sensitive being. In work on multispecies cognition by Franz de Waal, Ed Yong, and many others, *Umwelt* is still a generative concept not only for bypassing the subject-object divide that has structured post-Cartesian philosophy but also for rejecting a parsimonious attribution of sentience to other-than-human animals. Moreover, recent theorists and literary scholars, like Elizabeth Grosz and David Herman, use *Umwelt* to explain the possibility of artistically modeling nonhuman perception and imagining animal perception as the basis of art's world-making.[25] In this section, I consider the relevance of both terms, but I ultimately favor "milieu" because it expresses how multiple *Umwelten* relate: animals do not share an *Umwelt* with other species—it is always quite literally *specific*—but we do share a milieu. Shifting from *Umwelt* to the more explicitly relational paradigm of milieu ultimately accounts more powerfully for the broader convergence of phenomenality across species worlds, explaining how separate and mutually opaque perceptual worlds interrelate in multispecies communities. It also ultimately offers a stronger connection between ethology and ecology, highlighting vulnerability and interdependence.

Von Uexküll offers a biosemiotic understanding of each organism's perceptual world that generates meaning in response to a biological "demand." Perception is autotelic and self-regulating: "environment forms a self-enclosed unit, which is governed in all its parts by its meaning for the subject."[26] This framing suggests an isolated and foreclosed set of sensory possibilities: other-than-human *Umwelten* are "opaque" from the outside, as Yong writes. Yet von Uexküll's emphasis is on the reciprocal genesis of meaning that affords action, and action that makes meaning.²⁷ His concept presents living creatures as self-contained, impressible, and vulnerable, but also as responsive, active, and capable. As in James Gibson's now-familiar midcentury concept of affordances, developed with respect to animal cognition, the environment and the creature collaborate in generating an integrated suite of potentials for feeling and action. Each creature experiences a world that emerges through its perceptual capacities—a fundamentally formal matter because relations are themselves perceptual structures, and perceptual structures are relations; as Alva Noë explains *Umwelt*, "all animals live in structured worlds."²⁸

Umwelt is self-organizing: a world is actively produced according to its own potential for perceptibility by a given creature, creating what Canguilhem would call that creature's "vital norms" of response to material conditions. Each creature norms itself within the parameters of its species and experiences a reciprocal if delimited relation with a meaningful world because it exists in response to specific distributions of perceptibility. The concept is indebted to Kantian ideas of the subject, but "the subject" here is without the disciplinary self-sovereignty, self-reflexive consciousness, or human distinction that we usually associate with that word. Subjectivity remains immanent to the process that elicits it—an understanding that Jennifer Fleissner, identifying Canguilhem's understanding of the interaction between self and world, calls "a novelistic view—that we need the entire story in order to make sense of what precedes."²⁹

Umwelt is a deep structure of sentience that can foster connections among disciplines. After a long mid- to late-twentieth-century period in which the study of animal cognition downplayed animal sentience as unverifiable, philosophers of comparative cognition have become eager to recognize that "animals are sentient beings who live in community," in Kristen Andrews's words.³⁰ *Umwelt* has played a significant role in advocating for animal cognition as a legitimate object of study. The term has advantages of "elegance and utility," as Rachell Powell puts it, because it suggests that "the unified structure of experience is not a radically contingent accident of human, primate, or even vertebrate evolution. Rather, it is a law-like feature of the evolutionary process that is intimately connected to the emergence of image-forming sensory modalities."³¹ In understanding *Umwelt*'s "unified structure of experience" as the result of evolutionary convergence, Powell emphasizes that what we call "experience" structures all sentience. This claim is not unlike Pheng Cheah's phenomenological account of worlding, where the terminology differs but the point is markedly similar: "the unification of the world as a meaningful whole is associated with practices of collective existence."[32] *Umwelt* also ultimately suggests how much human sapience shares with that of other animals.[33]

Turning to Canguilhem's concept of milieu helps extend von Uexküll's concept to humans, particularly because his idea of milieu comes to play an underrecognized role in biopolitical theory, as I discuss shortly. But first, it is worth differentiating von Uexküll's work from that of Martin Heidegger, whose account of world has been more obviously central to biopolitical thought. Giorgio Agamben emphasizes the privative dimension of *Umwelt* as developed by Heidegger, prefacing a brief discussion of von Uexküll with the Heideggerian epigraph, "No animal can enter into relation with an object as such."[34] For Heidegger, fundamentally, "the stone is worldless, the animal is poor in world, man is world-forming," but world-formation happens primarily through an orientation toward death. Humans die, anticipating and experiencing death as "as such," whereas animals merely perish: Heidegger writes, "Let the term dying stand for the way of being in which Dasein is towards its death. Thus, we can say that Dasein never perishes. Dasein can demise as long as it dies."[35] Heidegger's distinction between human and nonhuman asserts a fundamental and abyssal difference governed by the conceptualization of death as the end of life. Von Uexküll's framing of animal perception, in contrast, focuses on competencies during life, and his work is generally understood as anti-anthropocentric because it stresses the underlying logic of world-formation and world-maintenance that is consistent across life forms. Antoine Traisnel comments that von Uexküll offers a way of thinking of the interdependency of our "absolutely enclosed worlds," while implying that for humans too, "what we take to be the world is but a worldview conditioned by the horizons of our own singular perceptual facilities."[36]

Canguilhem's development of the term "milieu" in his essay "The Living and Its Milieu" builds upon *Umwelt* to account for relationality beyond the scale of an individual creature's perceptual sphere. His goal is to explain how an environment affords human knowledge-production, yielding an idea of milieu that is more clearly social and nondeterministic, and less opaque, than von Uexküll's *Umwelt*. Canguilhem differentiates between *Umwelt* as a "a specific behavioral milieu" that reflects the norms of perception *within* a species and "milieu" as the relations among these centers of meaning-making—the medium in which perceptual worlds can interact and converge.[37] In other words, despite the mutual opacity of *Umwelten*, relationships and interactions are afforded by what the environment offers. As in the idea of *Umwelt*, a milieu is accessible because of the semiotic richness of a material world produced reciprocally through sensation, perception, mood, appetite, and emotion; it is a proceeding from the "middle" of the sensory surround that unites species.[38] Thus, as if in answer to philosopher Kelly Oliver's question "How can we share the earth with creatures with whom we do not even share a world?," the notion of milieu shows that even if the world of a given species is distinct, worlds are always in relation and share the fact of their structuredness.[39]

For Canguilhem, the key implications are indeed for considering the structure of human thought: milieu frames the senses as foundational to any explanation of historically contingent human structures of meaning. Human knowledge-production—like any other-than-human-animal cognition—requires, responds to, and recursively produces a milieu:

> if science is the work of a humanity rooted in life before being enlightened by knowledge, if science is a fact in the world at the same time as it is a vision of the world, then it maintains a permanent and obligatory relation with perception. . . . From the biological and psychological point of view, a sense is an appreciation of values in relation to a need. And for the one who experiences and lives it, a need is an irreducible, and thereby absolute, system of reference.[40]

For Canguilhem, emphasizing the role of milieu in human thought and behavior means reflecting on the production of knowledge from within disciplinary formations, in which the meaningfulness of claims is context dependent. As in Sylvia Wynter's later idea of the sociogenic principle, in which the stories we tell and knowledges we make dynamically impact our physiological and neurobiological being, methods make environments for thought.[41] The word "milieu" in this sense has often cropped up to describe cultures of literary criticism in recent years. For example, Rita Felski's *The Limits of Critique* (2015), she identifies "routines of scholarly life" that "suffuse our milieu," while in Nathan Snaza's *Animate Literacies* (2019), critics must contextualize the act of reading as occurring "within a much wider milieu" that involves "a range of material and nonhuman agencies."[42] Such emphasis on how environment and method mutually predicate one another highlights the contingency of disciplinary structures of knowledge-production on the material affordances of the environment. As when we describe a concept as a "site" of value, a theory of milieu as a mode of disciplinary formation suggests that meaning is an emergent, reciprocal quality of a situated response to an environment.

If we understand milieu in this way, its potential as a multidisciplinary concept becomes clear. For my purposes, I emphasize that literary analysis offers an underrecognized contribution to theorizing multispecies inhabitation of worlds because milieu is a formal and often narrative concept. Indeed, philosophers of cognition rely on technical narrative concepts to express problems of conceptual access to "other" experiences. For example, Thomas Nagel's influential essay "What Is It Like to Be a Bat?" (1974) turns on the use of simile that raises the possibility of achieving an "objective phenomenology."[43] Nagel argues that we cannot know "what it is like" to be nonhuman. The problem, Nagel suggests, is epistemological, but also *narrative*, a problem of the conflation of objectivity with a "third-personal" voice: "The fact that we cannot expect ever to accommodate in our language a detailed description of ... bat phenomenology should not lead us to dismiss as meaningless the claim that bats ... have experiences fully comparable in richness of detail to our own."[44] Sylvia Wynter asks of Nagel: "What kind of methodology, analogous to that of the natural sciences, yet different from it, would such an 'objective phenomenology' call for?" Reading Nagel with Frantz Fanon, she emphasizes the value of first-person accounts in understanding not only the physical laws but also the sociogenic laws that determine inward experience, making "the human" look like an "artificial" and "relative" category rather than a biological one.[45] For Wynter, Nagel's "what is it like?" can be repurposed as a provocative question for understanding the racial predicates of phenomenal life within a given, recalcitrant context, where systematic ontological negation becomes the ground of lived experience. I will return to Wynter's account shortly, but I stress here her point that attending to the perspective from which we narrate experience matters deeply, and that another of those "methodologies" for grasping an objective phenomenology might be even more explicitly literary. We humans are, she suggests, ultimately a "storytelling species."[46] Along with elegance and utility, then, milieu has an underrealized *literariness* that registers across disciplines.

The figurative dimension of Nagel's "what is it like?"—the idea that simile could be the basis of validating an irreducible and perhaps even unshareable phenomenological reality—suggests (however unintentionally) that *style* makes the rich worlds of nonhuman species *imaginable*.[47] To return to von Uexküll, he too anticipates that narrative forms afford and constrain radically different images of creatures' inner worlds: in the midnineteenth century, he argues, "'homology' became the basis of an entirely new theory about the relations between different bodily forms, whereas 'analogy' came into disfavor, and in this way dead spatial relations took the place of the vital reciprocal influence of the organs on each other."[48] Here, he distinguishes a term that highlights correspondence of structure with one that emphasizes resemblance of form or function; it is the active "response to the motions of the other" that is implicated in the very form through which animal thinking is conceptualized. More recently, too, when someone like Powell argues that "*Umwelt* is a first-person portal on the world" when reflecting on the priority that the philosophy of cognition has long accorded to third-personal perspectives, she likewise implies that aesthetic strategies have explanatory force.[49]

Recovering the ethological origins of the idea of milieu highlights its fundamentally aesthetic conception of other-than-human embodied living. It is aesthetic in Jacques Rancière's sense of the work of art "as the means of participating in the configuration of a specific milieu."[50] The medium of the artwork accomplishes a certain "distribution of the sensible"—its milieu emerges from the "delimitation of spaces and times, of the visible and the invisible, of speech and noise."[51] Similarly, in Gilles Deleuze and Félix Guattari's expansion of von Uexküll, milieus emerge and change aesthetically, through "rhythm." First, they establish a definition of milieu as immanence:

> Every milieu is vibratory . . . a block of space-time constituted by the periodic repetition of the component. Thus the living thing has an exterior milieu of materials, an interior milieu of composing elements and composed substances, an intermediary milieu of membranes and limits, and an annexed milieu of energy sources and actions-perceptions. Every milieu is coded, a code being defined by periodic repetition.[52]

As in Canguilhem's account of the "betweenness" in which perception happens, here milieu depends upon but differs in scale from the centeredness of experience within an *Umwelt*. Applying this vision of milieu to animal behavior, Deleuze and Guattari present rhythm as an aesthetic category that affords the immanence of territories from within milieus. Far from anarchic or formless, it is manifest through structure: "Territorialization is an act of rhythm that has become expressive, or of milieu components that have become qualitative. The marking of a territory is dimensional, but it is not a meter, it is a rhythm."[53]

Citing the emergence of a milieu from rhythms of repetition and difference that make a world out of perceptions, these theorists offer an affirmative vision of art that originates in other-than-human world-building.[54]

To affirm "having a world" or "world-making capacities" has become a nearly ubiquitous marker of value across many disciplines far beyond the sciences of mind. Rendering the explanatory force of "world" as milieu reveals surprising convergences across disciplines, from a path not taken in biopolitical thought to Black and Indigenous studies to the philosophy of comparative cognition. An everyday recognition of phenomenality subtends a wide range of critical practices oriented toward social justice—this central notion of world-making proves extraordinarily mobile across disciplines.[55] Wynter, as I discussed earlier, offers a revisionist account of Nagel's interest in the psychoaffective dimensions of embodied life in order to ask how a Black subject is "made to experience objects in the world, in the terms of its specific culture's system of perception and categorization as being to its own adaptive advantage (good), or not to its own adaptive advantage (bad)." She emphasizes how the social and cultural determinants of a human life depend upon an often pernicious logic of milieu, underlying the individual organism's embedded responsiveness to a social environment that is "culturally Westernized in the ethno-class terms of 'Man.'"[56] Snaza highlights the uneven possibilities of milieu in Wynter's approach: "While literacies form the material and affective milieu in which any human (or other entity) takes shape, it is only statist literacy that makes some humans Man."[57] It is on this kind of basis that Stefano Harney and Fred Moten offer an alternative image of environments for thought, insisting upon of the "blackness of the surround" as a strategy for preserving a "common" life. Their approach highlights that an emphasis on the "individual organism" is what makes being in "the world" a felt harm.[58] In Moten and Harney, opening out from Wynter's insight into the link between phenomenal experience and cultural surround, the injunction to perceive the surround qualitatively evokes the distinctive capacities of the concept of milieu to suggest *both* the profound limitations of a concept of individual autonomy *and* the common vulnerability and openness that constitutes the grounds of sentience.

This work demands recognition of both the value and the challenges of milieu for questions about difficult allegiances. Bénédicte Boisseron affirms that *Umwelt* affords an "essential" additive understanding of worlds that are intersectional without phenomenally intersecting.[59] Jen Rose Smith, working in critical geography on Indigenous landscapes, establishes that the notion of milieu activates the interdependent emergence of material spaces and more-than-human socialities, but she also stresses the pernicious racialization that conflates Indigenous people with their environments.[60] Milieu, in this framing, is a problem concept if it is captured by "managerial" scientific frameworks like statistics that tend to intensify this conflation. For Smith, a multidisciplinary approach is more accommodating of nondeterministic visions of situated environmental relationships. Fields oriented toward social justice seek "epistemologies that are nonhierarchial and nonhuman centered," as Dian Million describes the basic tenets of Indigenous studies. Such perspectives invite self-reflection about how presumptions about what counts as knowledge and as knowable impacts conceptions of "world," including multiple-world ontologies.[61]

Thinking in terms of milieu also invites reflection on what is *not* knowable and how to proceed from there: conceptualizing the opaque (a word important to Yong's popularization of von Uexküll), Édouard Glissant presents the fundamental opacity of the "world" of the other as nonetheless accessible via a nonhierarchical "poetics of relation." For Glissant, what this poetics "relates, in reality, proceeds from no absolute, it proves to be the totality of relatives, put in touch and told."[62] He offers an apt description of multiple milieus as representing a nontotalizing multiplicity of phenomenal worlds. Indeed, Glissant's "touch," which does not depend on *penetrating* an other's opacity, offers a compelling image of intimate proximity within an environment.[63] This approach neither romanticizes nor denies opacity, but supposes a set of functional relationships among differently structured modes—precisely what Canguilhem identifies as a milieu.

If milieu indexes the convergence of phenomenal experience, "world" as a synonym also indexes the coming together of commitments to the phenomenological relationality of embodied life across many academic fields. This sense of world—*this idea of worlds as sensed*—which is so portable across disciplines also reframes human consciousness in the creaturely terms of milieu without equating or even minimizing differences. "Milieu" and "world" are terms that bring fields together, making it possible to recognize already shared conceptual commitments. Isabelle Stengers, like Canguilhem, emphasizes that milieu (which she terms "situation") demands reflection on the production of knowledge: "Being capable of situating oneself—situating what one knows, and actively. Linking it to questions that one brings in and to ways of working that respond to it—implies being indebted to the existence of others who ask different questions, importing them into the situation differently, relating to the situation in a way that resists appropriation in the name of any kind of abstract ideal."[64] So if explaining concepts like *Umwelt* and milieu prompts other-than-literary scholars accounting for the sensual aconceptuality of these concepts to turn to an aesthetic and even narratological vocabulary, this suggests an opportunity to observe the distinctive contributions of the novelistic imagination to recognizing the convergent structure of sentience across species.

2. FROM ALLEGORY TO MILIEU

By arguing that novels present "world" as milieu, I emphasize the specific resources of literary fiction for making the perceptual worlds of animals appear without appropriating them. In attending to animals—both in the novel as a form and in the world—I pose what looks like a biopolitical question about who counts or belongs to fiction; yet I emphasize that biopolitics remains a framework that struggles to account for the milieus of human and other-than-human creatures except in abstract terms that belie their phenomenality.[65] The deep formal structure of experiential "world" complicates the otherwise all-too-compelling idea that literary form reinforces biopolitical capture. Thus I elevate alternatives to biopolitical criticism by emphasizing the conjunctions of animal studies with rejections of crisis narratives in Black studies, Indigenous studies, and postcolonial studies, which offer essential accounts of world-formation.[66] Drawing on these sources legitimates a wide-ranging comparatism and its goal of foregrounding how narrative strategies make multispecies worlds perceptible and thinkable.

The concept of milieu often functions negatively in biopolitical critique, as when Jacques Derrida describes the effects of industrial modernity's technical domination of animals' existence as the erasure of "the milieu and world of their object."[67] What is lost by biopower's constitution of living beings is that sense of milieu, and milieu as sensed. Derrida's orientation to animal questions has crucially attuned literary studies to the profound conceptual manipulability of animals' lives. But attending to milieu can also provoke a different set of questions: in Deleuze's words, "It is no longer a matter of utilizations or captures, but of sociabilities and communities. How do individuals enter into composition with one another . . . ? How can a being take another being into its world, but while preserving or respecting the other's own relations and world?"⁶⁸ Contemporary literature's animals often follow something like Deleuze's lead, taking fiction beyond mournful allegories of biopolitical capture, and taking criticism beyond biopolitical critique.

Allegory has been absolutely crucial for indicting what Dinesh Wadiwel and Dominic O'Key memorably call "the war against the animals."⁶⁹ But this vision of both literary form and literary critique does not account fully for the anti-allegorical, anti-conceptual turn in recent novels. The resistance to abstraction built into milieu has likewise contributed to the broad anti-cognitivist turn in theory of mind, affect theory, and beyond.⁷⁰ As I have suggested, it points to a creature's cognitive competence in mapping the colors, shapes, movements, and points of contact that generate its habitat's salient dimensions, and it understands affective valences like mood as integral to those perceptions. It neither heightens nor ignores creaturely agency; it assumes no particular distribution of power even as it recognizes that power relations may shape or even determine the possibilities of sensation.

Allegories explicitly and implicitly address the need for a more inclusive vision of rights, often using animals figuratively to evoke a yearning for the autonomy that animals themselves are not considered to have. Because allegory is a widely used strategy by many writers who care deeply about oppression, I hope not to take an entirely adversarial stance toward allegory that presents nonhuman animals as revelatory of specifically human concerns, or toward the way cultural critique gravitates toward reproducing this kind of allegory.⁷¹ Contemporary allegories often quite powerfully explore a long-standing alignment of the lives of animals with politically marginalized human subjects in order to think through the social, economic, ethical, and political consequences of overturning the presumption of the eurowestern, liberal subject's mastery. Donna Haraway recuperates figurative language as the "necessarily tropic quality of all material-semiotic processes," and this kind of position has been generative for the study of animals, like Mario Ortiz-Robles's investigation of "what it is like to be a trope," Heather Keenleyside's study of the eighteenth century, and Anishinaabe scholar Gerald Vizenor's account of the inextricability of tropes from animal representation, exemplified in Indigenous literature, such that "language . . . is one of the real environments of . . . authored animals."⁷² Yet allegory has striking limitations in contemporary literary practice, limitations that reflect the exclusions of much of biopolitical thought.

Historically, allegory has externalized and made public the virtues and vices of the human soul—the private inward states that have been thought to constitute the novel's terrain manifest as characters. For Walter Benjamin, allegory renders character even as it marks its own melancholic failure to adequately condense history into human individuality:

> History, in everything untimely, sorrowful, and miscarried that belongs to it from the beginning, is inscribed in a face—no, in a death's head. And though it is true that to such a thing all "symbolic" freedom of expression, all classical harmony of form, and everything human is lacking, nevertheless in this figure, the most fallen in nature, is expressed meaningfully as enigma not only the nature of human existence in general but the biographical historicity of an individual. This is the core of the allegorical vision.[73]

Allegory's anthropomorphic consolidation of political meaning involves a fundamentally violent as well as melancholic oscillation between depicting the "otherness" of the given and individuation as "capture." As Gordon Tesky argues, "What the act of capture exhibits is the truth over which allegory is always drawing its veil: the fundamental disorder out of which the illusion of order is raised."[74] In other words, allegory fundamentally seeks to constrain modes of embodied "life," a critique that resonates with my sense of the recuperative possibilities of the milieu. "Capture" is a term that arises quite often in critical discussions of figuration, and as Antoine Traisnel argues, the term's strong association with the production of art from the nineteenth century onward makes for an aesthetic that presumes violence against animals. For allegory's adherents, capture is precisely what makes it so revelatory: allegorical narratives especially highlight the discontinuities between subjective experience—Benjamin's "biographical historicity of an individual"—and supervening systems in postmodernity. As I will discuss further in Chapter 1, animal allegory offers many contemporary writers a mechanism for the searing indictment of social damage in the biopolitical state, where the capture of the body is the criterion of political inclusion.

Yet allegorical form, deeply entrenched in both contemporary fiction and biopolitical theory, often occludes animals' sapience, subtly reinforcing and reinventing individuality as an anthropocentric measure of a living creature's significance, however inaccessible that standard remains for many living beings. We have yet to understand how the concept of having-a-world has typically been rooted in an investment in exclusionary human exceptionalism. In Alexander G. Weheliye's words, biopolitics tends to "neglect and/or actively dispute the existence of alternative modes of life alongside the violence, subjection, exploitation, and racialization that define the modern human" even as it critically analyzes that process. By exclusively emphasizing the violent consolidation of the human, we lose the opportunity to articulate a multispecies "alternative"—"to insist on relation rather than difference," as Sharon Patricia Holland puts it, reflecting on Weheliye's critique.[75]

For an example, we have only to turn to how the use of the term "milieu" changes in the work of Canguilhem's most influential student, Michel Foucault. The term appears most significantly in his 1977–1978 lectures, published as *Security, Territory, Population*. Here, he connects milieu to security, the process of planning for human habitation: "Security will try to plan a milieu in terms of events or series of events or possible elements, of series that will have to be regulated within a multivalent and transformable framework."[76] Human populations gain the ability to make social meaning within the artificial environments of towns and cities: "We see the sudden emergence of the problem of the 'naturalness' of the human species within an artificial milieu," whereby a milieu becomes a political "territory" to be negotiated by sovereign power.[77] Even as a territorialized milieu is artificial, regulation occurs from within rather than being imposed from without; all political meaning emerges *within* this perceptual framework for existence. This milieu is maintained, Foucault continues, through a regulatory dispensation of sovereign power *allegorized by* multispecies relations but no longer routed through multispecies practices.

For Foucault, milieu becomes more pointedly political than it was for Canguilhem: the maintenance of a sufficiently conducive human milieu secures populations through the exercise of pastoral power that is compared to and originates in a human relationship with herd animals. Foucault's departure from Canguilhem occurs most pointedly through the animal fable he produces in *Security, Territory, Population*. It is a fable that occludes interest in the condition of nonhuman animals themselves, turning away from direct consideration of the ethological underpinnings of securitization.[78] When Foucault remarks that "the form of power so typical of the West, and unique, I think, in the entire history of civilizations, was born, or at least took its model from the fold, from politics seen as a matter of the sheep-fold," the word "model" signals an allegorical move to abstraction when it suggests that ongoing human relationships with other-than-human animals are no longer at stake. The sheep, like the human population, need sufficient conditions for physical survival or flourishing, but they are otherwise of less interest to Foucault than the consequences for the human shepherd: he writes, "The shepherd's power manifests itself, therefore, in a duty, a task to be undertaken, so that—and I think this is also an important characteristic of pastoral power—the form it takes is not first of all the striking display of strength and superiority. Pastoral power initially manifests itself in its zeal, devotion, and endless application." This "power of care" demands "keeping watch" and preventing "suffering" through routine tasks exercised with "zeal, devotion, and endless application," tasks that balance the needs of the individual with the needs of the entire population.[79] Foucault's emphasis is on this epistemic protocol for the maintenance of pre-modern political power. Foucault's tracking of the sovereign-as-pastor allegory places human organisms on a different perceptual plane in order to highlight their distinctive epistemic labor, exemplified by the highly allegorical and morally freighted "character" of the pastor.

The consolidation of the pastor's selectively individuating modes of knowing underwrites the distribution of privative milieus for the maintenance of biopower. Foucault theorizes that as population becomes a key political category in the nineteenth century, political power collapses distinctions between politics and biology, rendering territory a medium of sovereignty rather than a deep logic that affords the possibility of perception. State power is now "addressed to a multiplicity of men, not to the extent that they are nothing more than their individual bodies, but to the extent that they form, on the contrary, a global mass ... directed not at man-as-body but at man-as-species."[80] The collective orientation toward species at the core of Canguilhem's conception of milieu becomes a way of thinking about the origination of the management of human life by way of analogy to animal husbandry. At this juncture, milieu as ecological relationship passes out of Foucault's argument. Traisnel argues that Foucault's vision of pastoral power "is predicated on an immemorial presupposition of capture: of having the (human) animal already in hand."[81] And for Traisnel as for Derrida, the idea of "capture" is itself committed to a history of real and conceptual violence against animals—with enduringly dire consequences.

"Capture" also returns the work of criticism to the excavation of the ideological consequences of whatever conditions are being represented for the formation of the human in such a way as to drive everything marked as given and as body into the realm of the aconceptual. Pervasive models of critique reallegorize fiction, further inviting us to read representations of bodies as powerful expressions of human struggles against biopolitical and existential abjection, even when texts themselves treat allegory as an internal challenge rather than an interpretive key. When critics read allegorically, literary particularities have a socially diagnostic function. Biopolitical allegories represent an effort (however difficult) to "capture" or condense systemic geopolitical violences that highlight the exclusions associated with the human self. The importance of biopolitical analysis as a mode of critique that reveals the policing of decisions around who counts as human or animal, animate and inanimate, tends to perpetuate the privilege that critics accord to conceptual over aesthetic concerns. Elizabeth Anker and Rita Felski observe that allegorical critical practice has at times seemed synonymous with "critique" itself: an intellectual operation of ideological decoding, in which "allegories operate in literature as a manifestation of larger social hierarchies and inequalities."[82] This logic occludes specificity and at the same time, tends to reintroduce, however subtly, a hierarchic structure of meaning. Critique's overreliance on allegorical reading presumes a conception of animals as creatures constituted by biopolitical violence—their creaturely life is brought into being by external control. Traisnel turns briefly to von Uexküll's ethology as a potential way forward from the nineteenth century's aesthetics of capture, commenting that he offers "[a] different ethics of relation to this elusive animal: neither at hand nor at large, beyond both restitution and loss.... acknowledgement of distance as the ground for a new ethics of care and knowledge, as the condition for regarding other animals as well as ourselves."[83] As I argue in this book, such an ethological and ecological vision is often contemporary fiction's starting point.

3. THE NOVEL AS MILIEU

Milieu demonstrates that recent animal-centered narratives have gravitated away from allegory, or at least *only* allegory. Rather, they theorize milieu as a convergent, formal ground for relational sentience not dependent on what we normally think of as a centered, individual consciousness that instantiates a set of political manipulations. Recovering milieu as an underlying, convergent formation of sentience, I argue that this concept opens post-allegorical interpretive practices and explains how animals have come to prompt shifts in literary style.[84] As Peter

Boxall writes, "the world-making power of prose fiction arises from the capacity of the novel to reject or suspend the forms of community it helps to create" by "proposing a narrative form for common experience."[85] In what follows, I explain the importance of literary style to narrating multispecies world-inhabitation—structures that support the perceptibility of what is common.

"World" is certainly a key term for theory of the novel—a highly portable term with "rhetorically unmatched prestige," as Eric Hayot puts it.[86] But it operates in at least two divergent senses. Some accounts of world literature focus on the system in abstract or massively scaled terms very different from the interest of many narratives in small-scale experiences. For most accounts of world literature, novels' focus on the scale of the individual life serves as an allegorical index of the operations of global capital; David Damrosch and Pascale Casanova, among others, argue that world literature reflects circulation and crossings through a world-system.[87] In contrast, in phenomenological frameworks "world" signals a kind of irreducible value and often reflects the kind of sensory processes involved in the production of the milieu. For instance, Boxall argues that the novel offers "intimate access to the minds of others so that we might build collective life-worlds"; novels depict "the ways in which we inhabit our bodies in space and time, under the authority of the law" but often work also to evoke "the contours of a body and a world to come."[88] Debjani Ganguly evokes the sensory pleasures of the palimpsest to argue that "many worlds . . . travel with, haunt, layer, and disrupt other worlds," while Pheng Cheah uses Heideggerian concepts to theorize "world" as temporal openness: "world literature that is an active power in the making of worlds, that is, both a site of processes of worlding and an agent that participates and intervenes in these processes."[89] Taking inspiration from these perspectives, in this book I understand "world-making" and "life-worlds" as sharing the simultaneously phenomenological and ecological quality of "milieu." The literatures I examine in this book contribute to theorizing the very milieus they construct by at once constituting worlds and redistributing who counts as *having* a world. Not a single, abstract world-system *grasped abstractly*, then, but an account of how the perceptibility of a milieu—including our disciplinary ones—depends upon embodied life. Not world literature, then, but *Umweltliteratur*. I argue that the ethological dimensions of milieu offer a way to understand why recent global fiction so often becomes multispecies in order to promote capacious but also, often, non-nationalized and fugitive accounts of lived, embodied experience.

I would note that a sense of milieu inheres in many influential accounts of literary form. Using Gibson's environmental psychology, Jonathan Kramnick proposes that we consider literary texts themselves as "part of the encountered world," while Caroline Levine, accounting for the interaction between text and reader, argues that narrative structure's spatial and temporal affordances demonstrate that the process of being read is implicated in a novel's procedures of world-building.[90] Looking to texts as internally self-organizing, Hayot redefines fictional "world" as a *form*—a "container that is identical with its content and its containing." These perspectives suggest that we might see *novels as themselves milieus*, constituted by what is perceived by their readers—as Hayot puts it, the interaction between the artwork and the world "is the ground of activity, eventfulness, subject-and-objecthood, and of procession." He emphasizes how texts from many social contexts and global locations operate as theories of themselves: "Aesthetic worlds, no matter how they form themselves, are among other things always a relation to and theory of the lived world, whether as a largely preconscious normative construct, a rearticulation, or certain active refusal of the world-norms of their age."[91] While a novel may itself be a world—an integrated, sensory environment—that world emerges relationally through its reading. In other words, a novel not only models but also, *itself*, constitutes an environment that affords certain routes of percipience through its style.

As I will demonstrate, novels that evoke a milieu through the depiction of other animals develop an especially ambivalent or tense relationship to subjective character as the locus of these structures. They use the affective subtleties of sensibility, mood, tone, pace, and sound to reorient the incoherence of treating both human and other-than-human animals as having interiorized characterological selves.[92] The majority of the novels I discuss are first-person narratives, which might appear peculiarly unpromising for promoting an alternative to individuality.[93] Nancy Armstrong argues that early first-person novels—especially those narrated by women, culturally marked as more "inward" subjects—have long offered especially powerful documents of a "core fantasy" of "self-possession."[94] I hope to show that close examination of the complexity of first-person narrative, whether by human or other-than-human speakers, warrants my claim for its registration of milieu as formalizing worldedness. Literary realism, more broadly, can also have this capacity: despite its ostensible complicity with the most bourgeois investments of geopolitical neoliberalism, realism has long centered ongoing, lived relations as representative imaginings of what Raymond

Williams calls "structures of feeling"—the potential for apperceptions and affective relationships that reflect still-emergent historical conditions.[95] Rather than a retreat to the inner life, a commitment to the milieu makes sapience more impersonal and more common to all. As in Jacques Rancière's conception of the distribution of the sensible, the novels I will examine politicize their style less in the vein of "critique" but primarily in the sense that "politics revolves around what is seen and what can be said about it, around who has the ability to see and the talent to speak, around the properties of spaces and the possibilities of time" rather than through characterological exemplarity.[96] Animals have indeed frequently appeared as literary characters since the eighteenth century, typically as pets or working companions in the service of humans, who, as in Alex Woloch's influential account of character systems, receive the benefits of a deep interiority that minor characters are denied—and in the case of animal characters, might have been deemed incapable of in any case.[97] According to Woloch, realism is structured by a fierce "tension between allegory and reference," where the former mode confirms that minor characters are in the thrall of social power reinforced by the inherently hierarchic structure of allegory as a form. Animal characters often play an allegorical role that is particularly at odds with the interiority akin to what novels purportedly ascribe to human protagonists. But even "deep" *human* character can be read allegorically in highly politicized contexts, as in Fredric Jameson's infamous claim that "Third World" novels offer national allegories, in which *"the story of the private individual destiny is always an allegory of the embattled situation for public third-world culture and society,"* or Joseph R. Slaughter's more palatable argument that the *Bildungsroman* plot becomes a test case for the viability of human rights in contemporary fiction through the trajectory of an exemplary subject who instantiates a political positionality.[98]

Literary studies has long worked to complicate Ian Watt's foundational but universalizing notion that novels offer "a full and authentic report of human experience" by presenting individuality as an ideological norm.[99] Marta Figlerowicz's *Flat Protagonists* argues that "novels can undercut the ease with which one might come to treat one's first-person experience as a sufficient measure of the vastness of the surrounding world," while Kornbluh identifies rejection of characterological depth as key to ecologically urgent fiction in order to "actuate dimensions other than the immediate, the personal, the literal."[100] Yet I would stress that affective flatness (common as it is in contemporary fiction) is hardly the only strategy on offer, as exemplified in animal-centered novels today: their narrators are not "cardboard cutouts" or put into the service of a "provocatively immoderate, granular sense of commitment to material and social reality" beyond but rather emerge in relation to that material surround.[101]

Contemporary novels grapple with long-standing formal problems associated with character's condensation of the interaction between an individual consciousness, embodied life, and larger social structures. Histories of novelistic character shows that character expresses an allegorical logic, through which population is captured in, transfigured by, and instantiated as an exemplary interiority. For Deidre Lynch and Catherine Gallagher, literary character condenses the general into the particular, offering us an appealing image of type or what Gallagher suggestively terms "species" through the belated production of inwardness as a sign of individuality.[102] For many scholars focused on the novel's engagement with biological life, the sociological register of fiction's allegorical capture of population often reiterates biopolitical problems of inclusion through what are explicitly identified as allegorical strategies of compression and transcendence.[103] In the context of animal fiction, because these perspectives highlight that character is typically less individualistic than what have assumed, they would also, Ivan Kreilkamp points out, seem to raise a question of whether the imaginative process by which one "invests life in a fictional character," who is after all ontologically nonhuman, might resemble the process by which a human being grants consequence to an animal's experience.[104] In other words, whether we might see animals—and indeed literary characters of any species—as companion species. For Gallagher, the "differential accessibility or knowability of character is only one feature inviting cathexis with ontological difference." And after all, if an early worry about novels was that readers "imagined that to care for fictional personae was to mistake them for real persons," a common criticism of animal lovers is that they make the same anthropomorphic mistake.[105]

All of this is to say that the new centrality of animals in contemporary fiction suggests a reorientation toward character that acknowledges but also moves beyond the functions of allegory, often toward a more affectively oriented framing of "what it is like" to be a living creature. Jameson's more recent work offers a suggestive division between affect and allegory: the human "self," he argues, "is another one of these allegorical objects that the analysis of allegory is likely to transform beyond recognition, an advance which will not be possible until we begin to think of the 'self' as a construct and to acknowledge the allegorical nature of what may henceforth be called the *construction of subjectivity* as such."[106] This statement, consonant with Woloch's understanding of the crucial role of allegory in character systems, positions "affect" as what lies on the other side of allegory—nameless bodily states that have yet to find abstract form because they are nonproprietary. Theories of affect typically define the term as that which cannot be reduced to reflective, contemplative, or stable subjective states recognizable and namable as "emotions." In the novels that interest me, mood or tone often marks the departure from a centralized or normative investment in character, as well as the difference between reading an other-than-human perceiver as an allegory for human subjectivity or for itself. Because mood and tone feel diffuse despite sometimes very precise textual strategies for evoking them, they remain at odds with the allegorical logic of character and of critique even as they make space for literary practices pursued by humans.[107] Many of the novels I examine engage or compete, explicitly or implicitly, with other knowledge-making practices (law, biochemistry, geography), where tone is less overtly a consideration. In doing so, they seem to emphasize their own distinctive literariness. Still, their interest in how narrative voice makes novels into worlds as they are read resonates with comparative cognition's emphasis on how sensory strands generate an integrative scope, creating what Powell terms "phenomenal scenes."

Mood in all its diffuseness is an especially important register for assessing novels as milieus because mood is often understood not as individual but rather as diffusive and environmental. Mood is also as fully relevant to other-than-human sentience as it is to pre-emergent dimensions of human structures of feeling. For Heidegger, whose account of mood has proved influential to postcritical methods, mood preconditions cognition. It has a shaping effect upon the very possibility of perception and interpretation. In *Being and Time*, mood "implies a disclosive submission to the world, out of which we can encounter something that matters to us."[108] Felski and Susan Fraiman suggest that, as Heidegger posited, mood attunes us, "informing the questions we ask, the puzzles that intrigue us, the styles and genres of argument we are drawn to. Mood impinges on method."[109] What feels subjective—"what matters to us"—comes only belatedly, after the ineluctable "submission" to circumstances, environment, habitat. In von Uexküll's account of *Umwelt*, mood affects an animal's global affective orientation toward its environment, not unlike in Heidegger, but it also attaches specifically to individual objects within a habitat, which have what he calls "effect tones." An object has an "effect tone" once it becomes perceptible and meaningful to an animal and generates effects—once it can facilitate sensory interactions of some kind, whether taste or touch or more distanced evaluations.

The novels I examine are often quite interested what it means for an environment to develop effect tones for a perceiver, an emphasis that diminishes the allegorical logic of the character-as-exemplar. But this is a matter of *Umwelt*, while—per Canguilhem—these novels also consistently emphasize the relation between centers of habitation; play with tone or mood becomes an especially provocative way of making narrative voice relational.[110] A nonproprietary or impersonal term for the diffusion of feeling, tone emerges from a wide range of formal devices. It indexes, for instance, an optimistic uncertainty associated with the subjunctive "mood," or a restless unsettledness prompted by metalepsis. Tonal shifts are often a first signal that narrative stance is at stake. The impact of tone is especially palpable in lyrical moments in narrative prose where a lingering enactment of perceptuality is privileged over more cohesive assertions of personality, sociability, and agency.[111] Min Hyoung Song argues that lyrical style in contemporary fiction is a distinctively environmental style because it highlights "the space between a first-person speaker and a second-person addressee"—voice becoming a milieu in Canguilhem's terms, an in-between. Here lyric is less a specific set of formal devices than a registration of how mood presents relationships. Tone also diverges somewhat from the structures Levine and Hayot identify as facilitating literary world-building because tone tends to appear unstructured. Nonetheless, tone is perceptible and influential for many kinds of readers and readings, and it can be analyzed narratologically.

Narrative voice redistributes consciousness as sentience, as I show by building on narratology's tools for assessing narrative as milieu and milieu as form. I take particular inspiration from Eve Sedgwick's attention to tone; Elizabeth Freeman's term "sense methods" as the "visual, haptic, proprioceptive models of apprehension" that are central to narratives of unexpected social alliances; Harmut Rosa's claims for "resonance"—a term that evokes ambient auditory situatedness; and Daniel Heller-Roazen's attunement to the history of philosophy's subtle representations of the "inner touch" as an effect of animal "sensation[s] of life" with their "sweet familiarity."[112] These conceptual orientations toward the aconceptual are the basis of contemporary experiments in *narrative form*. I draw, as well, from work in the environmental humanities by Jennifer Wenzel, Heather Houser, and Min Hyoung Song that emphasizes the processual and affective dimensions of reading as an ecological practice.[113] Aligning with these frameworks, I read the animal novel not for exemplary characters but for the formal signatures of responsive sensation.

At the same time, this approach demonstrates how attention to narrative style offers a corrective to common but often undertheorized assumptions in animal studies and ecocriticism. Some ecocritical accounts of interspecies intimacy emphasize entanglements so complete as to appear to advocate the dissolution or nonexistence of boundaries in a multispecies world: for Haraway, influentially, "species of all kinds are consequent upon worldly subject- and object-shaping entanglements."[114] Against species identities that appear normative or constricting, entanglement seems like a reparatively anti-ideological becoming, elevating that open form to an ontology. The concepts of *Umwelt* as well as milieu suggest that there are many nonequivalent modes of percipience that are highly dependent on species different yet nonetheless in interdependent relation, and, further, that it is their *formal deep structure* that remains common. And the narrative style that conveys that environmental relationality, however lyrical or immersive, likewise remains analyzable as structure—or even as infrastructure, supporting the perceptibility of multiple and at times mutually opaque sentiences without collapsing them.

When novels shift their focus from human individuality to milieu, they tend to depict quite modest forms of interspecies attunement and often refuse to systematically analyze or represent substantive social change. Still, these milieus facilitate a range of critical orientations toward their own narrative style. I align here with Anahid Nersessian's suggestion that we might read for how a literary text "variously valorizes, eroticizes, strains against, and surrenders to the decision to be [literary] instead of another kind of practice, specifically one without a systematic and penetrating relationship to crisis."[115] As I noted earlier, it is "postcritical" interventions that tend to describe the culture of criticism as itself an ecology or a milieu. In contrast, Kornbluh decries the resignation associated with the postcritical turn as disastrous for activism in a time of environmental catastrophe. She enjoins: "Do critique: assess the environments for thought, and build necessary alternative environments. . . . The dispersive poetics of attunement to the material world, romancing precarity, and dissolving binaries entice us to lie down."[116] Kornbluh asks critics to make "the world" into an "environment for thought."[117] But this, too, is a logic of milieu. In centering the milieu as a way of thinking about "the world," I would argue that there is some possibility of bringing together a "dispersive poetics of attunement" (which certainly manifests in many of the novels this book considers) and the critical "work" of building. What I want to argue, in other words, is this: that contemporary engagements with animal milieus imagine world-building without *Bildung*.[118]

4. ANIMAL NOVELS AFTER ALLEGORY

By drawing attention to the aesthetic richness involved in representing the worlds of animals, I contribute to a growing body of criticism that moves away from a crisis-driven biopolitical model centered on privation and suffering, even as we share a commitment to animal lives as grievable. In animal studies specifically, that model is typically indebted to Heidegger's emphasis on animals' "nonsymmetrical [relation to] suffering and death," an analysis that has prompted influential accounts of the violence against animals in the grip of biopolitical institutions where their silence is a given.[119] Many theorists make animals' deaths central to the constitution of the privative category of "animal" itself—even when they do not depend on the Heideggerian notion that there is an *ontologically* significant difference that determines various species' ways of dying. Comparative work by Catherine Parry and Evan Maina Mwangi on contemporary animal fiction is motivated by biopolitical analysis and understands criticism as advocacy in the face of pervasive animal suffering.[120] In contrast, I argue for the value of formalism, as much to help theorists of the novel understand why animals bring out underrecognized dimensions of fictional narrative as to advocate for animals through literature.

The word "creature" does this double work because it operates in two ways. The first stresses the material connections between animal vulnerability and human political subjugation. For biopolitical thought the term "creature" marks a politically manipulated and allegorically rich dimension of human lives. For Eric Santner and Julia Reinhard Lupton, creaturely life is a dimension of the political human animal: in Lupton's words, "*creature* marks the radical separation of creation and Creator ... or ... between anyone or anything that is produced or controlled by an agent, author, master, or tyrant," though as Colleen Glenney Boggs points out, such approaches risk "locat[ing] the creaturely within the human."[121] Nonetheless, many in animal studies endorse the creaturely as a registration of bodily life constituted by the possibility of violent erasure. Hilary Thompson's *Novel Creatures* and Dominic O'Key's *Creaturely*

Forms, which document how urgently contemporary literature attends to "creaturely" need, use the term primarily to index shared exposure to climate and political catastrophe. These books argue for crisis-driven accounts of fiction's alternatives to anthropocentrism—for Thompson, a distinctively "millennial" and even apocalyptic mode, and for O'Key a postwar melancholy.

Yet animals may also be creaturely in a second sense that more strongly emphasizes bodily responsiveness. Anat Pick draws on the work of Simone Weil to define the creaturely as the preciousness of all living bodies that are "material, temporal, vulnerable"—an approach more focused on phenomenal conditions, including the importance of compassionate attention to the creatureliness of others.[122] To be a creature in this second sense, in Harmut Rosa's phrase, is to be "capable of resonance."[123] The "creaturely," then, has dual implications: on the one hand, it can index how allegorical structures in fiction register the political manipulation of bodies, but it can also explain how animal narratives imagine the world-founding qualities of sentience.

My formalist approach, which makes this book as committed to novel studies as to animal studies, differentiates *Milieu* from scholarship on animals in literature that ranges across literary modes or offers a more culturally, historically, or thematically specific scope. My focus on non-normative sensation aligns with scholarship on "ordinary multispecies" relations in specific contexts, particularly scholarship on Indian literature and culture, like work by Suvadip Sinha, Sundya Walther, and Naisargi Davé; Sinha's vocabulary, in particular, resonates because he occasionally uses the term "multispecies milieu" to describe what anti-anthropocentric fiction might offer us.[124] Refusing to center damage and celebrating multispecies alliance is an important focus not only of scholars of contemporary national traditions but also of more historical scholars, like Keenleyside, Traisnel, Laura Brown, and Ivan Kreilkamp, as well as comparative scholars working at a range of scales, such as Susan McHugh, Kari Weil, Mario Ortiz-Robles, David Herman, Nathan Snaza, and Julietta Singh. Interdisciplinary theorists and creative writers, too, like Haraway and Linda Hogan, celebrate multispecies existence by emphasizing real-world human-animal alliances. All of this work, in Herman's words, "affirm[s] the power of narrative to reframe the cultural models or ontologies that undergird hierarchical understandings of humans' place in the larger biotic communities of which they are members."[125]

Herman's account centers on texts that imagine animals as "experiencing, agential subjects" and strive to equalize the textual distribution of agency. My focus on milieu shows, however, that what it is to be "agential" is negotiated by the aesthetic form through which the milieu becomes perceptible. As Vinciane Despret puts it, "the milieu 'captures' the animal, and affects it, while on the other hand, the milieu only exists because it is an object in being captured, in the way that the animal confers to the milieu the power to affect."[126] Or, in the terms of Boxall's defense of novels, "novels give narrative expression to the ways in which we inhabit our bodies in space and time, under the authority of the law" as well as to "imagine and make new worlds."[127] The idea of milieu helps to interpret fictions in which a creature's environment may be harmful and where the robust mode of self-determination we typically call "agency" remains unavailable.[128] There is nothing *inherently* liberatory about milieu, even as it redistributes world-making sentience. Such narratives at their best can, in Susan McHugh's words, "cultivat[e] a politics based not on the rights of homogenous, atomized individuals so much as the affects that have always held together the heterogeneous, molecular groupings made so apparent in cross-species companionship."[129] With McHugh, I would not tie affirmative representations of animal lives to "agency"; in this regard my account aligns particularly with animal scholarship in Black studies by Boisseron, Joshua Bennett, and Sharon Patricia Holland. Their work values the affective richness of alliances with animals that refuse narrow conceptions of agency while also refusing the allegorical coding of Blackness as animality as agency-constraining, and instead employ more "open" techniques of representation, understood as "attempts to refashion a world."[130] Pivoting on the centrality of having-a-world to these projects of attention to living, I recall that, from its origins in the nineteenth century, the word "milieu" complicates a binary opposition between determinism and plasticity or openness. Through the lens of species diversity, contemporary novels arrive at a more distributive and convergent depiction of action and self-constitution, where action looks less like reflectively chosen interventions made in a world conceived as separate from and often hostile to the self, and more like a responsive creatureliness.

This book's investigation of the contemporary aesthetics of milieu does not offer a complete survey of recent animal fiction. The topic's explosive popularity is certainly one spur to this investigation (and many novels that I do not treat at length are discussed briefly in the notes). But a completist approach might be impossible, given how many relevant titles appear each month in the United States alone. The fact that I am working primarily with Anglophone texts, a disproportionate number of which are from the United States, reflects my own disciplinary environment, a U.S. Department of Literatures in English. I purposely treat several novels that have won major literary prizes for Anglophone fiction like the Man Booker Prize and the U.S. National Book Award and achieved a high level of visibility. Insofar as these novels create cultural capital, they allot some for animal lives too, garnering attention from readers perhaps otherwise unlikely to seek out animal fictions.

Rather than make a context-driven claim about why animals feature today in mostly Anglophone fiction, my approach is primarily formal, assessing how narrative voice creates environments for perception.[131] Each chapter pairs formally convergent texts from the mid-1990s through the present, usually across cultural origins, to argue for the novel's capacity to theorize milieu, which motivates robust grounds for convergence or resonance, rather than direct comparison, across states of oppression, intimacy, and pleasure. I would affirm Katarzyna Bartoszyńska's contention that a "robust formalism" can reorient a comparative discourse of world literature dominated by a center-periphery model that treats realism as a telos and downplays the stunning variety of innovation across cultural domains.[132] The book moves from allegory to realism, but that is not meant as a teleological move toward a more "accurate" formal vocabulary for milieu, even as I stress allegory's constraints. Narratives of milieu use gestures of defamiliarization that have long marked other-than-realistic animal narratives, often oscillating between what read as "realistic" and more surreal or fantastical modes—as in Victor Shlovsky's account of defamiliarization, "the purpose of art is to impart the sensation of things as they are perceived and not as they are known."[133] By attending closely to how novels position their own narrative strategies, I show how specific formal configurations can (and in a few cases, cannot) make possible the renovation of consciousness into sentience, and character-driven plot into creaturely milieu.

I open by arguing that allegorical critique is too limited an approach to recent fiction's investment in depicting animals' convergent milieus, especially in texts that themselves turn away from allegory. This book centrally recognizes the literary challenge posed by the hierarchical and anthropocentric structure of allegory. However, even as a version of allegory that reinforces human privileges remains an oft-used narrative form associated with animals both within and beyond realism, I argue that many recent authors present milieu as an alternative to the liberal humanist interiority that structures both influential theories of the novel *and also* the modes of biopolitical critique through which we have conventionally attempted to counteract dominant ideologies of individualism.

Chapter 1, "Breaking the Zoo," demonstrates the codependency of biopolitical critique and allegorical form, while showing the limits of animal allegory as a novelistic practice. Arguing that biopolitical thought is dependent upon a zoological approach to allegorical capture, I demonstrate that recent novels depicting destroyed zoos show the political limitations of allegory. Recent texts feature a persistent trope: the suffering tiger, struggling to survive a zoo ravaged by wartime. In most of these texts, from Yann Martel's *Life of Pi* (2001) to Haruki Murakami's *The Wind-Up Bird Chronicle* (trans. 1997) to Téa Obreht's *The Tiger's Wife* (2011), big cats allegorize human subjection to violent regimes, while zoos represent neoliberalism's regulation of biological life through its manipulation of specific a feline *Umwelt*. These narratives, recounted by human characters, demonstrate the challenges of recognizing the opacity and interdependence of animal and human milieus. Nonetheless, even from within potentially reductive allegorical structures, a lyrical orientation becomes a resource for emphasizing shared conditions that make perception possible, even under conditions of privation.[134]

Chapter 2, "Speaking Otherwise," further develops my argument that style complicates allegory. I contend that recent novels narrated by animals showcase ambivalence about the category of character itself through their approach to narrative voice. Fields like comparative cognition and anthropology validate animals' biosemiotic capacities, while recent novels that feature talking animals tend to highlight the awkwardness of translating other creatures' sapience—their "sensations of things"—into human modes of knowledge, critiquing linguistic anthropocentrism. Written in paradoxical animal voices, Yoko Tawada's *Memoirs of a Polar Bear* (trans. 2016) and NoViolet Bulawayo's *Glory* (2022) can be understood as allegories that present speech as necessary to political inclusion and claim to find voices for animals. Yet these novels center the voice as a mode of communication that uncouples affectivity from a narrowly defined, individualistic framework of citizenship or belonging. I argue that these texts promote a relational rather than subject-centered validation of the grounds of speech through their use of metalepsis. If allegory means literally a "speaking otherwise," Tawada and Bulawayo are interested in how animals speak otherwise from within human language—how animals' voices resonate and solicit response.

The second half of *Milieu* turns to literary realism, arguing for its distinctive contribution to interspecies thinking. In the texts I discuss in this section, animals tend to figure more naturalistically, even as I do not take for granted what this means in contexts where multiple sources of oppression either facilitate or block animal identifications. Certainly, the animals in this section appear in more ordinary contexts, and sometimes as more ordinary characters. Chapter 3, "Dog Friends," considers the narrative treatment of domesticated animals as non-allegorical friends. I briefly observe that "public dog" narratives—especially Pilar Quintana's *The Bitch* (trans. 2020)—depict human and canine homelessness as allegories of racialization and class consciousness under neoliberalism. Such narratives present dog worlds as privative. In contrast, I examine narratives of dog friendship that are more generous to shared if precarious milieus. Sigrid Nunez's *The Friend* (2018) and Jesmyn Ward's *Salvage the Bones* (2011) imagine dog-love as world-founding and thus offer a counter to the deathliness of biopolitical animal studies. Emphasizing the role of rhythm and mood in the constitution of first-person narrative voice, I argue that noncognitive dimensions of human sentience that diverge from traditional models of character emerge in these novels as a way of understanding dogs not through melancholic attachments to concepts, but as living companions in a shared milieu.

The final two chapters most explicitly concern how realism addresses animal endangerment as an effect of climate crisis. Chapter 4, "Cat Kin," refuses a politics or aesthetics of mourning, examining the depiction of wild big cats as occupying separate, imperiled milieus in Linda Hogan's *Power* (1998) and Lucy Ellmann's *Ducks, Newburyport* (2019). Though written from culturally divergent perspectives, both novels insist on a noncompanionate vision of two worlds. Both *Power* and *Ducks* work in dialogue with Indigenous ontologies, presenting what it feels like to think through multiple, simultaneous logics of two not entirely mixable "worlds"—Indigenous and settler-colonial, human and feline. Both first-person narrators experiment with strategies to avoid cognitive mastery and respect the opacity of a particular cat's distinct phenomenal world. Grappling with animal sentience prompts a decisive shift of narrative voice, calling attention to the limits of the first person and the possibilities of the third. The well-known impersonality of free indirect discourse when applied to animals evokes a common knowledge that begins to look less like human-centered sociology and more like a surprisingly precise evocation of how different species' modes of sapience converge. I argue that free indirect discourse has a distinctive value for representing a multispecies world because, used in a multispecies context, its orientation toward the embeddedness of individual thought within norms of communal knowledge gets traction on the coordination of first- and third-person perspectives that the field of comparative cognition needs in order to account for the convergence of the deep structure of sentience.

Chapter 5, "Wilder Things," reflects on realism's generic capacities and limitations in representing multispecies milieus where populations are in conflict. Realism struggles to represent the clashes and convergences of populations rather than one-on-one encounters, a problem that has motivated ecocriticism's preference for sci-fi. I argue, however, that realism has been undervalued in ecocritical discourse, connecting third-person narrative's distinctive capacity to juxtapose lived experience of systemic violence to comparative cognition's interest in the dimensionality of animal sentience. In Amitav Ghosh's *The Hungry Tide* (2005) and Aminatta Forna's *Happiness* (2018), scientists attempt to track threatened human and animal populations while their own movements, too, are traced by third-person narration. In both novels, scientific epistemologies are supplemented by nonwestern cosmologies as well as literary, hypothetical "as ifs" that open up sentience-based accounts of knowledge-production. The tentative structure of the subjunctive mood—as Nagel implied—insists on the world-making capabilities of other-than-human knowers while emphasizing the affordances of third-person narrative for a tentative making-knowable.

The contemporary animal novel tells us, then, how grasping a multispecies world means a diminishing investment in novelistic character. Novels like these allow that inwardness and a capacity for symbolic representation are the markers of human personhood and political belonging, and some of them even advocate this idea in the politically agile allegorical forms that would seem to reinforce that privilege. But most end up emphasizing environmental responsiveness as a convergent criterion of belonging, bespeaking fiction's truly long-standing fascination with perceiving in relation. Ultimately, this book positions contemporary fiction as a theoretically serious answer to core questions of ecofeminist ethics, like Maria Puig de la Bellacasa's "What does caring mean when we go about thinking and living interdependently with beings other than human, in 'more than human' worlds?"[135] For the discipline of literary criticism to answer this question depends upon how narrative makes "worlds" appear.

ONE

Breaking the Zoo

This chapter examines highly lauded works for the global mass market in literary fiction that center on zoo animals' escape or the destruction of zoos during wartime. This prevalent trope, I argue, should prompt us to evaluate the limits of allegoresis for our contemporary moment in literary criticism. Zoobreak novels often make immediate, valuable political interventions through allegory: zoo animals, though excluded from the polity, are constituted by it; their precariousness allegorizes crises of biopolitics, state sovereignty, and late liberalism, which turn on questions of autonomy and self-regulation. Yet I argue that in depictions of the broken zoo that turn away from allegory, the institution's desolation replaces large-scale organization with small intimacies, opening interspecies milieus and acknowledging the proximity of animals' and humans' experiences without assimilating them.

In this chapter I develop my argument about allegory through discussion of three works of fiction: Yann Martel's *Life of Pi* (2001), Haruki Murakami's *The Wind-Up Bird Chronicle* (1997), and Téa Obreht's *The Tiger's Wife* (2011). These zoobreak texts specifically concern the fate of tigers in order to indict the failed maintenance of the state's security. "What is it like to be a trope?" asks Mario Ortiz-Robles.[1] Jacques Derrida warns that it can be difficult to maintain the distinction between a "real cat" and "the *figure* of a cat," noting the "immense symbolic responsibility with which our culture has always charged the feline race."[2] Lions, allegorically fertile in western traditions, have long been associated with sovereignty: consider *The Faerie Queene*; recall the resonances between *The Lion King* and *Hamlet*. Tigers—solitary animals with a reputation for anthropophagy—have more recently become iconic. Perhaps building on the incendiary associations of William Blake's "Tyger," the tiger's celebrity may be due to its distinct allegorical potential: as charismatic megafauna, the tiger conjures absolute negative freedom from or resistance to social regulation.[3] Yet the tiger has emerged in recent texts not as the figure of revolution it once was but as an index of humanist values.[4] Today, tigers no longer herald unbridled power, though they retain rapacious connotations. And there might be more tigers in fiction than in forests now; the global wild tiger population has declined by 97 percent in the past century. Now figures of extreme precariousness, these literary cats embody a paradox: they may be instinctive killers, figures for rage and rapacious power, but they are also particularly patent victims of global capitalism, their populations waning as conservationism attempts to manage the collective life of a species increasingly defined by threat.[5]

Life of Pi allegorizes the pull of allegory itself; escaped zoo animals' renewed agency figuratively serves a neoliberal ideal of unfettered human autonomy and resilience. After a reading of this novel, this chapter reexamines the conceptual problems posed by the close connection between allegory and biopolitics and asks how they can be overcome. I then turn to *The Tiger's Wife* and *The Wind-Up Bird Chronicle*, which especially concern the relationship between disabled humans and "zoo animals." These less allegorical texts use the zoo's destruction to explore minimally politicized interspecies relations and reflect a less intense investment in a strong concept of human character. Rather than propose an alternative account of political sovereignty that can reinvigorate human agency, these texts are interested in how species relations take shape in a shared milieu, a term that originates in biopolitical thought, as I showed in the Introduction, but that ultimately motivates a less anthropocentric critical practice. If milieu is a historically telling concern at a time when neoliberal subjectivity and modes of relation no longer answer to insecure state institutions, its aesthetic manifestations cannot be fully explained in ideological terms. Murakami and Obreht use what Elizabeth Freeman calls "sense methods"—modes of narration that evoke "ephemeral relationalities . . . neither reducible to institution nor population," and value alliances between sensate bodies even when not recognized as such.[6] By doing so, their narratives suggest an important but nonreductive alliance between human disability and animal captivity. As disability theorist Sunaura Taylor advocates, this alliance revolves around an embrace of dependency, alongside an emphasis on sensory experiences not dependent on speech (a criterion that frames other-than-human animals as ontologically deprived) to foster awareness of a shared milieu.[7]

While grounded in narratives of human experiences, these novels retain only a tenuous commitment to the human protagonist; neither could be accurately called a *Bildungsroman* despite featuring youngish first-person narrators seeking accommodation in a defamiliarized world.[8] "Waning protagonicity"—Fredric Jameson's term, applied in different circumstances—shifts narrative emphasis to milieu while avoiding modes of figuration that confirm human privilege.[9] If these texts allow that animals of many species share a milieu, they also suggest that, to draw on Neel Ahuja's words, "power in a multispecies world is redirected on scales and in spaces that often elude perception"—or, like ecocritics Jennifer Wenzel and Min Hyoung Song, I would say *redirect* and *revalue* attention or perception.[10] *The Tiger's Wife* and *The Wind-Up Bird Chronicle* put pressure on companionship, often featuring relationships that don't conform to companion-species narratives of "ordinary multispecies living," in Donna Haraway's terms. Neither do they feature indifferent mutual regard, in Naisargi Davé's terms, *or* even much direct mutual care.[11] But still, animals and humans are touched, smelled, heard—and sometimes tasted—as narrators emphasize shared capacities for sensory perception and environmental situatedness after the destruction of institutional structures that capture and display animal lives, even if recognizing these common orientations cannot restitute the security formerly supplied by government or revalidate the forms of subjectivity it licenses.

In other words, I observe that these texts make quite minimal claims for the politically transformative power of privileging the sensory milieu. We might be disappointed by this apparent reluctance to offer a political vision to redress the failed state, perhaps lamenting that we shouldn't have expected more from works with such excellent sales numbers. But I make the case for the contribution of literary forms that resist allegorical reading to an inclusive image of milieu not fully accessible through still-prevalent models of biopolitical critique. That there is no clear, future-directed possibility in any of these texts underlines their skepticism about systematized approaches to animal and human lives—above all the zoos that continue to be arenas of occluded colonial history and neoliberal indoctrination.

1. THE ALLEGORICAL ZOO

Contemporary literature is not a zoo, but animal lives, in their vulnerability to external manipulation, are especially given to capture through allegory.[12] The popular and spectacular image of an escaped or unmanaged menagerie animal seems to readily aestheticize political conditions in urgent need of redress by figuratively evoking the destruction of a carceral state.[13] One might well imagine that the zoo is a biopolitical technology like the prison or the madhouse: the zoo is an effective figure for the sovereignty of institutions that regulate biological lives and engineer the border between human and other-than-human. Still, recent shifts in approaches to zoo management complicate the notion that the zoo figures the carceral state in miniature: zoos increasingly use affective strategies to affirm shared environmental situatedness and emphasize pastoral conservation, even as they nonetheless, in Brian Massumi's words, allow human visitors to "hold themselves at a distance in the role of unimplicated observer."[14] Irus Braverman makes the crucial point that the contemporary zoo should not be understood as instituting carceral discipline but instead as reflecting pastoral power. For example, the contemporary zoo's conservationist context demands that zoos keep biometric records and follow international protocols for mating, but the zoo's mission to "save" endangered species reflects the theological concept of salvation as the pastor's burden.[15] Many of today's zoos create elaborate environments or "experiences" rather than display animals in cages, countering any hints of the carceral state yet still motivated by modes of figural representation that return the value of animal lives to the human. Changes to zoo exhibits reflect increased attention to pastoral efforts to conserve wild species and their environments.[16] Sticking with the tigers that dominate this chapter, I will note that beginning in 2014, San Diego Zoo visitors could weave through a "Tiger Trail" evoking a Sumatran rain forest threatened by logging operations. The overall message is positive nonetheless. The zoo's marketing campaign advertised the new exhibit by asking visitors to identify with tigers: its slogan, "Tiger Power: See It, Feel It, Live It," communicates a goal of total immersion ("agency") but also positions the tiger as a figure for the human visitor's own imaginative engagement.[17] Braverman points out that even if this cagelessness is an illusion and no less spectacular than older zoo designs, contemporary zoo management "discipline[s] the public into caring" through techniques that create visual, tactile, and olfactory illusions of an unconstructed, non-anthropocentric environment.[18]

The contemporary zoo treats "caring" as a function best taught by cueing the senses—bodily responses to the environment—to affective, subconscious effects imagined to affect both human visitors and animal residents that adhere to a norm of wildness. As Matthew Chrulew documents, midtwentieth-century western zoo directors influenced by von Uexküll used the idea of *Umwelt* to reshape the psychological adaptation of animals, normalizing the institutional space to make it available for animal perception: "The task of zoo biology was to eliminate such captivity-effects through the provision of biological conditions of enclosure and exhibition. Captivity produces abnormality; refined captivity, expert biological care, ameliorates it"; this process demands an intensified pastoral relationship between animals and keepers.[19] Meanwhile, these strategies are underwritten by the vigilant management of health and reproduction behind the scenes in utilitarian spaces not meant for visitors. Such polarization of space suggests that affective strategies ultimately affirm and capitalize upon human imaginativeness and technical ingenuity—returning to the values of neoliberalism—while at the same time subtly regulating human bodies, perhaps beneath the level of conscious perception. This spectacle risks eclipsing visitors' awareness of propinquity and its ethical consequences, especially when it "renders" or "captures" zoo animals as figures for uniquely human experiences.

Using animals' lives to represent distinctively human experiences makes the animals themselves "disappear," as John Berger puts it in his foundational essay "Why Look at Animals?" (1986). "In zoos [animals] constitute the living monument to their own disappearance," he writes.[20] Cultural histories of zoos track their institutionalization to the rise of liberal government, typically contending that from the nineteenth century forward, zoos functioned as symbols of imperial dominion and European Enlightenment. Institutions like the London Zoo functioned as living museums that displayed animals captured through imperial expansion and global trade.[21] The design of the Berlin Zoo shifted over the course of the twentieth century to reflect Nazi ideologies of *Lebensraum* (a people's "natural" territory) before it was bombed and reconstructed to reflect socialist ideals.[22] The spectacle of captivity reinforces a hierarchical worldview that weighs human power relations—and reemphasizes the mastery of those who top the scale. Alternatively, in some contexts reports of zoos destroyed by war make *humans* disappear: their focus on animals distracts readers from the violence of the state upon human bodies by redirecting attention to the exotic, singular, even sublime animal: for Sarah Salih, "relatively apolitical" "stories of animals in war zones always carry with them the sense that we're looking away from another, contiguous catastrophe of the human lives destroyed by human violence," thus "obviating the need for a contextualized, politically engaged response."[23] The implicitly colonizing, comprehending gaze involved in reporting on zoos in conditions of political distress effects a double disappearance—first, the vanishing of the animals, often living and dying in dire conditions, even as they are consigned to a figural servitude that glorifies them, and second, the effacement of human suffering.[24]

Zoo allegories nonetheless constitute a robust, diverse trend in contemporary fiction, and before turning to *Life of Pi* in detail, it is worth briefly examining some other examples to showcase the broken zoo trope's range. While some are more fantastical than others, these narratives typically use animals to signal biopolitical manipulation. However, insofar as these texts reify or consume tigers and other animals as representing liberal humanist values (freedom, autonomy, unfettered self-expression), the zoobreak text itself becomes a zookeeper.[25] Allegory offers contemporary fiction a powerful mechanism for indicting social damage, particularly the plight of real as well as transcendental homelessness in the biopolitical state, where the condition of the body is the criterion of political inclusion. The state-sponsored captivity of real bodies is at stake. "Decolonization is not a metaphor," as Eve Tuck and K. Wayne Yang argue, in a brief for literary language that avoids the usurpations of figurative language, but conversely, figuration often works in the service of an explicit goal of decolonization. For example, in South African novelist Lauren Beukes's cyber-noir *Zoo City* (2011), animal affinities mark those who have been permanently excluded from citizenship, and whose efforts to reclaim power are tenuous, deeply dangerous, and likely to fail.[26] The novel portrays a securitized, dystopian Johannesburg experiencing a new version of apartheid: in the early 2000s, criminals and political refugees begin to be paired with animal familiars, granting them magical powers. The novel bleakly depicts the precarious lives of the "animalled," who struggle to survive in a burgeoning slum—a "zoo"—where the too-visible presence of their familiars always risks deepening their disenfranchisement.[27]

Like *Zoo City*, other recent zoo allegories centrally concern the relational development of the embattled human self progressing sequentially through the possibilities of social reconciliation and potential alignment with a national future—the postcolonial *Bildungsroman* as routed through animals' images that may not be as posthuman as they seem. Although the *Bildungsroman* is historically the "genre of demarginalization," as Joseph R. Slaughter argues, "human rights and the *Bildungsroman* are mutually enabling fictions: each projects an image of the human personality that ratifies the other's vision of the ideal relations between individual and society."[28] Arvind Adiga's *The White Tiger* (2008) explicitly investigates national identity fractured by globalization; although characters do not magically embody animals—as they do in Eka Kurniawan's more spiritual *Man Tiger* (2004, trans. 2015)—they identify as animals to signal their position in a postglobal India still structured by caste.[29] A crucial moment in *The White Tiger* comes when the protagonist—the White Tiger—visits a real specimen in a zoo. The narrator recounts, "The tiger's eyes met my eyes, like my master's eyes have met mine so often in the mirror of the car."[30] Yet the masterful tiger emblematizes the protagonist's own constrained strength, which he ultimately uses in the murder of his employer. As Sundhya Walther argues, "The narrative concludes with an emphatic insistence that modern capitalism is an animalizing force and that, in the contemporary urban context, the sanctity of the human is under threat."[31] Indra Sinha's *Animal's People* (2009) makes this biopolitical critique even more forcefully. The protagonist identifies as a creature who has lost his human status and now walks on all fours. His "animality" results from his disfigurement in the aftermath of an industrial accident, a fictionalized version of the 1984 Bhopal disaster, a gas leak at India's Union Carbide plant that caused many immediate deaths as well as disabilities in the longer term. Condemning the violence inflicted upon a postindustrial, postglobal population, Sinha portrays the main character, who calls himself Animal, as refusing the "transfor[mation of] humanity into human capital," opting out entirely by identifying as nonhuman.[32] While Sinha insists that the inner life of the individual subject emerges from the body's conditions, the novel nonetheless uses the term "animal" to critique the globalized regulation of human communities. As in Joshua Bennett's account of African American literature, these postcolonial texts "turn to the animal kingdom, that which had so often been used as a tool of their derision and punishment, as a site of futurity and fugitivity."[33] The vitality of allegorical meaning would seem to license the expression of transgressive energies that had previously been culturally excluded by being marked as animal; as Julietta Singh argues of *Animal's People*, "To mobilize one's animality is to dispossess oneself from the sovereignty of man, to refuse the anticolonial reach of becoming masterful human subjects."[34] At the same time, these animal representations risk serving anthropocentric positions.[35]

While these novels depict animals with varying degrees of figurativeness, the stories they tell defend the distinctive integrity of human consciousness, which only becomes more profound under conditions of political abjection. Animal allegory offers an especially potent form for such critique because animals have long been used to both allegorize and abject the colonial and postcolonial subject. Achille Mbembe argues that racial oppression "stems from the racial denial of any common bond between the conqueror and the native. In the eyes of the conqueror, *savage life* is just another form of *animal life*, a horrifying experience, something alien beyond imagination or comprehension."[36] Indeed, this mapping of race onto species suggests that allegory is a master trope of biopolitics: the long history of the animalization of racial others as a mechanism of political control has been devastating. For Adiga and Sinha, to claim an animal affinity is to question a self-sovereignty—and especially a masculinity—that has been barred for certain kinds of citizens; similarly, for Beukes animal affinities mark those who have been permanently excluded from citizenship, and whose efforts to reclaim power are tenuous, deeply dangerous, and likely to fail. These novels indict the state's capacity to make live and put to death and illustrate a key paradox of human rights discourse under the biopolitical power that controls bodily life: in Elizabeth Anker's words, "a person's potential to authenticate the liberal dictates of freedom and autonomy is constitutively predetermined by the relative limitations of—as well as opportunities afforded by—that person's embodiment."[37] It is also quite possible to allegorize animality as national future even in a novel that attempts to more fully disavow human agency.[38] Lydia Millet's *How the Dead Dream* (2008) is a particularly clear example, depicting a financially successful but dissociated young real estate developer's personal transformation into an "anti-protagonist" after he hits a coyote with his car. He begins breaking into zoos, gradually realizing a profound sense of responsibility for other species. Face to face with a wolf, for instance, the protagonist experiences a depersonalizing realization: although he registers its being as "self-contained," he finds "a fleeting awareness that in the wolf's gaze there was a directness unlike the directness of men."³⁹ Yet this recognition takes place within the walls of the zoo—an institutional space that makes animals the fully administered creatures of the human imagination, and reflects the protagonist's sense of helplessness. Such melancholy fictions, whether about species or individual animals, "index histories of modernization and colonization and ... articulate skepticism regarding their consequences," as Ursula Heise points out, noting also that such novels tend to depict characters who are drawn into contemplating animal experience "quite against their own intentions" and without any form of scientific or philosophical expertise."⁴⁰ Can the zoo ever really be destroyed?

As counter to the figural use of the zoo to represent carceral government or its opposite, neoliberal subjectivity, the logic of milieu also pervades the literature of the broken zoo. Martel's *Life of Pi* dramatizes a core tension between these modes: the idea that milieu, evoked through descriptive modes like mood, tone, pace, and sound, can constitute an alternative to allegory is especially clear in *Life of Pi*. In this novel, Pi's family closes the Pondicherry Zoo before the 1975–77 Emergency, when the Indian government suspended civil liberties, suggesting the zoo as a potent metaphor for what the novel presents as a repressive political institution. However, the novel evades this crisis by imagining a nonsecuritized and noninstitutional—which is to say, a less knowingly allegorical—model of species relations. Pi's family dismantles their zoo, and he accompanies some of the animals on a sea voyage, only to be shipwrecked in the Pacific Ocean. This shipwreck sets the stage for a more affectively attuned and individualized mode of care; the novel emphasizes the common bodily responsiveness that creates a shared milieu, yet also suggests that a recognition of separate sensory worlds might motivate human care for animals. As in Davé's account of "interspecies praxis," in *Life of Pi*, this care at its least anthropocentric looks like a "relational ethic premised on mutual regard rather than curiosity, love, or animus."⁴¹

Martel's novel stresses human responsibility toward animal captives even as it downsizes its model of care from the carceral zoo to the open life raft. Pi's survival depends upon attentive care that recognizes profound differences as well as shared conditions. The narrative provides a wealth of detail describing how Pi trains the tiger, named Richard Parker, in order to cohabitate with it. He wonders, "Animals in the wild lead lives of compulsion and necessity within an unforgiving social hierarchy in an environment where the supply of fear is high and the supply of food low and where territory must constantly be defended and parasites forever endured. What is the meaning of freedom in such a context?" This query would seem to reject the possibility that the tiger might emblematize human freedom.[42] Pi understands his efforts to grasp and even master the tiger's *Umwelt* as ensuring their mutual survival. He sees his power as pastoral in Foucault's sense, lamenting during an especially difficult stretch: "I had failed as a zookeeper. I was more affected by his imminent demise than I was by my own" (242). As I noted in the Introduction, Foucault in *Security, Territory, Population* stresses that pastoral power does not demand obvious displays of dominance. Rather, "pastoral power initially manifests itself in its zeal, devotion, and endless application."[43] It is not really about the animals, but about their keeper's distinctive moral authority.

Pi's pastoral orientation suggests a need for human domination. Still, Pi speaks admiringly but not idealistically about the extent to which an animal's world might remain inaccessible to a human observer. He makes a conscious effort to avoid anthropocentrism, though as I'll explain shortly, the allegorical structure of the novel undermines this epistemic tactfulness in the end. Not unlike Berger, Pi acknowledges, "we look at an animal and see a mirror." He insists that in living together, he must recognize a fundamental aporia: "that an animal is an animal, essentially and practically removed from us" (31). A story about a tiger, the narrator insists, will inevitably be in part a story about how humans create structures of value. But crucially, because everyday habits are suspended by crisis, this recognition of difference allows him to negotiate an intimate form of supervision. As in Foucault, Martel emphasis the moral consequences for the shepherd, but he also stresses that caretaking orients Pi toward the tiger's individual salvation, underlined by the tiger's clear function as a secondary character with a too-human name.

Pi's narrative emphasizes his strenuous efforts to feed the tiger and stresses the tiger's physical pain and satisfaction, describing his needs, his beautiful fur and musculature, and his eyes at great length: he is "charismatic in his vitality" (170), mobile and multiple. There is plenty to be said for how an affective orientation can benefit from the recognition of difference. Derrida stresses both the absolute "alterity" of an animal's gaze and the "finitude that we share with animals," the vulnerability and mortality that we hold in common. "Difference" is not a stable or static rupture, but rather "a heterogeneous multiplicity of the living" that can motivate admiration as well as compassion.[44] When Pi and the tiger part ways, the tiger leaps into the sublime, and Pi recalls, "I saw his body, so immeasurably vital, stretched in the air above me, a fleeting, furred rainbow" (284). Even in frightening moments, Pi is attentive to tigrine beauty in the protracted crisis that has become their everyday life: "[His] stance had something of a pose to it, as if it were an intentional, even affected, display of mighty art. And what art, what might. His presence was overwhelming, yet equally evident was the lithesome grace of it" (151). Pi goes on to describe "formidable sideburns, a stylish goatee and some of the finest whiskers of the cat world," the "perfect arches" of his ears, and nose-fur of "rufous lustre [that] shone nearly with a radiance" (151–52). Martel demonstrates thematically and formally how a human might offer intimacy through pastoral care based on an assertion of aporetic difference.

Indeed, floating in a transnational oceanic space, the novel suspends political categories, particularly the category of citizenship, that depend on a human-animal aporia. Theories of human rights upon which western models of citizenship depend have historically divided off the rational from the animal, distinguishing those aspects of the human that can be construed as free and autonomous from those that appear as biological givens: in Roberto Esposito's words, "subjective right, rather than being inherent to the entirety of the human being, applies only to the upper part, which is rational or spiritual in nature, exercising its dominion over the remaining area, which is devoid of these characteristics and therefore thrust into the regime of objecthood"—or animality.[45] Anker observes, "It is the predicament of the animal that exposes the liberal individual posited by rights logic to be a strangely fleshless, decorporealized abstraction, an entity divested of those affective dimensions of selfhood."[46] When a narrative like *Life of Pi* emphasizes the corporeal experiences of humans and other-than-human animals as an alternative to political categories of belonging, it makes clear that creaturely lives are not fully recognized in the terms of human rights or even animal rights.

But the novel's conclusion troublingly rescinds its emphasis on shared milieu, permitting an allegorical return to the human. When Pi tells his story to insurance adjusters, they doubt that his tale is true. Though Pi protests, "tigers don't contradict reality" (302), his tale is nonetheless revealed as an allegory or fable, and his tiger as a mere figure. Fables, of course, have long served as narrative alibis for telling unpleasant truths. Looking at animals, Pi admits, generates a "fiction that guarantees their social well-being and staves off violent anarchy" (85–86); even when he marks his awareness of this logic, inevitably animals become figures for fiction itself. When he retells the story without animals, it turns out that the story of survival with a tiger may be his way of telling a story of surviving with a vicious man. As Hilary Thompson argues, "A novel that seems to be about coexistence and sensibility becomes one about singular survival and sovereignty, the power to make extraordinary decisions in exceptional circumstances."[47] Pi asks the insurance agents: "So tell me, since it makes no factual difference to you and you can't prove the question either way, which story do you prefer? Which is the better story, the story with animals or the story without animals?" (317). They reply: "The story with animals.... Yes. The story with animals is the better story." This preference allows Pi to affirm, "So it goes with God" (317), implying that he needs to believe in a God, as up to this point he has believed in the tiger, in order to survive the unthinkable. The tiger is in the service of an apophatic theology, where God's protective power is best represented negatively or indirectly, appearing here through Pi's devotion to an animal who might always overpower him yet who also, subtly, nurtures him. And *this* insight, indicative of Pi's *Bildung*, comes at a significant conceptual cost: the tiger becomes not only other, but *immaterial*. The elaborate details involved in the narrative of caring for the tiger are rendered incoherent retrospectively because they have no corollary significance within the novel's allegorical structure.

Certainly, most of the novel develops an approach that points in a different direction from this final allegory, and in fact Pi's question—"Which story do you prefer?"—conveys ambivalence toward this recentering on exclusively human modes of value, even as its being framed *as* a choice only confirms that recentering.[48] After all, the fable suggests that there is condemnable likeness between killing humans and killing animals. Still, the final affirmation of the human capacity for storytelling, imagination, and religious belief renders the tiger figural, his tigerness drafted into the service of Pi's distinctive humanity. Derrida insists that "fabulation" "remains an anthropomorphic taming, a moralizing subjection, a domestication. Always a discourse *of* man on man, indeed on the animality of man, but for and as man."[49] In *Life of Pi*, the lived messiness of propinquity is belatedly subordinated to allegoresis, underlining the power of storytelling to generate empathy and highlighting the cognitive autonomy of the human imagination, which can powerfully imagine the world as it is not. From such a perspective, storytelling allows us to transcend embodied vulnerabilities and valorizes the purportedly most distinctive human faculties, while shifting attention away from recognition of shared environmental embeddedness.

2. THEORY IN THE MIDDLE

Allegory remains a major challenge for an anti-anthropocentric, postcritique agenda because both fiction (in its long history) and theory depend heavily on allegory: they reveal the *difficulty* of maintaining a lateral rather than hierarchic understanding of shared vulnerability and bodily finitude in our multispecies "community of the living." To dwell with animals outside of this "anthropological machine," we must insist on the lived reality of the animals we encounter, and thus resist turning them into figures, abstractions, or concepts that deny the sensate density of their living bodies, and their sapience as they navigate our shared milieu.[50] Animals-as-tropes prompt considerable disagreement among scholars eager to find the lives and vitality of actual animals recognized and represented. Following Derrida's critique of the notion of "the animal" as a stable category, Ortiz-Robles and Heather Keenleyside argue that animals, in their otherness, are what tropes are, while Philip Armstrong, Susan McHugh, Hilary Thompson, Sundhya Walther, and others seek representations of animal agency that refuse "substitutive logics."[51] Like the latter group, I am indebted to those critics who claim that allegory is an "openly violent" conceptual reduction of a "lower," natural or given level, to an "upper," abstract or hierarchic one. Angus Fletcher, for instance, argues that despite the "internal conflict" at the heart of allegory, allegory became ultimately associated with political authoritarianism during changes in the early modern period's struggles over sovereignty; as for Fredric Jameson, allegory arises out of political need—a need for management.[52] This section—moving past the allegorical rupture of *Life of Pi*—makes a step toward this book's larger contention that that the contemporary novel offers a corrective to biopolitical theory's own dependence on allegorical figuration, as in Giorgio Agamben's image of western metaphysics as an "anthropological machine" or in Foucault's conception of the pastoral.

In *Zoo City* and *Animal's People*, animalization indexes the logic of exclusion-as-captivity that constitutes biopower. But as theorists reflecting on biopolitics have noted, this discourse offers a critical reconstruction of the pernicious consolidation of a normative *humanity*. Nicole Shukin's *Animal Capital*, for instance, points out that while "discourses and technologies of biopower hinge on the species divide," the discourse ultimately remains interested only in the conceptual negotiation of the human—an emphasis she aims to rectify by focusing on the consequences of the regulation of lived animal existences. Shukin argues that deconstructive accounts of the animal such as Derrida's are less free from the burdens of figuration than they acknowledge: she argues that using animals as tropes risks "envisioning animals as pure intensities and undying specters"—all too exploitable by a capitalist economy that "renders" animals imaginary and fungible.[53] Moreover, allegorical critique emphasizes ideological content while placing the critic in a privileged yet attractively counterhegemonic position. For Anker and Felski, when "the hermeneutic project is . . . conceived in terms of an ethical disclosure of structures of Otherness or oppression," it implies not only a "trust in the transgressive or oppositional impact of critique," but the heroism of the critic, who absorbs these values through performances of ideological exposure. I share these "growing doubts about such claims of political efficacy and about the romantic image of the critic as heroic dissident."[54] In particular, I note how prevalent this ethos is in theories of allegory, whether in the deconstructive mode of Paul de Man, in which the critic recognizes that allegories reflect the impossibility of representation, or the work of Jameson, which treats the ideological function of literature as allegorical. An allegorical critical method is very effective at explaining, in Alexander Galloway's succinct formulation, "how and why something might appear in the form of its opposite" under late capitalism.[55] The rupture between representational levels reflects the disjunctive structure of ideology itself. When critique highlights this rupture, it attends to depictions of lived conditions of experience but risks overemphasizing ideology's determining force.

Biopolitics manages the concept of the animal through allegory. I want to point out that *as itself a narrative*, biopolitical theory tells an allegorical story of authoritarian power—the power to determine who counts and what means. According to Agamben and Esposito, the differentiation between human beings and animals is a fundamental mechanism for conferring human distinction; the animal comes into being as a privative category to mark what the human is not.[56] When biopolitics marks out those who count as human, it "requires the sacrifice of the 'animal' and the animalistic, which in turn makes possible a symbolic economy in which we can engage in a 'noncriminal putting to death,'" in Cary Wolfe's summation.[57] In Chapters 2 and 3, I will give more attention to what I view as the harms of the emphasis on death in biopolitical critique. Here, I observe that just as biopolitics is allegorical, allegory is biopolitical; allegory obscures animals from the analysis of biopower's making live and letting die by analyzing how the animalization of humans has served biopolitical ends. To work conceptually with animals is to expose the links between political sovereignty and the forms of representation that distribute bodily capacity. What we miss when we prioritize critique-as-allegory—and allegory-as-critique—is sentience.

Allegorical form is famously multiple and misaligned, offering both a literal and a figurative level that attempts to entirely subsume the literal, though for most critics fails *despite* its self-reflexivity. In Walter Benjamin's famous account of the baroque *Trauerspiel*, he articulates a melancholy version of allegory that both ruins and sanctifies the given, the natural, the *merely* biological. "The word 'history' stands written on the countenance of nature in the characters of transience," making a "ruin" of the nature elevated by this conscription's very awareness of its own discontinuity.[58] This is logic is exemplified by yet another literary zoo moment, in W. G. Sebald's *Austerlitz* (2001). As the novel opens, the narrator gazes at animals in the Antwerp Zoo seeking some insight into their opacity—the very space that makes possible an allegorical reading of the zoological capture of human lives (crucial to the novel's reflections on the Holocaust) precludes an account of commonality not dependent on capture. This is a fundamentally "melancholic" connection, in which capture is at once openly inadequate yet also, symptomatically, constitutive.[59]

As I noted in the Introduction, allegory's consolidation of political meaning involves, for Gordon Tesky, a fundamentally violent oscillation between depicting the "otherness" of the given and "capture": "What the act of capture exhibits is the truth over which allegory is always drawing its veil: the fundamental disorder out of which the illusion of order is raised."[60] For many, "capture" is precisely what makes allegory so critically productive; allegorical narratives, in DeLoughrey's words, "capture the lack of continuity between self and world" in postcolonial postmodernity.[61] Yet as Antoine Traisnel has crucially shown, "capture"—a term associated with artistic representation as such from the nineteenth century onward—is conceptually indebted to the hunt and depends upon settler colonial violence: "the desire to capture live animals in representation in the nineteenth century responded to and normalized the systemic disappearance of animals effected by unprecedented changes in the land, the new awareness of species extinction, and the automation of mass slaughter and the mass reproduction of farm animals . . . unknowable yet understood in advance."[62] This final phrase—"unknowable and yet understood in advance"— evokes the interpretive predicament involved in reading allegory and of reading allegorically. Traisnel's account of the term helps to explain why the treatment of animals is such a powerful test case for understanding the limits of allegoresis as a critical procedure writ large. Ultimately, pushing criticism of the novel beyond allegoresis is consequential for the prevalence of biopolitical analysis as a framework that has increasingly become synonymous *with* critique.

As an example of that mode of critical allegoresis, in *The Political Unconscious,* Jameson viewed realism especially as revealing "post-traditional life and its bewilderingly empirical, 'meaningless,' and contingent *Umwelt*" as an allegory of late capitalism, where *Umwelt* refers to the enclosed, affectively void space of bourgeois subject who believes in a measurable world.[63] Indeed, this description reflects, to a certain extent, von Uexküll's ideas insofar as the constriction of demand and sensation reciprocally captures a world through perception. Still, I advocate further revisiting the concept of *Umwelt*, as it first emerged as a concept in comparative cognition and as it developed into an account of milieu that undergirded the work introducing biopolitical critique.[64] Thus, even as I argue for the milieu as a conceptual model with explanatory power, I will show that its resonance is best discerned aconceptually, in writing that evokes the process of perception—and in the interpretation of narrative poetics.

In turning to contemporary fiction as a counterdiscourse, I want to highlight that allegorical critique has consequences not just for the novel form generally but especially for its treatment of the protagonist as a moral center whose ethos at once indexes sovereign power and gives significance to those marked as "other." The function of the protagonist is key to allegorical interpretation of fiction, as in Jameson's claim, mentioned in the Introduction, that all Third World literatures offer national allegories, in which *"the story of the private individual destiny is always an allegory of the embattled situation for public third-world culture and society."*[65] This claim for the compression of collectivity into individuality resonates with Jameson's assessment that allegory is currently re-emergent precisely as an index of current population pressures: "The immense and inconceivable proliferation of otherness in our now unrepresentable 'globalized' species population which take precedence over and indeed subsumes all these other undeniable developments."[66] According to Ivan Kreilkamp and Emily Steinlight, even older novels compress population into protagonicity, a logic that strikingly aligns with Foucault's account of pastoral individuation: Foucault writes, "Pastoral power is an individualizing power. That is to say, it is true that the shepherd directs the whole flock, but he can only really direct it insofar as not a single sheep escapes him. The shepherd counts the sheep; he counts them . . . *omnes et singulatim*."[67] Connecting Foucault to nineteenth-century novel, Kreilkamp and Steinlight draw on Alex Woloch to emphasize that minor characters (whatever their species) tend to play a more openly allegorical—indexical, exteriorized, functional—role in character systems that associate depth psychology with expansive character space with real-world social status. Still, in this account even the protagonist's relation to political and social power remains profoundly instrumental. It is in this way that, for Woloch, novels constantly call attention to the uneven distribution of allegory: "The novel gets infused with an awareness of its potential to *shift* the narrative focus away from an established center, toward minor character."[68] The allegorizing function of protagonicity is (like other allegorical structures) a signal of failure, rupture, and potential ruin, becoming an anthropological aesthetic of capture or containment.

Throughout this book, I suggest that a diminished commitment to the human protagonist and to the "private individual destiny" is key. Whereas Jameson contends in *Allegory and Ideology* that "humanism is a symptom" only of "bad allegory," he also acknowledges in *The Antinomies of Realism* (the previous volume in his series, *The Poetics of Social Forms*) that "allegory and the body . . . repel one another and fail to mix."[69] There, he argues that narrative, particularly realism, is structured by tension between the meaning-giving momentum and structure of storytelling, and the affective immediacy of sensory experience. Distinguishing allegory from the synesthetic sensory "intensity" of narrative style from the midnineteenth century onward—both of which emerge in historically contingent ways—Jameson contends that narrative creates an "irreconcilable divorce between intelligibility and experience," registering formally the interruption of "narrative by a kind of non-narrative perceptuality."[70]

I find this a productive division of energies and rhythms. Even in texts that allegorize animals, then, that does not mean we cannot notice their investment in animal milieus. Indeed, Jameson points out that "in an age that prizes difference and differentiation, heterogeneity, incommensurability, a resistance to unification, this failure cannot continue to be a reproach, and it is our fault then, as readers . . . that we fail to acknowledge the reality of the literal level of the allegorical text."[71] Thus even for Jameson, allegory may be less *merely* socially symptomatic but rather an emergent registration of when beneath this or that seemingly stable or unified reality the tectonic plates of deeper contradictory levels of the Real shift and grate ominously against one another and demand a representation, or at least an acknowledgment, they are unable to find in the *Schein* or illusory surfaces of existential or social life. Allegory does not reunify those incommensurable forces, but it sets them in a relationship with one another in a way which, as with all art, all aesthetic experience, can lead alternatively to ideological comfort or the restless anxieties of a more expansive knowledge.[72]

Connecting this passage to realist fiction, Anna Kornbluh writes, "Whether oppressive or liberating, realism appears as the referential *capture* of what already exists, even if what exists, as in bourgeois modernity, is flux and change."[73] Indeed, the rhythm of reading, even critical reading, is itself at stake, and does not always decode ideological mystification, but instead prompts a shift in what can be perceived. Attending to the rhythms of reading (as Jameson does here) motivates a return to some conceptual underpinnings of biopolitics that point in a different methodological direction, away from an aesthetics of capture and toward the novel as a site for imagining the interspecies possibilities of the milieu.

3. MILIEUS, NOT ZOOS

Even if *Life of Pi* frustratingly revokes its interest in the intimate, material challenges of human-animal relationship, several other texts imagine escaped zoo animals not merely as figures that redound to the human but as experiencers themselves. The final destroyed-zoo texts I consider attend more closely to milieu shared by humans and other animals alike without insisting so painfully on the clash between capacity and vulnerability. *The Wind-Up Bird Chronicle* and *The Tiger's Wife* use sense methods to emphasize the experiential dimensions of material, sensing bodies (whatever their capacities) that cannot or should not be fully legislated by institutions. Both texts depict "mute" humans responding to animals; by removing the division of spoken language, they are concerned neither to deflate nor elevate the dignity of humans as protagonists nor to conflate human and animal capacities. As Dinesh Wadiwel argues, the specific concept of *Umwelt* has the potential to create nonreductive alignments: "The capacity to elaborate an Umwelt also demands social and economic arrangements that enable participatory worlds, that allow beings to participate in determining their own futures, including futures in relation to others."[74] Following upon that observation is another: neither is a *Bildungsroman* that would provide a road map to the restitution of human consciousness or citizenship—neither treats the human's ability to provide care as an index of human sovereignty over biological life. Each of these novels, for its own reasons, offers limited revelations of the narrator's own inwardness. Moreover, neither treats animals as characters—they are not companion species in any conventional sense—not minor enough to start the machine of flat versus deep and allegory versus reference. These narratives develop non-allegorical aesthetic strategies—especially through their approaches to lyrical description—to evoke a shared milieu without dictating any particular degree of collaboration. With Min Hyoung Song, I would identify narrative lyricism here less as a distinctive set of formal devices than as a "mode of literary attentiveness" that "turns away from the demands of plot" to "linger on details," often with the effect of emphasizing the mutually constitutive relation between perceiver and perceived.[75] In these novels, interspecies relationships are openly matters of fantasy that mark projected if not necessarily fulfilled desires for intimacy. They have admittedly limited power because they may not translate into the creation of durable community or strategy for political change—or even something that could be articulated as a wish for these outcomes. Nonetheless, the "sense methods" that emerge in moments of lyrical description—which I will continue to highlight in the chapters that follow—might reframe our understanding of belonging in a time of exigency.

Murakami's *The Wind-Up Bird Chronicle*—the story of Toru, who searches for his missing wife and missing pet cat, discovering a series of enigmatic strangers along the way—includes a subplot that presents an effort at reframing relationships across species lines. One of the strangers, the healer Nutmeg Akasaka, befriends the narrator, aiding his search and seemingly facilitating the cat's return. One night, Toru discovers on Nutmeg's son's computer a file titled "The Wind-Up Bird Chronicle," which seems to beckon to him. There, he reads a story about Nutmeg's father witnessing the "liquidation" (401) of the Xinjing Zoo in Manchukuo at the demise of the Japanese occupation. The tiger is the first to go.[76] The story's narrator stresses the hideous interchangeability of bodily matter as the zoo animals are "reduced to hide, meat, organs, and bones, as if those elements had originally been quite separate and had just happened to come together for a little while" (410). Murakami communicates visceral horror through the disbelieving eyes of traumatized soldiers who cannot believe they have killed an almost mythical creature for the sake of efficiency. This scene has been interpreted figuratively. According to Randy Malamud, this episode in the novel "depicts pain—the pain of zoo animals, metaphorically representing the pain facing the entire planet—concentrated into a few moments of horrific barbarity, so repulsive that one can barely process it," and ultimately "remind[ing] us how painfully people are capable of treating each other."[77] But the zookeeper's daughter, who years later repeats the story to her nonverbal son, experiences it differently, reframing this catastrophe as an ongoing scene of affective responsiveness. Murakami's decision to give this dimension to the event shifts the emphasis away from analogy or allegory. Nutmeg Akasaka recalls of her father, "We would talk for hours about the names of the animals in the zoo, about the sheen of their fur or the color of their eyes, about the different smells that hung in the air, about the names and faces of the individual soldiers, about their birth and childhood, about their rifles and the weight of their ammunition, about the fears they felt and their thirst, about the shapes of the clouds floating in the sky" (444). Her tale is explicitly a fantasy of bodies bound through execrable violence, and of telling stories about it. The zookeeper's daughter emphasizes the story's material effects and sensuous resonances without ascribing to it an allegorical function.

Crucially, Nutmeg's nonverbal son Cinnamon also participates in the telling of these stories, a telling without language that diminishes the specificity of human privilege, for Cinnamon is said to be able to communicate clearly, his silence facilitating rather than "obstructing any mental exchange" (440). These stories emphasize bodies' unexpected scents and textures. The zookeeper's daughter recalls: "My father always smelled like the animals. All the different animal smells would mix together into one, and it would be a little different each day, like changing the blend of ingredients in a perfume. I'd climb up onto his lap when he came home and make him sit still while I smelled him" (405). Nutmeg recalls snuggling into her father's body, which carried the scent marks of many others in a kind of anti-taxonomy. This passage undoes hierarchies of sense, elevating touch and olfaction over the achievements of vision associated with power, regulation, and care, just as the characters' chosen names—Nutmeg and Cinnamon—refer to spices that call attention to, or resonate with, calming sensory effects. Thus, although the zoo's destruction makes up only a small episode in a long, episodic novel, it concretizes what up to this point has been a burgeoning affirmation of embodiment as against a nationalistic image of biopolitical putting-to-death. The humans associated with this story, Nutmeg and Cinnamon, are healers, suggesting that an embrace of the human as constituted by milieu might itself be a gesture of caretaking. And while these charismatic characters attract Toru, the distribution of caretaking between the two, and their at best indirect facilitation of his recovery from mysterious loss, suggests Murakami's refusal to overinvest in characters as sites of distinctive moral capacities or agential centers.

Despite Toru's strange, psychic affiliation with the zookeeper's daughter, his development of unaccustomed mental capacities is not associated with any form of educational growth, definite revelation, or progressive achievement—markers of the human as indices of a liberal plot of *Bildung*. Rather, he begins to experience himself passively, developing sensually specific animal affinities. The fascinations of animal bodies build as Toru comes to understand his own body's lateral coexistence within a shared milieu. Thinking back to the disaffiliated animal parts, we might note that in Murakami's novel, the narrator's shift of consciousness begins when, having lowered himself into a neighborhood well and discovered animal bones beside him, he imagines his body as a part of a larger life cycle: "The darkness and cold were swept away in a moment, and warm, gentle sunlight enveloped my naked body. Even the pain I was feeling seemed to be blessed by the light of the sun, which now warmly illuminated the white bones of the small animal beside me. These bones, which could have been an omen of my own impending fate, seemed in the sunlight more like a comforting companion" (165). In this underground world, he senses his own embodiment passively. Lying beside the remains of an unspecified animal, he begins to attend to his sensations, whereas before he understood himself as embodied only during intermittent sex acts. It is not that he becomes one with the animal bones in a mystic way: he and the bones retain their separateness, but their presence together, or alliance as bodies sharing a space for an unmeasured period of time, allows the narrator to state, "This was my body: my flesh" (256). His realization of fleshliness is morbid, yet it appears to emphasize pleasure as much as the potential for pain. Throughout, Murakami's novel is particularly interested in the dimensionality and responsiveness of "flesh." Beginning with his relationship with an animal corpse, Toru begins to notice and take pleasure in his own corporeality.

Pleasure's anti-allegorical alliance with caretaking is equally at stake in Obreht's *The Tiger's Wife*. To some extent, the first reviews of this novel misunderstood its message as similar to that of *Life of Pi*, where relations of care are ultimately put into the service of a portrait of distinctively human capacities. For instance, in the *New York Times* review, the tiger appears as a figure for the creation of myth: "Obreht shows that you don't have to go back centuries to find history transformed into myth; the process can occur within a lifetime if a gifted observer is on hand to record it."[78] The reviewer is not wrong in claiming that the novel suggests that the capacity for storytelling enables humans to survive situations that tax them beyond their physical and psychological breaking point. (Perhaps the same could be said of the computer file, "The Wind-Up Bird Chronicle," within *The Wind-Up Bird Chronicle*, which is explicitly marked as a written and probably fictitious narrative.) However, in *The Tiger's Wife*, narrative structure that decenters character-building, alongside its refusal to make its tigers analogies, means that it cannot be read solely as a fable about fabulation. This novel, like Murakami's told in the first person, recounts a journey undertaken by the narrator, Natalia, a young doctor living in a Balkan country. Grappling with her grandfather's recent, mysterious death on her way to a coastal orphanage to immunize the children, Natalia continually places animals at the center of her reflections on the nation's political precariousness; however, a lyrical style pulls against the allegorical force of the tiger-as-failed-nation trope.

The Tiger's Wife features several tigers, mythic and real, figurative and not. First are the tigers of the recent past, living in the zoo that the narrator, Natalia, and her grandfather frequent. This zoo, and the "fortress" (93) or "citadel" (94) where it is housed, fails to protect the captive animals, much less secure the integrity of the city. Its tigers' behavior registers their vulnerability to the human structures that contain them. A newspaper report on the bombing of a city zoo "focused on the tiger, and only on the tiger, because, despite everything, there was still some hope for him."[79] Traumatized by their experiences of a war they cannot comprehend, the tigers turn on themselves. Their acts of self-harm are never made analogous to a human condition, though the war in question, modeled on the Balkan wars of the 1990s, could be understood as violence against the self. Obreht underlines the tiger's uncomprehending trauma:

> For weeks and weeks after the bombing ended, Zbogom the tiger continued to eat his own legs. He was docile, tame, to the keepers, but savage on himself, and they would sit in the cage with him, stroking the big square block of his head while he gnawed on the stumps of his legs. The wounds were infected, swollen and black.
>
> In the end, without announcing it in the newspaper, they shot that legless tiger there, on the stone slab of his cage. The man who raised him—the man who nursed him, weighed him, gave him baths, the man who carried him around the zoo in a knapsack, the man whose hands appeared in every picture ever taken of the tiger as a cub—pulled the trigger. (302)

This tiger functions as a potent synecdoche for hope in a threatened nation, but tellingly, he is eventually euthanized—an outcome that links the figurative use of animals with institutionalized death. Obreht contrasts the persistence of relationships of care when the institutions of the state have failed, creating a collapse in the managed *Umwelt* of the tiger's previous zoo experience. This intimacy is not merely an analogy for that condition of the state. The passage also details how the female tiger responds to bombings by eating her young, so "the keepers took the remaining cubs away from her, raised them in their own houses, with their own pets and children. Houses without electricity, with no running water for weeks on end. Houses with tigers" (302). If the keepers here appear heroic, it is under the conditions of a shared vulnerability that creates a new kind of community. Whereas the pastoral care of the zoo normally involves maximizing health and norming *Umwelt* in order to reproduce the species and promote their attractive, exotic nature through spectacle and display, the keepers' new recognition of shared embodiment renders their care less hierarchic. New community also emerges at the zoo itself, when citizens protest the bombings by visiting in animal costumes, a surreal scene that speaks to the failures of the human population to protect the animals they have made their wards. It also suggests, as it insists on the propinquity of human and animal lives, a resistance to viewing animals merely as victims.

The other tiger in the novel escapes during World War II and becomes an object of village legend without becoming an emblem of the enduring human imagination. Through this tiger, Obreht more fully explores the affective dimensions of cross-species relationships. While narrating her present-day concerns, Natalia also recounts her grandfather's childhood, emphasizing his rewriting of Rudyard Kipling's *The Jungle Book*. In Kipling's tales, the human child Mowgli outwits Shere Khan, the tiger, handily gaining authority over all the animals of the jungle through his use of fire, his ability to strategize, and above all, his dominant gaze. Kipling's stories not only valorize human dominance over the natural world, from which humans remain apart, but also constitute an allegory of empire that suggests the natural fitness of paternalistic power. When Natalia's grandfather encounters a tiger, he thinks of Mowgli's effort to "subdue" Shere Khan, but he instead, more subtly, "put his hand out . . . and touched the coarse hairs passing by him" (116). He finds pleasure in the fleeting contact. Furthering his nonhierarchical impulse, he later retells the story of *The Jungle Book* to the titular tiger's wife, a mute young woman who has developed her own tiger affinity. As with the nonverbal Cinnamon Akasaka in *The Wind-Up Bird Chronicle*, the communicative silence of a disabled human character seems to indicate diffused borders between human and animal modes of being.[80] When the boy retells *The Jungle Book*, he refuses to comply with Kipling's narrative of domination: "Somehow he could never reveal the way the man-cub claimed the tiger's life" (227). Instead, he keeps the conflict vibrant, portraying an agonistic but ongoing relationship between the tiger and the boy, a relationship less legible in terms of domination. As the boy grows up to become a doctor, he must contend with this fantasy of deathlessness and recognize more fully the shared vulnerability that binds animals and people together.

Villagers recount how the tiger changes form to become the "husband" of the battered, nonverbal young woman no human will defend. Using the terms "husband" and "wife" for this unusual pair, the villagers gesture to the larger suspension of social regulation during wartime. They also evoke the marriage contract that these two lack the standing to initiate, setting their relationship apart from the legal and religious contract administered by institutions and dependent upon communicative action. The villagers find it difficult to imagine this interspecies bond, but curiously they never claim that the tiger must become human in order to be the woman's husband. Despite some physical changes, he stays more or less a tiger in their stories. "People have seen it," says one villager. "The tiger is her husband. He comes into her house each night and takes off his skin" (259). The apothecary imagines the scene in more detail: he "could see the tiger rise upright and embrace the girl, and the two of them would sit down at the table together to eat—and always they were eating heads, the heads of cattle and sheep and deer, and then they ate the head of the hermaphroditic goat from the pasha's trophy room" (260). The passage concatenates dehumanized images:

shared carnivorous hunger stands in for bestial sex; the head of a hermaphroditic goat suggests boundary blurring; eating heads, particularly, would seem to signal an attack on cognition—except for the fact that these heads are those which ostensibly lack the power of rational thought, further eroding familiar demarcations between human and animal categories.

Narration focalized through the tiger's perspective similarly deemphasizes human-animal differences. At first, the narrator makes it clear that her perspective on the tiger is filtered through her own, very human, perspective. Imagining the tiger's flight from the zoo, she ponders, "I like to imagine his big-cat paw prints in the gravel, his exhausted, square-shouldered walk along my childhood paths, years before I was even born—but in reality, the way through the undergrowth was faster, the moss easier on paws he had shredded on city rubble" (95). Acknowledging anthropomorphism from the outset, she does not take it on as an urgent problem. When the narrative later describes a human town as if from the tiger's perspective, the novel appears willing to grant each species its unique set of saliences: if humans cleave to memory, tigers home in on scent as a kind of embodied remembrance. Outside the zoo,

> the smells were pleasant and distinct, entirely separate from one another: the thick, woolly smell of sheep and goats; the smell of fire, tar, wax; the interesting reek of the outhouses; paper, iron, the individual smells of people.... The smells also made him more and more aware of his hunger, his lack of success as a hunter, of the length of time since his last meal, the calf that had blundered into him that bitter afternoon when he'd seen the man turn and run. The taste of the calf had been familiar; the shape of the man had been familiar. (108)

The passage does not make an issue of species difference: like humans, Obreht's tiger has a rich perceptual world. His affective responses are neither particularly inhuman nor particularly human: he is attributed an olfactory sensorium that allows for a degree of self-awareness, memory, and familiarity. The novel, then, appears invested in the tiger's *Umwelt*, the appetites by which his environment becomes salient to him and the emotions that lead him to pursue further sensations. The tiger experiences the woman through "the warmth of the village and the smokehouse smell of her hair" (261) as expressions of interspecies love. The world-making senses of the tiger create a bond. The narrator's use of free indirect discourse makes embodied consciousness familiar without cautioning that the tiger's perspective is radically unknowable (a strategy I will discuss further in Chapter 4). The novel ends by refusing to claim authority over the tiger and his stories; if the overall narrative constitutes a defense of the human imagination, the imagination's power is surprisingly weak. How to explain the attachment between a battered woman and an escaped zoo animal? "Maybe it's enough," Natalia ponders, "to say he enjoyed the sensation of her hand between his eyes. She liked the way his flank smelled when she curled up against it to sleep" (336). There is no contract between the two, but their worlds overlap. Moreover, although *The Tiger's Wife* centers upon storytelling, this passage is the first of several concluding professions of unknowingness that vie against any vocabulary of mastery or valorization of human capacities. With vulnerability and nescience come ample and specifically rendered pleasures.

In focusing on the sensory dimensions of world-making that humans and animals share, Obreht's novel, like Murakami's, presents fragile alliances of care between living bodies without valorizing uniquely human capacities. I have focused on certain parts of it, but taken as a whole, *The Tiger's Wife* is something of a strange beast, an affirmation of storytelling that recognizes fabulation's limits, and a coming-of-age story that persistently decenters the storyteller herself, refusing to allow the novel to become about her while recognizing that it inevitably will return to her to some degree, whatever her ostensible topic. From a human-centered point of view, much of Natalia's story appears strangely impersonal, lacking any eros to motivate the plot, or even a keenly emotional sense of loss to drive recuperation. Though the narrative is spurred by Natalia's process of grieving for her grandfather, he remains shadowy, and his loss is taken with the stoic attitude of the professional doctor. A considerable portion of the text uses the register of collective narration—"Some say...," "Others believe..."—a textual strategy that deemphasizes or de-aggrandizes individual acts of human cognitive exemplarity and instead presents storytelling as one form of species instinct, a human way of organizing a milieu.[81] Moreover, it tells stories in whorls, rather than full circles, never allowing that a tale could be a complete achievement: "In the end, I cannot tell you who or what she was," Natalia says of the tiger's wife, just as the townspeople have largely forgotten the tiger, or incorporated him into their instinctive lives, "in their movements, in their speech, in the preventive gestures that have become a part of their everyday lives" (337). The tiger's "sound is lonely, and low, and no one hears it anymore" (337). The narrator, certainly, hears it, takes pleasure in it, and shares it, but only with the recognition that human reflection, too, depends upon its sensory milieu.

4. CONCLUSION

Moving away from allegory, and at times thinking through disability, the broken zoo does more than perpetuate pernicious modes of representation that, even as they ostensibly undertake political critique, return us always to ourselves at our most disengaged. If there is "capture" in contemporary zoobreak fiction, it often feels like what Anahid Nersessian describes as the paradoxical "capture [of] the active and in-depth knowing of nothing, and the peculiar achievement of being on close terms with incomprehension."[82] At the same time, this approach registers a shifting presentation of human obligation even despite not "knowing" animals' otherness. *The Wind-Up Bird Chronicle* and *The Tiger's Wife* suggest an alternative to a path in animal studies that centers on the negotiation of conceptual aporias as its primary problematic. They also offer an alternative to a path in literary critique, similarly invested in conceptual difference, that would reject interest in the nonhuman in order to avoid politically suspect conceptual conflation, exoticism, or distraction. Rather, affinity and proximity matter, because they reframe the too-often reimposed boundary between forms of life and suggest only quite tentatively the need for a political system, or a mode of care, that responds to life's fragile conditions within a given milieu.

TWO

Speaking Otherwise

One might well assume that allegorical novels struggle to "entertain the viewpoints of other beings."[1] In *Memoirs of a Polar Bear*, an ursine narrator attends a performance of Chekhov's *The Seagull* and comments only, "The performance was delectable. The part I found the most appetizing was the dead seagull on the stage."[2] In a world where a polar bear attends the theater and forms her own aesthetic views, *of course* this is what she would appreciate in Chekhov. Humor marks the narrative strain of acknowledging the distinctness of the talking animal's worldview. Animal narration would seem to be a limited means of rethinking the relation between literary form and animal life; Alice Kuzniar complains that "the imaginative leap into the [animal's] thoughts arises from the desire to supply what is missing; it is compensatory for both the animal's silence and human incomprehension." The effort, she argues, often "descends into banality and insipidness."[3] Why should animals have to make words? The aporetic line of animal studies would urge extreme caution in speaking as though from an animal's wordless perspective—"to imagine a language we cannot understand," in Cary Wolfe's phrase.[4] Indeed, the posthuman turn often avoids the problem of the animal word, instead asking scholars to "learn to hear or enhance our receptivity for 'propositions' not expressed in words"—not unlike the nonverbal scenes of affinity I discussed in chapter 1.[5]

Talking animals make paradoxical characters—a banal observation.[6] Often starring in allegories without knowing it, animal protagonists and especially animal narrators forcefully translate the meaning of their own existence into anthropocentric terms. Character often entails "the importance of stance, attitude, and relationality," qualities that *can* be extended to animal protagonists.[7] Yet animal characters often function in non-individualistic ways even while highlighting the extremely strong association in the history and theory of the novel between protagonicity and interiority, individuality, and a capacity for moral growth. But this paradox, as I argued in the Introduction, reflects the predicament of "character" itself. Individual character has, both historically and critically, appeared as an allegorical form reliant on a logic of capture: Foucault's claim that "pastoral power is an individualizing power" suggests that narrative attention produces the unique, psychologically nuanced, morally exemplary individual protagonist as a way of capturing, condensing, or exemplifying a population.[8]

Animals also make paradoxical narrators. Animal narration refuses the option offered by feminist standpoint theory, in which, as Josephine Donovan argues, "human advocates are required to articulate the standpoint of animals... that they do not wish to be slaughtered and treated in painful and exploitative ways."[9] Given the centrality of an exclusionary model of speech to political representation from Aristotle onward, novels have historically used first-person animal narration to justify animals' need for access to political representation, most famously in Anna Sewell's *Black Beauty* (1877). Criticism handling nonhuman speakers often asks whether it is possible for a story—necessarily structured by narrative conventions associated with human character—to evoke nonhuman cognition with any authenticity. Ludwig Wittgenstein famously claimed, "If a lion could talk, we could not understand him," but typically, nonhuman animal narrators or speakers are at once strategically strange yet familiar enough to be empathetic. In these texts, we can understand animals, but they don't mean only *for* us. Narratology debates whether "experientiality of an anthropomorphic nature" is a fundamental quality of narrative even when characters are not human.[10] Some scholarship on animal autobiography contends that when these "acts of speaking-for that cross the species boundary," in David Herman's words, they take seriously animals' worldedness.[11] At the same time, argues Frederike Middelhoff, first-person animal narratives often "call attention to the limits of language as well as to the epistemological anthropocentrism mirrored in our conceptions and representations of animal phenomenology." Much of this work, inflected by deconstruction, offers what Middelhoff terms a "zoopoetics of negativity," in which animal narratives that purport to offer cohesive evocations of animal consciousness function ultimately to allegorize linguistic limitation.[12]

Recent allegories of speaking animals show that what looks like paradox is really ambivalence.[13] What looks like character really isn't, quite. I argue that allegorical novels centering animal voice demonstrate ambivalence toward character itself, as well as toward the modes of critique that sustain it. This chapter suggests that these fictions do not fully confirm a zoopoetics of negativity; in making this argument, I draw from Peter Boxall's reminder that throughout much of the history of the novel, the form has drawn attention to the "mechanics of its own . . . vocal presence." Yet this is not to insist only on the "artificiality" and "emptiness" of voice, but instead to offer "self-reflexive analyses of the ways in which . . . imagined worlds are shaped by a progenitive voice."[14] Even allegorical narratives can desist from the contrarian strain of their own paradoxes by offering openly literary, experimental practices that diminish claims for humans' cognitive mastery. In this chapter I focus on two ambivalently allegorical, transnational, profoundly polyphonic novels: Yoko Tawada's *Memoirs of a Polar Bear* (2016) and NoViolet Bulawayo's *Glory* (2022). Their anthropomorphic animal narrators call (often humorous) attention to the coercion they experience in their use of language, using defamiliarizing strategies to highlight what they present as a disconnect between their species assignment and their narrative capacity. Both stress the necessity of language as essential to the project of biopolitical critique, particularly their searing assessments of the ways in which personhood is distributed by authoritarian regimes rather than existing prior to it. But they valorize animal speech only to *complicate* the force of their verbal critiques of the social order. For Bulawayo in particular, drawing on the Zimbabwean cultural heritage of orature, polyvocal narrative constitutes a forceful rejoinder to exclusionary understandings of voice.

The predicament of speaking animals in these texts counteracts historical traditions that exclude nonhuman animals from personhood, rendering them silent beings defined by their ability to suffer and die. It is important to recognize that contemporary allegories like *Glory* or *Memoirs of a Polar Bear* absolutely *do* observe, even fixate upon, the production of the self through the biopolitical regulation of state-sponsored death. Yet the allegorization involved in biopolitical dilemmas of animal finitude, and the paralyzingly negative affects that accompany them, is not the only register in which these novels present animals' narratives. Indeed, they use animals' voices to propose alternatives to the biopolitical logic that makes death central to how we conceive of creaturely lives. *Memoirs of a Polar Bear* and *Glory* call self-reflexive attention to the poetics of narrative voice, especially through experiments with metalepsis and collective narration. In fact, another way to articulate the agenda of this chapter is to ask: Why do recent politically pointed animal allegories seem so enamored of metalepsis?[15] I argue that their multispecies voicings highlight the unworkability of the ideal of the self-representing, independently acting, rights-seizing individual that divides humans from other species and refuse a centering narrative consciousness that would definitively code the allegory by demonstrating the biopolitical distribution of who counts as a person. Rather, they demonstrate the mutual dependency of a narrative's representational scope with a sense of milieu: what is perceptible depends upon how feeling, sensing, and knowing are distributed.

Allegory means literally a "speaking otherwise": these texts are interested in how animal voices speak otherwise even in human language—how they resonate and solicit response. They do not, for the most part, evoke animal vocalization directly; if the novel can occasionally function as a "biotechnology for preserving animal sounds," strongly allegorical novels refuse that option.[16] Evan Maina Mwangi points out that letting animals speak does not in itself give them agency, but rather "show[s] the dehumanization of everything under a cynical postcolonial regime."[17] Yet these novels' emphasis on their own vocality, even as it redistributes political attention and even if it motivates a human critic's engaged response, raises an unanswered question of how a *polis* can represent the interests of those who cannot use language symbolically, a question pressed in political discourse of the twentieth century, for instance, by Hannah Arendt in *On Revolution*, and more recently and specifically in regard to animal citizenship by Will Kymlicka and Sue Donaldson. Either eliminating or minoritizing human characters, however, arrives at a more distributive concept of action and self-constitution in part through the idea of species, where action looks less like reflectively chosen interventions made in a world conceived as separate from and often inimical to a protagonistic self, and more like responsiveness. Bulawayo and Tawada use allegory to explore vocality as an alternative to the liberal-humanist interiority that structures influential theories of the novel, and especially theories of character. Speaking back against allegorical capture, these novels participate in a mode of collective communication that uncouples voice from a narrow view of individual consciousness, selfhood, and citizenship. Allegorizing animals' vocality, then, makes novelistic interiority look at once less central and more aspirational than it has been taken to be.

1. CREATURELY VOICES

Voice has long been a rationale for the exclusion of nonhuman animals from the human political community. Aristotle conceives of "man" as a "political animal" (*zoon politikon*) thanks to the use of language:

> Man is the only animal who [nature] has endowed with the gift of speech. And whereas mere voice is but an indication of pleasure or pain, and is therefore found in other animals (for their nature attains to the perception of pleasure and pain and the intimation of them to one another, and no further), the power of speech is intended to set forth the expedient and inexpedient, and therefore likewise the just and unjust. And it is a characteristic of man that he alone has any sense of good and evil, of just and unjust, and the like, and the association of living beings who have this sense makes a family and a state.

For Aristotle, only those capable of speaking can be members of the human political community; conversely, reserving the capacity for "linguistic agency" for humans only has historically constituted grounds for excluding animals from political representation because not only are they dubiously capable of intentional action in legal terms, but they are also unable to verbally represent their own interests in the public sphere.[18] Drawing on the Aristotelian tradition of the *zoon politikon*, Arendt tracks a shift in what constituted politically significant participation from "action to speech, and to speech as a means of persuasion rather than the specifically human way of answering, talking back and measuring up to whatever happened or was done."[19] This move away from communication as an expression of species-being and toward the founding of political institutions thus raises an unanswered question of how a *polis* can represent the interests of those who cannot use language symbolically.

Indeed, as animals began to gain legal recognition in the nineteenth century, animal advocates increasingly stressed that other species could *not* communicate to highlight their vulnerability at human hands.[20] Their capacity for suffering, rather than communication, became more important. Although these activists typically drew on anecdotes of animals' inherent moral wisdom to elicit concern, they also persistently used an exclusively human notion of voice, and of communication as purely linguistic, as the ontological basis of a rigid human-animal binary to justify animal protection, emphasizing human political and social agency by citing animals' lack thereof. For Cora Diamond, "our hearing the moral appeal of an animal is our hearing it speak—as it were—the language of our fellow human beings"; moral attunement is not just an act of translation, marked between dashes as a figurative move, but, as for activist-oriented criticism, it also demands a strategically anthropocentric speaking-on-behalf. Other influential thinkers in animal studies worry about animals' speechlessness because it seems to authorize not protection but rather a strong formulation of humans' economic and political authority over animals' bodies; Derrida's influential "The Animal That Therefore I Am," for example, centers on this concern as it protests the ubiquitous killing of animals.

Derrida traces animals' unprotesting givenness to death—the central problematic of his concern—to the work of Martin Heidegger. For Heidegger, as I discussed in the Introduction, speech and death converge in the animal's inability to conceptualize the "as such." Heidegger writes, "The leap from living animals to humans that speak is as large if not larger than that from the lifeless stone to the living being": if access to *logos* is the basis of a distinctly human capacity for self-conceptualization, this exclusivity matters because it opens the concept of death: "Mortals are they who can experience death as death. Animals cannot do so. But animals cannot speak either. The essential relation between death and language flashes up before us." Derrida comments in his *Aporias*, "Since [Heidegger] links this possibility of the 'as such' (as well as the possibility of death as such) to the possibility of speech, he thereby concludes that the animal, the living thing as such, is not properly a mortal: the animal does not relate to death as such. The animal can come to an end, that is, perish (*verenden*), it always ends up kicking the bucket [*crèver*]. But it can never properly die."[21] Derrida draws an urgently political point from this reading of Heidegger: the ability to be put wordlessly to death is the ultimate wedge between species.[22]

Literature's experiments with first-person singular and collective animal voices offers an angle on interspecies relations that reflects a point of departure from Heidegger in early biopolitical theory: the contrast between the role of speech in Heidegger and Arendt. Arendt views not death but birth as a ground of commonality because of its sense of "initiative, an element of action," as she puts it in *The Human Condition*, that culminates in the capacity for political speech. Philosopher Kelly Oliver explains that for Arendt, there is a distinction between humans as an animal species and humans as special kinds of beings: "as an animal species we *live* on the earth, and only as human beings do we inhabit a world."[23] We begin to inhabit and make the "world" the through the exercise of "natality," a value that reflects the importance of initiative and action but also emphasizes the grounding of existence in living bodies. For Arendt, natality is exemplified by *speech* because speech is plural and initiates ever new ideas.[24] To have a cohesive "world" in Arendt is not only about survival or perception, but it means to exist communicatively in relation: "With word and deed we insert ourselves into the human world, and this insertion is like a second birth, in which we confirm and take unto ourselves the naked fact of our original physical appearance."[25] On this account, speech "inserts" human individuality into a pluralistic collective: "speech corresponds to the fact of distinctness and is the actualization of the human condition of plurality, that is, of living as a distinct and unique being among equals.[26] "Action" becomes configurable as voice, and if we are thrown into the world through our birth, our natality, it is ultimately our voices that give our world meaning.

Arendt's orientation toward speech highlights that voicing is the result of embodied conditions, an alternative to a framework in which it is *only* a capacity for political speech that forestalls letting-die. The commonsensical implication is that even what seem the most distinctively human of actions are dependent upon, and often interrupted by, having a responsive and vulnerable creaturely body. This perspective, as Oliver points out, opens Arendt's approach to far more robust interspecies perspectives than Arendt herself offers. If political rights emerge from our ability to speak freely from the physical safety of a home, conversely, political rights are not only protection from "the violence of homelessness and statelessness," Oliver points out, "but also the protection of a shared common world and access to the world of meaning."[27] Heather Keenleyside offers a formulation I find helpful in glossing the kind of role Arendt's natality offers for stressing the connection between multispecies world-inhabitation and human language: "Society comes together neither through voluntary consent nor forced enslavement, but by means of activities like eating and breeding, as well as speaking reconfigured as an effect of animation."[28] These connections among birth, the basic labor of survival, and speech highlight the role of an accommodating milieu in creating the opportunities for initiation that ultimately give rise to a sense of collective endeavor. It also means taking especially seriously Boxall's use of the word "progenitive" to mark how narrative voice is often not only unstable but *also* world-founding.

In what follows, I argue that Tawada and Bulawayo highlight the animality of communication. Rather than author a divide that reserves linguistic agency (as a shorthand for agency *tout court*) for humans by highlighting the anthropocentric failures of language, these texts propose that communicativity unites all living creatures. In their own figurative plurality of levels, these novels present ways of understanding what voice makes legible outside the human frame. It shows how despite their allegorical structure, these novels also envision a speaking-otherwise than in what they themselves mark as political discourse, calling attention to humans as animals, "a storytelling species," as Sylvia Wynter puts it.[29] By turning to obviously fractured narratives I could highlight their continuities with postcolonial fiction's fragmentary aesthetics as facilitating biopolitical critique of institutional failures. Yet I want to show how these texts treat style itself as source of initiation, renewal, plurality, and collectivity grounded in the body, reframing fragmented experiences of oppression by imagining narrative voice itself as a milieu that coordinates multispecies existence.

2. POLAR POETICS

Yoko Tawada dramatizes the distortions of animal character when her first bear narrator struggles with writing her life story for a human audience; editors and promoters manipulate her narrative into a sentimentality at odds with her persistently matter-of-fact bearness. After beginning her writing in the USSR, she emigrates to Berlin, where she is pressured to continue by German editors and journalists. She resists human manipulation with patent inauthenticity: "'All penguin marriages are alike, while every polar bear marriage is different,' I wrote in Russian and demonstratively placed the manuscript page on my desk so Herr Jäger would see it right away if he visited unannounced.... They showed up again several days later and immediately found the sentence I'd left for them. Wolfgang translated it into German and exclaimed euphorically: *'Weltliteratur!'* " (58). The moment openly satirizes the idea that animal narratives might produce authentic accounts of either universal human values or situated, human transnational experiences. But ultimately, I argue, *Memoirs of a Polar Bear* might better be considered *Umweltliteratur*. It is interested in how, despite the manipulations of speech or writing, voice at once creates and responds to a sensory milieu.

This novel comprises a multipart, trans-species, transnational narrative through a series of three "studies" or memoirs: an unnamed grandmother bear's meditations on life after the Soviet Circus; her daughter Tosca's examination of circus life in East Germany, told collaboratively with her human trainer Barbara; and her grandson Knut's account of his experiences as a global warming poster child at the Berlin Zoo before his unexpected death in 2011. Knut—the real, famous polar bear who lived in the Berlin Zoo from 2006 to 2011—is legible as a historical actor; though he narrates as if from after his death, the novel is interested in how animal narratives open unexpected perspectives reflecting the logic of natality and validating animals as, if not exactly historical or political agents in a strong sense, then as creatures whose lives occur in a historical milieu. Despite their historical individuality, however, Tawada's bears are not particularly cohesive as characters. The novel's many shifts in telling the stories of its self-defeating speakers also evokes an unending process of initiation through natality in both senses, while recoiling from a consolidated model of character. Each narrative involves diegetic manipulation, shifting the historical perspective and narrative voice, moving between singular and collective first person, or between first and third. Moreover, each narrative evokes a polar dream-space as a site of shared sensory pleasures not confined to an individual's, or one species', consciousness. There is no frame narrator or character, meanwhile, to impose a centering subjectivity. For the grandmother bear, to be a character comes belatedly: eventually, she admits, "While copying out these passages from [a] book, I entered the story being told as its protagonist" (71). As in this moment, the novel's many shifts of narrative voice suggest the absurd difficulty of speaking from an "authentic" animal character's perspective, even as it grudgingly takes a centered subjectivity as the condition of narrative writing.

Memoirs of a Polar Bear was read by scholars first as an allegory of transnational labor and migration, a move that largely ignored its ursine qualities, and more recently as an intervention in the human-animal imaginary.[30] I draw attention back to its allegorical style to make a case for its value as offering its own theory of the novel: while *Memoirs of a Polar Bear* makes use of the anthropocentric structure of allegory, it uses animal voices to allegorize the centrality of a capacity for communication and representation to a seemingly exclusionary definition of the character itself. In a brief but suggestive account of *Memoirs of a Polar Bear*, Rebecca Walkowitz proposes that Tawada "rethinks the migrant novel," suggesting that "normalizing multiple origins may create a more ethical, more inclusive basis for collectivity," "organized around mutable collectives rather than walled-off beginnings and destinations."[31] While Walkowitz only neutrally acknowledges the ursine status of the narrators, her take on the novel evokes its interest in using transnationalism as an allegory of multispecies existence, as well as using multispecies collectivity to allegorize transnationalism. Rendering the allegory reversible allows the novel to stress the poignancy of social critique made through the eyes of creatures who, despite those communicative capacities, are trained and captive.[32]

An ambivalent anthropomorphism pervades the text. Its three generations of literate polar bears, male and female, insist that they have bear *Umwelten* and do bear things, but they record many humanlike experiences: they perform in circuses, attend conferences, do some filing, read Kafka, write best sellers, go grocery shopping, invest in the stock market, and send email. Each polar bear is representative not only of their species, but also their gender, their proletariat class status, and their national origins, all of which demonstrates their thorough regulation by the biopolitical forces that accelerate across the novel's historical account of globalization from the 1950s into the early 2000s. Throughout, the bears take their intersectional identities as a matter of course. Yet, constantly emphasizing the bears' species-specific corporeal pleasures, the novel also stresses the dependency of these bears upon the humans who put them to unnatural uses, including by ascribing to them a novelistic subjectivity that authorizes their writing.

When they reflect on their own literacy and translatability, the bears work according to Paul De Man's well-known account of allegory as a trope that "simultaneously asserts and denies the authority of its own rhetorical mode," reflecting the novel's concern with surviving political authoritarianism: on this view, the novel's allegory carefully asserts the authority of the animals to speak while also undercutting their status as "real" authors.[33] The novel's own status—Tawada wrote it in Japanese and translated it into German as *Etüden im Schnee* (2014) before it was translated into English by Susan Bernofsky—especially invites *Memoirs of a Polar Bear* to be read as "about" transnational identity, migration, and exile. In the first narrative, the narrator enters a bookstore in order to study German, where she is told that the section labeled Philosophy has been replaced by "literature of migration" (69) as if flagging the pivot from epistemic to political concerns this novel ostensibly invites.[34] The first narrative is especially legible as allegorizing the experience of ethnic minorities: the narrator offers conventional recollections of her school days when she was bullied for her facial differences; she attends conferences where her ability to engage in verbal debate appears unproblematic even when her opinions are unpopular; and cross-species sexual desire appears only mildly surprising.

Reading the polar bears as transnational ethnic subjects constituted by sovereignty as theorized by Foucault, Suzuko Mausel Knott argues that "it is difficult to divorce the image of the captive but personified polar bears of Tawada's novel with the dehumanized and exhibited colonized peoples" who circulated in Germany during the late nineteenth century when zoological exhibitions included both animal and human examples. Tawada's bears certainly toy with their allegorization as ethnic minorities.[35] The first narrator identifies strongly with the Soviet Union before emigrating to West Germany and then Canada. She feels herself in exile in a too-warm western European city, even while the next generation imagines that "for polar bears, national identity has always been a foreign concept. It's common for them to get pregnant in Greenland, give birth in Canada, then raise the children in the Soviet Union. They possess no nationality, no passport. They never go into exile" (86). While the novel opens the question of whether migrancy is a fully determining reading, it certainly echoes the biopolitical implications that the concepts of human rights and political inclusion depend upon the demarcation of bodies as nonhuman. This message plays out as a gesture of alliance as well as the pride of species difference: when an activist hopes to interview the first bear "about the situation of artists and athletes in the Eastern Bloc" (53) like herself, the narrator acknowledges, "locked in my invisible cage, I am living proof of human rights violations, and I'm not even human" (59). Whereas some species "couldn't care less whether or not human beings find them cute" (212), the polar bears' status as charismatic megafauna inevitably means exploitation. As transnational, trans-species figures whose lives span the fall of communism in the global North, the bears present their experiences as revealing the predicaments of migrancy, translation, class struggle, and climate crisis, encoding their itinerant, contingent lives as stand-ins for human experience. They also, however, use their voices to less immediately revelatory ends.

The first narrative reflects cynically on speaking animals. Tawada takes

Franz Kafka's fable of captivity, "A Report to the Academy" (1919), as a predecessor when the grandmother bear, whose first language is Russian and/or Bear, reads it in her efforts to learn German. In Kafka's story, the ape Red Peter addresses an academic gathering; he has learned human language, and in doing so, he lost access to the experience of animality that he now has the language to conceptualize. This influential story emphasizes the violence of humanity's appropriations and manipulations of animals' difference.[36] Tawada's first narrator reacts in disgust at Red Peter's desire to be human and claims for transformation despite his patent condition of exploitation, even as she experiences similar pressures as she begins to publish her life writing.[37] A publisher tells her not to write in German but to "write in your own mother tongue. You're supposed to be pouring out your heart" (51), but translation is as painful as the possibility that one *could* have a linguistic origin. The crucially unnamed grandmother bear contests the pressures of producing the sentimental image of an authentic self, instead presenting a compressed redux of the anxieties of deconstruction, noting what she calls the "spooky" (4) quality of writing as mode of presence or (self-)possession, a Derridean gramophone that disappears the self it attempts to evoke and evacuates the very concept of the mother tongue. In an interview, Tawada observes that "foreign languages draw our attention to the fact that language per se, even one's mother tongue, is a translation" that distorts preverbal perceptions.[38] In stressing Tawada's attention to allegory's translation of animal sapience into human terms, I follow Emily Apter's argument—highly consonant with Tawada's own sensibility—that world literature is not universally comparable or readily translatable. If animal consciousness, construed as fundamentally inaccessible or inevitably *translated* into human terms, is highly visible in the contemporary world novel, it justifies Apter's "approach to literary comparativism that recognizes the importance of non-translation, mistranslation, incomparability and untranslatability."[39]

The refusal of compelling translation, underlined by this self-negating understanding of linguistic authenticity, is clearest in the novel's repeated recourse to evoking a shared polar dream-world as outside of language. The magnetic pull of an aestheticized north disrupts the binary east-west axis that orients the transnational reading. Tawada seems to imagine such nontranslatability as an impersonal experience at the core of writing, explaining, "When I write, I am not a fisher fishing with a net but rather a knot in this net. And then I am ready to be powerless, so to speak. . . . It's exciting, too, to lose yourself. You do lose yourself at first in a foreign language. This is a condition similar to meditation or the trance of the shaman in that you empty yourself in order to be receptive, to accept foreign voices which, in fact, are not foreign but very familiar."[40] This fantastical milieu, I would argue, eludes biopolitical allegorization because there is no question of what the dream-world represents. Rather, it constitutes a milieu because it exists as a cohesive space of perception within a given frame, however temporary. In an allegorical reading of the novel, these polar fantasies would appear only as compensatory relief from the burdens of bearing a personal identity.[41] Such daydreams withdraw assent from an agreed-upon reality that does not amount to an agential social intervention, political claim-making, or achievement of reflective knowledge. They appear especially this way in Knut's narrative, where sleep relieves his overscheduled and hypercommodified existence: "As soon as he entered the sleepers' realm, the air around him grew sharply colder, with glittering silvery particles of light falling all around him. He watched the miniature flakes floating, they danced, liberated from gravity, yet still went on falling: falling ever farther until at last they alighted on the frozen earth and disappeared" (170). Knut enters a milieu of animacy that offers him respite outside the identity categories of species, class, and gender that shape his biopolitical life. This fantasy is, appropriately, "as sweet and nourishing as mother's milk" (251)—an opening associated the everyday vulnerability of new bodies in need of care.

The importance of these scenes as impersonal lyrical suspensions, bearing witness to the novel's ambivalence toward animal allegory's investment in character's political legibility, is much clearer in the novel's substantially different German title. As many have observed, *Etüden im Schnee* does not feature the openly paradoxical category of animal autobiography but instead emphasizes different perceptual angles—*Etüden*, case studies, musicological or ethological—of the experience of snow. Describing her novels, Tawada argues, "You have to create the enigmas in order to create the gaps. If you don't do that, everything looks normal and comprehensible, although I believe the world to be incomprehensible."[42] Resistance to subject-centered and centering order erupts in the novel's polar fantasies, which often substitute for clear narrative endings.[43] In the second narrative, Barbara and Tosca envision polar fantasy as a space that dissolves the mother tongue into a wordless but collaborative arena of interspecies collaboration:

> There, in darkness, the grammars of many languages lost their color, they melted and combined, then froze solid again, they drifted in the ocean and joined the driving floes of ice. I sat on the same iceberg as Tosca and understood every word she said to me. Beside us floated a second iceberg with an Inuk and a snow hare sitting on it, immersed in conversation (98).[44]

As in the Knut passage quoted earlier, where falling and floating occur simultaneously, "drifting" and "driving" evoke both the force of natality and the unexpected, anti-teleological quality of the (pleasurably alliterative) mutual voice it originates. Moreover, this moment inaugurates the collectivization of two homodiegetic narrators, Tosca and Barbara, in metaleptic shifts that structure the remainder of the section. The diegetic shifts in this second narrative particularly suggest a link to Arendt's idea of initiation as the social voicing that makes a home in the world; again, pace Lupton's gloss on Arendt, initiation means "new births delivered by . . . our own signifying practices."[45]

The three studies appear as a historical series, but the novel is complicated by metalepsis both between them and within them that furthers the novel's presentation of "character" as what it calls a "super-imposition." In the first narrative, metalepsis is a matter of historical compression. The time frame in which this story is told is unclear; it ends in a quick report of life events: migration to Canada, marriage, vocational retraining, a return to East Germany, and pregnancy. "How much longer do I have?" she asks, balancing on an in imaginary ice floe, evoking the coming threat of climate emergency as well as the imminent end of her narrative, but the very question is muddled by the circularity of the ending, in which, notably, Tosca's birth is reported twice, once as an event in the past, and again as an event in the future. The refusal of a linear historical perspective redounds in the other two narratives. In the second, it turns out there are two Toscas that Barbara has worked with. "In Barbara's memory," Tosca reports, "two bears intermingled later—the older one was named Tosca, just like me, and Barbara had already kissed her in the 1960s. I too was born in Canada, but in 1989, and I came to Berlin just before the Fall of the Wall. I am Old Tosca reborn and carry her memory within me. We look the same, and there is scarcely any difference in how we smell" (162). Historical personal identity is subordinated to a sensuous relational milieu. In the third section, Knut dreams of this amalgamated Tosca as "beautiful aged queen . . . wearing a gleaming white fur coat" who declares, "I am the super-imposition of numerous ancestors" (213), as if confirming an accelerating indifference to a strong model of bounded personal or ursine identity, even as it insists that these voices emerge through the unfurling of historical time, not *only* existing in a fantasy outside of history. Knut's narrative, because it ends with his death and because he is a well-known historical individual, appears to be a retrospection from beyond the grave and thus returns to the "spooky" critique of presence from his grandmother's narrative, while one of his dream-interlocutors, Michael Jackson, is also dead. If the appearance of Michael Jackson has been especially puzzling to critics except insofar as he and Knut are both dead boy-celebrities, a framework that focuses on the impossibility of his voicing as only one among the novel's many metaleptic experiments can offer some help.

According to Elaine Freedgood, "flamboyant instances of metalepsis" are central even to the realist novel, which is far less stable than we assume; this is why fictional characters can exist in real-world spaces like the Berlin Zoo. Tawada's novel—far from realist—also lets real-world characters exist in fictional spaces, the kind of reference all but historical novels typically renounce because it disrupts the feel of wholeness in a novelistic world. Though Tawada's bear narratives are not alternate histories, they aren't *not* them. Real historical figures—Knut especially—are key to the novel without being exactly characters, and they are not involved in counterfactual events that rise to such a level of importance as to alter real-life historical outcomes, or avert real historical deaths.[46] Their initiation is more consequential to their agency as individuals. In other words, their presence creates aestheticized milieus—homes in the world, as in Arendt—that are not part of the historical record.

Ambiguous voicing and natal alliances emerge against the ultra-allegorized history of the zoo as well as the Soviet circus, which historically sought to encode highly didactic political messages about social cohesion and collectivity, particularly where animals were concerned. During the Cold War, historian Miriam Neirick argues, "the circus offered proof of the Soviet Union's seemingly incompatible claims to be the world's best guarantor of peace, its most advanced military power, its sole sponsor of world revolution, and its most favored nation."[47] As co-narrator, the human trainer Barbara is deeply aware of the overt ideological and allegorical function of the circus. A lover tells her, "The circus is nothing more than a metaphor," trying to dissuade her from circus work, and indeed, she spends her career resisting explicit political messaging in her acts. Barbara announces, "I abhor the human stupidity and vanity that takes pride in forcing tigers, lions, and leopards to sit nicely side by side. It reminds me of the government choreography that displays brightly garbed minorities in a parade, minorities granted a crumb of political autonomy in exchange for providing an optical simulation of cultural diversity in their country of residence." Rather than reject the politicization of the circus, she offers a vaguer notion of a seemingly purified circus act, one that resonates with the Soviet circus's own emphasis on individual trainer-animal bonds: "I hoped that the national circus would decide to drop the mixed wild-animal act, since its primitive brutality was not in keeping with a modern state's notions" (80). Here, the biopolitical critique in the novel requires emphasis. These bears, who live as companions with their human trainers, are unquestionably victims of physical and psychic violence—a perspective that differentiates Tawada from prominent advocates of training as a redemptive mode of interspecies collaboration like Donna Haraway or Vicki Hearne.[48] The first narrative is open and casual in depicting the abuse of the grandmother bear, who comes into consciousness around a sense of bad touch—being tickled, then trained to dance with electric shocks by Ivan, her first trainer. A literary colleague later tries to convince her, "Ivan was your mother. Have you forgotten? The age of female mothers [is] over" (52), but the idea that training is a reliable source for having many-gendered multispecies mothers of the heart rings false.[49] The humans who participate in animal training are also, often, drained and harmed. At the same time, however, the novel rejects as too instrumental the idea that an animal's story "might be used as proof of the Socialist abuse of animals" (34). Both bears and humans are victims of regimes of signification and narrative meaning that offer inadequate accommodations to both human *and* nonhuman bodies.

The second narrative, "The Kiss of Death," demonstrably recognizes and resists the way changing human social norms frame animal experiences, particularly at its end, when Tosca and Barbara defend their circus act from a specifically western misogynistic critique:

> Tosca was so harshly criticized for having rejected her son Knut. Some said that Tosca had relinquished her son to strangers because she was from the GDR. Others wrote in their newspapers that Tosca had lost her maternal instincts while working in a circus known for its animal abuses, under typical Socialist stress levels. Invoking 'stress' in this context struck me as misguided. . . . With animals, childrearing is a matter not of instinct but of art. (92)

Knut's narrative reiterates this stress argument in a quotation from an article the young polar bear reads about his mother, but he presents the argument without commentary or excuse, perhaps making it sound as if Tosca and Barbara's self-justification doesn't in fact quite undercut the possibility that animal captivity provokes depression. Much the same for human captivity: Barbara eventually leaves her own child in her mother's care after struggling with postpartum depression, which she terms *tristesse* (90)—her maternal identity competes not only with what she presents as an East German indifference to maternal care, but also with her vision of herself as a circus *artiste* (130).

Tosca substitutes writing, or voicing, for maternity. Without their children, she and Barbara find one another. A refusal to fetishize maternity is crucial to Tosca's vision of bears as cultural actors. Tosca, even more directly than Barbara, reframes her art as in competition with maternity. She admits that to be an artist, she cannot mother. Her own mother, in the first narrative, sucks milk, then her trainer's finger, then a pencil, substituting the weird extimacies of language for an originary maternal relation. Tosca confidently reports,

> I entrusted Knut's care to another animal. This wasn't an easy decision, but because of my literary work I didn't have enough time for him.... My dream bore fruit, and Knut grew up to become a noteworthy environmental activist who made his mark on the global struggle for conservation. And not just that: Knut showed us that we no longer needed circus acts to draw the public's attention to us polar bears, to move human hearts, and awaken admiration and love.... Among the mothers of Homo sapiens, there are some who treat their sons like capital. My task, on the other hand, is to narrate the magnificent life story of my friend Barbara, who otherwise would long since have vanished in Knut's shadow. (164)

Here Tosca closes out the narrative in which she and Barbara move in and out of controlling the first person, sometimes even speaking in a collective voice. The newness of living being, which requires mutual caretaking, appears most valued in its transfiguration as the process of initiation itself—the surprise of deep intimacy as the condition for speaking in an unexpected voice. Barbara reflects, "From time to time Tosca looked deep into my eyes and seemed to be alluding to something. Apparently it wasn't just in my imagination that we'd spoken: we really were entering a sphere situated halfway between the animal and human worlds" (102). As if in a dream-space, in which they read one another's minds, Barbara and Tosca "come inside" one another (138), a profoundly intimate, erotic process very much at odds with a stable conception of character, for it can often be difficult at first to determine who is speaking when they say "I" for one another, telling one another's experiences. When Tosca complains, "My mother already described me as a character in her book," Barbara replies, "Then I'll write for you. I'll write your life story so you can escape from your mother's autobiography" (110). The unpredictable exchange of narrators itself appears to be what disentangles sensation from character. Toward the end of "The Kiss of Death," the narrative appears to shift definitively into Tosca's voice at this point, where there is a bear paw printed on the page. Ivan Kreilkamp has argued that such a graphic functions to "acknowledge the signifying fullness of [animals' prints] . . . as signs by a nonhuman agency.[50] In the deconstructive context established by the grandmother bear and many of Tawada's own writings, however, such a mark of presence evaporates as in the Derridean fantasy of the ideogram. Still, even if Tosca belatedly and somewhat spuriously marks her territory as frame narrator, what she tells remains collaborative as she tells the story of Barbara telling hers.

They ultimately come to care for one another through what Elizabeth Freeman calls sense methods: ultimately Tosca and Barbara touch, kiss, speak, taste, and "laugh[] with one voice" (138). If communicating personal, subjective experiences is the initial rationale for their connection, it ends in indifference to the investment in the individual ability to speak that subtends it. What they trade first are early memories of the instability of maternal care and the dependency of being newly born—Tosca's recollections of suckling in fearful darkness, Barbara's of how her early understanding of the language of animals followed directly upon her mother leaving her for a gynecology appointment. What discarding maternity initiates, and where the narrative ends, is in an circus act called "the Kiss," which they perform around the world. Tosca concludes her narrative by evoking that intimacy in the present tense, as if it occurs in a fantastical polar vagina outside of historical time: "I stand on two legs, my back slightly rounded, my shoulders relaxed. The tiny adorable human woman standing before me smells sweet as honey. . . . I see the sugar gleaming in the cave of her mouth. Its color reminds me of snow, and I am filled with longing for the far-off North Pole. Then I insert my tongue efficiently but cautiously between the blood-red human lips and extract the radiant lump of sugar" (165).

This "radiant" love that feels as if it could last "a thousand years" (165) is as potent as it is distorting—it can still be manipulated by biopolitical control, and still be subsumed to an aesthetic of allegorical capture; it is an alternative palpable only *as* aesthetic, as style. The potential that many critics have seen in this queer interspecies intimacy as an alternative to the deathliness of biopolitical domination not only fails to avert a tragic conclusion in Knut's death at the end of the novel but *itself* constitutes an allegorical reading that could better account for the novel's own relation to allegory.[51]

Knut suffers an untimely death after the human zookeeper and "male mother" (188) he most loves, Matthias, leaves him and dies of cancer. The novel's depiction of Matthias's maternity evokes a strong, fostering connection between Knut's arrival in the world as a perceptive, vulnerable creature and his function as the narrator. Knut remains vulnerable throughout his narrative thanks to his outsize fame; he consistently resists becoming a "character," the kind of figure who can be easily and endlessly commodified in the service of the zoo's self-defeating environmental mission. (In 2013, the Berlin Zoo won a trademark lawsuit against a UK company for the use of his name.) Though Tosca lauds him as an environmental activist—an identity that implies empowered self-motivation and ignores any differences between the bear's largely passive relation to his life in the popular press and what one might legitimately term human activism—she utterly misunderstands his commodification.

This section offers an especially hostile assessment of the pressures of character as a governing framework for narration. Knut initially speaks of himself in the third person until teased by a sun bear into calling himself "I." This first-person narration is painful: "schooling left deep wounds" (210). This shift to the first person, which is fairly stable from this point forward in Knut's narrative, reveals the uncomfortable fit of speaking or writing human language. Initially it is only his hunger for milk that he identifies as "Knut," while he is confused by the first-person pronoun because everyone uses it, and thus it strikes him as *impersonal*. But still, he dutifully begins to narrate as "I," and here, metalepsis is disciplinary, a constraining shift of tone as well as stance. Joy drains from him. He becomes all too aware of both his language and his space at the zoo as captivity. When newspapers write up his first swim lesson, he complains, "They took a piece of my life away and locked it up in newsprint. When I went swimming, Knut should have stayed contained within this swimming 'I' rather than being consigned to newsprint one day later. Perhaps I should have kept so many people from learning that my name was Knut. They used my name whenever they felt like it, to amuse themselves" (223). Like the too-human name of *Life of Pi*'s tiger Richard Parker, which I discussed in Chapter 1, Knut's existence as a character is outwardly imposed; he prefers the sensations of his swim to his capture in human language and especially in the human aesthetic category of the cute, which as Sianne Ngai demonstrates encodes a violent diminishment.[52] Whether "contained" or "consigned," Knut registers the role of boundedness in his own ability to formulate a perspective from which to narrate.

Against the hyper-individualization imposed upon him, Knut himself appears curious about his surroundings in the zoo and fascinated by other animals. Even if what they say to him when he is walked around the zoo is usually insulting, he remains fascinated by their sounds. This attunement appears to be first encouraged by Matthias's guitar-playing, which the infant Knut enjoys. A little later, the maturing Knut enjoys the zoo's soundtrack as a way to map the space of the whole zoo—to understand it as a milieu. Sound is another sense-method for cross-species alliance. Listening at night, "in each voice, he heard something like a tautly strung bow: every animal must constantly attend to his own life with the utmost care, making full use of his abilities and intelligence, otherwise his chances for survival would be nil" (183). But the seeming individualism and Darwinian self-interest that piques Knut's curiosity gives way to an inkling that voices constitute a milieu: "Knut always listened, regardless of what there was to hear. The subtle differences between the individual voices and the combination of these differences gave each night its own unique color, and to Knut this appeared magical" (184). Such moments in his narrative suggest that milieu emerges from voice, whereas individuality is tied to proper speech. But his ability to access this milieu shuts down once he is kept strictly in his enclosure with its pool and terrace. He complains, it "didn't constitute an environment for me" (249)—an especially poignant lament given that the historical Knut, suffering from encephalitis, drowned while swimming in this pool. As I discussed in chapter 1, zoos' manipulation of *Umwelt* aims to normalize animals' psychological experiences by opening tailored spaces to their perception. In Tawada's ending, this zoo enclosure no longer constitutes even a delimited *Umwelt* for the bundle of sensations that Knut has been trained to call "I."

The final narrative, much like the first, suggests that a capacity for symbolic representation is the marker of personhood and political belonging, and advocates this idea in an allegorical form of a personal narrative that would seem to reinforce precisely that privilege. At the same time, however, Tawada emphasizes animals' capacity for communicative gesture as a more inclusive criterion of belonging. Being born and giving voice initiate alliances through which "divergent forms of life . . . enter into world-building and future-founding relationships with each other"—and these relations subsist primarily within style itself.[53]

3. GLORIOUS VOICES

Glory further extends metalepsis as style for multispecies living. Hailed in reviews as an allegory that explicitly reinvents George Orwell's *Animal Farm* (1945), *Glory* tells the story of the overthrow of Old Horse, dictator of the fictional country of Jidada. Bulawayo's human-free nation clearly refracts the 2017 military overthrow of Zimbabwe's former president Robert Mugabe, even as it moves away from the hierarchical dynamics of the allegory it ostensibly pursues. If it is an innovation on Orwell, the robustly polyphonic *Glory* to some extent reflects the positionality of its transnational author, NoViolet Bulawayo; she uses a patently western literary form to critique the neocolonialism of Black national power in Zimbabwe, cast as a political desire for the glorious sovereign power over life and death.[54] However robust, the allegory is only part of the story—and allegory is not a word that Bulawayo uses to describe her own text.[55] Bulawayo herself has claimed that even if Orwell was "on the syllabus" for a secondary education in Zimbabwe, "the novel is powered by orature" referencing familial and national storytelling traditions.[56] These sources are not fully reconcilable: Mukoma wa Ngugi argues that Bulawayo inherits an African literary tradition "that privileged the English language over African languages, calling for a new African canon" that takes as given a world "fractured" by globalization.[57] In *Glory*, these fractures are legible in the very Benjaminian residue of allegory itself as the genre of ruined synthesis.[58] The centrality of animals to this novel's portrayal of the vulnerability of Zimbabwean citizens, however, matters more deeply than an emphasis on globalization's fractures would suppose. If part of this novel's vision of the experience of postcolonial world-fragmentation is coded by the talking animal's paradoxical state of being, I would argue that Bulawayo's animals offer vocality as the criterion of a plural sense of belonging.

But it is tempting (and easier than with *Memoirs of a Polar Bear*) to minimize the animality of the novel's animals, like one reviewer proposes in the *Washington Post*: "That the characters are animals—furred, feathered, scaled and all—is almost incidental."[59] Such a claim suggests that the animal characters operate as cover for historically recognizable agents. But it also reflects long-standing concerns in Black studies about the harms of aligning the dehumanization of Black people with the treatment of animals, which risks perpetuating violent historical occlusions within the category of the human. Furthermore, if *Animal Farm* is one of Bulawayo's source texts, it too has often been de-animalized when it is treated narrowly as an allegory of Stalinism.[60] As a corrective, McHugh and Ortiz-Robles argue that Orwell in fact allegorizes the treatment of animals, which to some extent may be true of Bulawayo's text as well, especially in her choice of species assignments (as I'll discuss shortly).[61] At the same time, *Glory* appears less concerned with the treatment of nonhuman animals per se than with moving past biopolitics' account of the exclusions of personhood; instead, in Joshua Bennett's words, it seeks "to combat certain foundational claims within the Western philosophical tradition regarding the limits and lacunae of personhood" through an aesthetic examination of what that tradition marks only as excluded.

Thus, the novel should also be read in the context of Black studies' recent efforts to claim and document interspecies alliance. Bennett, Bénédicte Boisseron, Sharon Patricia Holland, and Evan Maina Mwangi (among others) have argued in both American and African contexts that nuancing Black allegiances with animals also provides alternative means of rethinking "personhood *as such*"—that Heideggerian and biopolitical category—so that it is no longer so predominantly a matter of critiquing the sovereign conferral of the biopolitical right to belong. *Glory* does not, in its openly unrealistic depictions of animal life, "engage[] the fullness of non-human worlds" that Bennett looks for (nor does *Memoirs of a Polar Bear*). But as an allegory working at the limits of allegoresis, it most certainly does ask "how to delight in a precarious life" by asking how "Black love enters the world through the figure of the animal."[62]

Glory envisions the demise of Robert Mugabe as the overthrow of the "Old Horse" and his donkey wife by his profoundly corrupt former second in command, another horse called Savior of the Nation, and a team of military dogs. It includes no humans, while the animals, who wear clothes, use social media, and engage in a wide range of anthropomorphic activities, refer to themselves as "mals"—cutting out the *"anima,"* or soul, leaving behind the malodorous "mal."[63] The way what Bulawayo calls "mals" map onto the political allegory is uneven, particularly because the novel has no central character. The general, vulnerable, and largely sympathetic population comprises various barnyard animals—cows, pigs, sheep, cats, and especially goats.[64] As I will discuss below, one goat in particular, Destiny, becomes something like a protagonist late in the novel, and indeed she is legible not only as a character but more or less as a human person.[65] Throughout, species assignment matters: as for McHugh writing on Orwell, narratives about meat animals call particular attention to the "wavering status of metaphorical forms."[66] *Glory* largely excludes charismatic nondomesticated megafauna, as if to imply that its figures need to be understood as in relation to the bodily exploitation of an unmentioned or even unmentionable farm-as-state/state-as-farm motif.[67] Mwangi highlights that in the cultural context of Zimbabwe, eating animals is the only excuse for killing them; from this perspective, Jidada's rampant necropolitics present a fundamental violation of prohibition without needing recourse to the challenges posed by exclusionary discourses of human rights.[68] Simply put, *Glory*'s animalized characters highlight the unacceptable manipulation and putting to death of vulnerable bodies.

Species difference maps onto some arenas of political privilege (horses are leaders, dogs are military), but friendships as well as sexual relations commonly cross species lines, the latter often nonconsensually. The racial coding of animals is unspecified; although there are "Black animals" and "white animals," reflecting concern with the aftermath of imperialism, this character system appears to exclusively focus on the victimization of Black animals.[69] Still, species does not resolve all identity questions, and the degree of anthropomorphism also varies considerably. Horns and tails express political emotions—often, incendiary rage—but the characters are also indistinguishable from humans in their uses of technology, including, often, the technology of their own bodies. The mals commonly make power moves by intentionally "hinding"—rearing into an upright position that many sustain for long periods; others hind without meaning to in expressions of strong feeling. Their animal bodies also matter to one of the most provocative but ineffective protests in the novel, when a group of "females" called Sisters of the Disappeared disrupts a rally by appearing topless to protest sexual brutality against women during Zimbabwe's first Liberation War—an act of what Naminata Diabate identifies as strategic public nakedness, through which African women across several national contexts have historically claimed political visibility.[70] If the forcible stripping of women has also been a tactic of police brutality, the "threat of disrobing against police brutality" is also a tactic for protest. For Diabate, women's exercise of "naked agency" openly acknowledges its biopolitical foreclosure.[71] Still, this paradoxical collective expression is a gesture of initiation that does not depend on the logic of the public sphere, or even of the contingent distribution of personhood to citizens. Bulawayo renders an exaggerated version of this paradox in the strategic disrobing of animals. Likewise, the inventive term "mal" as shorthand for animals, and especially the adjectival portmanteau "persomal," reflect the paradoxical naked agency of *Glory*'s animals. These terms express the personhood of an animal being while seeming openly to mar or distort the concept. Through these essentially biopolitical insights, the novel underscores that captivity to political power becomes the ontological category of a creature's being. Conversely, the only mechanism for the expression of dissent is understood as core to the very category that can exclude them from the category of the person.

Even as the novel develops these incisive critiques in its very framework, Bulawayo's animal character system simultaneously offers aesthetic, and not immediately political, routes out of these bleak conundrums. *Glory* insists on the necessity of public, political speech and agency despite its foreclosures with a fascination with the material dimensionality of sound and voice, especially the poetics of narrative voice itself. The mals comprise a diverse and vocal public, actively engaged in political speech both in the streets and on Twitter (a platform named in a play on animal speech), to which Bulawayo gives substantial attention. A fixation on sound is not in itself a signal of virtue, for it can become captive to habit and suppress diversity. As an example of this logic, many of the namings of this animal nation emphasize the pronunciation: it is, we are constantly reminded, Jidada "with a *-da* and another *-da*": the doubled sound appears intrinsic to the mals' nationalism. In the novel's opening, the disoriented Old Horse holds a rally (the one the Sisters of the Disappeared disrupt), where

> even the animals who had been trying to leave were now part of the uproar, standing on hind legs and cheering His Excellency, not just with their voices and bodies, no, but also with their hearts and minds and souls. Cows mooed, cats meowed, sheep bleated, bulls bellowed, ducks quacked, donkeys brayed, goats bleated, horses neighed, pigs grunted, chickens clucked, peacocks screamed, and geese cackled—the cacophony reaching deafening levels as the entourage of power came to a final stop in front of a raised platform. (17–18)

While the passage explicitly insists that individual viewpoints have been captivated by the glorious power of political emotion, Bulawayo's narrative energy remains absorbed by its noise. This nightmare version of a baby's barnyard book initiates a strong connection between animals and voices. Although later in the novel, crowd noise is threatening—"a devastating storm of sound" (181)—here even while the variety of voices temporarily overtakes the passage, there is little doubt about the powerlessness of all these conventional voices that are taken by the powerful to express political assent. Nonetheless, such a passage de-individualizes these voices, and crucially, the opening of the novel refuses focalization through a situated observer. If, as Roberto Esposito argues in *The Third Person*, "it is difficult for [western] tradition, soaked to its roots in political theology, to sever the category of decision from its connection with the categories of the individual and of sovereignty, to ally it with the impersonal instead of the personal," Bulawayo's novel experiments with how captive its voices really are to what a biopolitical thinker might call the *dispositif* of the individual.[72] In other words, *Glory* explores the collective and often spontaneous voice of the "impersomal."

Through ceaseless polyphony and restless metalepsis, the novel explores the aesthetic potential of the impersomal voice in many registers. Most obviously, Bulawayo studs the entire narrative across many configurations of diegetic frame with the term *tholukuthi*. The term means "only to find that," but it appears so often as to function as an inflection, an incantation, an unshakable habit of continual emphasis, a mark of orality—and yet also an unattributable utterance that seems to pervade the atmosphere, as if waiting for a narrator or a character to emerge to enunciate it.[73] Bulawayo seems to allude here to the viral 2017 song "Tholukuthi Hey" by South African artists Killer Kau, DJ Euphonik, and subsequently singer Mbali Sikwane. The song may not be directly mentioned in *Glory*, but the logic of popular dispersion (and the viral marketability of Black joy) reflects aspects of the term's function in the text. "*Tholukuthi*" works, too, as a manifestation of the collective consciousness that constantly asks from what perspective it is being uttered. In other words, it raises the question of the milieu in which a surprised perception emerges and the mode of consciousness that follows. Its ubiquity across narrative levels suggests that even those sections not explicitly focalized either through a character or a collective's experience bears the mark of a perceived world that is ultimately not individual. This is one of the most distributive, least character-centered, of the novel's several strategies of collective narration to evoke group political witnessing.[74]

Refusing a singular narrator, who might be able to speak even partially for a larger collective, the novel also remains ambivalent about whether this collection of individual mals constitutes what narratology calls a "collective agent" capable of "shared group intentions and acting on them jointly."[75] Some sections of the novel use "we-narration" not to bolster but to diminish agency in a strong sense. We-narration in *Glory* is especially tied to the election that is supposed to legitimate the Savior of the Nation. "We" emerge not only in the streets and polling booths but simultaneously on the Internet, suggesting that we-narration not only serves as political witness but reflects the group's epistemological tools and limits.[76] Within this metaleptic shift, Bulawayo also uses numerous microstylistic techniques, from syllepsis to internal rhyme to anaphora, to unmistakably highlight that this collective experience is also a voicing: "We enter. We confront the booths. The levees inside us threaten to give again but we hold ourselves fast. We hold and vote for change at last. We vote without fear at last, for the new Jidada we want at last" (202). The vote does not achieve change; this hope ends in despair. Collective narration, juxtaposed with political action, implies the possibility of synthesis through the unification of multiple voices into a single national consciousness.

As these strategies begin to suggest, Bulawayo makes exceptionally frequent use of metalepsis as if searching for a mode of collective narration. Not only does the novel not have a central character, but tense changes from past to present, narrators from hazily heterodiegetic to explicitly collective, tone from comic to incendiary. Bulawayo identifies "spontaneity" as a core investment of this aesthetic.[77] In third-person sections, focalization is often general, evoking widely perceived phenomena but without the "we" pronoun. These shifts embed a critique of political dialogue. Chapters emulating Twitter feeds demonstrate the failure to engage in real debate among interlocutors while raising the question of the extent to which the medium produces or refracts that fragmentation. These chapters feature Twitter's multiplicity of voices, each with its own sardonic handle, speaking past one another in an unresolved, ever-circulating struggle of assertion rather than debate. The presentation of a set of threads and hashtags itself appears fragmentary—who could ever represent the whole of Twitter?—redoubling the novel's critique of media hyperliteracy.[78] A sylleptic hashtag—#freefairncredibleelection—heightens the satire evident throughout. It also functions as a subtle reminder of the role of unvoiced speech in writing: "incredible" emerges as if *audibly* from the unavoidable synthesis imposed by hashtag style.[79] If, as Garrett Stewart has argued, even in the ordinary prose of novels "what is called up is voice but only under suspension," Bulawayo's use of Twitter (after all, a kind of animal cacophony) heightens that sense of suspended orality—or rather, orality under forced erasure, as through the censorship of life under a military regime.

The novel's depiction of viral media's repetitions is perhaps spontaneity's vicious flipside. Newish statements are at once recycled and offer no intervention. So are pages in which a single sentence gets repeated ad infinitum; is this the stuckness of a traumatized group consciousness? Or is this a version of vocal renewal, where inflection is everything? Both, perhaps. This repetitious narrative mode initiates when Jidadans respond to seeing viral footage of George Floyd's murder in the United States: "When we gather the courage to look at our phones, we find the video trending on WhatsApp, Twitter, Facebook—everywhere. We're ill at ease but we press Play." The passage narrates, in short sentences, violence inflicted by a "Defender" upon a "Black brother." After this collective, hypermediated witness, "I can't breathe" flows over nearly a page, across a break. The repetitions not only evoke the virality of the video—"trending... everywhere" but also, of course, the inescapability of what it reveals.[80] As Joelle Mann puts it, "A sense of virality within vocality locates the ways in which the viral aesthetics of the contemporary novel move voices out of context, and hence destruction and creation become two sides of the same coin."[81] The temporary salve for watching the video is a group trip to the house of a cat medium, Duchess or Nomadlozi (meaning "with the ancestors"). The collective narrator explains that after viewing the video too many times on too many platforms, "we do find ourselves"—a passive phrase that highlights the catastrophic disjunction between collective voicing and collective agency—entering Duchess's garden. "We" explain that this space was reclaimed after British violence during Jidada's first struggle for independence. Nomadlozi has planted a tree "from the seeds on the very tree on which Mbuya Nehanda [a historical nineteenth-century Zezuru Shona medium] was hung by the British during the struggle for independence. The tree bears these curious pods—Nehanda's bones" (208).[82] "But for now," the tree is redemptively full of butterflies that "float to the Nehanda tree and start to land land land land land land land land land land land land land land land land land land land" (208)—obscuring visible reminders of the tree's violent past with a new but also stuck image of land sovereignty. Both planting the tree and encountering it here emphasize that recuperation occurs through the *voicings* of the action as much as the action itself. Thus, even as Bulawayo casts doubt on the stability of any collective mode of discourse—an insight with direct ideological consequences that bear on the allegorical force of the novel—the very frequency of these shifts in narrative voice offers a continual being, acting, and feeling anew. The function of initiation works not purely in an allegorical sense but as an experience that *must unfold as narrative*.

No one approach to collective narration is sustained. The temporary quality to any style highlights the fragility of any perspective as offering a durable sense of milieu; any perspective can be shattered at any moment. Still, the novel valorizes the effort to find an enduring mode of speech despite its impossibility in the chapters focused on Destiny, as a belated protagonist. Pace Cheah on Arendt, "an agent is disclosed when [s]he becomes the protagonist in the unique life-story told about [her].... The dynamic web of worldly relations consists of many life-stories."[83] After all, Destiny's perspective metaleptically absorbs the image of the butterflies, and it becomes central to her own writing. Through Destiny, Bulawayo highlights women's role (or burden) in maintaining creaturely life and cultural continuity in the face of largely masculine violence, existing less as an individual than a part of network of caretaking relations.[84]

Destiny returns from expatriate life as a transnational figure experienced in exile. She reappears in Jidada, ultimately to reclaim her family history, which her mother, Simiso, has never shared with her. Her return provokes a particularly forceful set of metaleptic initiations. At first, she is observed through the eyes of a collective of "bent-double femals" working to "prove their femalness and earn the attendant respect": "They do not ask her where she's going because it'd be cruel being that this obviously solitary child of Simiso has, since her arrival, offered absolutely nothing more than the quiet fact of a presence so hushed the goat has escaped answering the usual questions asked of returnees" (183). These early Destiny scenes emphasize a "femal" self-silencing that preserves an in-group, gender-normative identity. Destiny's departure from this norm, in contrast, is ultimately associated with sound and voice, which the narrative itself anticipates when it moves from third person, collective, past-tense description to a present-tense voice that sometimes addresses Destiny as "you." So just pages later, the narrative has shifted: "This country, she thinks, with bitterness. This country! This country! But then was it even wise for you to return, Destiny? To the very same country that broke you?" (186). These moves from free indirect discourse to second-person address—or is the second person embedded within the free indirect discourse?—reflect her own interest in narrative writing.[85]

Destiny's plot centers on the role of communication (both the affectivity of sensations and the meanings of words) in reclaiming this history. Yet it also expresses doubt in the adequacy of straightforward speech. In her old bedroom shortly after her return, Destiny picks up an old tape and listens: "The voice rings and doesn't stop ringing until the goat realizes the voice is not coming from the relic anymore, but from somewhere else, and that somewhere else is actually her own throat"—a song that leads others to "walk out of their houses trancelike, yes, tholukuthi leave whatever it is they were doing whether they want to or not—your voice doesn't give them time or choice or permission" (192, 193). This moment diminishes individual choice even in its own use of the second person, in which Destiny is addressed along with Bulawayo herself (for whom Destiny appears to be at least in part a metafictional stand-in). It also calls upon the reader. Two collectives, then, simultaneously lose their shape as groups of individuals when it is the fact of making a new sound, not belonging to any "one," that matters.

Destiny's mother, who has long resisted retelling her own traumatic experiences, at last reveals the story of her abuse during the Liberation War, and comments that there is "obvious trauma in the voices" (225). As if in rejoinder to what narration alone does not adequately register, she shows off her scars and asks, "Why am I telling you when I know my words can't really show you what I mean?" (242). What Destiny's mother tells her galvanizes her to learn more about her family history. Destiny's trajectory contrasts the fact of speaking anyway with speaking otherwise, and with speaking as voicing, a process that de-individualizes the act of speech. The second-person voice offers slightly sarcastic, conversational encouragements: "Isn't it amazing, Destiny. That these many years . . . after your family's murders, there are animals who will still say their names?" "Yes, it is amazing, she thinks" (342). Returning to the area of Bulawayo, where her family had their original home, "Destiny Lozikeyi Khumalo talks to the dead and talks to the death and talks to the dead . . ."—a phrase that repeats eighty times "until she forgets time" (347). Destiny's absorption in the expanding present of this voice evokes, in a more historically pointed key, another desistance from the pressures of conventional modes of political speech. Lengthy repetition here looks less or not exclusively like a trauma aesthetic.[86] This discourse ends in the liberating vision of butterflies that has migrated from the collective consciousness to Destiny's own. The butterflies return in the novel's final, redemptive image of "a new national anthem" (400). It's a song rather than a speech, and heard, once again, collectively.

Destiny is killed speaking what is represented as one sentence over and over on a public stage—she "read in a voice that was full of the dead, and read in that voice that was full of the dead, and read in that voice that was full of the dead" (359). What began as eighty repetitions is curtailed to merely three. Conversely, only a crowd wielding a tornado of strategic silence, frightening the military dogs before trampling them to pieces, succeeds in averting the execution of Simiso. If, as the collective voices acknowledges, "some stories will mow an animal down" (211), some collective silences can be equally potent. The sonic and semiotic dimensions of giving voice continually redistribute the narrative milieu. Despite its constitution as an allegory that centers the failures of mediated political speech to penetrate the crisis of state sovereignty in the context of nationalism, *Glory* eschews the systematic relation to its analysis of crisis that its allegorical form would imply.

4. CONCLUSION

While their allegorical form suggests that a capacity for symbolic representation is the marker of socially and politically recognizable personhood threatened by authoritarian regimes and put under pressure by transnational migration, *Glory* and *Memoirs of a Polar Bear* end up underscoring the communicative gesture as a more inclusive criterion of world-making. Bulawayo and Tawada allow impersonal—and nonhuman—voices to generate, moment to moment, distinctive and robustly literary stylistic practices that are not legible solely as conceptual interventions in the constitution of the citizen or nation. So even while allegoresis remains a critical approach that turns depictions of animal sapience into revelations about the production of citizenship, *Glory* and *Memoirs of a Polar Bear* offer animals' voices to explore alternatives to the rationalist sensorium that allegory presumes.

My account of these animal allegories shows, against the odds, how much perceiving a world depends upon the impersonal range of sensation afforded by a milieu, rather than the paradoxical localization of systemic abstraction within an individual consciousness. In each novel, the capacity to make "radiant" art—Tosca and Barbara's kiss and Destiny's book, *The Red Butterflies of Jidada*—is the site of a very precarious, temporally foreclosed optimism. *Memoirs of a Polar Bear* and *Glory* are not, themselves, those art forms. Their emphasis on voice, as well as speech, affirms animals as allegorical figures rather than individual characters. But for both Bulawayo and Tawada—allegory unexpectedly leads *away* from merely reinforcing or reinventing human interiority. To return to Walkowitz's suggestion that "normalizing multiple origins may create a more ethical, more inclusive basis for collectivity," I would argue that *Glory* and *Memoirs of a Polar Bear* both do this by reimagining a transnational public sphere as a shared milieu, rather than a site of individual validation. Representing talking and writing animals, then, allows these writers to explore alternatives to the allegorical novel's commitment to an exclusionary understanding of individuality and to character itself—even through the very allegorical mode that would seem to confirm it.

THREE

Dog Friends

When is a pet is "not just my dog, but my friend"?[1] In Marlen Haushofer's *The Wall*, for example, the milieu makes the difference. *The Wall* presents a dystopian scenario—a woman living in a remote hunting lodge, suddenly separated by an invisible wall from other human beings and trying to survive. Consumed with the labor of caring for herself along with a companionable dog, a pregnant cow, and a pregnant cat, the narrator is at once disturbed and comforted by her sense of responsibility to the creatures she calls "my animals." *The Wall*, published in 1963 and freshly translated into English in 2022, would seem fraught with postapocalyptic allegorical significance for the postwar atomic age, if only its narrator were at all interested in reflecting on the origin or purpose of the wall itself, and not so fully absorbed with describing the details of the milieu the wall creates. These concerns overwhelm an allegorical reading. Reflecting on her keen sense of the enclosed environment that establishes their strange community, the narrator creates a retrospective description of her daily, monthly, and yearly activity log. This activity increasingly denies any sense of human privilege. If at first the narrator insists, "A human being can never become just an animal," she gradually divests from this binary as her unique, attentive relationships with each of these animals and later their offspring—the happy dog, skittish cats, gentle cattle, and even the deer she must hunt—shape her daily activities. While she continues to see herself as more aware of the passage of time and of their predicament than they are, she also loses interest in having an individual past or identity: "remembering is dangerous," she reflects. Rather, "it was almost impossible, in the buzzing stillness of the meadow, beneath the big sky, to remain a single and separate Self, a little blind independent life."[2] Haushofer's protagonist is less concerned with revealing much of her unrecoverable past than with documenting the endless carework that sustains her precarious existence with her beloved animal companions in their mysteriously enclosed world. Even when reflecting on the devastating losses of some of these animals in the novel's conclusion, the narrator can do no more than accept how the forest continues to challenge and afford their mutual survival; she thinks, but isn't sure, the cow is again pregnant.

As I argue throughout this book, these issues are ever more prevalent within contemporary fiction, which often proceeds with a keener sense of how scrupulous attention to a milieu reframes an individualistic model of character, plot, and voice. Yet in considering animal friendship, they also contend with a counter-impulse exemplified by J. M. Coetzee's influential *Elizabeth Costello* (2003), in which a fictional philosopher of mind proposes that it is impossible to be friends with an animal. Elizabeth's response is no *Companion Species Manifesto*. She replies by suggesting that humans try to imagine accompanying livestock to their deaths, sidestepping a much more ordinary answer—petkeeping.[3] Though she does not speak of pets, Elizabeth lives with several cats. By avoiding any mention of them, she insulates herself from being written off as an elderly cat lady, a stereotype some of her interlocutors would be too eager to apply. In fact, the novel avoids representing any lived relations with domestic animals: it prefers instead to explore the paradox of dismantling the anthropocentrism of rationality using the tools of language and reason. Rationalism, Elizabeth indicates, leads to the biopolitical devaluation of animals' existence—to unacceptable practices of exploitation ranging from factory farming to global extinction.[4]

For Elizabeth and for Coetzee, to think about animals is first to focus on how they die. The intimacies of domestic petkeeping—Haraway's "ordinary multispecies living"—are far less urgent.[5] The absence of domestic animals from *Elizabeth Costello* aids Elizabeth's argument for their moral significance insofar as they are not being put into the service of anthropocentric abstractions. Yet their elimination echoes accusations by Haraway, Susan Fraiman, and others of critical animal theory's allergy to companionate relationships with animals, whether in Deleuze and Guattari's scorn for the feminine "fool" who loves a pet, or even Jacques Derrida's more affectionate yet quizzical exchange of unknowing stares with the "little cat [*chatte*]" who saunters into his bathroom.[6] If, in "The Politics of Friendship," Derrida imagines the possibility of calling "the friend by a name that is no longer that of the neighbor [*prochain*], perhaps no longer that of a man," the infinitely varied yet abyssal difference he positions between humans and other-than-human animals inhibits friendship and produces the famously awkward roommate scenario at the heart of *The Animal That Therefore I Am*.[7] For Derrida, and for Elizabeth Costello, it is not companionship but mortality that is "the most radical means of thinking the finitude that we share with animals, the mortality that belongs to every finitude of life, to the experience of compassion, to the possibility of sharing the possibility of this non-power, the possibility of this impossibility, the anguish of this vulnerability and the vulnerability of this anguish."[8] This emphasis in Coetzee's novel has made it an extremely influential reflection on the political status of animals and on biopolitics more broadly. Yet *Elizabeth Costello*'s centrality to animal studies raises a question that might be answered by attending to a broader range of novels: Does death have the same implications in narratives of the living room as it does in parables of the slaughterhouse?[9]

Like other critics who want to redeem the affective richness of companion species narratives, I must contend with how allegories of death dominate even in domestic contexts. This is an especially canine problem. Karalyn Kendall-Morwick observes the frequent "figuring of the dog as tragically sublime," marking a sense of lost origins in modernity and beyond, while Karla Armbruster describes the likelihood that a dog novel will end with the dog's death as the inevitable denouement: in American literature's allegorical "classic narrative of the good dog," "in order to prove itself a good dog as defined by its human caretakers, the dog must do no less than conclusively demonstrate its loyalty to culture over nature, usually to the extreme of placing human interests above self-interest. In many cases the dog ultimately proves its loyalty by dying to protect a human being." Susan McHugh, likewise, observes the "logic of substitution through which the animal's sacrificiality (its real and representational consumption) supports the human."[10] This logic persistently attributes a sacrificial meaning (or dysphoric and thus still-diagnostic lack thereof) to canine death.[11] Biopolitical allegory remains an established and ubiquitous technique of acknowledging constraints on animals' power, in this case because the deathliness of dog narratives reflects their long-standing ability to represent both real and transcendental *human* homelessness. Homelessness is a major theme of dog narratives from the eighteenth century onward, as Laura Brown and Philip Howell demonstrate. The figure of the unowned "public dog" endures as a comment on the conditions of survival in threatening milieus that are not adequate homes.[12] As for Colin Dayan in *With Dogs at the Edge of Life*, the representation of a dog's life speaks to "disregard, forfeiture, and extinction."[13]

A particularly searing example of an novel that explores this homelessness is Pilar Quintana's *The Bitch* (trans. 2020). This brief but devastating account of a working-class Colombian woman struggling to keep a dog as a pet emphasizes the dog's refusal to be kept. In *The Bitch*, neither the narrator nor the dog she grudgingly adopts has a stable home; the narrator and her husband are house-sitting in a tragedy-haunted coastal home where she once worked as a child. The dog, much like the narrator, cannot settle in, but the dog's agency often outpaces the narrator's own, especially after the dog becomes pregnant. Disgusted and fascinated with the dog's maternity in the wake of her own reproductive challenges, the narrator rejects finding common ground in motherhood. Indeed, she becomes obsessed with *not* owning the dog, and fascinated by the possibility of the dog's death as a reckoning with her own disposability. The novel concludes by resisting redemption: the narrator watches the dog recede into an impenetrable jungle on the edge of town and feels an overwhelming sense of alienation from herself. This chapter, in contrast, examines two novels that refuse such a biopolitical allegory of the dog friend, while emphasizing that humans are also animals.

Some of the critics mentioned previously, along with David Herman, respond to the pervasiveness of sacrificial allegory by valorizing narratives that in his words imagine animals as "experiencing, agential subjects," often by presenting animals as characters. I am especially interested, however, in novels that still emphasize powerlessness and vulnerability, openly disavowing a strong sense of individual agency for any party, but that nonetheless refuse to allegorize the dog's death. Instead, they focus on how dogs and humans inhabit the shared milieu of the home. I discuss two first-person realist novels, both National Book Award winners, both written by American women of color and featuring women protagonists living, unexpectedly, with dogs (*The Bitch*, too, was a National Book Award finalist for literature in translation). Sigrid Nunez's *The Friend* (2018) depicts the meditations of a middle-aged woman author of unspecified background, living in New York City, who has been tasked with caring for a large dog, the pet of an old friend who has committed suicide. Jesmyn Ward's *Salvage the Bones* (2012) is narrated by a young Black girl who has recently discovered she is pregnant; she lives a precarious existence in a rural community, which includes her brother's pit bull, as they survive Hurricane Katrina. Despite the considerable difference in the ages, racial identities, and economic positions of these two narrators, both novels explore what it means to become invested in loving a dog. *The Friend* and *Salvage the Bones* come as close as any novel I discuss in this book to treating animals—pet dogs included in the domestic circle—as characters in an ordinary sense. The dogs are named and individuated. They are accorded their own perceptual regimes by individualized human narrators, who observe them first with detached attention and later with affection. But as Herman argues, "narratives ostensibly centering on human protagonists nonetheless raise important questions about the scope and limits of selfhood in a wider world of selves, non-human as well as human."[14]

In both novels, the dog is not "owned" by the observing narrator who finds herself in the middle of an interspecies relationship she did not choose; in the case of *Salvage the Bones*, the narrator never even touches her brother's dog, who so intensely fascinates her. Unlike the training scenarios at the heart of Haraway's understanding of interspecies collaboration, the intimacies in these books are not chosen and sometimes indirect; they are not friendly assertions of power but, rather, reflect divestments from self-assertion at all. Non-ownership not only allows for "sharing the possibility of . . . non-power," in Derrida's formulation, but it also permits an intimate detachment that attunes the narrator to their shared milieu. Shared milieu and shared if non-equivalent disempowerment are both crucial to these narratives, where animal friendship becomes a cautious alternative to human social life riven with sexual violence. Even as *Salvage the Bones* and *The Friend* acknowledge the very profound differentials of power between human and animal companions, their narrative modes "balk at domination," as Nunez's narrator puts it.[15] The narrators are often melancholic, especially in the presence of an animal companion who has no comparable knowledge; damage and death—the end of one's perceptual world, perhaps as the result of structural violence—loom, and after all, petkeeping and death are hardly at odds. Yet mortality is not the only shared condition of powerlessness in *The Friend* and *Salvage the Bones*, because they treat dog-love as a world-founding experience. These texts rethink, first, the deathly temporality associated with biopolitical readings of creaturely lives, and second, how postallegorical narrative forms foster non-appropriative creaturely allegiances.

The Friend and *Salvage the Bones* particularly concern women's roles in meeting creaturely needs and affirming multispecies intimacies in the home. Their emphasis on milieu occurs in part through their interest in *birth* as a ground of commonality—which I discuss in terms of Hannah Arendt's concept of natality alongside Jennifer C. Nash's affirmative account of Black maternity as the potential basis of institution-building, rather than always a site of crisis. Taken together, then, these frameworks allow me to extend a point Joshua Bennett makes about *Salvage the Bones* specifically: both of these novels "unsettle normative, anthropocentric modes of imagining kinship and relation" by extending their conception of creaturely needs and caretaking.[16] They prepare the rhythms and spaces of the household—the milieu that is also the familiar domestic terrain of the realist novel.

For Arendt, labor in the *oikos* creates the foundation for others to participate freely in the political sphere, facilitated by the capacity for speech. While Arendt creates a dichotomy between the *animal laborans* and human autonomy in the political realm, she also suggests that action begins in the household before reverberating beyond, a "need for home," Kelly Oliver points out, "that we share with all of earth's creatures."[17] For Arendt, natality is literal and figurative, domestic and political—and deeply creaturely:

> The new beginning inherent in birth can make itself felt in the world only because the newcomer possesses the capacity of beginning something new, that is, of acting. In this sense of initiative, an element of action, and therefore of natality, is inherent in all human activities. Moreover, since action is the political activity par excellence, natality, and not mortality, may be the central category of political, as distinguished from metaphysical, thought.[18]

The spheres of *oikos* and *polis* are not in a hierarchic or even binary relation, but in a rhythmic relation imagined as what Julia Lupton describes as a "variable threshold" sensitive to "seasonal and bodily cycles; the kinds of thinking they enable and inhibit; and their world-building and conversation-supporting capacities."[19] Nash makes the entirely consonant point that allegories of death obscure the fundamental linkage between the carework of birthing, mothering, and parenting, and the genesis of political institutions that protect and enable alliances. Her perspective, with its more contemporary American context and pragmatic orientation, brings forward the dependence of political communication on alliances grounded in bodily vulnerability. Though neither of these accounts turns on other-than-human relationships, their work nonetheless highlights the ways in which birth is a beginning for the creature newly entering the world, a mode of expression, and the ground of collaborative affirmation—the kind of "deep praxis," as Sharon Patricia Holland writes, that forwards the multispecies remaking of "*this* world" as "a world."[20]

In the novels I discuss, multispecies friends share an environment that becomes a condition of relational as well as narrative possibility. That environment is not only the represented domestic map but the ecology of the narrative voice itself, crucial to the perceptibility of the common milieu.[21] Both *The Friend* and *Salvage the Bones* explore the rhythms and moods of lyrical first-person narration—which might risk seeming *more* rather than less anthropocentric—to evoke the possibility of sharing a world. Thus, even while the narrative techniques of first-person dog-companion novels remain overtly tethered to human-centric perspectives marked by loss, their lyrical use of rhythm, tone, and mood as hallmarks of human sapience are conditioned by sharing an environment with a dog. In these texts, lyricism suggests an anti-allegorical convergence between being born and giving voice—common ways of being together through which "divergent forms of life ... enter into world-building and future-founding relationships with each other."[22]

1. DOES THE DOG DIE?

First, for a moment, a cat: Sigrid Nunez's *What Are You Going Through* (2020) places a storytelling cat in the center of a narrative that deeply probes internal anguish. The narrator briefly encounters a voluble cat while visiting a friend suffering from terminal cancer. Before and after this encounter, the novel dramatizes the difficulty of really paying attention to another's painful experiences. Nunez opens with an epigraph from Simone Weil—"The love of our neighbor in all its fullness simply means being able to say to him, 'What are you going through?'"—a question demands an attention to others' creaturely afflictions that is anything but "simple."[23] In Nunez's rendering, this attunement can be difficult to achieve or even to tolerate: the narrator and her friend struggle to communicate, often "lapsing into silence." "I can't bear the sound of my own voice anymore," the sick friend comments. It is shortly thereafter that a charismatic cat jumps into the narrator's lap, offering her his own attention and fluently presenting his life story: "I had a decent home, the cat said, his words muffled by the purr but still clear." While the narrator has not asked him Weil's question, the cat answers it "simply." He retells his experiences of human violence on the street and praises the love of his adoptive human, his "second mother." The narrator merely listens, reacting appreciatively, "He told many other stories that night—he was a real Scheherazade, that cat."[24] *What Are You Going Through* never considers this anthropomorphism a problem, whether by asking how the cat and the narrator communicate or by flagging the moment as a singular violation of realism. The cat is what he is: a charismatic minor character capable of keen attention who voices the importance of care on a difficult night.

In *What Are You Going Through*, the human narrator's attention to the cat assuages the narrator's need for comfort whether or not we accept that he literally speaks to her.[25] However unusual this emotional-support-cat incident may be, his impact is temporary: Would the novel really be so different without him? *The Friend*, in contrast, fully commits to an investigation of animal companionship through grief. And yet *The Friend*, as Christina Fogarasi argues, invokes only to set aside a trauma plot of damage and recovery.[26] Dog plots usually *are* trauma plots: that is, they typically absorb relations of mutual care between humans and animals into an anthropocentrically therapeutic model of trauma recovery. *The Friend* pivots from this model to emphasize an interspecies milieu that emerges through its narrative form. As if refracting Weil, the novel imagines interspecies attention as a way for vulnerability to be fully recognized and valued.

Admittedly, death is central to what becomes *The Friend*'s ultimate project: the defense of "a life in which a person's most significant relationship is with a dog" (111). The novel is premised on the narrator's adoption of her closest friend's Great Dane, Apollo, after his suicide. Interrupted in her solitary, writerly existence by a dog in mourning, the narrator begins to experience her own loss in a new way as she observes first the dog's melancholic relation to his former owner and later, his own aging. At the outset the novel appears to perfectly illuminate Alice Kuzniar's central claims in *Melancholia's Dog*: "To own a pet . . . means refusing to give up the lost object. It is a shield against recognition of forsakenness; and it allows for an intimacy that would otherwise be forbidden with the pre-oedipal object of desire. The dog, of course, is a remarkably efficient substitute, who always exists in the immediate present in its companionship, love, and capacity for affection."²⁷ In Nunez's novel, a mourning that begins with the loss of the human friend after a complex but long-enduring mutual regard ultimately shifts its ground as the eponym starts to refer more to the dog than to the human "you" whom the narrator frequently addresses. "He has to forget you," she resolves, hoping to alleviate the dog's own sadness. "He has to forget you and fall in love with me. That's what has to happen" (123).

And it does happen. The dog falls for her, but still the novel remains seemingly captivated by death. *Spoiler alert*, the dog dies. "Why, having saved him, must I watch him suffer—suffer and die—and then be left alone, without him?" (168) asks the narrator? The narrative is fascinated with suffering—a key term for Weil, for whom suffering can be answered only through a mode of heightened attention distinctive to humans.²⁸ Nunez's novelist narrator is highly self-conscious about her emotional attachment to a powerful cultural symbol: the dog as an abject creature defined by its capacity to be wounded, to be ill, and ultimately to die. "There's a certain kind of person who, having read this far, is anxiously wondering: Does something bad happen to the dog?" (57). This kind of person has good reason to pose such a question. Disgusted with the human self-regard structuring these sacrificial narratives of dog-companionship, *The Friend* reports dryly, "Stories like these are one of the main reasons I have always preferred cats" (57).²⁹ Reacting to this clear-eyed assessment of the trend in which the novel itself participates, it also raises the question of how to construe an animal's death in nonsacrificial terms.

In depicting ongoing intimacy between the narrator and Apollo as a response to death, *The Friend* offers a feminist rejoinder to the novel it identifies as its "mirror," J. M. Coetzee's *Disgrace* (1999). Linking common abjection to the inevitability of death is central to *Disgrace*, perhaps the most commented-upon contemporary novel in literary animal studies. Nunez's narrator calls it "a book that you read with your skin" (45). In Coetzee's novel, the self-involved David Lurie flees his career as a literature professor after he is investigated for sexual misconduct, making a new life at his daughter's small farm. In the wake of a violent attack on the farm, which resonates with the political divisions of post-apartheid South Africa and culminates in his daughter's rape, Lurie—himself a sexual predator—begins to shed his sense of privilege and at the same time develops a new affinity for animals that he does not fully understand. Working at the local animal shelter, he participates in the euthanasia of homeless dogs and disposal of their bodies. Much of the critical dialogue about the novel centers on a scene toward the end, in which Lurie decides to "sacrifice"—euthanize—a dog with whom he has formed a bond. He thinks he can do "little enough, less than little: nothing" for the dog as he cares for the disposal of its corpse.[30]

Lurie purportedly exchanges sexual exploitation for animal affinity. Haraway praises the final "sacrifice" scene in *Disgrace* as less disembodied than *Elizabeth Costello*; Derrick Attridge, Philip Armstrong, Alice Kuzniar, and others point out that the menial tasks Lurie takes on at the dog shelter attempt to share in the dogs' own abjection.[31] His sacrifice is purposeless and perhaps even unwarranted, but these critics find value in Lurie's acceptance of purposelessness as an ethical impulse toward an "other" who is not usually deemed to be significant. Crucially, David's choice lacks the reasoned basis we might normally expect of an ethical principle, which might be especially important given that he is doing volunteer work for a biopolitical institution. If no sense can be made of reasoned choice in such a context, the novel expresses "doubts about the claims of instrumental reason," as Attridge writes. Elizabeth Anker comments further that by "submit[ting] himself to other lives" and "divesting himself of the instruments of domination," Lurie finds the plight of common embodiment.[32]

Coetzee's evaluation of Lurie's final gestures remains an open question. It is difficult to assess the degree to which the novel valorizes his actions, given that Coetzee's use of free indirect discourse invites considerable suspicion of Lurie's self-perception throughout. (In *Elizabeth Costello*, too, the non-totalizing and evasive qualities of free indirect discourse allow Coetzee to avoid anthropocentric rationalism as well as the rigidly hierarchical allegorical figures that would seem to bolster it.[33]) This sense of filtered evaluation is especially challenging in the novel's final, forbiddingly allegorical, and Christ-like image of Lurie bearing the dog in his arms "like a lamb"—in other words, like a biblical scapegoat that will symbolically purge the novel's tiny final community of its guilt.[34] Josephine Donovan and Marianne DeKoven are especially critical of Lurie's commitment to a fruitless sacrifice in the place of some enactment of a more positive commitment. Donovan acknowledges that "few . . . human characters exhibit the intense empathetic identification with animal suffering and loss of dignity as do Coetzee's"; yet, in his "inability to move beyond absurd, ineffectual gestures," Lurie remains caught in a dominating "male narcissism despite [his] awakened ethical awareness."[35] The dog fulfills the function of an emotional supplement, a pattern Keridiana Chez argues has attached to masculine dog companionship narratives since the nineteenth century.[36] Lurie exercises a power that only a human can. Despite his claim that he shares in the dog's abjection, his actions resonate with the biopolitical concept of sovereign decision rather than present a sustained allegiance with the occluded category of bare life.[37]

Certainly, Coetzee seems cautious about the prospect of turning his novel into a fable by too clearly adumbrating an abstractly reasoned principle—even a principle of submission—that could provide a moral doctrine, much less a political road map for the people of South Africa. Yet in *Disgrace* the power of human thought and choice in relation to death pulls against the novel's efforts to refuse rationality, a tension that registers in the resurgence of the allegorical. As Anat Pick argues, in this novel "championing ulterior subjectivities does not in itself generate a new ethics if the question of power is left unaddressed"— whether we understand this as the power of humans to choose animal death, gendered power, or their troubling intersection.[38]

Reflecting on *Disgrace*, Nunez's narrator asks, in exasperation or disbelief rather than with exegetical dispassion, a question in keeping with the most skeptical critical responses to *Disgrace*:

> Something very bad happens to a lot of dogs in *Disgrace*. The question persists, why won't David Lurie save the one, a mutt that has clearly come to love him and for which he, in turn, feels a special affection. Why can't that dog—a good dog, crippled but still young, and apparently sensitive to music—be spared the fate of all the other unwanted dogs destroyed at the animal welfare clinic? Why, instead of keeping this one dog, does Lurie insist on sacrificing it? (173)

The question chimes with one she asks about Apollo—"Why, having saved him, must I watch him suffer—suffer and die . . . ?" Though *The Friend* too confronts the inevitability of death, Nunez's answer to this particular set of questions has to do more with bodily vulnerability than Coetzee's, and ultimately much less to do with anthropocentric abstractions like sacrifice and salvation.

Although making an anti-theoretical fiction is not *un*fraught in *The Friend*, Nunez aims for a form that might not excessively valorize its own origins in human reason, subjectivity, and language. Certainly, in its concern about the pervasiveness of male sexual exploitation, the novel follows the model of Coetzee. In fact, it is explicitly interested in what it is to be following in another's tracks, to be captivated by a charismatic masculine master. Isn't the narrator in love with her dead friend, after all? "Is this the madness at the heart of it?" she asks, writing of her adoption of Apollo. "Do I believe that if I am good to him, if I act selflessly and make sacrifices for him, do I believe that if I love Apollo—beautiful, aging, melancholy Apollo—I will wake one morning to find him gone and you in his place, back from the land of the dead?" (169). The phrase between the dashes marks this as particularly strained logic, for it implies that she must value Apollo in his embodied specificity in order to then find that his ultimate significance lies beyond himself. The implication is that writing itself allows for such magical substitutions that subordinate the materiality of the figurative vehicle for its spiritualized, purified tenor.

And writing, the narrator suggests, is a narcissistic enterprise plagued by the unavoidable problems with human subjectivity in its capacity for self-reflection:

> The problem of self-doubt.
> > The problem of shame.
> > The problem of self-loathing.

She adds, remembering her friend:

> You once put it like this: When I get so fed up with something I'm writing that I decide to quit, and then, later, I find myself irresistibly drawn back to it, I always think: *Like a dog to its vomit.* (76)

It might be said that *The Friend* literalizes the metaphor by being "irresistibly drawn" to the vehicle rather than the tenor (while featuring a more dignified dog, whom we never encounter eating his disjecta). And the friend has chosen not an animal's death but his own.

Anti-theoreticality that manifests as a complex relationship to allegorical and fabular structures—perhaps to rationality itself—is a commitment *The Friend* shares with *Disgrace*. At one moment late in the novel, the narrator tries the gambit of offering her work as an allegory of writing, in which her depiction of the dog stands in for the capacity of fiction to invent and distort. Imagining the dead human friend as alive and well, she envisions a conversation in which he is shocked to hear that she has liberally rewritten his story. He is horrified. She defends herself:

"I unnamed everyone. Except for the dog."

"Jip? Jip's in it, too?"

"Well, not exactly Jip. There's a dog. He's an important character. And he has a name: Apollo."

"Rather a grand name for a miniature dachshund, don't you think?"

"He not a dachshund anymore. As I said, it's fiction, everything's different. Well, not everything. But you know how it works. You take some things from life, you make other things up, you tell a lot of half-lies and half-truths." (195)

But rather than rest with this explanation, in which the dog's significance becomes much diminished—cut down to dachshund size, with a name cribbed from Dickens—the narrator gives this thought experiment a kind of Schrödinger's dog status.[39] Is the friend really dead, or not? Is the novel an allegory of the human imagination, or not? Rather than resolve these questions, though, the narrator offers a single blank page, then moves on to a final, elegiac chapter that lyrically evokes the gigantic Apollo's sensory capacities—only rarely more Dionysian than Apollonian—and how they encourage her to notice her own. In other words, while the narrator explores what it would mean to transform this story into an allegory of human creativity in the face of mourning, in which the dog remains a conceptual stand-in, that move is rejected.

The melancholia that begins with mourning the loss of the human friend gradually transforms into epistemophilia: while the narrator seems confident she knew her human friend well, the dog in his dog world prompts uncertainty. He requires infinite observation. After all, for von Uexküll, "In the dog world there are only dog things."[40] For Kuzniar, this means a melancholia specific to dog-love because "however close we are to the canine pet, that closeness can never be enough and we are always conscious of the obliqueness and imperfection that govern our communion with it and, hence, of a fundamental muteness."[41] All of this would be to suggest that the concept of world, too, is ultimately exclusionary—no creature can access the world of another. As Martin Wallen explains, for Kuzniar, "unwillingness to impose an understanding on her canine friends" is the grounds of a "cynical friendship."[42] However, Nunez allows secondary characters, such as a veterinarian, to articulate cynical attitudes about the possibility of knowing a dog's world, while her narrator reflects intimately and attentively upon her new companion's habits and needs, as well as the cultural and literary history conditioning the possibility of their cross-species friendship.[43]

How to attend to a dog's world? It is worth returning to Heidegger, whose reading of pets prepares for and resonates, to a limited extent, with Nunez's attention to how the dog interacts with the narrator in her apartment. Here is Heidegger:

> We keep domestic pets in the house with us, they "live" with us. But we do not live with them if living means: *being* in an animal kind of way. Yet we *are with* them nonetheless.... Through this being with animals we enable them to move within our world. We say that the dog is lying underneath the table or is running up the stairs and so on. Yet when we consider the dog itself—does it comport itself toward the table as table, toward the stairs as stairs?[44]

Heidegger, Derrida points out, makes the distinction between human *Dasein* and animal living on the basis of the animals' inability to encounter things as tools—a move that requires a distinction between their way of encountering death, for "from the possibility of being dead . . . one can let things be such as they are."[45] Without being able to interact with objects "as such," animals lack the autonomy and flexibility of human beings and are thus merely captives to the few objects that are available to them within an otherwise incomprehensible environment.

Heidegger's awareness of von Uexküll's work shows here, as it also does in his comments on the way inhabitation structures environment—or milieu—in *The Fundamental Concepts of Metaphysics*:

> The animal's *way of being*, which we call "*life*," is *not without access* to what is around it and about it, to that amongst which it appears as a living being. It is because of this that the claim arises that the animal has an environmental world of its own within which it moves. Throughout the course of its life the animal is confined to its environmental world, immured as it were within a fixed sphere that is incapable of further expansion or contraction.[46]

Heidegger emphasizes the pet's ontological captivity in the home, focusing on the pet's lack of autonomy in relation to the object-world. Yet the distinction Heidegger makes between how a domestic animal and the human companion encounter the objects in a household has an entirely different and less hierarchical significance in ethological frameworks.[47] Von Uexküll treats environment as less fixed, using a dog's encounter with domestic space as an example of how objects acquire "tones" or modes of encounter that turn them into tools over time.[48] An environment's objects become meaningful when they have a functional significance—they can be interacted with. Certain pieces of furniture like a stool or a toilet that have a "human sitting tone," for example, do not read to the dog as having a "sitting tone," and vice versa. Other objects, meanwhile, may be perceptible only in their "obstacle tones" and indeed this feature can be read as privative in Heidegger's sense. The animal "misses" many of the objects that might be said to exist in the environment, while it is captivated by others. Only insofar as a dog can act upon an object like a table does it acquire an "effect tone," and indeed "the number of dog objects remain far less than the number of human objects."[49] Kendall-Morwick comments on this basis that von Uexküll's account of canine *Umwelt* is impoverished, and thus anthropocentric.[50] And although von Uexküll argues that each species has a world unto itself, organized by its own way of perceiving space and time, he also explicitly rules out the idea, like Heidegger's, that an animal's *Umwelt* has a permanent, immutable structure.

Rather, animals and human companions collaborate, *especially* through domestic cohabitation: "With the number of actions available to an animal, the number of objects in its environment also increases. It increases as well in the individual life of any animal capable of accumulating new experiences, for each new experience conditions a new attitude toward new impressions. By this means, new perception images with new effect tones are created. This is especially evident in the case of dogs, which learn to handle certain objects useful to human beings insofar as they make them into things of use for dogs."[51] Von Uexküll is also attentive to the affective dimensions of the object map in a given environment: it may appear object-rich and potentially overwhelming, or relatively spartan, leading to a sense of safety (or boredom).

This remapping applies well to Nunez's compassionate representation of how the bereaved Apollo first enters the apartment, uncertain of how to interact with it:

> Since he moved in with me, he has spent most of his time on the bed.
> The first day, after sniffing around the apartment—but in a listless way, without any real interest or curiosity—he climbed onto the bed and collapsed in a heap.
> *Down* died in my throat. (58–59)

The narrator acknowledges the mutually reinforcing effects of perceptions and emotions on what gives objects effect tones. She refuses to use her voice authoritatively to deny the disoriented dog the security of the one object that has a meaningful tone. Certainly, her apartment is initially "privative" for Apollo, held captive by the bed as the space's only signifier. But as she comes to realize, its tone can change over time and with collaboration. He still likes the bed, but the rest of the space eventually opens to him.

The novel's use of a concept of *Umwelt* is also applicable to its representation of humans. The book opens by exploring the notion of fit between senses and environment, yet with an anecdote seemingly disparate from the matter of animal companionship. The narrator plunges into the story of a group of Cambodian refugee women, living in the United States in the 1980s, who lose the ability to see. Their loss of sight is determined to be psychosomatic: "The women's minds, forced to take in so much horror and unable to see more, had managed to turn out the lights" (5–6). The narrator recounts this episode in medical anthropology, she says, because it was the topic of the last conversation she had with her friend. But like many of the anecdotes the narrator recounts, it resonates with other concerns, particularly the way that never-ending mourning, or trauma, affects how the senses might construe or curtail the world. She does not compare her own suffering to that of these women, or to the women rescued from sex slavery to whom she later teaches creative writing.[52] Her persistent concerns with extreme cultural violence, sexual captivity, and inequality point to, on the one hand, an enduring search for an anti-dominative style, and on the other, a refusal to present human beings as either rational or autonomous. This initial case, introduced sympathetically if impersonally, allows the novel to foreground the vulnerable sensory conditions of even human subjectivity. "Find the right tone and you can write about anything," the narrator remarks (108).[53]

While emphasizing potential limitations on the human *Umwelt*—humans' own dependency upon tone—the narrator offers a generous reading of dogs' sensory world consonant with von Uexküll's own.[54] In her initial observations, Nunez's narrator discovers that Apollo's *Umwelt* is not primarily visual. Eye contact appears human-centered: toward the beginning of their cohabitation, the narrator reports, "Mostly he ignores me. He might as well live here alone. He makes eye contact at times, but instantly looks away again. His large hazel eyes are strikingly human; they remind me of you. . . . Having your dog is like having a part of you here" (58). The "you" in this passage is not Apollo but the human friend; looking remains a human endeavor. Predictably, olfaction leads to richer intimacies. The narrator gives the impression of writing short, occasional compositions, often the result of solitary, sometimes idle googling of dog-related information, and of course some of what she turns up relates to the dog's remarkable sense of smell. She depicts the dog's sensory capacities as not only making meaning of his own world but as enabling mutual knowledge. By the end of the novel, her apartment smells of dog—a condition she is willing to put up with—because it has been occupied by a dog, smelling. (A casual friend remarks, "Your whole house smells of dog, says someone who comes to visit. I say I'll take care of it. Which I do by never inviting that person to visit again" [175]). She writes, addressing the dog, "Whenever [the wind] blows our way you lift your head to sniff, and I know your three hundred million odor receptors are picking up far more than the salty tang coming through my measly six million." She continues,

> Talk about too much information. A power like that would drive any human being insane. Thinking back to when you used to wake me in the middle of the night, inhaling every inch of me as I lay on the floor. Searching for data. Who was I and what might I have up my sleeve. You still sniff me all the time, but never with the same investigative fervor.
>
> I think it's fair to say that, thanks to your superior gift, you can read me better than I can read you. Hormones and pheromones keep you updated. My open wounds. My hidden fears. My loneliness. My rage. My never-ending grief. You can smell all that. (201)[55]

Rather than reinforce difference, the dog's own attunement to mood through his olfactory sensitivity allows the narrator herself to feel known in her own species-specific body.

Apollo's access to her feelings through her scent offers an alternative to the narrator's own limited capacity for self-revelation *despite* her seemingly sensitive and cerebral personality. She presents herself as often caught off-guard by the personal comments of acquaintances (e.g., "Aren't you the one who's in love with the dog?") and persistently skirts the open secret of her love for the dead friend, avoiding, for instance, any representation of her one sexual encounter with him. Despite its many reflections on the category of autofiction, the genre in which the novel appears to participate, the narrative itself turns out to have quite limited capacities to reveal "interiority." The narrator devises a series of miniature essays that explore positing of beliefs, interpreting facts and histories, and working through positions without particularly celebrating the achievement of the consciousness that performs all these tricks. The essays are neither impersonal nor confessional; their tone is curious, understated, perhaps slightly evasive, but neither histrionic nor affectless. Although there might be plenty to read into her interest in conditions of exploitation, the narrative does not particularly encourage this depth-psychological approach.[56] Inward, unacted upon desire seems not to be the key to this text—rather, its form itself models the horizontal modes of relation between bodies the narrator comes to value. Its organization might be said to give objects, relations, and situations a *writing-tone* more than to reveal a human self. In short, often in one-line paragraphs, the narrator often appears to fall into simultaneously tactful and puzzled silence. Rather than see arguments through to their conclusions, she leaves images and, in the end, sounds, hanging, refusing a fuller line of mastery, letting them accrue a mood that at once evokes curiosity and sadness at the many kinds of suffering, cruelty, and unkindness that concern her. She exhibits none of the intellectual satisfaction that would make her definitively superior to any of these conditions—nothing that would make her scent an inadequate way of knowing her, despite her vocation.

Voice—that writerly tool, so evident in the curious tone that pervades the novel—turns out to be another surprisingly valid world-making sensory modality that she and Apollo share. But voice is different from language, the other wedge that differentiates humans from animals, as the narrator articulates: "If we could talk to the animals, goes the song. / Meaning, if they could talk to us. / But of course that would ruin everything" (175). The vet, a mouthpiece for beliefs about animals that the narrator rejects, insists "dogs are a lot more mysterious and complicated than we ever thought, and unless they develop our language we'll never know them at all. Which goes for any animal, of course" (120). In contrast, her cohabitation with Apollo reaches its fullest expression in a voicing:

> I have talked to him, sung to him, and read him some poetry. I have trimmed his nails and brushed every inch of his coat. Now, watching him sleep, I feel a surge of contentment. There follows another, deeper feeling, singular and mysterious, yet at the same time perfectly familiar. I don't know why it takes a full minute for me to name it.
>
> What are we, Apollo and I, if not two solitudes that protect and border and greet each other? (202)

In this passage, which quotes Rilke, the notion of world encounters the necessity of care—protecting, bordering, and greeting are all grounded in the rhythmic procedures of daily, creaturely life. The narrator takes from Rilke what might be an effective description of the relationship between worlds in Canguilhem's use of von Uexküll. And it's crucial that it comes from a lyric poem: the narrator cites reading aloud as a particularly effective way of making companionship, alongside rituals like grooming, walking, or feeding, because reading is connected to objects that have the most significant "tones" to her as a writer.[57]

As the narrator begins to identify poetry as a key to thinking about their shared milieu, *The Friend* accords particular significance to vocalizing as a mode of companionship. At least from Darwin onward, studies of canine cognition show that dogs are the "opposite of mute" and "may have developed a more elaborate barking language precisely to communicate with humans." Alexandra Horowitz, introducing the science of canine cognition to a general readership, argues that the difficulty of interpreting dog *sounds*, more than other forms of dog communication, "strikes at the heart of the trouble in determining the subjective experience of an animal of which you cannot ask questions," precisely because of the voice's paralinguistic status.[58] Nunez's novel emphasizes the shared capacity for communicative voicing, a fascination with, in Tobias Menely's words, "the passionate expressivity and vulnerability of finite being [as] the first condition of common life."[59] Non-normative habits of voicing structure much of the interspecies relationship in *The Friend*, functioning as an alternative to an orientation toward language that would reveal interiorities. Part of the initial strangeness between the two is Apollo's use of his voice: "Every once in a while, he'd make this noise, this howling, or wailing, or whatever it was. Not loud, but strange, like a ghost or some other weird thing" (51). The narrator interprets this howl as an expression of his loss, which he eventually stops voicing. The relationship to the previous owner, too, is framed in terms of voice: "He may be my dog now (*my dog!*) but I don't believe he's forgotten you. What might hearing your voice do to him? How can he understand?" (145). The narrator presents herself as sympathetic to the idea of animals' communication, recollecting in one of the few childhood memories in the text, "I liked to pretend that I was some kind of animal, a cat or a rabbit or a horse. I would try to communicate through animal sounds rather than speech and refused to eat with my hands. At times I kept this up for so long and with such conviction that it became cause for parental concern" (172).[60] Her interest in animals' relationship with sound initially leads her to play music for Apollo, following the advice of therapeutic websites she scours on the Internet, but she finds that reading aloud works better. "Apollo never appears to enjoy the music I played for him, was never soothed—not my music, not by massage—as he appears to be soothed now," she writes, acknowledging that the effect is mutual. She notes,

> When I reach the bottom of the page I pause, thinking. Apollo pokes me with his nose. He barks, very low, just once. He takes a step forward, a step to the right, a step back, all the while cocking his head from side to side: his way of saying WTF.
> He wants me to keep reading! True or not, that's what I do. But soon I stop.
> Read your sentences out loud, goes the advice, and you'll hear what doesn't sound right, what doesn't work. I hear, I hear. What doesn't sound right, what doesn't work. *I heard*" (178–80).

Both give voice in the passage, and both "hear." And although she finds this mutuality embarrassingly outside human-canine social norms, "I read on." She reads "as clearly and with as much expression as I would to someone who could understand every word. And I too find it soothing: the lyrical prose in my mouth, the great warm gently heaving weight on my legs and feet" (184). Reading aloud gives the narrator a new and more visceral experience of words as well as of her body, which is sparingly depicted in the narrative. Her reading creates their milieu, the join between their separate *Umwelten*.

Such an interaction is proposed in *Disgrace*, too, just before the sacrificial plot shuts it down. David Lurie, supposedly writing an opera, notices:

> The dog is fascinated by the sound of the banjo. When he strums the strings, the dog sits up, cocks its head, listens. When he hums Teresa's line, and the humming begins to swell with feeling (it is as though his larynx thickens: he can feel the hammer of blood in his throat), the dog smacks its lips and seems on the point of singing too, or howling.
> Would he dare to do that: bring a dog into the piece, allow it to loose its own lament to the heavens between the strophes of lovelorn Teresa's? Why not? Surely, in a work that will never be performed, all things are permitted?[61]

Of this turn in Lurie's thought, Carrie Rohman remarks that it "reveals the artistic to be [something that] reorients us to the most fundamental forces of the earthly and creaturely, rather than to the self-importance of the human."[62] Yet Lurie's curiosity about the dog's voice emerges amid markers of human distinction, a certain scorn for the dog's "loose" and unreasoned song in contrast to the containment of bodily resonances Lurie notices in himself. The passage appears only two pages before the final scene in which Lurie euthanizes the dog. Canine vocality is not, ultimately, permitted. Nunez answers the question more affirmatively.

Rather than present reading aloud as an unequal experience of language, in which the dog experiences its materiality and the narrator its semioticity, the importance of the differences is diminished. Two key effects seem to follow from their reading together: first, it confirms that informational mastery is not the novel's ultimate domain. "An analysis of the full benefits to canines of being read to by humans is not something my research turns up" (191), the narrator remarks dryly, suggesting that aesthetic experience offers a phenomenality not captured by official knowledge of cognitive or subjective function. Second, this ongoing practice ("I decide to make reading aloud part of our routine. Knowing how this might look to others, though, I don't tell anyone" [191]) seems to affect the narrator's formal choices, leading to increasingly short, utterance-like sentences. "It's all about rhythm," the human friend said of writing. "Good sentences start with a beat" (9). Rhythm or tone, it is the sonic qualities of writing that come to feel most significant by the novel's conclusion.

And finally, the novel ends in the vocative. They are at the beach, Apollo ailing, the narrator worried:

> Oh, what a sound. What could that gull have seen to make it cry out like that?
> The butterflies are in the air again, moving off, in the direction of the shore.
> I want to call your name, but the word dies in my throat.
> *Oh, my friend, my friend!* (212)

As it did earlier, an utterance "dies in [her] throat," only now with respect to her vocative call, rather than to ordering a negative command. These two passages bookend this sharing of a world by the narrator and Apollo, emphasizing the role of voicing and sound to call that world into being, juxtaposing death to the vitality of sound produced in the living body's vibrations. As it does so, this final passage reechoes the restrained formal qualities that lead the novel to its animal-centricity. What lingers is not a cognitive achievement—a self remade or freedom won—but an unvoiced sound, felt in the flesh. Did something bad happen to the dog?

Although *The Friend* remains captivated by death, its interest in voicing ultimately allows it to turn toward birth as another shared condition of vulnerability that constitutes an entrance into, rather than exit from, having a world. *The Friend*'s other named mirror-text is J. R. Ackerley's memoir, *My Dog Tulip* (1956), about cohabiting with an excessive dog. Ackerley, a gay writer preoccupied with his dog's sexual voracity and ability to breed, seems to coordinate queer desire for canine sexuality; according to McHugh, Ackerley's dog allows him to "unleash[] desires that otherwise seem doomed."[63] Nunez's narrator observes this theme in *My Dog Tulip*, but notably, she does not register how fully sexual urgency dominates the text. *The Friend*, in contrast, repudiates sexual desire, quietly condemning the human friend's coercive sexual appetites. The narrator is single, childless, and does not show any present-day sexual impulses, all of which might symptomatically signal her unavowable devotion to her friend on a depth-psychological reading. Apollo does not breed, and he comes to the narrator fully grown ("Not to have known him as a frisky young dog, to have missed his entire puppyhood!" she exclaims. "I don't just feel sad, I feel cheated" [170]). Still, the narrator connects *the fact of being born* to the voicing that makes their shared world:

> I believe the intensity of the pity you feel for an animal has to do with how it evokes pity for yourself. I believe we must all retain, throughout our whole lives, a powerful memory of those early moments of life, a time when we were as much animal as human, the overwhelming feelings of helplessness and vulnerability and mute fear, and the yearning for the protection that our instinct tells us is there, if we could just cry loudly enough. (127)

Linking the conditions of being born to giving voice, the narrator's blossoming anaphora seems to echo a key aspect of natality. This rejection of embodied finitude opens onto an idea of responsive, creaturely spontaneity that makes a home through compassionate attention, and is nowhere more evident than in Nunez's style itself.

2. TWO MOTHERS

In *The Friend*, natality is a hint or a wish, but it forcefully counteracts biopolitical allegory in Ward's *Salvage the Bones*. The novel is narrated by a pregnant fifteen-year-old Black girl, Esch, who awaits the arrival of Hurricane Katrina with her multispecies family. Throughout, the novel attends to the daily processes of keeping a pack of siblings and a dog fed, clothed, and clean in the gradually accelerating crisis of the impending storm. From the novel's opening, when Esch watches her brother Skeetah's pit bull, China, give birth to a litter of puppies, the novel is interested in how creaturely needs are felt under exposure to shared but unequally threatening conditions. Partaking of realist traditions in representing domestic space, the novel is keenly attentive to the details of the home. Esch demonstrates their home's effect tones in what she pays attention to, and she also highlights the many acts of care that sustain the meanings with which their underresourced domestic milieu is precariously invested: how, where, and when each character eats, goes to the bathroom, manages injuries, and sleeps, as well as when others help or hinder them as they meet these needs. As Min Hyuong Song points out, Ward's attentiveness to the family's environment means that *Salvage the Bones* subverts expectations around disaster fiction because "natural disaster only compounds the precarity already endemic to their experiences of the everyday."[64] As I will argue, Ward's novel accords value to devalued lives in many ways, but interspecies kinship, and the formal choices through which it emerges, are among the most significant dimensions of Ward's "salvage" work.

Allegiance, if not exactly affection, between mothers living in a shared milieu redresses the narrator's loneliness in a masculine world (and in this way, its message is almost diametrically opposed to *The Bitch*). Ward's novel depicts dog companionship as emerging from within conditions of intense structural sexism and racism without being easily reduced to an index of them. The bright white pit bull of *Salvage the Bones* is "blackened by her breed," as Bennett puts it. Black studies documents the profound violence of the white supremacist logic that uses animals, especially pit bulls, as figures for Blackness, while scholars like Bénédicte Boisseron, Joshua Bennett, and Sharon Patricia Holland have worked to redeem and complicate the possibilities of alliance.[65] The novel builds upon what Dayan describes as the "one-on-one lamination of the pit bull onto the African American male," an association that stirs up white fear of both parties at the same time that it highlights their heightened regulation by the state's capacity to put to death, directly or indirectly.[66] Rather than actively contest stereotypes, Ward's novel unsettles them to suggest incipient alternatives—alternatives that resonate with what Boisseron presents as a Black "interspecies alliance against the hegemonic (white, human, patriarchal), dominating voice."[67] In the novel, these alternatives are not articulated as particularly politically powerful. *Salvage the Bones*, too, is an anti-theoretical fiction, one that resists conceptual substitution and conceptual abstraction, through its use of a lyrical narrative voice.[68]

To be sure, the novel actively resists the biopolitical formulation of certain lives as disposable. As Christopher Lloyd argues, the novel depicts "Katrina as revealing the persistence of southern history, arguing the storm's effects on black southerners recollected the historical legacy of denigrating African Americans to a form of 'bare life.' Those who were marginalized before the storm's arrival—through entrenched poverty and structural racism—were further marginalized after it."[69] The novel's hopeful ending on maternity does not necessarily provide a counterpoint: Rebekah Sheldon points out that

> the salvation promised by the reproductive woman and her child ... recalls the history of generational racial slavery and, in particular, the centrality of reproduction to plantation-based slave labor camps, particularly after the closure of the Atlantic slave trade, and thus to the making of American wealth.[70]

In other words, relying on the reproductive capacities of a Black woman's body—*especially* one likened to an animal's—as the basis of a collective future is ethically suspect. To take animals as figures for Blackness is violence. Documenting the historical pervasiveness of this logic, Boisseron advocates "expos[ing] a system that compulsively conjures up blackness and animality together to measure the value of existence" in order to explore the conjunctions of "black and animal defiance."[71] Alongside critiques of reproductive futurism, Ward's picture of this kind of interspecies defiance also calls up Nash's defense of Black maternal alliance. Nash points out that "the rhetoric of crisis is part of an enduring, troubling tradition ... of reading Black mothers ... into symbols, even if now Black mothers are symbols of tragic heroism rather than deviance." Alternatives to the symbolic presentation of Black maternity, for Nash, range from Black feminist institution-building to what she terms "a noncrisis style." *Salvage the Bones* appears to lean into the romanticized crisis stereotype that worries Nash, but only to complicate it profoundly. Ward offers a vision of interspecies allegiance that, as in Nash's account, generates "joy, playfulness, and even sensuality" that cannot be reduced to the "shared grief and trauma" it may involve.[72]

By working within rather than breaking stereotypes, Ward creates a defiant alliance between dog and human histories within a specific cultural and geographic milieu. Ward builds on Toni Morrison's meditations on racist associations between African Americans and animals, cemented by nineteenth-century racial pseudoscience (such as Josiah Nott and George Gliddon's 1854 *Types of Mankind*). Morrison's novels, particularly *Beloved* (1987), explore a fraught relationship with animal life; Sethe kills her baby to prevent her from being classified as an animal, yet the narrative dwells on a fascinated, respectful, and powerful visionary attitude toward the natural world through Baby Suggs. As Vera Norwood points out, "Morrison is not suggesting that humans are separate from animals and that the whites' only error is in conjoining blacks to a 'lower' species"—the allegorical reading of the animal analogy. "Rather," Norwood argues, "she critiques whites' dealings with all other life forms as though they were only meat for the table, [or] beasts of burden."[73] Following Morrison, Ward aligns violences against any "othered" lives. *Salvage the Bones* shifts the emphasis of the stereotypes it uses, so that instead of defending a dignity unique to human beings, she lights up the creaturely dimensions of the precarious modes of living that both humans and other animals in the novel experience.[74]

Salvage the Bones thus offers a non-anthropocentric and anti-racist portrayal of a profound crisis of human and canine survival, especially through its depiction of Hurricane Katrina. Some have been cynical about the national attention garnered by stranded "Katrina dogs" while the plight of thousands of Black people was dismissed. Brigitte Fielder comments that the problem is more complex than white "affective prioritization... of dogs over black people." Rather, Fielder suggests, "perceived similarity is not a prerequisite for sympathy. ... sympathy that can be transferred across species difference also has the potential to be transferred across racial difference."[75] Accommodating difference along multiple axes at once, *Salvage the Bones* can be seen as advocating, in Lloyd's words, an "ethic of survival, home, and family across species lines, emphasizing the ways in which precariousness and creatureliness—exposure to biopolitical forces, such as those engendered by Katrina's effects on the Gulf region—is not confined to human life."[76] But I would also argue that the novel's impact cannot be understood as a re-allegorization of biopolitical exposure. While Ward acknowledges profound inequalities of power along lines of race, gender, and species, gendered intimacies between species in *Salvage the Bones* repartition difference and sameness without eliminating them, giving a perceptual world to those to whom worldedness is too often denied.

In Ward's novel, devotion to animals initially seems melancholic in

Kuzniar's sense, given the children's loss of their mother in childbirth and their father's ongoing struggle with alcoholism.[77] Dog-love offers a compensatory and futureless intimacy, underscored by the probable death of China in the hurricane in the novel's conclusion, as well as the loss of her puppies one by one as the novel progresses. Nonetheless, the persistent and affirmative link Esch identifies between her own impending motherhood and China's giving birth suggests the value of reading this novel as more invested in birth than death as a common condition of embodiment. Before discussing this maternal identification, however, I want to demonstrate the novel's investment in depicting the challenges and pleasures of a companion-species relationship.

Esch is an observer of China, rather than her direct companion. In contrast, her brother Skeetah's deep intimacy with his pit bull—which complicates cultural discourses connecting the breed with Black masculinity, in turn a highly intensified version of dog's long-standing emotional supplementation of the masculine—is the most profound example of the many interconnections between humans and animals throughout the novel. The novel does not disavow or erase the social and political histories involved in human manipulation of animal life. It does not underestimate the pitfalls of identification with a pit bull, who is literally property. Skeetah's desire to fight China at times appears as an exploitative effort to gain power and recognition in a cultural scenario in which he is nearly powerless. She is a flagrant status symbol: "They will throw their own dogs into the ring, each hoping for a good fight, a savage heart, a win, to return home from the woods . . . to be able to say, *My bitch did it* or *my nigga got him*" (160). Rather than reject cultural stereotypes about dogfighting or pit bulls, Ward shows Skeetah as, at least to some extent, perpetuating the image of the dog as vicious, associated with drugs, criminality, and an image of Black masculine toughness. He chants to her before he fights her:

> *China White*, he breathes, *my China. Like bleach, China, hitting and turning them red and white, China. Like coca, China, so hard they breathe you up and they nose bleed, China. Make them runny, China, make insides outsides, China, make them love you, China, make them need you, China, make them know even though they want to they can't live without you, China. My China*, he mumbles: *make them know, make them know, make them know.* (171)

Here he sees her as a powerful possession, her glamor that of cocaine, her prestige all too clearly that of whiteness. Esch—who does not try to prevent the fight from happening—echoes this angle of admiration: "Manny would talk shit whenever we were all out under the trees as if he could lessen the wonder of Sketch's prized dog. He thought he could dim her, that he could convince us she wasn't white and beautiful and gorgeous as a magnolia on the trash-strewn, hardscrabble pit, where everything else is starving, fighting, struggling" (96). Their idealization reinforces the idea that Skeetah abuses his pet to reinforce his own masculine power, which the other boys all question. Bronwyn Dickey describes this compensatory capacity for violence as "the romance of the urban pit-bull": "In the pit-bull, a young man could see whatever version of himself he wanted, from family defender to resourceful hustler to unbowed survivor."[78] Skeetah wants to be all three. And in Esch's eyes, thanks to his care for China, he is.

At the same time, Ward complicates Skeetah's interest in dogfighting by also evoking the pleasures of his cross-species companionship. Dayan's reflections on how to avoid moral judgments of dogfighting are helpful, invoking a spiritual dimension to the practice that seems to explain Skeetah's sense of exaltation when he is with China:

> There is always something outside the human world. It is the world of men who believe in and pray to God, to Christ and the angels of mercy, at the same time as they fight dogs or chickens, hunt all manner of game, or run through the woods, dog head low leading the way to catch wild pig. It is hard to say what matters more to them: animality or spirituality. They are in between and exist for, with, and through the impalpable and fleshly in their midst.[79]

Dayan's passage captures well the furtive companionship between Skeetah and China in the woods beyond the threshold of the home. Ward also makes Skeetah a self-aware proponent of species as well as gender equality, emphasizing the importance of his own understanding of their bond. Acting huffy when others scorn his care for the dog and defending his choice of a premium dog food despite the family's food insecurity, Skeetah remarks, "Some people understand that between man and dog is a relationship." The bag of chow "hangs even, covers half his chest. 'Equal'" (29). And when entering China into her first postpartum dogfight, he rejects both species and gender inequality:

> *How you going to fight her?* Randall scream-whispered at Skeetah after Rico started laughing and led Kilo across the clearing to rub him down. *She's a mother!* The boys

and their dogs spread around the circle of the clearing; the knot loosened, frayed. *And he's a father*, Skeetah said, motioning toward Kilo, *and what fucking difference does it make?* China nosed Skeetah's side. *Her titties*, Randall said. *Are for the puppies, and you don't have to worry about that*, Skeetah breathed. *The puppies*, Randall said, *what about the puppies? We all fight*, said Skeetah. *Everybody.* (169)

Randall's attempt to discourage Skeetah is not motivated by concern for the dog or the puppies—he hopes the puppies can be sold to pay for his basketball camp. Skeetah, no less self-interested, seems to easily reconcile his claims of equality with his authority over China by insisting upon a trans-species condition of fighting, birthing, and care. In contrast to Esch's notion that China stands apart from the "starving, fighting, struggling" human beings she lives among, Skeetah strategically disavows distinctions.[80]

As caretaker, he often appears as China's lover and heterosexual partner, a relationship less horizontal than he thinks it is, given the novel's depiction of masculine domination, and yet meaningfully distinct from the pride of absolute ownership. Skeetah sees himself as the puppies' father, telling Esch, "'You know how you hear daddies on TV talking about birth being a miracle? For all them pigs and mutts and rabbits I seen giving birth, I ain't never felt nothing like that. Them puppies is *real*'" (21). Esch has only a sexualized concept of the home to understand and represent such an alliance. Building on the highly gender-normative relationship between her parents—her mother, represented as a loving femme caretaker, and her gruff, alcoholic father, who struggles to provide and maintain an income and infrastructure—Esch reads Skeetah's relationship with China as a heterosexual marriage. When he builds her a doghouse meant to shelter her from the storm, Esch comments wistfully, "I always thought it was something a man did for a woman when they married: build her something to live in" (60). She presents Skeetah as offering a distinctively masculine contribution to the home: "It is what makes him so good with dogs, with China, I think, the way he can take rotten boards and make them a kennel, make a squirrel barbecue, make ripped tile a floor" (74–75). These are all modes of care crucial to survival. "He is building her a house," she declares. "He is watching over her, gauging her for sickness. He knows love" (103). Pace Arendt on the *oikos*: "That individual maintenance should be the task of the man and the species survival the task of the woman was obvious, and both of these natural functions, the labor of man to provide nourishment and the labor of the woman in giving birth, were subject to the same urgency of life. Natural community in the household therefore was born of necessity, and necessity ruled over all activities performed over it."[81] The novel, thus far, rewrites the sexual binarism of the *oikos* as interspecies marriage, a move that turns the power imbalance between species into that of gender.

Yet this interspecies household also allows for some flexibility, some queerness, within a rigid gender system. A mode of intimacy Dayan cites as specific to the alliance between pit bulls and Black men: "Theirs is another kind of love, something close to attachment and awe."[82] Esch recognizes Skeetah's distance from the sexual norms of his peers, and presents his growth into a kind of dog-boy as an alternative trajectory for pubescence:

> I'd always assumed he missed more than half of what went on at the Pit; seemed like all I ever saw around him, once he brought home a pit he told me he stole out of somebody's yard when he was twelve, were dogs.... His voice was a bark, his step the wagging thump of a meaty tail. We lost each other, a little. And now I wonder what Skeetah's seen, what he's been paying attention to when his dogs are sleeping.... What does he know about lovers? He's the odd one, the one that always smells like sweaty fur when all the boys are together, the one the girls probably think stinks. But even I know that there's one, always one, who likes the boy like Skeetah. There's always one for everybody. But I don't think he believes that. (33–34)

Perhaps standing in for a queer sexuality Esch doesn't know how to articulate, Skeetah's love of China becomes heterosexualized; she articulates his dog-love as compensatory for the kind of sexual attachment he perhaps cannot frame even to himself. Katherine Bond Stockton observes that relationships with pet dogs are a prevalent trope in narratives of queer childhood because the dog offers the child a way of "confounding [their] parents and [their] future," while delaying realizations that would disrupt the domestic order.[83] In his alliance with China, which seemingly reshapes his own body, Skeetah creates an interspecies chosen family.[84]

Finding love and power within the oppressive and dominating structures of the gender-normative home likewise orients Esch's fascination with China. The novel is deeply invested in the distinctive feel and function of maternal care. Having lost her own mother to her youngest brother's birth, Esch looks to China as a role model for a more powerful image of maternity. She lives in a condition of extreme masculine domination. Unlike *The Friend*, *Salvage the Bones* features an unprivileged, unworldly narrator: a Black child, barely parented by her abusive father and surrounded by brothers and their friends, many of whom take sexual advantage of her. Esch's agency is in doubt from the beginning, especially where sex is concerned. On the one hand, Esch describes herself as desiring sex, particularly with Manny, the father of her baby, and it is important that Ward refuses to treat as anything other than normal the sexual desires of a young Black girl. On the other hand, Esch is so young and her sexual encounters occur so entirely on the boys' terms that her consent is out of the question. Meanwhile, her pregnancy takes on a life of its own when her consideration of abortion evaporates, in part because it would be logistically difficult and in part because, seemingly, she wants to become a mother, but it is not framed as an active choice. When Esch tells herself, "These are my options, and they narrow to none" (103), her situation is a keen reminder that the concept of milieu (psychosocial and physical) can be as constraining and normative as it can be liberating.[85] Still, Esch has unusual imaginative and affective capacities that are not stymied by her environment, but rather respond to it in innovative and ultimately restorative ways. She yearns for authority and significance—which Ward emphasizes by depicting Esch's fascination with Greek myth, particularly the tumultuous romance between Jason and Medea, who kills their children. Most of all, she hopes for a female ally and finds it in China. Ward does not play this attachment primarily for pathos—a sign of the absolute failure of human care—or as solely melancholic, but rather the novel takes seriously what Esch's creaturely identification can mean.

She remembers her mother cleaning the children's faces and tending little wounds with scarred but "sure" hands (52) that knew how to cook "the wild out of" (85) caught seafood—her mother knew how to preserve the home as a zone of protection. When Esch sees China giving birth, she is surprised to see the fighting dog offering the kind of maternal care she recognizes: "China is licking the puppies. I've never seen her so gentle. I don't know what I thought she would do once she had them: sit on them and smother them maybe. Bite them. Turn their skulls to bits of bone and blood. But she doesn't do any of that. Instead she stands over them, her on one side and Skeetah on the other like a pair of proud parents, and she licks" (17). Yet she seems to admire the dog when she acts more characteristically and kills one of her puppies: "China is bloody-mouthed and bright-eyed as Medea. If she could speak, this is what I would ask her: *Is this what motherhood is?*" (130). Can motherhood accommodate aggression—can

Esch, if she is angry, be a mother? Can Esch, when she becomes a mother, still be angry? China allows Esch not only to see mothering as caretaking, but also to find a mode of being that allows for the expression of anger. Watching the dogfight between China and her mate, Esch imagines their dialogue: "*Hello father*, she says, tonguing Kilo. *I don't have milk for you.* China blazes.... *But I do have this*. Her mouth is a mousetrap snapped shut around the mouse of Kilo's neck" (176). Whereas Esch projects a harmonious image of domesticated heterosexuality onto Skeetah's alliance with China, in which China is the passive recipient of Skeetah's husbanding, she sees China's ability to inflict violence on both her mate and her babies as enabling action. Her identification with the fighting dog's new maternity begins to grasp a violent yet loving vision of corporeality that makes few species distinctions.

Esch persistently frames China's action as speech while reflecting on her ability to tell her own story; the possibility of speech attends moments of particular gender identification and legitimates her own use of her voice in self-defense and self-definition. Watching China give birth, Esch emphasizes the dog's voice: "She yelps. She sounds like I do when I let go of the swinging rope that hangs from the tall tree over Wolf River: terrified and elated. Her clipped ears curl forward. The puppy slides from her" (13). Describing her early sexual encounter with Manny, Esch invokes the canine voice to begin: "China barked, knife sharp. I was bold as a Greek; I was making him hot with love, and Manny was loving me" (17). China's speech, according to Esch, will make sense of the mystery of shared embodiment. As the siblings enter the woods—about to steal medicine from a neighbor's house for China—they gaze around:

> Insects root under our feet, squirrels leap from tree to tree, crows glide between the tops of the pines, cawing. The beat of their wings sounds soft as the swish of Mudda Ma'am's [their grandmother's] broom when she sweeps pine needles from her sandy front yard. Skeetah watches them the way he watches China like any second she might speak, and he's sure when it will happen, she will reveal all the answers to all the things he has ever wondered about. (45–46)

Over the course of the novel, she imagines their shared maternity as provoking conversation. Always attuned to China's barks and yelps, Esch yearns for a more direct mode of communication. Finally confronting Manny for his cruel rejection of her pregnancy, she attacks him with China as her role model: "I am on him like China," she reports (203). Afterward, she imagines that her baby's emergence into the world will be an act of speech. "'The baby will tell,' I scream. 'It'll tell!'" (205). Even if it is unclear exactly how Esch imagines the baby will "tell," she imagines its birth as a vocalized claim for attention and care that will redistribute justice.

Still, the novel's endorsement of Esch's voice in the context of Hurricane Katrina's threat to survival raises biopolitical and ecological questions. After all, a key problem for ecocriticism engaged with the Anthropocene is precisely how to understand gestures of individual action against the excessive scale of apocalyptic environmental events. Just after Esch shouts at Manny in the preceding passage, the wind "grabs my voice up and snatches it out and over the pines, and drops it there to die" (205). As in *The Friend*, the human voice dies out, creating a link between living and voicing. Any gains in Esch's confidence or agency are overwhelmed by force of the hurricane, even if the human family's survival remains hopeful. Furthermore, the association of hope with childbirth—very far (phenomenologically, socially, historically, biopolitically) from an event occurring at the scale of individual choice—may appear more problematic than reassuring for its aggressive allegorization of the birthing body. Sheldon's *The Child to Come*, concerned with narratives in which birth appears as an allegorical event indexing hope in contemporary fictions of crisis, articulates the kind of concerns I have in mind:

> Racially marked reproductive labors perform a kind of ideological sleight of hand: they appear to iconize the reproductive woman of color and the community her fertility prophecies by proffering birth, labor, and the child against a backdrop of ecological devastation. But the promise she engenders through the fact of her fertility in fact reinstates a complacent nature capable of enclosure. In her fleshly surplus lurks a new form of wholly economized life.[86]

Sheldon's counter-allegory appears in the context of readings of novels in which pregnant and birthing women are seen as objects. Indeed, *Salvage the Bones* presents Esch as not at all a self-determining agent. But she is also far from reduced to a suffering teen mother figure, as Nash might remind us. Rather, she is a perceiver and a maker of her milieu. Certainly, she may at times appear ideologically blinkered—another of the many checks on her autonomy—and yet the novel's interest in her telling of her own story suggests a refusal to reduce her to "the reproductive woman of color." Her lyrical style of attending to her world becomes a way of finding, as Bennett puts it, "joy and vitality where we might see only blight."[87]

Esch begins to see herself enmeshed within a process at once biologically rooted and culturally complex, and she often proposes animal similes in her observations of the fragile world around her. But the novel's overall treatment of animality is not as anthropocentric as this figurative impulse would imply—especially because it is so pervasive that Esch's consciousness seems fundamentally zoopoetic. She is given to "slippages between the human and nonhuman at the level of description," as Bennett puts it, that evoke and validate the phenomenal richness of her milieu.[88] Especially in the early sections of the novel, her narrative offers a profusion of similes for making sense of her interconnection with animals' lives. Despite the skepticism I have expressed toward allegory as a form that partitions the world of living creatures, not all figurative language need be understood as having this function. Heather Keenleyside, starting from the eighteenth century's newly zoological imagination, argues that "we best apprehend the specificity of animal life—including, potentially, our own—by way of conspicuously figurative uses of language, generic literary forms, or recognizable rhetorical configurations," such that we might "conceive literary form as an engine for incorporating individuals into a species or community."[89] The ubiquitous applicability and reversibility of simile in *Salvage the Bones* suggests its world-reshaping capacities. Keenleyside defends the notion that "when we apprehend animals (including humans), we are never in the territory of strictly literal description, relying solely on the evidence of our sense," where our application of figurative language means we recognize animals' vitality, animacy, and unpredictability.[90]

Watching China give birth, Esch animates the scene through a profusion of similes: "[Skeetah] curled around China like a fingernail around flesh" (2); "He is focused on China like a man focuses on a woman when he feels that she is his, which China is" (3); "China's skin is rippling like wind over water" (8); "Manny was holding the ball as tenderly as he would a pit puppy with pedigree papers" (9); "I want [a particular puppy] because he comes out of China chanting and singing like the New Orleans Indians, like the Indians that gave me my hair" (12); "She yelps. She sounds like I do when I let go of the swinging rope that hangs from the tall tree over Wolf River" (13). China is a book Esch reads with her skin. The similes emphasize environmental and fleshly embeddedness, racial and species mixing, exploitation and tenderness. Food, like birth, prompts figurative language and rampant asyndeton that proliferates connection. Gathering chicken eggs to ensure food for the coming storm prompts a particularly lyrical passage that uses similes to emphasize common reproductive vitality: "I wonder if inside eggs, the kind that need the shelter of a body—horse eggs, pig eggs, human eggs—are so light. Would they look clear as jelly with firefly hearts, or would they look as a solid and silent as a stone? Would they show their mystery, or would they cover it like a secret? Would a human egg let itself be seen?" (24). Similes link these common eggs to substances (stone and jelly) that appear many times elsewhere in the novel, underlining their figurative as well as literal fecundity.

As with the eggs, eating turns such figurative attunements almost literal, as when Esch tastes squirrel Skeetah has caught and cooked in the woods:

> By the time the meat is done cooking, has turned brown and small with as many hard edges as a jewel, the boys have come. . . . the meat is stringy and hard, tastes of half red spice from the hot sauce, which has turned the bread pink, and half wild animal. I bite and I am eating acorns and leaping with fear into the small dark holes in the heart of old oak trees. (49)[91]

Aware that everything she ingests transforms into nutrition for her baby, Esch opens herself to food as figurative transformation, imagining that she becomes the squirrel whose flesh she (nauseously) eats. Animalizing herself, Esch lends vitality even to death.

The novel's final chapters, centered on the hurricane, echo this pathway, emphasizing the creatureliness of the human family, Skeetah in particular, as they struggle to survive. Lloyd notes, "the exposure of the South's inhabitants to social, historical, and natural forces during Katrina revealed a kind of creatureliness; humans and nonhuman animals were simultaneously stripped of security, defenses, and bodily stability."[92] Skeetah's queer orientation toward the dog means that he can be oblivious to the human needs around him, especially in the eyes of his siblings. As Esch and her other brothers scramble to buy enough food to get them through the storm, Skeetah suggests "we can eat like China" as he embraces his dog, "each kneeling before the other, eyes together." "I want to kick her," Esch thinks to herself. "'We ain't no dogs,' Randall says. 'And you ain't either'" (193). The hurricane presents a not quite leveling situation. While the father in *Salvage the Bones* usually maintains what he sees as domestic order by insisting that Skeetah keep China out of the house, Skeetah ultimately gains entry for the dog and her remaining puppies by insisting that he will not come inside unless they do too. The rising water forces them all out into a condition of shared marginality. "He and China step as one, a new animal, toward the light opening of the hallway where the wind whistles in a thin sheet under Daddy's door," Esch reports (225). After Skeetah lets go of China to help his human family members make their way to safety and the dog flees into the woods, probably never to return, Esch describes him as "trying to shake himself apart" (238). Afterward, he appears shattered with regret, and when he decides to find her, plunging into the water that has flooded their property, "he was one animal again, or at least he thought he would soon be" (240). Being an animal, in this context, means *having* a world—being able to act.

The hurricane's effects on the family seem equivocal rather than outright disastrous. Their father—his too-careless hand mutilated in an accident in the preparations—takes a renewed interest in his daughter's welfare, offering to bring her to doctor's appointments where he has been dangerously leery of seeking medical care in the past. Meanwhile, friends step up, proclaiming that Esch's baby will have a community of "daddies" to make up for Manny's lack of interest. These expressions of commitment constitute acts of domestic renewal within an extended human kinship network. Still, the novel's final note of hope turns not so much on recovering China herself but on the alliance with China that the siblings have formed. The novel concludes with what it is reasonable to assume is the dog's death (albeit not presented as self-sacrifice on China's part). When Skeetah releases China into the water, freeing himself to rescue Esch, China disappears looking like "a water moccasin" cutting through the flood, in a context in which the flood itself is presented as a "fanged" snake. Esch's biological imaginary otherizes China as Skeetah lets her go. Moreover, if China dies, it is in the service of both Esch's individual self-realization and heightened solidarity among the human family. Yet I would not read this as an allegorical transubstantiation of China's life or maternity. Just as Armbruster cites narratives that resonate with feminist care ethics as alternatives to the sacrificial narrative, the novel's final passage lands instead on birthing as a basis for common practices of world-making and inhabitation.

Esch hopes that her story will not end in China's death at all. Admiring Skeetah, desolately camping out on the property waiting for China's return, she predicts—though with the wistfulness of anaphora—that "he will feed the fire so it will blaze bright as a lighthouse. He will listen for the beat of her tail, the padding of her feet in the mud." Here, sound will constitute the most important sign of her presence and suggests a lingering faith that she will come back unharmed. She will remain "in the middle of the world." The last paragraphs, however, are more ambiguous:

> He will look into the future and see her emerge into the circle of his fire, beaten dirty by the hurricane so she doesn't gleam anymore, so she is the color of his teeth, of the white of his eyes, of the bone bounded by his blood, dull but alive, alive, alive, and when he sees her, his face will break and run water, and it will wear away, like the water does, the heart of stone left by her leaving.
>
> *China.* She will return, standing tall and straight, the milk burned out of her. She will look down on the circle of light we have made in the Pit, and she will know that I have kept watch, that I have fought. China will bark and call me sister. In the star-suffocated sky, there is a great waiting silence.
>
> She will know that I am a mother. (258)

The acceptance of her own maternity that Esch demonstrates depends upon interspecies kinship—an aesthetics of sisterhood, in Nash's framework. Despite the possible figuration of China as an anthropomorphic angel, upright and looking down, surrounded by flame, the passage is also legible in entirely literal terms, given the topography of the family's land. Moreover, the dulled coloration of the passage undercuts the idealization of China that has at times prompted Esch's jealousy and led her to devalue her own impending maternity. Now difference is diminished—not absent, but less stark and less significant. Esch portrays herself as gaining her bearings by hearing China's voice. Her bark makes possible a silence that is there to be broken by Esch's own newborn's cry.

3. CONCLUSION

I want to conclude by observing that these novels have accrued considerable cultural prestige, with consequences for their depiction of dog love. As National Book Award winners, *Salvage the Bones* and *The Friend* each grant cultural visibility to the women who authored them—in fact, Ward is now the winner of two. In Ward's acceptance speech for her 2017 novel *Sing, Unburied, Sing*, she explained the challenges she has encountered in writing ambitious novels about poor Black people in the rural South: "Throughout my career when I've been rejected, there was sometimes subtext and it was this: People will not read your work because these are not universal stories."[93] Even as some critics of the National Book Award and other literary prizes have presented prize-giving as a "thoroughly social, economic, and (racist) political instrument," as James English explains, they have also chosen to credit it with "real, even potentially decisive power in determining long-term literary valuations."[94] If this "decisiveness" means that these novels are now part of an evolving contemporary canon, it is especially important to notice that the dogs at their centers cannot be read in either symbolic or sentimental terms. Readers are being encouraged, by virtue of the award alone, to take dog friendships seriously.

As Fielder claims, we should not immediately be *only* cynical about the attention dogs attract if the stories of animals suggest that there are grounds for optimism about identification despite difference. *Salvage the Bones* and *The Friend* endorse visions of a social milieu in which interspecies alliance is central to the making of an environment in which a creaturely self can survive. Hence the prominence of dogs in novels also concerned with sexual abuse, intergenerational racial violence, and even the threat of human extinction. Even while they recognize the dangers their environments pose, in other words, they underline commonness not only in death, but in living on in relations of mutual care.

FOUR

Cat Kin

In Lucy Ellmann's *Ducks, Newburyport* (2019), a middle-aged white Ohio mom cooking in her kitchen finds herself pondering "the fact that it can't be easy to be a Florida cougar, stuck in the Everglades, feeling damp all day, unless it's one of those *underwater panthers*, the ones in charge of storms, waves, whirlpools, skookumchuck, waterfalls and white-water rapids, Mishipeshu."[1] Ellmann's narrator seeks an accessible image of an opaque animal world. Her curiosity about an endangered animal's bleak existence leads her to evoke a more active spiritual world of animal power, an image culminating in an Ojibwe word she has learned. An associative rhythm first diverts her from imagining the bleak, tedious existence of a Florida cougar and then suggests the inadequacy of her own eurowestern framework for understanding its life. And then the mom moves on.

What is it like for a human to commit to imagining an animal having its own world—even or especially if that animal is in peril? Perspectives from Indigenous studies suggest that endangerment narratives demand recognitions of kinship, which may elicit grief in response to the ecocidal logic of settler colonialism: in the words of Deborah Bird Rose, "The animals and plants that are dying out are not so much vulnerable, endangered, or extinct species, but more significantly are vulnerable and dying members of the family."[2] When endangerment fictions aren't paralyzingly apocalyptic, they tend to express a melancholic or elegiac mode dependent upon a powerfully subjective sense of individual sensitivity and loss, as Ursula Heise points out.[3] Expressions of endangered-species love make poor compensation for the structural violence the prospect of extinction implies (as I suggested in Chapter 2, the Knut section of *Memoirs of a Polar Bear* offers this critique).[4] In part because of these limiting affective patterns, environmental studies tends to privilege speculative science fiction over more traditional novelistic approaches to ecological crisis that represent terrestrial, domestic reality experienced by interiorized human individuals.[5] Still, if from the eighteenth century onward "the novel" broadly has disclosed inward life, first-person novels are exceptionally well suited to evoking the *experience of thinking*—in this case, thinking about other animals' worlds, conveying both their relatedness and their separateness.[6]

Building on my examination of first-person voice in Chapter 3, this chapter reads *Ducks, Newburyport* alongside Linda Hogan's *Power* (1998): first-person novels of two worlds that react to crises of endangerment by interweaving representations of animals' and humans' sapience. Both novels work in dialogue with Indigenous ontologies, presenting what it feels like to think through logics of two not entirely mixable "worlds"—Indigenous and settler-colonial, human and feline. Eileen Crist argues that ecological devastation is profoundly connected to the historical denial of animal minds: "alongside destroying biological kinds, natural habitats, and populations of animals," she writes, "we are deleting the Earth's noumenal dimensions, elaborated through emotion, intention, understanding, perception, experience—in other words, through varieties of aware beings shaping and adorning the world-as-home."[7] *Power* and *Ducks* are structurally committed through their use of first-person narration to representing the ebb and flow of a human narrator's awareness, but they accord substantial attention to the separate awareness of a big cat. The separation of worlds opens onto the question of how a person might think and feel about an animal's own, distinctive sentience: how sensations, desires, obsessions, hesitations, and decisions make multispecies convergences possible, and *also* make divergences and recognitions of opacity necessary. *Ducks, Newburyport* begins with a "Proviso": "This is a work of pure supposition"—evoking the way that first-person narration both presents and performs a conditional "supposing" in response to that opacity.

In Linda Hogan's *Power*, a panther dies. The novel depicts a teenage girl,

Omishto, one of the last members of the fictional Taiga tribe, navigating a growing chasm between the western context that has dominated her assimilationist childhood and the remote tribal culture where she seeks reconnection. Exacerbated by a tribe member's mercy killing of one of the very few remaining Florida panthers, the rift between these two worlds is framed in terms of sovereignty, particularly the power of judicial decision over death. The middle of the novel juxtaposes Omishto's navigation of the U.S. court system and the tribal court as they pass divergent judgments on the panther's killing. However, *Power* is ultimately more oriented toward "sense-methods" rather than providing documentary witness to necropolitics.[8] The divergence of these two worlds and the divisions in kinship that follow increasingly become a matter of what Omishto can perceive—an affective rather than institutional matter marked by the possible or desired convergence of Omishto's consciousness with the panther's. While the panther is no longer living, its "world" becomes one Omishto believes she can access while acknowledging its separateness; the narrative's ruminative, repetitive structure centers her reshaping of her sensations, making possible the perception of a new milieu.

In *Ducks, Newburyport* (2019), a mountain "lioness" survives. The narrator laments that "the world seems so indifferent to mothers" (124), but Ellmann's text lavishes attention on two creatures united by motherhood though differentiated by species and narrative style. Most of the novel comprises the ruminations of the Ohio mother of four human children, but her stream of consciousness is interspersed with synchronic episodes that narrate the experiences of a mountain lion who births cubs, loses them, tracks them across Ohio, and is reunited with them at the Columbus Zoo after her capture. Their worlds are nonequivalent, but they touch—the mom follows news of the lioness, while the lioness enters the mom's yard, collapsing the henhouse and absconding with her dog. And so throughout, the novel proposes a collaboration between human and animal protagonicity without investing in an impossible companionship.

Milieu shapes the larger structures of both narratives, from their simultaneous use of and divestment from strong understandings of character to their ambivalence about the significance of plot events. Both texts, as in Susan McHugh's recent account of extinction narratives, "take loss as a starting point rather than the usual end point," but they also "refuse tragic outcomes."[9] The ubiquity of loss compounds "the fact that" (in Ellmann's parlance) these novels represent no achievement of social power beyond the work of reframing. It is worth noting that the protagonist of *Power* is a survivor of trauma—physical abuse by her stepfather, her older brother's recent death, and a painful awareness of ecocide—even before she witnesses Ama kill the panther. The human narrator of *Ducks* grapples with the death of her parents and her own recent bout with cancer before her family is threatened by a gunman who invades their home. Despite these traumas, their interest in animals is ultimately not, I think, the compensatory melancholic work that Alice Kuzniar associates with dog companionship, which I discussed in Chapter 3. Though Hogan and Ellmann depict violent events, they largely subordinate the drama of crisis to narrating the dual but kindred textures of human and other-than-human sapience. In their present-tense redistribution of the rhythms of attention, they evoke something like Lauren Berlant's redefinition of crisis as impasse, which her articulation caps with an animal simile. Crisis, in Berlant's words, "belies the constitutive point that slow death—or the structurally induced attrition of persons keyed to their membership in certain populations—is neither a state of exception nor the opposite, mere banality, but a domain where an upsetting scene of living is revealed to be interwoven with ordinary life after all, like ants discovered scurrying under a thoughtlessly lifted rock."[10] Or in this case, where panthers still roam, maybe defeated and maybe not. *Power* and *Ducks* offer a reduced commitment to plot that may reflect the logic of impasse. In doing so, they reinvent some of the distinctive practices of literary modernism, where the demotion of plot, according to Paul Ricoeur in *Time and Narrative*, not only substitutes for action the "complexity of moral and emotional existence" but also evokes "subtle ... changes affecting the temporal course of sensations and emotions."[11] Putting theory of the novel into conversation with Indigenous studies, I also argue that an examination of this process in these novels aligns with decolonizing approaches to human-animal solidarities that do not issue in decisive or salvific action. Their non-outcomes are consonant with the broader rejection of heroic narratives in Indigenous criticism.[12]

First-person narrative allows these novels to acknowledge animal lives without imposing on them through and despite their seemingly anthropocentric methods of narration. Oriented toward the depiction of inhabiting rather than transforming an environment, these novels emphasize that humans too are constituted by their milieu. First-person novels typically "orient readers toward *allegiance*" with their narrators as "moral centers," as Rita Felski puts it. The mode of attention modeled by Hogan and Ellman's gentle, empathetic, curious, but introverted women may be attractive, but does not suggest that they have particularly strong capacities for taking action.[13] The textures and rhythms of their moral orientations might be best understood as ruminative: according to Amanda Anderson (in conversation with Felski), the novel from the nineteenth century onward is fascinated by "rumination as a part of ordinary moral and psychological life."[14] Where outward drama gives way to inward event, rumination links sensation and evaluation in a nonhierarchical way associated with critical discourse around mood and tone. Rumination, for Anderson, "is not structured by sustained reflection awareness of the sort that we associate with deliberation. At the same time, however, it is characterized by persistence and repetition and a kind of attachment."[15] Anderson briefly mentions the animal orientation of the term, which she notes "stands out among verbs that describe modes of thinking . . . in its etymological connection to nonhuman animals; brooding, which in another meaning denotes the parental activity of instinctive care among bird species . . . but which when used figuratively is almost exclusively negative."[16] For Anderson these animal associations reveal cultural bias against rumination as an everyday mode of thought. Embracing them makes rumination potentially a way of valuing an affectively rich, neither anti-cognitive nor pro-rationalist, sentience that makes worlds. Moreover, I would emphasize that this term shows how present-tense, first-person novels might remain, in a curious way, impersonal. Despite their investment in the texture of a particularized, situated, and undoubtedly human narrator's temporally unfolding sapience, they might present that experience as emerging within a milieu, rather than exclusively valuing the achievements of sustained higher-order reflection—or valuing subjective consciousness as a particularly distinctive phenomenon. It becomes merely a way of mapping a world. Rumination's predominance in *Ducks* and *Power* means that these are anti-teleological texts even before their narrators explicitly express doubt about deliberative political action. In *Ducks*, the phrase "and there's nothing anybody can do about it" is a frequent, self-exculpating refrain. Yet the novel's creation of another, creaturely milieu makes attention matter without overinvesting in exclusionary models of human thought or action.[17]

Moreover, each text turns to free indirect discourse from *within* first-person narration to represent a big cat's sentience. Neither is well-known for its use of free indirect discourse, but in both cases, grappling with animal sentience prompts a decisive shift of narrative voice, calling attention to the limits of the first person and the possibilities of the third. If free indirect discourse mediates thought into "unspeakable sentences," in an animal context this style allows for the representation of an animal's nonpropositional sentience to proceed from within an openly human stance. Free indirect discourse, broadly and debatably, coordinates two perspectives—third and first—and has been taken both to instantiate hierarchies among these perspectives. According to Ann Banfield, free indirect discourse "solves the technical problem of silencing the speaker and his authority"; the narrator dissolves into impersonality while dramatizing without absolutely occupying or fully appropriating a character's experience.[18] But what in Banfield sounds like an ethical violation—free indirect discourse as coercive synthesis—for others suggests continuities, or evokes intimacies, some of *them* quite unspeakable. For Anna Kornbluh and Frances Ferguson, free indirect discourse demonstrates the embeddedness of individual thought within norms of communal knowledge. In the case of animals, it might seem especially fraught to narrate an other-than-human animal's sentience through a style that frames the act of thinking as occurring in language—not only to claim a transparent knowledge of an animal's inward state, but also to all too freely transform her wild opacity into propositional form.

Yet I would argue that in these novels it becomes a way for transparency and opacity to face off in the open, and perhaps even go so far as to say that nonspeaking, naturalistically represented animals *need* "unspeakable sentences" for their worlds to appear. Katarzyna Bartoszyńka proposes the style as a "space of plurality," "a meeting point for a multiplicity of conflicting perspectives whose tensions remain unresolved, an assemblage that is held together but not unified, yet speaks in one voice."[19] A style that offers two worlds within one sentence is, in this context, less a coercion than an interval of relation in which thresholds between worlds are, in Cherokee theorist Daniel Heath Justice's words, "strong but permeable."[20] The sentence as milieu, two centers in relation. In this sense, the style can offer a striking, if latent, environmental and multispecies ethos. By dallying with free indirect discourse as a dimension of their ruminations, *Power* and *Ducks* explore what it feels like, from a situated perspective, to recognize oneself and others as existing in bounded and yet connected perceptual worlds.

1. INDIGENOUS WORLDS, MORE-THAN-HUMAN MILIEUS

This chapter highlights that some contemporary American fiction's interest in milieu manifests the knowledge of other-than-human kinship specific to Indigenous traditions, a framework that animal and animality studies as practiced in the Anglophone academy has not adequately recognized.[21] *Power* and *Ducks, Newburyport* are written from culturally distinct contexts: Hogan's narrator, a teen girl from a fictitious tribal community in Florida, grapples with the killing of one of its last sacred panthers, while Ellmann's white protagonist, a former adjunct professor of American history, ponders her implication in settler-colonial violence. While both narrators hint at a biopolitical critique of the management of life and death, neither character models doing critique in this way; they are characters fully capable of thinking this thought, but critique is not their primary mode of engagement with their milieu, even when they display a lucid assessment of shared exposure to structural violence, especially along lines of race and gender. Rather than offer a negative critique of settler-colonial violence, these narratives—as narratives—evoke the process of recognizing the convergences and separations of multispecies living.

In bringing together Indigenous thought and theory of the novel, I want to pull through Anna Kornbluh's injunction to critics not to retreat from political action but instead to "build worlds" and "risk synthesis," discussed in the Introduction. This idea is newly inflected if put into conversation with Jodi Byrd's caution that the language of worlding can read as settler-colonial. Byrd, explicitly situating their argument with regard to Chickasaw heritage shared with Hogan, advocates "interrogating how the impulse to world is the setting-to-work of the colonizer, even if that work is to reconfigure the world so it might be kinder and gentler and be a world more possible to live, and grieve, within. The future anterior of such a world that exists outside the cruel optimisms and violences constitutive of liberalism's very structures must also be a future in which indigenous peoples will have been and will remain decolonized."[22] As Byrd's intervention stresses, "worlding" is not inherently admirable, especially in the colonizing singular. For neither critic does "world" refer to "the bounded earth as a single living, mutually interdependent organism with its own differences and kinds."[23] Rather, both use the term "world" to mean a created, cohesive phenomenologically accessible space—a meaning that is also consonant with comparative cognition's treatment of the term.

These novels of two worlds need Indigenous philosophy to explain their investment in twoness. An idea of two worlds is, in Heath Justice's words, less a dualism than "a dynamic and relational perspective, not an assumption of unitary supremacy," where thresholds between worlds are "strong but permeable."[24] Citing this moment, Byrd elaborates that "Southeastern indigenous phenomenologies understand the Middle World (the reality we all inhabit) as a bridge between Upper and Lower Worlds of creation. When the boundaries between worlds break down and the distinctive characteristics of each world begin to collapse upon and bleed into the others, possibilities for rejuvenation and destruction emerge to transform this world radically. The goal is to find balance."[25] Byrd's explanation demonstrates that critical use of "world"—a word that sometimes feels ubiquitous as a signal of value—is also a culturally specific provocation. Engaging with Indigenous ontologies (though to differing degrees), *Power* and *Ducks* are invested in decolonizing "world" itself as a perceptual category that allows for other architectures of perception, allowing world-building to include more-than-human kinship as an ecological necessity.

Indigenous theory is a crucial discourse if a given species difference is theorized with a two-world model rather than the kind of self-other model that compounds a chasmic human-nonhuman divide. It tends to reject what Jacob von Uexküll also rejected: the "widely held conviction" of the "existence of one and only world, in which all living beings are encased."[26] In complicating this conventional belief, von Uexküll's work provides a productive hinge for recent efforts to highlight convergences between Indigenous philosophy's "ethic of connection"—and comparative cognition. Hogan, in *The Radiance of Animals*, describes western science as recently "relat[ing]" what Indigenous science has known far longer.[27] The implication of the consilience of traditional Indigenous knowledge and recent eurowestern biology is that interspecies thinking needs Indigenous viewpoints, an argument explicitly made by Kim TallBear in her responses to Dorion Sagan, author of the introduction to the most recent English edition of von Uexküll's *A Foray into the Worlds of Animals and Humans*. For TallBear, "western science like Sagan's is only beginning to catch up to Indigenous insights into 'world,' which Vine [Deloria] understands as an interspecies community or networked set of social-biological relations among living beings that are both material and *immaterial*."[28] For Justice, in *Why Indigenous Literatures Matter*, a "mainstream" viewpoint is juxtaposed with "ethology . . . which continues to demonstrate just how little we understand about the complex subjectivities of our other-than-human neighbours" *as well as* with Indigenous traditions of other-than-human kinship, which present those lines of relation as ontologically foundational as well as "fraught," "partial," and non-"homogeneous."[29] In other words, Indigenous philosophy has long anticipated dynamics of interspecies dependency, collaboration, and distinction that eurowestern posthumanism is only beginning to postulate.

While many of these critics highlight the belatedness of eurowestern interest in multispecies kinship, Justice, TallBear, and others also propose that this cultural convergence has profound potential for a multidisciplinary rethinking of personhood that can center Indigenous scholarship, enhancing intellectual rigor and expanding categories of analysis.[30] The phenomenality of "worlds" in Indigenous studies is an important point of convergence not only with cognitive science and the new materialism, but also with Black studies and narratology, as I argued in my Introduction. In an Indigenous studies context, world or, more precisely, milieu can index the material co-constitution of place and identity in human and more-than-human communities.[31] For Jen Rose Smith, working in critical geography, milieus cannot be registered by a single discipline, and especially not captured by "managerial" scientific frameworks like statistics that make environments look static and deterministic. (Though *Power* and *Ducks* both depict some debate about the extent of the central big cat's endangerment, they also suggest that counting cats is beside the point.[32]) Rather, Smith argues that attending to the artistic rendering of Indigenous milieus "require[s] an adherence to the sovereignties of Indigenous polities, however they take shape. One such practice . . . is an attendance to poetic imaginings and articulations of space and sociality sidelined in favor of more 'legible' climate data."[33] The poetics of milieu here serves as "world-making" evidence "of emplaced historical and ongoing relationships in geographies" that are obscured by the datafication of crisis, as in counting the members of an endangered population.[34]

What these critics, along with the novels I examine, call "world" can thus be understood through the ethological and phenomenological dimensionality of "milieu." A broadly cognitive or phenomenological understanding of "world" bears across discourses; for Justice, it is central to the articulation of animal kinship or animal personhood: "As beings with priorities and personalities of their own that remain only partially legible to humans, the Animal People stand apart in their difference, yet as active co-inhabitants of the world"; for

Rose, animal extinctions mean, for some Indigenous groups, "the pain of losing nonhuman kindred whose existence in the world gave human life much of its meaning."[35] "World" both theorizes and prompts convergences, referring to the globe as well as more demarcated environmental spaces. It also refers to their phenomenal and spiritual perceptibility.[36]

2. GRIEVING OTHER WORLDS

In Hogan's *The Radiant Lives of Animals* (2020), she presents the meaning of "world" as a given—she states straightforwardly, "We need to have changed minds, to look at new ways of thinking about our shared world."[37] But throughout this book of essays and poems, two uses of "world" cohabitate. Sometimes Hogan adduces an ontologically "whole" and "undivided" world system of which humans only perceive a part: she writes to a bird nesting in her doorway, "I am a mere human being, slight in the world of all the other lives. Like your nest, there are depths in this world I do not know." Even when she acknowledges the profound opacity of another animal's perceptual experience, there is one "world"—a shared milieu—divided in two: "We are two different minds. Two species. Two ways of being. Two lives, both fragile for the moment . . . We live by different maps of this world."[38] At other moments, her use of "worlds" sounds very like the multiplicity of non-coextensive phenomenal spaces indicated by von Uexküll's concept of *Umwelt*. Reflecting on the presence of mountain lions near her home, she observes, "On the open page of some mornings I see that a cat has walked through, as if to let this mere human know this is still its own world, leaving prints, large and nearly rounded, in the sand or mud."[39] This passage strongly marks her own human worldedness by emphasizing her writerly orientation ("the page of morning"); the mountain lion too is a writer making her own proprietary mark. As Hogan puts it in her poem "Mountain Lion," included in *Radiant Lives*, she finds herself "Turning away / from what lives inside those / who have found / two worlds cannot live / inside a single vision."[40] Giving plurality both to the number of worlds and to the meaning of "world," this poem supposes the possibility of thinking about twoness from within one, continuously "turning"—trope-making—mind. Varying the emphasis and even the meaning of world from a phenomenal bubble to an ontological whole, Hogan presents herself as living with that concept, continuing to test its resonances.

Power centrally concerns the more-than-human worlds of animals. The sixteen-year-old narrator Omishto, one of the last thirty members of the fictional Taiga tribe, witnesses her "aunt" Ama kill one of the few remaining Florida panthers in the aftermath of a powerful storm. Omishto immediately responds with shock and grief, but the remainder of the novel opens questions of how to evaluate this devastating event. Hogan's depiction of the killing reinvents a 1987 legal case, *United States v. James E. Billie*, in which Seminole tribal chairman James E. Billie was charged with violating the Endangered Species Act (1973) for hunting a Florida panther. As Helen Makdoumian explains, Billie's defense emphasized his exception from the Endangered Species Act on the basis of his Seminole identity and specifically his right to religious freedom, claiming that panthers were part of Seminole religious practices. In this way, he occupied a biopolitical state of exception that permits action even as it bars belonging. Makdoumian argues that "by reimagining *Billie* with Ama and Omishto at the center and then extending jurisdiction of the case to the Taiga community, Hogan shifts legal authority from U.S. law to a tradition grounded in community, storytelling, and a connection to the land."[41] Hogan's perspective here resonates with burgeoning conversations in Indigenous studies around the possibility of finding alternatives to tribal traditions that necessitate killing animals, a key dimension of Billie's defense.[42] Hogan's choice to expel men from the center of the story implies a more direct divergence from such traditions, while nonetheless indexing an institutional if not more fundamental connection between a shadowy patriarchy and environmental degradation. Men are only the minorest of characters in this novel—sources only of distant traumas of abandonment and abuse—and the novel contains no heterosexual plot. Rather, the novel focuses on the loss of the panther through the eyes of a narrator who is "just a girl" (78) with little standing in either the legal or the tribal system. Omishto occupies a multiply disempowered position that links the experience of gender in the 1990s to the settler-colonial history of ecocidal violence. Through her perspective at the margins, *Power* emphasizes the experience of perceiving and thinking about more-than-human relationships from within a gendered account of endangerment.

Ama's act is simultaneously destructive and utopian. Her killing voids a biopolitical death for the panther; she short-circuits slow death, evacuates the possibility of allegorizing tribal-experience-as-endangered species.[43] The trial for the U.S. court attempts to classify and manage the panther even after its death—was it really classified as endangered or was it a hybrid that doesn't count? Does it matter that conservation efforts too sometimes kill panthers? But as McHugh asks of this novel, "what is Ama's crime of killing her sister compared with the crimes that condemn all to extinction?"[44] Ama takes it upon herself to evade "the biopolitical tendency to deny individuation, biotic value, and grievability."[45] Unlike Billie, she does not accept the legal designation of her agency as operating from within a state of exception. While the novel contains this biopolitical critique, it does not encapsulate the panther's loss as a story about sovereignty narrowly construed, a perspective that would downplay the absolute centrality of multispecies relations in Hogan's vision. Even as Ama's act is presented as not in accord with Taiga practices, it is also clear that her logic, by which the panther's death might produce renewal, "is no longer acceptable" and "accomplishes nothing through becoming yet one more instance of suffering," as Lydia Cooper points out.[46] Juxtaposing the U.S. Court system's arraignment of Ama for killing an endangered animal with a tribal court's decision to exile her, *Power* presents Taiga self-sovereignty as on the one hand, urgent, and on the other, problematic in its own ways. As several critics have already suggested, a reading of this novel focused on its critique of sovereignty "underestimates" the centrality of Hogan's multispecies vision.[47]

My reading further emphasizes Hogan's narrative form—how working *with* rather than *resisting* novelistic conventions, Hogan centers the animal milieu. The novel emphasizes Omishto's recognition of these incongruent institutions for the production of a truth of the event. Omishto does not endorse Ama's actions, describing her as "acted on" and reporting "we were under something that felt like a spell" (83); this middle zone of agency is not even something Omishto feels satisfied with her ability to explain. But explanation itself may be the wrong category of knowing for which to read Omishto's narrative. After the panther's killing she says, "I feel like weeping, at least a part of me does; the other part feels more awake and alert to the world than I have ever felt" (60). The effort of decisive evaluation gives way to description. Approaching the U.S. courthouse, she ponders,

> I am the child who followed, the quiet thing who has no mind. . . . They can't tell what I am inside. Neither can I. In the slow motion of time it takes to reach the steps, inside myself I am trying to find out what I really know, what is wrong or right, and all I know is that the birds are above us now, too many grackles looking for a place to settle in just two trees on this street and they displace each other, bickering. (116)

Certainly, this passage can read as post-traumatic dissociation—but it reads as another thing too. Omishto does not seem especially *troubled* by being a "thing who has no mind" (even as the passage shows its patent falseness, since Omishto is plenty precocious). She associates introspection with judicial fact-finding. Supplanting the labor of knowing is a sense of environmental situatedness.

Coming-to-value milieu becomes a way of renegotiating kinship throughout the novel. Before as well as throughout the two court scenes that constitute the centerpiece of the novel, Ama's own intentions and experience of grief remain obscure even to Omishto, while Hogan centers Omishto's process of feeling and observing. Omishto doesn't support the panther's death but does "understand it" in an opaque way, seemingly reframing what "understanding" might mean. Throughout the trials, Omishto is in the process of evaluating which "world" she belongs to—her assimilated mother's suburban home, complete with abusive stepfather, Ama's home at the swamp's borders, or the ancestral home at Kili Swamp, of which she has little previous personal experience. Ama is a liminal figure, a woman who gives the impression of being steeped in traditional lifeways but living in her own at the edges of tribal land after a divorce—Omishto finds it hard to imagine that Ama was married, and her home is a space of gender nonconformity, where one wears long dresses with heavy boots to track animals through the mud. Her mother, on the other hand, is a gender-conforming Christian who downplays her tribal ties. Omishto empathizes with her mother's desire to control her, recognizing that "it must be hard for her to bear, that I am becoming so fully another person, that my skin, made of her skin, is a boundary that closes her out and now she wants me in" (211). In contrast to her mother's rejection of boundaries, for Omishto, both Ama and the panther have the potential to initiate a chosen natal connection made possible by a tribal understanding of kinship. Omishto is disappointed in Ama's ability to help her through adolescence, however, because they do not occupy the same perceptual milieu: "Though there are only twenty years between us, we live in different worlds. We do not even hear the same sounds" (55). She recognizes, "I thought she would" "make a place in the world for me" (104), underlining her strong desire to reject conformity and renegotiate kinship.

Ama's sacrificial approach to world-renovation, which Omishto imagines as tearing a hole between worlds, is rejected.[48] In contrast, Omishto, whose orientation is often pragmatic in crisis, realizes that this is a process that she needs to undertake for herself, making a decisive break with her nuclear family: "Ama is saving a world," Omishto concludes, "but I am saving myself" (224). Such a statement clearly marks the narrative as a typical coming-of-age tale, albeit one that centers identification with animals as part of maturation, to a great extent in lieu of the role that sexuality tends to play in such narratives.[49] The novel may connect Omishto's rejection of compulsory heterosexuality to her stepfather's physical abuse, but it certainly does not reduce her investment in ecological awareness to a symptom of trauma. Moreover, the novel resists a strong *Bildungsroman* gloss on the plot of personal salvation insofar as Omishto no longer identifies as a subject by the novel's end: "Me, I am a dissolved person, like salt in water" (231). The simile at this conclusion echoes the subjunctive at the novel's opening, in which Omishto feels "as if I am curled inside an opening leaf" (1), even while suggesting a more complete immersion. Evoking milieu allows Omishto to more and more fully refuse human exceptionalism.[50] If *Power*, to use Rosi Braidotti's formulation, "evacuat[es] . . . socially constituted gender identities of women," it returns to a still-in-process, situated becoming within a milieu.[51]

Conversely, in the aftermath of the panther's death, Omishto's mother's house and her school lose their sensory accessibility; they cease to operate as a cohesive milieu. She recoils from them: "It's as if I have never lived here. I see the world this place has come from. I see the walls of the fallen forest, the floor of clay dissolving in time" (91). What here feels like a materialist critique also occurs at the level of sensory immersion. "I hate the smell of school" (150), she declares, and admits, "I can hardly picture my own room, even though I've walked out of it just moments ago, the room where I've slept for sixteen years of my life in a bed with a blue chenille spread, my head on the same pillow with its clean, white case . . . and the vase of artificial flowers my mother loves so much she even plants them outdoors" (151). Hogan highlights olfactory, visual, and spatial orientation to suggest that home loses its status as a milieu at the same time that Kili Swamp becomes one: "The place itself seems alive" (159). Even as *Power*'s vision of the future remains tenuous—Omishto ultimately joins the tiny Taiga community at Kili Swamp—the novel situates its approach to environmental loss within ongoing, lived relations palpable as milieu, even as Omishto withdraws from the ordinary domains of realism.

This novel's embrace of milieu is also legible in Hogan's ruminative style, especially its use of present tense. Through the sense-methods of the present tense, *Power* accumulates experiences that layer over evaluative positions. Omishto is knowledgeable about the prehistoric past, a perspective on the present that highlights its precariousness and renders the present grievable. From the beginning, Omishto's vividly stratigraphic fascination with deep time also suggests her attraction to an elegiac understanding of the Taiga's cultural life as past tense. And yet she tells it in the present:

> One day someone will find this world, our world, our time, our pieces, beneath a layer of limestone or silt. They'll find snake bones with their hundred ribs. They will be fossils in lime the way the old bones of mastodons are still beneath this land.... They'll find us like the treasure hunters who were searching for pieces of a wrecked Spanish galleon off the Keys found the sabertooths and mastodons. They broke through a layer of limestone and found a tusk from something large that had lived and walked before we were here.... There are layers to the world. And with time, the world changes, a new layer forms, and the old one falls or drifts. this much is always certain. (48–49)

Omishto acknowledges what Kathryn Yusoff describes as the present's "subterranean geologic debt."[52] Geologic deep time is not part of the past, consigned to the era of early colonial violence or of a prehistoric sublime, but actively shapes the present. The long, elegiac passage is a common literary device for representing deep time (this passage is reminiscent of the present-tense first paragraph of *Bleak House*, in which an imagined megalosaurus trundles up through central London). Hogan's ruminative protraction of the narrating moment suggests a fantasy of escape from human time, even as it also makes-present.[53]

Rumination allows for a stillness that is also a wildly capacious synthesis. For Omishto, present-tense repetition especially leads her to reflections on Taiga naming, offering many variations on phrases like "we Taiga call the wind Oni" and "Sisa, that's what we call the cat," as if perpetually trying to affirm her belonging while reminding herself of cultural facts she has to work to remember, often in subordinate clauses that showcase the effort of definition.[54] But Omishto also understands repetition as a way of contacting her cultural origins, as when she thinks about how Ama rejects chronological time: "Ama once said that space is full and time is empty; I think now I understand this. We are surrounded by matter, but time disappears from us" (55). To be cautiously synthetic, I would point out that this achronological aesthetic lends itself rather well to western novelistic approaches to first-person voice. Repetition may be, as Paula Gunn Allen suggests, a core rhythm of affirmation in some indigenous aesthetics, *and* it is also crucial to rumination in a more negative sense: as Anderson highlights, rumination is often pathologized and linked to depression, because it tends to highlight rhythms of "repetition," "distraction," "inertia," or "attrition" despite "some sort of orienting or nagging focus."[55] The meanderings of rumination lend themselves well to slow, potentially fruitful processing. As Carrie Bowen-Mercer points out, first-person present tense allows Hogan to show "that through a lived and narrated reality-story of recurring myth in both real space and time (the actual endangerment of panthers in Florida and the past and present domination over Native tribes in America) and fictional space and time (the text), myth and reality and space and time take on the characteristics of a dynamic stillness—a repeating pattern that changes contextually."[56]

Another of the narrator's preoccupations is the anti-conceptual concept of "world" itself, as many of the preceding quotations have already begun to suggest. This relatively brief novel uses the word eighty-nine times. Like Hogan in *The Radiant Lives of Animals*, Omishto vacillates between phenomenological, historical, and ontological understandings of a word that structures her thoughts and makes possible her sensory experiences, which do not always offer direct evidence for her conclusions about them. Rifts between worlds are at times historical, caused by colonization, and other times spiritual, marking ontological zones whose status in part depends on the epistemic labor of those who believe in them. Ama hopes to renew the world by breaking the boundaries between worlds, as in Byrd's rendering of the Upper and Lower worlds. Omishto, in contrast, retains a more contemplative relation to mediations among worlds. Midway through the novel, she tells herself, "Two worlds exist. Maybe it's always been this way, but I enter them both like I am two people. Above and below. Land and water. Now and then" (97). The boundaries are, pace Justice, "strong but permeable," a relationship made especially palpable by Omishto's modulation among articles. Especially provocative is Omishto's comment that her mother thinks industrialization is "the small price you pay for progress" but "I think, it's the way to kill a world" (27). Direct as Omishto is in her condemnation of her assimilated, Christian mother's progressivism, her indefinite article holds space for other milieus. Rather than try to reconcile the meanings of "world," the ruminative possibility that more than one meaning might bear at different times, in response to different circumstances, itself reflects the logic of milieu.

The idea of separate worlds is thought most intensively in relation to the panther in its spiritual form, Sisa. Part of Omishto's grief at the cat's killing is its obvious failure to thrive—it is already sick, with broken teeth and a shabby coat; protecting the tribe from having to witness its suffering is part of Ama's rationale for her rogue approach to sacrifice, whereas Omishto's relation to its endangerment is more straightforwardly one of grief. At the novel's conclusion, though, she sees a panther in the "middle world," "standing still, looking back at me, the golden cat, large and with tawny fur loose and healthy, lean-muscled." She says "No shi halo"—"I mean no harm, Aunt, Grandmother" and wishes it would run, rather than walk away, for "we are dangerous people, every last one of us" (232–33). This conclusion offers no possibility of a sentimentalized bond in which the two figures durably coexist or offer mutual care on the same representational plane.

Moreover, she struggles with the right representational milieu in which to embed the panther that stalks her thoughts. Telling herself a Taiga origin story, she recalls that

> the panther entered through the broken shell, the hold of creation, all golden eyes and secret pride and lithe stillness, stalking as if every cell of its muscular body was breathed awake and healthy. She, Sisa, God of Gods, entered this world with grace and sunlight and beauty. It was a world filled with the wind, with life-creating air. And everything in it began to breathe and move. (84)

Omishto's rhythm of stillness echoes the panther's own ontological status, insisting on Sisa's presence even as she tells a story from a deep cultural past. Omishto's understanding of the panther's qualities permeates how she perceives and narrates its presence. Here, despite the intensity of mourning for a real, endangered animal, the novel also evokes Hogan's designation of the big cat as an "other life" that elicits spiritual awe in *The Radiant Lives of Animals*: "Her own inner world still unknown to mine. With the unique dignity of other lives, I understand how they may have been the original gods while we were merely stick figures, known to others."[57] While insisting on the opacity of the animal's own *Umwelt* from a human perspective, Hogan also reverses predictable novelistic expectations about the relation between psychological depth and knowability—another relational duality.

Reflecting on *Power*, Hogan singles out her depiction of the panther's spiritual form: "A favorite part is where the cat watches the people, knowing they have broken their original covenant with other living animals of this world, the sacred law given at our beginning.... As in our past tribal stories, the watching, listening panther is one who gave humans the power of medicine."[58] McHugh emphasizes that the panther in *Power* is "approached as never simply human or animal, metaphor or referent." Thus, "the dynamic animal god opens a perspective through which narratives that revisit mass killings of the past can begin to make critical interventions in the present."[59] The narrative incorporates Sisa's perspective into Omishto's own as part of a long section after the trials in which Omishto lies in her boat, surrounded by wind. As in the novel's opening, Hogan highlights the milieu in which thoughts happen, and presents the culminating event of the novel as an act of rumination.

Omishto meditates on the outcome by inhabiting a range of perspectives—her mother's, several tribal members', and Sisa's own. Some critics (Olsen and McHugh) take Sisa effectively to become a "character" through Omishto's imaginative speculation; clearly, this is a moment of metalepsis.[60] Once again, I would emphasize the spiritual dimension of Genette's own account of metalepsis, which I noted in the Introduction: metalepsis offers "a shifting and sacred frontier between two worlds, the world in which one tells and the world of which one tells."[61] Genette's language captures something of the intimacy-yet-difference between Hogan's two narrative grammars. But I would present this shift into Sisa's perspective not only as metalepsis but more specifically as a situated use of free indirect discourse. Throughout this three-page passage, Omishto remains clear that the "world of the panther" is "carried toward me by Oni," rather than inhabited. After she says "I see it from Sisa's eyes," "I" remains Omishto, and "Sisa" is the subject of sentences that are attributable to her perceptions, until the narrative shifts very briefly into free indirect discourse when describing Sisa's knowledge of humans ("How straight they walked!" [191]). If free indirect discourse inherently "involves a representation of thought rather an than expression of it," this style allows for the narration of Sisa's sentience to proceed from within an openly human stance.[62] Sisa herself watches and ruminates on the state of humans as "pitiable and small and broken" (192) in a meditation that only rather indirectly winds its way back to explicitly flagging Omishto's role in thinking this thought: "She, the cat, hopes that the world still has golden evening light, will have it again, and that the Taiga and the panther will recover and breathe again, and that we will all sing once more in the swamps at night" (192). This vision of recovery does not depend, as Ama's did, on a broken boundary between two worlds except in a *narrative* sense—between two narrative grammars.[63] For Omishto, the cat has a certain vision of its environment that depends upon a shift in narrative frame—narrative "world."

The vision attributed to the panther insists thematically upon milieu as a source of enduring value, but I have been arguing that milieu is also key to the novel's approach to a first-person coming-of-age story that isn't really one. As Byrd argues, "Sovereignty, in the context of such philosophies, is an act of interpretation as much as it is a political assertion of power, control, and exception."[64] In *Power*'s ruminative narration, interpretation has no clear telos but, as a process of thought, it also subsumes outward events. Hogan makes living with the idea of "worlds" a sensory, lived process in itself.

3. RECOIL AND LEAP

Across its thousand, frequently repetitive pages of reactions, reflections, shopping lists, memories, and worries, *Ducks* is less a novel of centered consciousness than it seems. Rather, it unfolds a maternal organism maintaining a milieu. The Ohio mom stretches her narration through an endlessly "spiraling" sentence while she bakes cinnamon rolls, appropriately enough. If *Power* is agonized but meditative, *Ducks* tends toward the frenetic. And if its pattern of associations and dissociations evokes some of the newness of metalepsis, that endless novelty appears at least as much the product of late capitalist stress as the surprise of the new.[65] Still, in Ellmann's hands, rumination about the material minutiae of daily life produces a materialist *écriture féminine*, in which semiotic play, metonymic relation, and associative proximity evoke the permeability of material boundaries. At the same time, the logic of intimate proximity becomes itself a thematized value that bleeds over into the novel's endorsement of curiosity about other worlds.

Rumination is not freeing for the narrator, but her meanderings lend themselves well to slow, semiproductive responses to long-term preoccupations.[66] The additive function of repetition is especially provocative in this novel, in which repeated phrases orient the reader in the flow of ideas, producing unpredictable affirmations of the narrator's continuity between past and present self as her perceptions unfold, in ways not strongly temporally marked except by the intervention of mountain lion sections, over the time of reading. Without endstops, the predominance of short phrases throughout the narrative allows mood to dictate content, tones to accrue and abruptly disappear; we often have to read between the lines to establish a correlation between implied events and the mom's reactions to them. Repetition, moreover, eventually maps the mom's milieu—her world appears not through descriptions of her body moving through her home, of which there are rather few, but through repetitions of phrases, especially minimally encapsulated memories (i.e., "ducks, Newburyport," "the bee at Breadloaf," "Mommy") that punctuate her thoughts.

The novel's title indexes the narrator's mother's experience of running into a Newburyport pond as a toddler, wanting to touch the ducks and needing to be rescued—an impulse of cross-species contact thwarted. (Had her mother touched the ducks she might have drowned, and the narrator might never have been born, giving the entire novel a "suppositional" or optative sensibility, an orthogonal relationship to definite empirical knowledge.) This anecdote—it's not even the narrator's own memory—of her mother's early desire to enter an animal's world is only one of many repeated catchphrases, but it especially signals the novel's interest in linking narrative style to a multigenerational desire for animal intimacy. The mom's family includes four human kids, each with their challenges, and the household also includes cats, goldfish, chickens, and briefly a dog, not to mention "all the tardigrades and macrophages" (14). In the mom's overburdened life, the nonhuman creatures are at times sources of pleasure and companionship: while she admits "You never know how happy pets really are" (180), such epistemic doubt is rarely her default position. "At least the chickens really do love me" (27), she says to comfort herself when feeling blue. She frequently reminds herself of the existence of "boarlets" and reminisces about former pets—turtles, a mouse, guinea pigs, and especially a childhood dog named Pepito.

The novel explicitly marks these habits of noticing animals as feminine. As in *Power*, most adult men in this novel are threatening. "I've never been raped ... except almost" (61), the mom admits, and she wonders if self-defense classes could be "a new mom and daughter bonding tool" (432).[67] The mom links violence against animals to ecocide to toxic masculinity more broadly. Not only does she flag the sexual politics of meat ("the fact that yep, if there's fried chicken to be had, men'll be there" [263]), but she also emphasizes that human violence coincides with anti-animal sentiment. The delivery man Ronnie, who ultimately attacks the family with an assault weapon, gives creepy vibes throughout but especially once the mom notes his fear of mice. In contrast, she vividly revisits her love for her childhood mouse Edward, who birthed two litters of mouselings ("the fact that an adult mouse can have a friendship with a human child" [138]), and she recalls multiple incidents of trying to save "wild mice" trapped in human dwellings.

Her gendered animal affinity extends beyond the domestic context to suggest her biopolitical awareness: she recalls, "I once looked a mother orangutan right in the eye, when I took Stacy to some zoo somewhere, and we really seemed to connect for a moment, one mom to another, but then I left her there and never went back, so what good am *I* as an orangutan friend" (628). Despite her recurrence to interspecies friendship, she also recognizes the violence of zoos as institutions that maintain human privilege. She obsessively reflects, in fact, on the many anti-animal institutions in which she is complicit, especially the factory farms where she buys nonorganic chicken to feed her family.[68] She reacts in horror to the manufacture of chemicals, many of which appear in her food, medications, and household products, that contribute to the disappearing habitats she names again and again. She admits, in other words, that "no mode of being in the world is innocent."[69]

"The fact that what we've done to animals," she repeatedly thinks to herself, a thought connected to another recurring phrase, "the numbness of muted beings." The mom wants to think differently with animals. Considering an account she has heard of a salmon farm destroyed by a booming population of jellyfish, she reminds herself of "the fact that fish feel pain, the fact that they used to deny it, the scientists I mean, not the fish" (70). Recognizing that it is human presumption, rather than any inherent quality, that renders animals muted and purportedly unfeeling, she invests the many animals that she either encounters or imagines with complex inner lives and communicative capacities. Like an armchair Vinciane Despret, the mom suggests that scientists deny agency by basing research on exclusionary assumptions and supposes that the imagination constitutes a legitimate form of experiment.[70] Her confidence in animals' sentience is also a persistent source of pleasure as well as a provocation to critique, for instance, when she wonders "what must that be like," "to have a trunk" (149) or "to be born a pelican" (122). Pace Thomas Nagel, she doesn't tell us what she thinks it is like, but she knows that being other-than-human has holistic phenomenal qualities.

"I don't know how animals think," the mom reflects, "but I know I think in spirals" (321). Animal sentience is certainly not only the topic of her recurring ruminations, but it has special bearing on her reflections on literary form.

Writing about animals is difficult to do well, she reminds us: "Grandma liked to write terrible haiku about zoo animals, and longer poems too that went on and on about giraffes or pelicans or something, flamingos, the fact that we never told her how bad they were" (115). Poetry, generally, seems unpromising—the thought "the fact that what does a chick think when it looks at an egg" (139) hatches from the declaration "I never read poetry" (139). She seems to think novels a more generative form: much later, she chirps happily, "I think animals think a lot, the fact that they're the ones who have the *time*, birds too, the fact that birds do everything fast, the fact that birds could think up whole novels in twenty seconds, I bet, livelier novels than Ann Tyler's too" (891). *Ducks, Newburyport* itself does not attempt to be or imagine the proposed bird novel—very far from it, given its focus on the bothered experience of human mothering. Still, one of the things "we" have done to animals is tell their stories, and the novel attempts to do that, albeit in explicitly incommensurate terms.

The narrative by the human mom is framed by the mountain lion's story, told in a different narrative voice. (Any claim that the novel is all one sentence simply ignores these sections.) In the mountain lion's narrative, she rears cubs only to be separated from them accidentally—they are found by humans, presumed abandoned, and trucked to the Columbus Zoo, while their mother sets off to find them. The lioness's journey touches the mom's own life when the animal enters the yard, crushes the chicken coop, and captivates the family dog (a rescue dog who has failed to fit the mold of the family pet, as the mom acknowledges sadly).[71] Her sections of the novel aren't quite a feline version of the animal novel the mom imagines, but they undertake a related project. The second lioness section opens, "What we prize in poets, the lioness already had: every muscle toned to tread precisely, every sense alive to wind and moonshine and other creatures, whether rivals or prey" (81). Reframing "poetry" as a sensory attunement that has little to do with the use of language and opens the form to animal being, the passage also uses the only human-centered pronoun in the lioness's narrative—"we"—to suggest an external frame for valuing her worldedness. The lioness is neither numb nor muted.

Both sections serve to diminish species difference in the interest of a convergent experience of mothering.[72] In fact, the novel opens inside the mountain lion's thoughts while still insisting on an external frame that universalizes her experience: "When you are all sinew, struggle, and solitude, your young—being soft, plump, vulnerable—may remind you of prey" (1). The mountain lion's thought evokes the cuteness of the kittens along with their vulnerability, a proposition that acknowledges negative, even violent impulses within the obligation of care. It begins with being already enmeshed in a maternal milieu. Moreover, in using a second-person address to express this idea, the narrative frames her individual experience as generalizable to a broader, communal stance without reference to species. Most of the lioness's narrative, which *does* feature endstops, makes clear use of free indirect discourse that further diminishes species differences in representing the experience of maternity. There are plentiful parallels between the lion and human mothers: their children are a joy and an all-consuming burden; the sentences "Hers was a life of resentments, suspicions, and alarms" or "Her life was constrained by this new intimacy" (297) could apply equally to either, glossing as the most important facet of maternity, regardless of species, the uneven experience of *thinking about mothering*. "But they were hers, each one a necessity, a joy" (662): the mountain lion's story of heroic maternal care certainly functions as a trans-species gloss on Ellmann's maximalist presentation of human motherhood. Still, the lioness's story begins first. It is possible to read the lioness's narrative as a frame that gives the human's narrative a *secondary* significance. In this light, the comparative clarity of the mountain lion's inner life highlights the mental static of the human mom's. Either way, both narratives privilege the process of thinking as a core part of maternal caretaking, encompassing an ever-fluctuating range of affective orientations toward offspring.

It is worth mentioning that many reviews of the novel treat the lioness sections as unsuccessful or whimsical if they discuss it at all—a perspective I contest. Admittedly, the mom's narrative predominates over the mountain lion's in page-count terms and no external frame explains the relations of these narratives to one another. I would argue that there are two equally compelling if somewhat different ways of understanding the double narrative in *Ducks*. On the hand, if we take the "proviso" about supposition *as* a framing device, it seems to apply equally to the narration of any fictional sentience and thus diminishes sharp species divisions. As Paul Ricoeur has it in *Time and Narrative* (quite in contrast to Nagelian claims about imagination's limits when it comes to animal minds): "it is by any case by means of the imagination that we understand all other minds. The novelist does this, if not effortlessly, at least without any qualms, because it is part of the writer's art to supply expressions appropriate to thoughts."[73] In this light, a fictional animal is no different from a fictional character or from a real other person—its sentience is just differently organized. On the other hand, it is possible to read the mom *as* the narrator of the mountain lion sections, much as Omishto is the narrator of Sisa's meditations. The mom's fascination with the mountain lion is one of the more cohesive trajectories of the second half of the novel. We might also want to keep in mind that she takes Jane Austen—her mother's favorite novelist—as a major point of reference. If *for her* free indirect discourse might be, as Frances Ferguson has argued, "the novel's one and only formal contribution to literature," it is not inconceivable to imagine her as narrating the mountain lion's tale. (She would probably insist that she doesn't have the time, though, and she "just wish[es] they'd quit it with all that conceptual stuff" [637]—but Anne Tyler favors free indirect discourse too.) To read the novel's structure this way would certainly be to emphasize even further the mom's already powerful linkage between aesthetic form and excitement about unmuting muted beings. On this reading, the shifts between these two maternal milieus are again well explained by Genette's account of metalepsis as an intimacy-yet-difference between two narrative grammars.

Still, reading the mom as narrator, plausible though it may be, is not necessary to see that the novel takes very seriously the effort to register a mountain lion's *Umwelt* with a strong emphasis on her sensations, her knowledges, and her capabilities in orienting herself to her world. As I noted earlier, the mountain lion's narrative is not told in the first-person voice but through free indirect discourse that grants her inward experiences an objective status.[74] In using free indirect discourse, Ellmann avoids anti-anthropomorphic gymnastics that might undercut her affirmative depiction of the mountain lion's competencies in making and maintaining her milieu. In the novel's first paragraphs, the mountain lion sounds rather like a feline Mrs. Ramsay:

> Alertness was her new mode, but the cubs' easy slumber was contagious. She was always briefly astounded, on waking, by their contributed presence. They troubled her, they were so needy: if she died, they would die too, and soon. And she would forget them. But for now, she belonged to them. They were not so much a conscious concern as the whole purpose of her being—lives engendered by her body, created inside her and released through pain and panting upon the world. She had borne them, and now she fed them with her milk. They were part of her still.

The only marker of species difference here is the possibility of forgetting her young if they died. The human mom reflects painfully on her teen's gradual separation from her, while in *Power*, as noted earlier, Omishto emphasizes that "it must be hard for [her mother] to bear, . . . that my skin, made of her skin, is a boundary that closes her out" (211). As this lioness passage meditates on what is inside and outside the self, the prose modulates that question by its confidence in reporting the transparent nuances of her thought as they emerge through lived time. The mutual calibration of inward perception to outward environment that is a hallmark of free indirect discourse is also, in this context, legible as the logic of milieu.

The beginning of the novel showcases how the mountain lion moves through her world through lessons she imparts to her cubs in how to survive and how to act. She even has a maxim that is at once descriptive and normative: "For all of life is really recoil and leap, leap and recoil" (1). This chiasmatic idea becomes a marker of the lioness's distinctive rhythms of thinking—the recoil and leap of her thought (perhaps especially its use of entirely ordinary endstops, which feel extraordinary only in this context). "Recoil and leap" is also a fair description of the recursive dynamics of rumination.[75] The lioness's maxim itself reappears throughout her sections across the narrative. In such moments, she tends not to see herself as an individual, but as a member of her species, like when she thinks to her cubs:

> All mountain lions are one. You are just one example of a lion. Mountain-lionhood is strong and immense, and goes beyond the individual. Each lion is part of a continuum, and privy to everything good and bad that happens to other mountain lions. You tough things out on your own, but you're linked to the pleasures, pains, and drama, the leap and recoil and lonely deaths of others. (397)

The mountain lion seems to understand her individuality as on a continuum with the experiences of her larger threatened population, even as her own individual fate ultimately appears strongly exceptional. The mountain lion seems to grasp the logic of the style through which her sentience is represented: in free indirect discourse, Ferguson stresses, individual thought emerges from within a "projected communal stance."[76] Especially when the question of the individual and species population is centered, free indirect discourse appears very much as a logic of milieu.

Among the mountain lion's competencies are her searing indictments of human behavior: though she is "confused by the changeable stink of men," she is fully aware that humans "did not respect lions"; she fantasizes about unrealistic acts of revenge, as when she "dreamed of subduing [a car], forcing it to the ground, squashing the life out of it under her own weight and parting its hard, smooth, shiny hide with tearing teeth" (487). Once the lioness begins to search for her cubs, this arc highlights the precarious existence of wild animals under threat, living in the margins between human settlements. The novel's animal geography is, on the one hand, represented in a map that appears at the end of the book, and demonstrates the accelerating precariousness of a shrinking wild milieu. But on the other hand, thanks to free indirect discourse, we see the lioness herself as keenly aware of her constrained mobility—the pictured map is not *her* perceptual map.

Ellmann preserves the mountain lion as a site of alignment and even a moral center in her fundamental nonviolence, which is especially evident in her act of generous indifference to a woman she trees unintentionally:

> Slowly she ventured down to the woman's branch, offering a cautious purr. She came so close that for a second their noses touched.
>
> The sweet, sorry smell of the sobbing woman was briefly intriguing. Then the lioness dropped . . . and swiftly wound her way through the underbrush, the cubs trotting after her. (507)

The meeting occurs on the mountain lion's own terms; her aesthetic appreciation for the woman reads as moral purity, a quality that allows the novel to emphasize widespread *human* violence. Ben De Bruyn calls her "a surprisingly peaceful predator" whose orientation toward this human woman in particular underscores the possibility of coexistence and even collaboration. This possibility recurs throughout the novel, not least in its style. She knows perfectly well that humans "were merely her rivals in the forest, and dangerous ones, to be shunned. . . . Cub-stealers, all. Life-wasters" (733), and when she encounters animals escaping from a real-world abusive private zoo in Zanesville, Ohio, she distances herself from the "lost hollow creatures," thinking herself a "queen" (820). When finally captured and brought to the Columbus Zoo, she considers it a "catastrophe" for the distortions of smell and sound that compress modes of animal communication into "indeterminate utterances of animals whose needs were not met" (939). She lucidly indicts the zoo's failure to "constitute an environment" (to recall Yoko Tawada's phrase, discussed in Chapter 2). For De Bruyn, the upshot of the mountain lion's narrative is that "we should privilege narrative instead of physical contact with wildlife, it seems, and reimagine the cultural meaning of the cougar in a way that foregrounds its tenacity and fugitivity—and provides conceptual resources to women exposed to violence, like Stacy and her mother."[77] What needs amplification here is "narrative contact": that narrative builds a new environment rather than mourns the destroyed one. On the one hand, narratively the mountain lion occupies a world marked as separate by the use of free indirect discourse, but on the other hand, building the world of this animal, which emphasizes shared orientations and precarities, matters at least as much as its demonstration of exemplary survival strategies for apocalyptic scenarios. This two-worlds logic does not have the ontological specificity of the Upper, Middle, and Lower Worlds of an Indigenous ontology, but its interest in two narrative organizations as relational and complementary showcases how crucial Indigenous theory, like that of Justice and Byrd, is for grasping this narrative strategy for rendering milieu as multispecies.

The mom's narrative ends by risking a conceptual synthesis of the two worlds without confidently affirming its meaning. After the family has weathered the rebellious teenage Stacy running away for a night and later being threatened by an intruder with an assault weapon, they plan to visit "the runaway lioness at the zoo." The novel ends: "The fact that Stacy seems to feel some kind of rapport with that woebegone creature, the fact that whether this is because she feels fierce and free, or caged and cowed, doesn't bear thinking about" (988). Throughout the novel, the mom has been attempting to achieve a non-appropriative relationship with Stacy, to accept the unpredictability of her child's life. (The novel comes at this issue from the maternal direction, whereas *Power* sides with the rebel daughter.) If on the one hand the mom hopes Stacy might feel inspired by the lioness's wild resilience, imagining her as a "conceptual resource" in a convergent world of gendered violence, on the other hand she refuses to make a decisive, advance supposition about what concept is being encoded, an acknowledgment of both Stacy's and the lioness's opacity. Even while the novel refuses a decisive stance on the allegorical coding of the lioness's existence, it presents a convergent sentience as an inherent site of value, curiosity, and epistemic effort.

The mom's interest in the mountain lion reflects a certain degree of moral evolution in relation to wild animals; toward the beginning of the novel, when she is stranded in a snowstorm with a dead car, she is unrealistically terrified of being eaten by bears, whereas she is clearly on the lioness's side by the time it has entered the Ohio suburbs, unlike the pearl-clutching public. Her sympathy for the lioness as an object of human violence and a symbol of human freedom is a particularly emphatic site of her own counter-ideological world-making and an index specifically of her interest in reckoning with settler colonialism. I would call attention to how fully the novel validates an observation of Hogan's in *Radiant Lives* about a mountain lion's unexpected entry into human spaces. Hogan claims, "We live with the beautiful world and in it lives the lions, the other wildlife that don't have maps, don't follow human rules"; this articulation highlights the novel's interest in how decentering a eurowestern framework admits a multispecies world picture.[78] De Bruyn connects the lioness with positive images of animal fugitivity in Joshua Bennett's work: he points out, "Time and again, the lioness slinks away 'unseen' (787) and proves that she is 'good at keeping out of sight' (945), like the rats and other animal 'escape artists' revalorized by Bennett."[79] At least as relevant, though, is the mountain lion's intersection with Indigenous history, which the mom taught when she worked as a lecturer at the local liberal arts college. Somewhat consonant with Bennett's fugitivity is Gerald Vizenor's "transmotion" as a sovereign mode of movement: a "sense of native motion and an active presence is *sui generis* sovereignty. Native transmotion is survivance, a reciprocal use of nature, not a monotheistic, territorial sovereignty."[80] The big cat might be said to demonstrate either or both of these values. As the lioness cuts across Ohio, the mom rejects the accelerating moral panic among the right-wing, pro-gun population tracking her down, and especially the perception that the creature is a "non-native incomer that entered Ohio illegally" (900). Insisting on its "native belonging," the mom links the lioness's sovereign presence with her own urgent need to reckon with settler colonial violence. At the same time, the mom grasps the pathologization of Indigenous movement; Byrd writes, in contrast to Vizenor, that to be in transit "is to be in motion, to exist liminally in the ungrievable spaces of suspicion and unintelligibility. To be in transit is to be made to move," even if it is also to "exist relationally," a source of kinship and intimacy even within experiences of coercion.[81] Similarly, Ellmann's image of transit also glosses the lioness's eventual ability to settle into the zoo once she is joyfully reunited with her cubs; she is not preternaturally committed to wildness or freedom; her transit has opened her to coercion and reconnection.

The predominantly white trackers of the mountain lion racialize the space of Ohio as white, taking advantage of a logic of transit that frames her as ungrievable and unaccountable—and thus killable.[82] The mom thinks otherwise: when the mountain lion story spreads all over the news with varying degrees of implausibility, she reflects,

> *I'd* like to be in two places at once . . . the fact that there are lots of Indian names for cougars, the fact that Katalgar means Greatest of Wild Hunters, and Puma means Powerful Animal, Pitwal means Long-tailed One, and Ko-Icto means Cat of God, the fact that there's also Mishipeshu, the underwater panther, and Fire cat . . . the fact that their whiskers detect air currents, the fact that starving cougars sometimes eat beetles, the fact that it's weird watching the whole country mobilize itself against one little beetle-eating beast, the fact that, I mean, what is all this *costing*, what with the hound dogs, Mounties, man hours. (899)

Admiring the lioness's ability to elude "man hours," she also reminds herself of its cognitive differences and a wide range of cultural meanings besides her own projections. She is in two places at once experientially—fully ensconced in her kitchen while roaming mentally, invested in the partial Indigenous histories she has learned while entrenched in midwestern middle-aged whiteness. Part of her long woman-hours of milieu-making is acknowledging her limitations. The de-temporalized quality of her narrative style makes it is unclear whether the mom is googling the information about Indigenous terms for cougars as she goes along or whether she already knows it ("because I'd *studied* this stuff" [608]). Certainly, she strives to reverse the political allegorization of the lioness's journey and to avoid essentializing or romanticizing its Indigenous associations, even if over the course of the novel her decolonial self-education is unevenly implemented.

Her valorization of the mixed-race "Cherokee tracker" who ultimately locates the lioness is steadfast: when he names her Mishipeshu, she approves: "He chose the right one." She also highlights that his tracking skills can hardly be conflated with his heritage given that he grew up in the Bronx and survived being born with a "neonatal disorder" in which "his blood was incompatible with his mother's" (1036), a weirdly specific detail that scrambles any hint of biological essentialism. When she refers to him as "the Cherokee tracker," it is only partly an attempt to center his culture's epistemologies; it is also an opportunity to link the mountain lion with Indigenous people subjected to government-sponsored genocide. She notes "the fact that [the tracker] had to remind the police daily of their no-shooting agreement, treaty, broken treaties . . . the fact that he used conservation and extinction as two big reasons not to shoot her" (1060). He is a generational cycle-breaker whose Cherokee heritage seems aligned with his conservationist ethos without presuming it. (Indigenous identity, meanwhile, is not an object of fantasy. She mentions that her ex-husband, a Yale-educated and unmotivated partner, "shows no interest in his Indian heritage" (602), even if she is careful never to make these reminders contiguous with expressions of disappointment in Frank as a father or what a reader might extrapolate as signs of depression in him. She does not claim to be able to tell his story.) In this sense, Indigenous Americans are not solely the past-tense, "spectral," "lamentable casualties of national progress" that they too often appear but represent a varied response to the lived experience of settler colonialism; the mom wants to make Indigenous history a part of her understanding of the present—to recognize Indigenous lives in her world and also to acknowledge a separateness that might hold space for their sovereignty.[83]

I said *might*: she struggles to know what to put in place of American history's erasure of Indigenous people, and her own life seems to have gravitated toward reifying American whiteness. As her fascination with the mountain lion exemplifies, the mom pays attention to racialization and reflects on how her own racial identity shapes her perception, often needling herself about her complicity in settler colonialism. Just as she knows she is collaborating in climate emergency, she reminds herself often that her interests—especially the *Little House on the Prairie* and *Wizard of Oz* books, which she references frequently and passes on to her daughters as staples of white American girlhood—endorse genocide.[84] "The fact that they probably didn't see Indians as neighbors or even as people exactly," she reminds herself, even while encouraging her oldest daughter, the only one of her children who has Indigenous ancestry, to read the books aloud to the youngest child. She recounts many acts of government-sponsored violence while not doing much with these facts—in one of the novel's more extended meditations, she recounts the Gnadenhutten Massacre; perhaps this is a kind of land acknowledgment, because she now delivers pies and gets her car repaired in Gnadenhutten. She is a "good white person" who used to lead seminars about tribal burial mounds and eighteenth-century massacres, but she has withdrawn from college teaching. Her topic places indigeneity in the past (much like her academic career), and it often synonymizes history or anthropology with mourning. Still, it is not quite a simple elegiac relation, as one of her descriptions of mounds makes clear: "The fact that Florida was covered in Indian mounds made of crushed shells, but they all got destroyed to make the roads and railways, sand mounds, the fact that the shape of Indian mounds makes me think of pregnant women, or bras in the fifties" (290). The order of the ideas means that a somewhat ambivalent possibility of rebirth from the ravage of industrialization emerges in imagining burial mounds as first tumescent bellies and then as imprisoned breasts, even though the whole thought indicts necropolitics by implying that what was razed are reproductive organs. A reaction against gendered violence, even against gender *as* violence, that cuts across race and species categories often motivates the mom's thinking even as the scattered form of her thought means that these critiques are never sustained.

The prevalence of critique of settler colonialism throughout the novel highlights that there is nothing inherently powerful about inhabiting a stance—or a never-ending flow of stances. The mom's narrative meanders in such as a way as to highlight the multiple identity categories that are imperiled by settler-colonialism's violences without giving her a cohesive political stance. At most, the narrative's existence as a stream of tidbits protests the narrator's *own* cultural marginality by refusing the muteness or the "shyness" she claims to feel (or the "reticence" she was once accused of on a date). What could a more sustained encounter with Indigenous cosmology allow her to understand about her yearning for connection with animals? Still, it is worth connecting rumination to work in animal studies that emphasizes the value of the anecdote. Despret creates an abecedary of short explanations of research problems, including a defense of the YouTube animal video, many of which are reported watched in *Ducks*. Susan Fraiman defends anecdotes as "feminized by their brevity and intimacy," valuable "for their attentive, detailed, domestic materialism."[85] The domestic microrealism of *Ducks*, likewise, has enough space in the rhythm of rumination for the animal anecdote—though far less for longer arcs of historical critique.

In some ways the ruminative "worlding" of the mom highlights its antisocial and unproductive qualities. Her narrative presents the outer world only in a filtered way: featuring almost no reported dialogue, it is not even a polyphonic text, but rather one that presents sentience itself as activity. In contrast, the mountain lion's narrative offers little remembrance (except one episode depicting, in some detail, the acts of mating that led to her cubs). Without much of a sense of the past, the lioness is neither granted nor refused a prototypical image of psychological depth or stable identity; rather, the coherence of her progressive present is continually affirmed. Slightly ruminative, featuring only a few repetitions, this narrative does appear to confirm what the mom wonders: "Do [animals] talk to themselves all the time like we do?" (321). Yet hers is a narrative ultimately oriented toward activity—the search for her cubs—even as it is narrated as unfolding primarily through the representation of inner life as it is coordinated with the outer world.

The mom's narrative manages this coordination not through reported action but through the endlessly repeated phrase "the fact that." Despite her exasperation with her nine-year-old son's "pedantic" fascination with scientific facts, it's clear where he gets it from. The narrator has access to a worrisome Internetful of mis/dis/information; hers is a knowing consciousness marked by lack of any action, especially any act of political protest that might be taken in response to the litany of environmentally and politically disastrous facts she notes. She feels like she has little knowledge and authority, a self-image she seems to have gotten partly from her intimidating father but also more broadly from an overwhelming culture of information. "I don't know, but *they* know" is another frequent, self-flagellating refrain. The only action, it would seem, is the effect of the stating of facts itself—the flattening of the distinction between statements that would appear to be factual in an ordinary way—scientific tidbits, plot summaries of classic films, descriptions of cooking tools—along with shopping lists, word association games, rich memories, immediate sensations, and affects, granting them facticity. The mom suggests that her son Ben's exclusive obsession with facts means that he is "starving himself of fantasy," whereas as I've been suggesting above, the mom's ability to imagine or "suppose" other minds suggests an expansive understanding of fact. The narrative structure acknowledges that, as Jen Rose Smith articulates, "scientific discourse and data collection operate as dominant, and often preferred, forms of knowledge-production that draw conclusions about a changing climate" but also suggests that using literary forms as modes of "evidence upends an overreliance on Science as arbiter of truth" and deny "the statistical as superior."[86] Many of the mom's facts adduce knowledge of a phenomenon as "the most X in the world," as if the world in its totality can be known and organized according to statistics, but the sheer number of these declarations calls their validity into question. How could she possibly know?

The structure of *Ducks* means that numerical units of information are asserted to be on an epistemological level with scents or childhood memories, flattening a huge array of perceptual and cognitive modes into a single category of something like "having an acknowledged bearing on reality." The immense range of technical reference in the book necessitates an index of mostly real-world acronyms and abbreviations for chemicals, political organizations, and many more kinds of things. The index serves both to martial and to ironize the impossible array of knowledges that an ordinary citizen is supposed to possess. Canon Schmitt has argued, in defense of description as a narrative mode in contemporary fictions of extinction, that the work of description is to "lovingly, meticulously . . . tell[] over the things and the names we live amidst every day," offering a "luminously melancholy inventory of what is, and so what might be lost."[87] Such a claim at least partially explains the many lists that pepper the novel. But many of the objects and items named are lamentable products of industrialization where there is no love lost, or lists become so broad in scope as to be toneless. These lists might intimate a flat ontology, in which humans are just one of the many kinds of things in an interdependent material collectivity. For feminist materialism and object-oriented ontology, an awareness of the vitality of objects is said to induce an "affective openness" in the human object entangled in this awareness.[88] But as Byrd cautions, despite the appeal of flattened ontologies that "imagine against the self and state sovereignties that promise recognition as panacea for oppression," these framings risk perpetuating white fantasies of sovereign appropriation.[89] For Ellmann, the mom often has a paranoid relation to the objects she lists, whose material vitality and mobility is not a joyful source of posthumanist molecular jouissance but rather a terrifying signal of the permeability of human skin in a toxic milieu. It is, in other words, a violently post-political zone that threatens obliteration.[90] If a "fact" is, for Mary Poovey, the result of a system of agreements about a stable, commonly acknowledged reality that is politically and economically enforced, *Ducks*'s obsessive engagement with the "fact" is no less invested in pronouncing judgment on the many external enforcements and coercions that go into forging common experiences.[91]

Profoundly ironizing omniscience, these accretive descriptions and namings of supposed facts and factual things seem to undermine the authority of recognized knowledges but also to supplement them with a host of other ways of accounting for a milieu. At the same time, however, the mom's perpetual assertion of facts serves less to organize than to render permeable two *other* worlds, fictional and "real." For Elaine Freedgood, the novel from the nineteenth century onward is more suffused with veridical description than critics other than frustrated Marxists (from Georg Lukacs of "Narrate or Describe" to Franco Moretti's *The Bourgeois*) would like to admit; she hopes to recapture the weirdness of realism's interpenetration of two worlds. Borrowing Genette's sense of "world" in his account of metalepsis, Freedgood writes,

> The realist novel wants to refer to real people, events, and places, yet it also wants to distribute lots of fictional people, things, and places among that real stuff, creating a seemingly seamless integration of two very different diegetic and ontological worlds. We don't feel a sense of rupture or uncanniness when we think of the fictional characters who inhabit actual cities or when we think of actual wars interrupting or furthering fictional plot. I argue ... that we should.[92]

The novels I examine in this chapter offer a realism that permits both integration and rupture, both intimacy and opacity, explicitly foregrounding qualities that for Freedgood mark most realistic fiction to some extent. Their two worlds are at once deeply fictive—especially and somewhat notoriously the fictionality of the tribe in *Power*—and also referential. In *Ducks*, Ellmann offers a complementary if opposite twoness to the conclusion of *Power*, where Hogan interrupts realism with a vision of an actual spiritual realm, and insists that two worlds can be thought in one sentence, and one sentience. Ellmann's text, likewise, aims to make multiple milieus perceptible within one text that showcases all its ruptures, insisting that this is what thinking is like. If we acknowledge that it *isn't* unified, we can also acknowledge other worlds that touch, in their worldedness, one's own. The narrative itself is the milieu in which they meet.

4. CONCLUSION

These are novels of two worlds in multiple senses: human and animal worlds that converge without merging; fictional and nonfictional material that combines in unexpected ways; the rhythms of thinking and outward event. A similar duality appears in Frederic Jameson's *The Antinomies of Realism*, another narrative of two worlds where realism is structured by tension between the narrative momentum of storytelling and the affective immediacy of sensory experience. Emphasizing the synesthetic "intensity" of realist fiction from the midnineteenth-century onward, Jameson argues for an "irreconcilable divorce between intelligibility and experience" that interrupts narrative "by a kind of non-narrative perceptuality" or intensity that he terms "affect."[93] The ruminative logic of *Power* and *Ducks*, even as it does not turn its back on human thinking, falls on the affective side of the divide, in the kinds of relationship valorized by Indigenous and feminist materialisms that take the gendered work of care as central to the survivability of a milieu against the tide of despair. These frameworks allow for a twoness guided by rhythmic relations, a recoil and leap of intimacy, rather than hierarchic domination or aporetic difference.

Against companionship, a vision of non-appropriative kinship is proposed in both novels, across species and within human communities. Both novels embed their human protagonists in multispecies milieus: their narrators exist in what Arne Naess calls "mixed communities" of wild and domesticated animals that imply kinship. To sustain such a community requires substantial carework in the face of the accelerating threat of extinction—the kind of non-aggrandized carework that is central to much feminist ecocriticism, especially the work of Josephine Donovan, Lori Gruen, and others.[94] Yet these are novels of perception rather than novels of direct interspecies care that at once, to use Claire Colebrook's words, "open the classically feminist question of the *scale of the personal*" yet simultaneously pursue "a chastening of the human—because we no longer assume that world is reducible to the world *for us*."[95] Another way to put this is that the novels I have discussed in this chapter certainly do not propose that "women," especially Indigenous women, have any intrinsic bond with or obligation to animals, but rather suggest that gender "emerges from a history that is ecologically bound up with violence and depletion."[96] For many white feminist materialists, the alternative to this history of coercion is what Braidotti calls a materialist "experiment with intensity"—but in Hogan's and Ellmann's hands, that "intensity" is only one facet of ruminative narrative oriented toward historicizing the settler-colonial violence that shapes the milieus of the present.[97]

Insisting on non-companionate attention to animals positions thinking itself as a environmentally consequential site of repair. Even as these novels are told by situated human voices, these voices are associated with milieu rather than cohesive subjectivity. The same could be said of the novels I discuss in Chapter 3, but unlike *Salvage the Bones* or *The Friend*, *Ducks* and *Power* consider the possibility of valuing animal kinship without companionship and do not present their cats as characters living within the same representational plane as the narrators themselves. To speak of a cat requires a different voice. Thus, they experiment with norms of characterization, imbricating the representation of animal experiences with human efforts at self-understanding. In related ways, then, these novels take first-person narration to the limits of an implicitly eurowestern realism; both insist on thinking of non-companionate relations as necessary to positioning humans within a milieu—an environmentally essential shift in how we think about what it means to know another.

FIVE

Wilder Things

To reflect on how third-person realism's approach to milieu represents the endangerment of populations in a time of climate crisis, I want to circle back to the tiger, the emblem of threatened megafauna that I discussed in Chapter 1. Several recent novels feature scenes in which characters enter a trance in the overwhelming presence of a solitary tiger. In Carol Birch's *Jamrach's Menagerie* (2011), a historical novel, the protagonist's childhood encounter with a tiger in the streets of London launches his impossible dream of imperial conquest. In Fiona McFarlane's *The Night Guest* (2014), an aging protagonist loses consciousness in the embrace of a dream-tiger: the novel stresses the incapacity of a range of institutions (from government care agencies to banks, shops, and even families) to fully acknowledge the physical and mental experiences of aging. In Aravind Adiga's *The White Tiger* (2008), the protagonist faints when he visits the animal in a zoo and confronts his own powerlessness: "The tiger's eyes met my eyes, like my master's eyes have met mine so often in the mirror of the car. All at once, the tiger vanished." In Amitav Ghosh's *The Hungry Tide* (2004), an urbane translator loses his capacity for language just before he sees—or thinks he sees—a tiger in the Sundarbans jungle. Each scene of sublimity emphasizes the distortions of perception instigated by an encounter between the most charismatic of endangered megafauna and an existentially destabilized human individual, whose capacity for self-sovereignty is held in abeyance. When consorting and companionship are not possible, sublime awe transfigures the encounter with animal otherness, presenting it as an allegory of the limits of human perception—a "tool[] for . . . self-(re)fashioning," as Sundhya Walther puts it.[1] In these novels, a singular tiger encounter initiates a loss of human will in the face of animal power, questions the presumption of human mastery, and stresses corporeal vulnerability.

But what happens to human perception when the animal presence it encounters represents an entire population? The sublime is clearly an insufficient answer to questions of how humans are responsible to that population: we need, in Allan Stoekl's words, some "calculation of the true and total cost of things" without recourse to the allegorizing distortions of the sublime.[2] The specific sublimity that attaches to individual tigers, both within and across cultural contexts, is a particularly forceful index of this problem.[3] Writing of the plight of big cats under increasing environmental pressures, Nayanika Mathur proposes that the Anthropocene "requires a transformation in how we narrate the story of human-animal relations as well as the plotlines and who—or what—the characters are."[4] Indeed, recent realist fiction explicitly addressing climate crisis often emphasizes the fate of animal populations, rather than one-on-one encounters, by reflecting on human strategies of knowing even as it turns away from the singular individual protagonist, a break with Lukácsian biographical form that, as Aaron Rosenberg demonstrates, has its origins in late-nineteenth-century fictions of incipient ecological crisis.[5] This multicharacter approach reiterates realism's long-standing questions about how possible it is to conceive of the "total" or the aggregate.

Turning to populations opens the realist novel to questions of scale that have become central to critical discourse on the aesthetics of the Anthropocene.[6] This discourse has tended to undervalue realism: the resources of a minimally allegorical realism and especially of third-person, "omniscient" narrative for documenting environmental crisis have been underestimated. If we take realism as a genre that constantly reflects upon its own procedures for securing concrete knowledge of creaturely life in the aggregate, we can better understand fiction's recent interest in animals as central to its conception of environmental crisis. Realism's emphasis on interiority has sometimes seemed to directly negate this potential: for Pam Morris, "as anxiety about mass society, perceived by the educated classes in terms of brutish bodies, increased during the later decades of the nineteenth century, novelistic concern came to focus largely upon interiority."[7] For a critic like Ulka Anjaria, newer realisms can become anti-subjective insofar as they "strip[] metaphor away, replac[ing] metafictionality with an aesthetic of transparency that verges on the banal, and thematize[] the bearer of 'bare life' rather than the conflicted subject."[8] Anjaria's claim puts the novel in the conceptual service of biopolitical critique, potentially re-allegorizing its status as fiction. In this chapter, I contend that recent realist animal novels reimagine collective life in multispecies terms that avoid the category of bare life, instead making the scale of population a way of thinking aesthetically as well as scientifically about inhabiting a shared, imperiled world while retaining ambivalence about "character" or "subjectivity." In other words, these texts take human care about animals as environmentally consequential rather than as a hyper-individualist symptom of the late Capitalocene. They insist on the existential and psychological consequences of thinking at species scale. In the previous chapter, I emphasized that rumination in first-person narratives registers how caring makes perceptible a lived and livable world; here, I emphasize that third-person narration's attention to conflicts among modes of knowledge-production makes sense of its recent fascination with other than human animals. Representing multispecies milieus is a key way in which realist fiction gains traction on our shared environmental peril.

The novels I examine in this chapter concern how human scientists respond to populations under threat.[9] While several American novels tackle similar questions—most famously Barbara Kingsolver's *Flight Behavior* (2012) and Richard Powers's *The Echo Maker* (2006)—I discuss two Anglophone novels by writers of color that consider populations of liminal animals in a transnational context that heightens concerns about the cohesiveness of any given milieu.[10] Amitav Ghosh's *The Hungry Tide* (2014) and Aminatta Forna's *Happiness* (2018) each examine the challenges humans face in orienting themselves toward other species, juxtaposing the arduous efforts of scientists to measure animal populations with a range of other disciplinary and epistemic frameworks. Both texts align animals' sentience with aesthetic attunement, and thus engage in a distinctively literary way the conceptual crises provoked by the Anthropocene. In neither of these novels do animals themselves function as individuals, much less as characters; rather, they appear as members of populations. This restriction of character space to humans might imply a revived anthropocentrism. Yet *The Hungry Tide* and *Happiness* strongly emphasize the profoundly interdependent interests of different species encountered collectively while largely avoiding both the heightened agon of epistemic alterity and a sublimed pose of incomprehension.[11]

If animal studies and ecocriticism have sometimes functioned as separate subdisciplines—the former animated primarily by questions of difference and the latter by questions of scale—I contend that the concept of milieu helps to show how recent novels suggest that these are fundamentally shared concerns. Fiction that presents characters attempting to grapple with historically and environmentally situated animal populations at larger scales avoids representational problems that emerged in Chapters 2 and 3: the question of whether an animal might or might not work as a literary character, as well as the connected implication that human-animal relationships flourish primarily in dyadic affective bonds, however unsentimental. In these novels, animal behavior scientists clearly love and sometimes grieve for the animals they study, but they have a largely unsentimental view connected to their interest in the species scale. While they demonstrate the "zeal, devotion, and endless application" that Michel Foucault argues distinguishes the pastoral figure of the shepherd, these scientists are of course not caretakers but observers.[12] Coordinating their ethos of objectivity with third-person narrative style, population-oriented realist fiction demonstrates the keen relevance of a distinctively literary epistemology to grappling with the Anthropocene as a multispecies phenomenon rather than defer to the pastoral allegories of biopolitics. As it does so, it also addresses a key concern about the very concept of the "Anthropocene" itself posed by Indigenous studies: Métis scholar Zoe Todd, for example, argues that the term's abstraction obscures both art and scholarship's capacity to evoke multispecies interdependence.[13]

Depicting how the fields of environmental science and animal geography study the entanglement of human and nonhuman populations, these novels nonetheless offer a distinctively *literary* perspective on multispecies existence.[14] While the settings differ considerably—the Sundarbans and London—the characters and prose styles stage convergent questions about disciplinary epistemologies, animal lives, and human selves. As I discussed in the Introduction, an investment in the phenomenological constitution of "world" through environmental resonance or responsiveness brings together a wide range of discourses. *The Hungry Tide* and *Happiness* both portray a tentative romance between a cosmopolitan man and a professional female population biologist. In each novel, the devoted biologist tracks the behavioral patterns of an indigenous species altered by violent histories of human development. She is observed in her work by a man more concerned with the human psyche and initially bemused by the scientist's concern with animals' patterns. Ultimately in both cases, the plot turns not on consummated love—the future remains iffy—but on the how the scientist's modest yet sustaining commitment to mapping animal geographies is deepened by the encounter with humanistic epistemologies that reemphasize mutual interdependence. These rather remarkable similarities underscore the interest the two novels share in exploring how disciplinary epistemologies permit or inhibit access to multiple worlds. As is often the case throughout the long history of the novel, a scientist character's investment in objective, ongoing study is aligned with the work of a third-person narrator, self-consciously reflecting on the novelistic project's commitment to a one-culture model of literature and science.[15] Philosopher of cognition Kristin Andrews argues that "liminal animals who share the wild with humans . . . offer places to reconcile field and lab studies" precisely because multiple frameworks of evaluation, including multispecies sociability, come into play.[16] I would argue that the possibilities for consilience extend beyond subfields of comparative cognition to potential collaborations between literary and cognitive approaches to animal worlds.

Contemporary third-person realism evokes a creaturely milieu by exploring how and when to inhabit a stance toward that which evades rigidly disciplinary procedures for knowing. In the novels I examine, the precariousness of animal populations renders long-term crises as immediate emergencies in which the "narrating" moment becomes malleable, suggesting that compression and expansion are some common human strategies of world-building by which the realist novel makes perceptible the interdependence of multiple species. Indeed, the navigation of scale *is* central to the realist novel's negotiation of how the individual participates in the population. At the level of syntax, the expansiveness of the subjunctive vies with contraction of parataxis. Free indirect discourse aggregates and disaggregates objective and subjective views. Character systems filter when sensation itself is an adequate kind of knowledge and when disciplinary rootedness is necessary. In attending to these aspects of realist form, I highlight its processual, perspectival account of the production of knowledge. Realism's attention to the sensations and affects that attend the effort of coming to know resonates with recent developments in comparative cognition, such as philosopher Rachell Powell's advocacy for the concept of *Umwelt* in the field of comparative cognition. Not only does that term make sense of convergences between animals' and humans' ways of knowing the world, but even more fundamentally, it shows that "meaning is felt, not merely represented."[17] Such a claim makes the explanatory force of the philosophy of comparative cognition sound very much like realist fiction's distinctive fascination with how lived experience generates a knowable world.

1. REALISM'S CREATURELY IMAGINATION

Theories of the Anthropocene have undervalued realism's distinctive ways of attending to creaturely life. Meanwhile, the concept of "world" has been central to recent defenses of realism, often a political rather than ecological or ethological term, a reaction to Gayatri Chakravorty Spivak's foundational postcolonial redefinition of "worlding" as colonial epistemic violence.[18] A special issue of *Novel: A Forum on Fiction* defends the form as, in Lauren Goodlad's words, "both constitutively worlded (in taking the material world for its premise) and worlding (in making new ways of seeing, knowing, thinking, and being palpable to those worlds)."[19] Noting realism's ability to work across plural temporalities, the journal issue takes the geopolitical conditions of capitalism as the spur to realism's plurality, while only occasionally mentioning climate change as a secondary factor (and not one intrinsically linked to capitalism). Still, world's ethological sense feels relevant: for example, Jed Esty suggests that realism highlights "interrelated and trackable links leading all the way from intimate life to world systems." If we conceptualize Esty's term "life" along nonanthropocentric lines, not only might realism include nonhuman lives in that world-system—but could it also think life as itself systemic—structured and networked? "Disclosing connection," for Esty, means "offering an epistemologically grounded account of life inside the world system" rather than using the individual's consciousness primarily as a means of "negatively allegorizing the system's indescribability" as in the sublime moments I described in this chapter's opening.[20]

While defenders of realism could make far more of a contribution to debates about representing climate crisis, some ecocritics reject the genre, most infamously Ghosh himself in *The Great Derangement* (2016). Ghosh (whom Esty identifies as one of realism's "new masters") claims that realism's incapacity to compass unpredictable events demonstrates its anthropocentric commitments—it cannot accommodate "forces of unthinkable magnitude that create unbearably intimate connections over vast gaps in time and space" because of its emphasis on the everyday details that "conceal" the "exceptional events" that constitute evidence of the Anthropocene.[21] Ghosh follows Donna Haraway, Ursula Heise, Wai Chee Dimock, Mark McGurl, and Adam Trexler, as well as Benjamin Morgan and Aaron Rosenberg, working more historically with sci-fi's late Victorian inception, in observing that climate fiction often turns to the apocalyptic, outsize, and often allegorical sensibilities of epic, science fiction, and horror in order to capture the magnitude of ecological crisis.[22]

Third-person realism depends upon the logic of the "world" in its ethological sense; the fascination of animal sentience in realist multispecies fiction is crucial to its ability to participate in climate discourse by presenting human and animal experiences on the same plane. To make this argument, it is first necessary to acknowledge Ghosh's point that *events* may not define realism. Within realist novels, even on the most suspicious view, events do not stand on their own because they depend upon the modes of perception that constitute events, modes that in turn depend, in part, upon the scope of perception in the first place. Understood in this way, realism offers protocols for thinking the relation among ways of being, sensing, and knowing, and thus for positioning that thinking as a lived experience. Put differently: Ghosh contends that "the longue durée is not the territory of the novel," and that "within the mansion of serious fiction, no one will speak of how the continents were created; nor will they refer to the passage of thousands of years."[23] But his own characters themselves do refer to, speak, and think of it—more and more explicitly, as in his recent *Gun Island* (2019).[24] Moreover, at a structural level, his narrators mediate the conditions that make their thinking possible—even when climate is not an obvious thematic concern, narrative builds a structure, an environment, for this thought.[25]

Realism's theorists have long positioned the genre as committed to rendering a common construction of the material, collective conditions of living—as invested in *sentience*, though they do not usually call it by that name. Realist narrative brings together an array of strategies for sense-making, in other words.[26] In Georg Lukàcs's *Theory of the Novel*, the individual life is initially only metonymically attached to the stream of history from which the self is alienated, but becomes ultimately a synecdoche or allegory for the social totality which it expresses through the self's representativeness.[27] Building the distinction between individuality and totality in Lukàcs, Amanda Anderson describes realism as presenting a "representative social totality at a particular historical moment, focusing on the ways emergent conditions of modernity are affecting psychological, moral, and social life."[28] Such a definition allows for the possibility of disjuncture of scales—the scale that allows for the analysis or perception of that totality, and multiple, experiential scale of both individual and collective "life"—and not necessarily only a life that belongs to human beings. In its complex representation of historical situatedness, realism oscillates between systems-level "perspectives and practice—sociological, impersonal, and political—that exceed the domain of the individual" and those that are marked as personal and moral; moreover, it reflects upon what can feel like a "structural gap" between these modes of thought, allowing their inassimilability.[29] Peter Boxall calls this kind of gap a "beautiful disintegrated partiality," which in his view has been part of realist aesthetics from the beginning.[30] A related gap or oscillation structures Jameson's recent *Antinomies of Realism*, which offers a phenomenological account of novelistic time. He argues that realism involves a constitutive tension between a sense of the eternal present, in which new feelings and experiences are registered, and a more structured, Lukàcsian temporality that envisions the collective destiny of some geopolitical group. While either temporality can generate a sense of collective scale—in the former case through affective sensibility (or even the sublime), and in the latter case through something more like a chronicle, history, or report—Jameson is getting at the plurality of rhythms and scales that might ostensibly measure the same moment.

We recover the potential of realism for considering the plight of animals in the multispecies Anthropocene if we consider the role that perception plays in realism's deployments of what we usually call subjectivity but might rather call world-making—if we consider the centrality of realism's concern with the making of knowledge as the integration or lack thereof between stance, situation, and perception, all of which depend on the spatial, temporal, affective, and social dimensions of cognitive appraisal.[31] For critics converging on the dialectical value of realism, aesthetic dislocation enables reflection on how perspective authorizes perception. Harry Shaw contends that realism "involves a movement between positions in and above a given historical moment" in order to "insist[] that certain mental procedures are needed to make sense of those substantial aspects of the world it selects as significant"[32]—and that what is selected depends on the relation to a sense of historical time. Ayelet Ben-Yishai builds on Shaw to argue that while the realist novel works to create sense of epistemological commonality—a sense that a known community shares objects of knowledge that can be agreed upon to be stable or objectively existent—it builds up that commonality over time and in situ.[33]

We might call realism's coordination of these dimensions of perception "integration," however unevenly distributed it is among a character system. By choosing the term "integration," I highlight the relevance of comparative cognition's recent renewal of interest in von Uexküll's account of the phenomenal scene of animal perception. Biology-oriented approaches have emphasized the inaccessibility of animals' first-person experience and therefore avoided the burden of explaining how animals' phenomenal world is unified. But Powell argues that comparative cognition would benefit from reopening questions of animal psychology: "if we are to understand an animal's behavior, we should attempt to see the world through its eyes (so to speak), or as interpreted through its interconnected suite of sensory, nervous, cognitive, and motor systems." When studies examine the qualitativeness of animal perception through categories like "temporal thickness" or "affective valences," their underlying research goal is to show that sensory perception creates what is called a binding effect, giving an animal's *Umwelt* integration or coherence—for example, the sensory inputs that make a den feel like home. For Powell, "conceiving of consciousness in terms of the information integration that is implicated in . . . various forms of binding . . . renders the *Umwelt* an epistemically accessible target of evolutionary explanation," while avoiding the problem of inhabiting an animal's first-person point of view.[34] By connecting *Umwelt* to evolutionary adaptation, Powell emphasizes that its explanatory force is at the scale of the population of a species, rather than the individual subjectivity of a single creature.

Powell's approach offers two slightly different points of connection with theories of the novel. First, it ends up treating any animal's first-person point of view as something very much like a literary character's in a third-person realist narrative. There may be no absolutely authentic access to a nonhuman animal's inwardness, and yet the experiential thickness of its perception is available to and a legitimate object of descriptive analysis through attention to, in Powell's words, "things like shape, texture, color, motion, and relative position, which are bound (along with affective valences) into spatiotemporally differentiated objects that are in turn integrated into a meaningful Umweltian scene."[35] As I demonstrate shortly, the narrative challenge posed by animal consciousness—

the challenge that Thomas Nagel famously flagged with a simile—is finessed by the writers I consider here by the subjunctive, where an "as if" creates a bridge into an animal's world, or a kind of translation. The subjunctive openly admits speculation and uncertainty, and yet also conveys a willingness to make an animal's *Umwelt* thinkable. For Jennifer Wenzel, the subjunctive is a distinctively narrative method for "imagining a world": "those prefatory words 'It's like' and 'perhaps' invoke the metaphorical, the provisional, the possible. They are portals to the realm of the imaginary or counterfactual: the literary"; similarly, Carolyn Fornoff argues that the subjunctive is a provocative voice for ecological writing because it complements the need for accurate reportage of vastly scaled events with the more intimate scope and *feel* of thinking. These perspectives showcase the prestige attached to a phenomenological concept of world across disciplinary categories. They also imply, perhaps, that the subjunctive exemplifies the dual impulses of realist fiction.[36]

Second, comparative cognition's emphasis on how sensory strands generate an "integrated" "*Umweltian* scene" resonates with scholarship on narrative form, particularly with Eric Hayot's claim that realist texts create a sense of "worldedness"—a "diegetic totality"—through cognitive variables that essentially constitute the novel as a technology for producing an image of a qualitatively rich set of human milieus with varying levels of integratedness.[37] Here I want to highlight three of Hayot's terms: completeness, amplitude, and connectedness. Each quality indexes the scope of what a literary text renders perceptible by assessing its integration. Although Hayot is more concerned with realist *scope* than with how *style* produces these "variables," his account leaves room for considering how free indirect style, the subjunctive, or other narrative devices might conduce to a sense of "connectedness" or "networkedness" in particular, where density of relationships in a represented world indexes how "the mediation that permits communication itself acts on the nature of the world-structure, by placing all that is communicable on the same ontological plane."[38] Bringing this point together with Caroline Levine's argument for the representation of interlocking social networks as especially necessitating longer narrative forms, I would stress that novels highlight the process of coming-to-know networkedness as an ongoing process, a thought that emerges through the thinking of it.[39] And so even if Ghosh, other realist novelists, and/or their critics portray no single practice of knowledge-making as fully adequate to producing a total image of shared global peril, realism registers particular modes of thought through the conditions that elicit them. Put differently: realism too depends on the logic of the milieu.

2. KNOWING ANIMALS IN THE SUBJUNCTIVE

In *The Great Derangement*, Ghosh notes that climate crisis features only "obliquely" in his own fiction, but it is close to the surface in *The Hungry Tide*. The novel is set in the Sundarbans region on the India/Bangladesh border in the early 2000s, a time and place that he says proves our "substantially altered world."[40] This novel contests a neo-colonial, western environmentalism that separates humans and nature, and insists on the region's multiple, entwined histories. *The Hungry Tide* brings together an upper-caste Bengali translator, Kanai, a visitor to the region; Piya, an Indian American cetologist on a research trip, who puzzles but fascinates Kanai; and the local fisherman, Fokir, who serves as Piya's guide as they search for river dolphins, a population under threat. The novel does not entirely fit a prototypical postcolonial narrative that, in Ursula Heise's phrasing, would "contrast[] an indigenous, ecologically grounded past with the degradation of nature European imperialism has brought about," but it comes close: it presents the Sundarbans as staging encounters between competing attitudes toward an environment that it presents as challenging human inhabitants from evolutionary prehistory into the unevenly postcolonial present.[41]

The novel juxtaposes activist, indigenous, cosmopolitan, and scientific frameworks for perceiving and communicating about this increasingly imperiled environment. The storms that threaten the region are historically precedented, as the novel is careful to establish. Nonetheless, the translator's uncle Nirmal, a transplant to the region, alludes to ways in which the Sundarbans are ineluctably changing. He writes, "The nearby islands are sliding beneath the water and soon, like icebergs in a polar sea, they will be mostly hidden."[42] Piya, two decades later, observes the catastrophic diminishment of the river dolphin population. When Kanai asks why the dolphins are disappearing, Piya replies, "Where do I begin? . . . Let's not go down that route or we'll end up in tears" (289). Piya's refusal to give vent to climate anxiety, however, is far from the novel's only approach to the topic because it centers a multispecies approach to thinking through population.

The question of how animals should be known and treated condenses the novel's evaluation of its multiple epistemic frameworks, dramatizing their potential for conflict around the regional history of tigers. The present-day characters in *The Hungry Tide* experience the Sundarbans as shaped by the aftermath of 1979 Marichjhanpi conflict, in which refugees were violently expelled from the island of Marichjhanpi to make room for Project Tiger, a tiger preserve funded by western donors to protect endangered animals. As Mathur points out, the competition between tigers and humans in this region, a story often told as one of "man-eating," emphasizes that "big cats are active agents."[43] The Sundarbans show that there are very specific socioeconomic and political conditions in which humans are likely to be victimized by tigers, and Mathur suggests that the tigers here "allow for a bloodied mirroring of the larger inequalities of this world."[44] This mirroring, for Mathur, is encapsulated in the "beastly tale," but I would argue that in *The Hungry Tide*, which includes the folkloric telling of such a tale, a wider range of narrative forms are in contested play. Indeed, Ghosh's unequal exploration of alternative epistemologies has led many critics, including Victor Li, Hilary Thompson, Graham Huggan, and Helen Tiffin, to express concerns about the novel's ultimate investment in "hegemonic narratives of development and humanism," as Walther puts it, especially in the seemingly sacrificial death of its subaltern character, Fokir.[45] These interpretations tend to focus thematically or formally on dyadic conceptions of character and/or species; reading the novel's reflections on its own formal negotiations with the problems of knowledge, I argue, offers not necessarily a more politically redemptive reading of the novel's limitations but a stronger sense of realism's distinctive contribution to problems of multispecies existence.

Narratives like *The Hungry Tide* featuring conflict around endangered megafauna can, in Ursula Heise's words, "bring them home" to show "the potential of multispecies justice as a way of thinking about biodiversity conservation—a framework that foregrounds how cultural, political, and economic differences shape our thinking and talking about how species should live together as much as biological and ecological differences do."[46] In *The Hungry Tide*, clashes among tigers, refugees, and state police are narrated in a diary kept by Nirmal when he visits the island. In the diary, the person who most sharply articulates the environmental pressures in the region is a young woman, Fokir's mother, who even though she is on the brink of starvation lucidly assesses the dehumanizing effects of western, cosmopolitan environmentalism: "This island has to be saved for its trees, it has to be saved for its animals, it is a part of a reserve forest, it belongs to a project to save tigers, which is paid for by people from all around the world. Every day, sitting here with hunger gnawing at our bellies, we would listen to these words over and over again. Who are these people, I wondered, who love animals so much that they are willing to kill us for them?" (284). Stressing the conflict between human and animal dispossession, she highlights the uneven effects of anthropogenic restructuring of the jungle, the price disproportionately paid by the poor, and demonstrates the insight born of situated knowledge. It is for reasons like these that the novel has achieved a sort of ecocritical canonicity despite the critiques I noted earlier.[47] Pheng Cheah explains that *The Hungry Tide* "seeks to reworld the world of the subaltern inhabitants of the Sundarban islands, which is threatened with destruction by the alignment of global flows of funds for world heritage preservation, environmental and ecological movements, global capitalist interests, and economic development."[48] Where I diverge from Cheah's argument, which (like Mathur's account of the big cat) stresses the "nonhuman agency of divine and natural forces in . . . daily survival through religious rituals and folk practices," is in emphasizing how central the insistence upon animals' worldedness is. This novel's interest in animals' milieus structures its presentation of how climate crisis affects the *experience* of a multispecies scale.

As I noted earlier, the novel struggles to depict tigers except as figures of otherness filtered through a eurocentric lens, rather than as a population. The poetry of Rilke, which fascinates Nirmal, offers a persistent touchstone for thinking about animals conceptually. When Nirmal warns the young Fokir of coming environmental apocalypse, he emphasizes a human-animal divide in the experience of climate crisis. He asks, "How long can this frail fence last against these monstrous appetites?—the crabs and the tides, the winds and the storms? . . . Neither angels nor men will hear us, and as for the animals, they won't hear us either" (66). Like Stoekl, he insists on the importance of imagining the contingency of human presence on earth, and the subtraction of humans from the environment. Why won't the earth register our loss? Nirmal, a Marxist encountering the Sundarbans as an outsider, favors Rilke's reading of animal life as an explanation for the natural world's hostility to human meaning. He records: "Because of what the Poet says. Because the animals '*already know by instinct / we're not comfortably at home / in our translated world*'" (192). For Nirmal, Rilke's text juxtaposes animal with human cognition, suggesting that animals' at-homeness in their world comes from their use of "instinct," whereas humans feel a dislocation from the natural world that is figured as the linguistic, rational activity of translation. Through Rilke, Nirmal makes the transcendental homelessness sometimes associated with the novelistic subject into a matter of species difference. In doing so he creates a pessimistic human exceptionalism implying that animals, living in an immersive eternal present, will survive environmental disaster, a fantasy that often appears in apocalyptic climate fiction.[49] Nirmal, bearing out his vision of human difference, compresses the deep time of human extinction into three brief lyric lines, each multiply translated. Whereas Kanai, a successful translator, sometimes seems to believe that his linguistic abilities grant him godlike knowledge, Nirmal renders translation, and the recombination of literary forms, as indexing the kind of epistemic limitation that features in the aporetic thinking of animal studies (which is itself deeply if complicatedly indebted to Rilke).[50]

Kanai echoes Nirmal's Rilkean vision when he is left alone on an island by Fokir and believes that he sees a tiger coming for him: "It was as if his mind, in its panic, had emptied itself of language. The sounds and signs that had served, in combination, as the sluices between his mind and his senses had collapsed: his mind was swamped by a flood of pure sensation. The word he had been searching for, the euphemisms that were the source of his panic, had been replaced by the thing itself, except that without words it could not be apprehended or understood" (353). The tiger he sees, or thinks he sees, prompts appreciation of its sublime aspect in a moment of protracted attention that becomes a surreal absorption as Kanai cowers, beholding its immensity and its color "that shone like gold in the sunlight" (354). The great irony of this passage is its performance of the sublime through its own act of translation—capturing in simile precisely that which is said to elude it. Kanai experiences this moment as an experiment in self-abasement, asking himself, "Wasn't this why people who lived in close proximity with tigers so often regarded them as being something more than just animals? Because the tiger was the only animal that forgave you for being so ill at ease in your translated world?" (351). These questions show that this vision expresses rather than challenges his absorption of Rilke's juxtaposition of animals' phenomenal embeddedness in nature with human homelessness.[51] And after all, it is most likely an imagined vision—neither locals nor Piya spot a tiger when they haul a self-shattered Kanai back to the research boat. Moreover, the idea that humans respond to the gaze of an animal through an absorptive, atemporal stasis is so pervasive that even Piya seems to have recourse to it in a moment of erotic captivity: sharing a charged moment with Fokir on their final research voyage, we are told, "they sat unmoving, like animals who had been paralyzed by the intensity of their awareness of each other" (377).

The novel provides few decisive answers of how to think about tigers, beyond that each individual tiger's representation of a larger population provokes fear. The novel's vague handling of the tiger population is an almost ubiquitous complaint in criticism that considers this novel's animal politics.[52] Juxtaposed with Nirmal's and Kanai's cosmopolitan and literary view of nature's hostility to human thriving are Piya's techno-conservationist framework and Fokir's mythological one. Both are presented as disciplinary understandings of nature that Piya insists are compatible, though one "required the input of geostationary satellites while the other depended on bits of shark bone and broken tile" (148). But her hope for consilience founders when it comes to tigers: Piya, who has grown up in the United States and "never had much interest in terrestrial carnivores" (103), sees tigers as an endangered species worthy of conservation. When she encounters a village group killing a tiger they have captured, she attempts to rescue it; she is horrified that Fokir (whose grandfather was eaten by a tiger, unbeknownst to her) participates in the killing. Kanai warns her that she has idealized him as "some kind of grass-roots ecologist" without understanding his relationship to the peril that tigers pose to his community.[53] Still, Fokir's attitude is complicated by his spiritual relationship to the threatening figure of the tiger in the local legend of Bon Bibi—a goddess who mediates humans' and tigers' enmity as well as mutual dependence. As Bon Bibi rescues a child from the grips of a tiger demon and brings animal and human needs into balance, the goddess signals a common quality of agency in a world of scarce but shared resources.[54]

Despite the commensalist implications of the Bon Bibi legends, *The Hungry Tide*'s representations of tigers tend to index the limits of human cognitive capacity, and neither the characters nor the narrator envisions a tiger *Umwelt*. Tigers appear in glimpses, fears, and flashes—as bits of golden fur glimpsed through a cage. One appears whole only when threatened by a storm; in the eye of the hurricane, Piya observes a tiger climb into a tree before disappearing into the water:

> It became aware of their presence at exactly the same moment they spotted it; although it was several hundred yards away, she could tell that it was an immense animal, so large it seemed incredible that the tree could sustain its weight. Without

> blinking, the tiger watched them for several minutes; during this time it made no movement other than to twitch its tail. She could imagine that if she had been able to put a hand on its coat, she would have been able to feel the pounding of its heart. (416)

Empathetic as Piya is when she imagines a tactile contact with the tiger's fear, she understands tiger life in terms of individual survival. The individualism of tigers throughout the novel remains inextricable from an aporetic framework of encounter, and it underlines the undecidability of tigers' future in a context where their liminality remains contested. In other words, the novel frames tigers' situation less as an Anthropocene phenomenon than as a means of indexing human attitudes toward the concept of animal otherness. When Kanai ponders that tigers' aggression toward humans might have "something to do with overpopulation, or encroachment on the habitat, or something like that" and wonders if the tigers are able to "think things through" (259, 260) in response to human efforts to control their aggression, his fumbling shows an effort—not a very sincere one—to think at the level of population. Meanwhile, his aunt responds, "Don't you believe it.... These attacks have been going on for centuries" (260), positioning tigers outside of or accessory to human history.

The representation of the dolphin population, in contrast, offers the novel a fuller opportunity to create links between animal and human milieus. Piya's study of *Orcaella brevirostris* (Irawaddy dolphin) migration patterns allows the novel to reflect in substantial detail on the strategies of perception, behavior, and environmental orientation that are adaptive for the species. She observes and recognizes individual dolphins, but her investment is ultimately in knowing enough about *Orcaella* behavior broadly to both extend understandings of evolutionary biology and to create "protective measures" (131) for this species in this region. "Are they fetching, these beasts of yours?" Kanai asks. "Do they hold one's interest?" (243). Kanai's snooty formulation of attention as *only* stasis—what the novel marks, accurately or not, as the Rilke move—belies the novel's interest in depicting dolphins as embodying a complex temporal and historical rhythm. Dolphins do turn out to have held Nirmal's interest, precisely thanks to the dolphin's distinctive ability to map their own territory and manage their own time. Observing them on one of his boat journeys to Marijhampi, he records:

All the time our boat was at that spot, the creatures kept breaking the water around us. What held them there? What made them linger? I could not imagine. There came a moment when one of them broke the surface with its head and looked right at me. Now I saw why Kusum found it so easy to believe that these animals were something other than what they were. For where she had seen a sign of Bon Bibi, I saw instead the gaze of the Poet. It was as if he were saying to me:

> Some mute animal
> raising its calm eyes and seeing through us,
> and through us. This is destiny . . . (253)

The passage from Rilke's "Eighth Elegy," which Nirmal excerpts, more emphatically stresses temporal dislocation as a frustration with finitude:

> Always turned so fervently toward creation,
> we see only the reflection of the Open
> which our own presence darkens. Or sometimes
> a mute animal looks up and stares straight through us.
> That's what destiny is: being opposite,
> and nothing else but that and always opposite.[55]

As Kári Driscoll explains, such a moment in Rilke "implies an interpretation on the part of the (human) observer, to whom it seems that to the [animal] it must seem as if there is no world."[56] It also (again) implies human alienation from nature. But seeing these dolphins as world-makers, Nirmal selects from the original text to emphasize connection. By eliminating both the idea of freedom "darkened" and a destiny of opposition, Nirmal resists the gesture of foreclosed communication implied by "muteness." He also frames the poet's communication to him through the subjunctive, a grammar Driscoll identifies as crucial to Rilke's zoopoetics because "even as [the 'as if'] seems to declare that there is no world, in fact it has the potential to create a world that is shared by human and nonhuman animals alike."[57]

The dolphins that prompt this moment of connection elicit more productive models of ecological thinking throughout the novel, probably not least because their needs are in less urgent competition with those of human populations. This is a limitation, indeed. Yet it is also worth noting how much narrative style frames questions of how human epistemologies make sense of dolphins' milieu. The dolphin narrative is less directly concerned with the impossibility of an authoritative or accurate translation of animal subjectivity into human terms, and more interested in the way perception of time and space can expand and compress for dolphins as well as for human beings, and for some of the very same reasons.

For Piya, *Orcaella* are the living representatives of a long chain of evolutionary changes that centrally include anthropogenic ones, reflecting coevolutionary pressures. As she observes the river, she notes coastal *Orcaella*, who need salt water, adapting their movements to chase the changing salinity of the tides. Wondering about the physiological mechanisms that allow these *Orcaella* to react to constantly changing microenvironments, she reminds herself,

> These microenvironments were like balloons suspended in the water, and they had their own patterns of flow. They changed position constantly, sometimes floating into midstream and then wafting back toward the shore, at times being carried well out to sea and at others retreating deep inland. Each balloon was a floating biodome filled with endemic fauna and flora, and as they made their way through the waters, strings of predators followed, trailing in their wake. (131)

Robin Chen-Hsing Tsai notes that Piya's observation of the "balloon" seems to echo von Uexküll's imagery in *A Foray into the Worlds of Animals and Humans* when he describes "worlds strange to us but known to other creatures, manifold and varied as the animals themselves.... To do so, we must first blow, in fancy, a soap bubble around each creature to represent its own world, filled with the perceptions which it alone knows. When we ourselves then step into one of these bubbles.... A new world comes into being[;] ... the world as it appears to the animals themselves, not as it appears to us."[58] The image of the bubble, I would add, evokes the logic of the subjunctive: blown "in fancy," the bubble presents an imaginative leap into another, self-contained space. For Piya, this image allows her to posit that the Sundarbans *Orcaella* create local mappings of microenvironments that prompt their unusual patterns of stasis and migration. Her hypothesis positions these dolphins' perceptual mechanisms as performing a kind of local history, while at the same time, Fokir's knowledge of their habits, gained through his lifetime of fishing for crabs, allows him to predict their movements well enough to show Piya. If before her dawning understanding of the *Orcaella* she "had thought of these concepts—keystone species, biomass—as ideas that applied to things other than herself" (150), this multispecies insight leads her to think of herself and her friend in species terms.

Species terms shape the narrator's representation of both dolphin perception and of Piya herself. What initially brings together Piya and Fokir is her near-drowning when she attempts to shield him from extortion by river guards. The narrative protracts her endangerment to make a foray into a factual mode (but also counterfactual, because it describes something that isn't happening). When the chapter begins, Piya is already underwater, but the narrator pauses to dwell on the adaptivity of dolphin perception in muddy water: "In the clear waters of the open sea the light of the sun wells downward from the surface in an inverted cone that ends in the beholder's eye" (58). This optical phenomenon, identified as Snell's window, becomes a means of suggesting dolphins' access to not only perceptual but aesthetic world-making. The circle of light, "like a floating halo," is a "prism" "creating a single clear opening in the unbroken expanse of shimmering silver" (58). Then the narrator juxtaposes these lucent images to the experience of being underwater in the Brahmaputra river, where silt causes light to

> lose its directionality within a few inches of the surface. Beneath this lies a flowing stream of suspended matter in which visibility does not extend beyond an arm's length. With no lighted portal to point the way, top and bottom and up and down become very quickly confused. As if to address this, the Gangetic dolphin (found in the Ganges) habitually swims on its side, parallel to the surface, with one of its lateral fins trailing the bottom. (58)

The passage calls for thematic as well as formal attention to questions of perception and filtration. Because the passage is not filtered or focalized through Piya's perspective, it offers an evolutionary, behavioral account of dolphins' perceptual world-building, even while also not claiming access to a first-person *Orcaella* point of view. This "as if," another subjunctive, translates dolphin adaptation into an everyday vocabulary for human action ("habitually") while legitimating the lengthy description of dolphins' perceptual capabilities. Despite the slight discomfort perhaps evoked by that subjunctive, the tools of evolutionary biology are presented as factually explaining dolphins' precarious thriving. In turn, these tools permit the novel to reframe Piya's own consciousness comparatively as an *Umwelt*, and for her to value her own capabilities for perception in equivalent terms to those of the dolphins. Unlike them, Piya cannot orient herself in the muddy river water, but the narration of her awareness stresses sensory integration, often attending not only to her visual/spatial perceptions, technologically amplified by her depth sounder and GPS, but her frequent attunement to nonlinguistic, emotionally resonant sound and smell.

Piya's connection with animals makes her a skeptic when it comes to language; at the beginning of the novel, she wants only minimal language, "empty of pain and memory and inwardness" and used as a "surgical" tool oriented toward the future (98). Part of her instant attachment to Fokir seems to come from his lack of interest in trying to communicate with her in Bengali. She idealizes dolphin communication; while she and Fokir share a boat, they listen "to echoes pinging through the water, painting pictures in three dimensions—images that only they could decode. The thought of experiencing your surroundings in that way never failed to fascinate her: the idea that to 'see' was also to 'speak' to others of your kind, where simply to exist was to communicate" (168). Piya has no worry that she cannot know or access the animal world: there is enclosure without a sense of aporia. Attending to the dolphin *Umwelt* reflects unflatteringly on the need for linguistic translation in human interaction, however: "Whatever [Fokir was thinking], she would never know: not just because they had no language in common but because that was how it was with human beings, who came equipped, as a species, with the means of shutting each other out" (168). Thinking of humans in species terms means a painful reckoning with the trade-offs of human complexity; "the most primeval divide in creation" (96) is among humans, rather than humans and nature. The novel's trajectory, however, offsets the seeming valuation of animal *Umwelt* over an impoverished human one by augmenting Piya's evolutionist endorsement of animal world-making with a literary sensibility, embodied in Kanai's gift to her of a translation of Fokir's recitation of the Bon Bibi myth. In other words, a literary perspective supplements the biological one to connect these *Umwelten*—in doing so, it may itself constitute a milieu, a middle between worlds.

The novel makes literature's capacity for rhythmic, temporal oscillation part of its presentation of a broader human milieu as fundamentally narrative in structure; Ghosh suggests that animal worlds need narrative forms to be made perceptible, especially at species scale. The novel's characters all eventually conceptualize humans as one species among many, thinking in temporal terms that register oscillation between individual and systems analysis, between absorptive stasis and sweeping compression. Ghosh's novel, its omniscient narrator, and its characters are explicitly concerned with the way the worlded experience of the present contains a deep past. Early in the novel, the narrator provides snippets of social and ecological history of the region, complemented by the attempts of characters themselves to generate historical narratives. Nirmal offers the most complex and most explicitly literary meditations on scale in his diary, excerpts of which are reproduced, as if translated by Kanai, in the body of *The Hungry Tide*. For Nirmal, the idea of the deep past is integrated with images of reading and especially of translation. Nirmal's diary is a hybrid historical document (the kind of text that realism has long associated with the "authenticating" reproduction of written documents from Samuel Richardson's novel *Pamela* [1740] onward). Nirmal's text initially aims to present facts about the Sundarbans—Nirmal's wife, trying to keep her dreamy husband busy, asks him to write it up as a brochure before it takes on a life of its own. Nirmal never renounces his commitment to faithful documentation from the historically lofty perspective of a bookish and conventionally well-informed cosmopolitan participant-observer, and his diary includes many moments of historically oriented synthesis. But it also enfolds other literary modes, from Nirmal's own lyrical description of landscape to excerpts from Rilke's meditations on animals as indices of human alienation. Kanai, who is given this diary many years after his uncle's death, reads it (in Bengali) during the novel's present-day time. Along with him—but also not with him, because it is translated—the reader experiences this past unfold in the present time of reading, dilating the present and presenting numerous perspectives on the past by aligning multiple texts with divergent attitudes toward history.

As I've suggested, Rilke's poems are key to how the novel both dilates time and highlights the concept of translation, which it renders as central to ecological thinking. As Ghosh explains in the acknowledgments section, he presents the text of the poems as multiply translated, primarily using a 1977 English translation, while Nirmal quotes translations published in Bangla in the late 1960s. The Rilke excerpts always appear at the ends of chapters in which the diary is excerpted; they function as something like the opposite of punctuated equilibria, absorptive non-events that shift the frame of perception around what has just been narrated. Such moments require a different pace and readerly orientation because they take lyric rather than narrative form, calling attention to the materiality of the text on the page as well as its translatedness. With Cheah, I would agree that "the interruptive reading experience" produced by these multiple, embedded diegetic modes "suggests that there is something deeper than the values of secular modernity according to which the cosmopolitan middle-class characters process their immediate perceptual experience."⁵⁹ Protracting the time of reading, rather than compressing it, as in synoptic historical narrative, these excerpts suggest the need for multiple epistemologies and temporalities of knowing, especially of knowing the limits of knowledge.

Nirmal's diary documents his transformation from the resolute secularity of traditional Marxism, where religion is false consciousness, to a more open-ended view that values the myths local to the Sundarbans, myths that he reads printed in a verse form readable as prose and poetry, that depend upon Hindu and Muslim traditions, and that Kanai later translates into English for Piya after she hears Fokir sing the legend of Bon Bibi orally. As Nirmal comes to appreciate myth, he imagines that he will become a teacher in Marijamphi, where he will show that

> there's a lot . . . in common between myth and geology. Look at the size of their heroes, how immense they are—heavenly deities on the one hand, and on the other the titanic stirrings of the earth itself—both equally otherworldly, equally remote from us. Then here is the way in which the plots go round and round in both kinds of story, so that every episode is both a beginning and an end and every outcome leads to others. And then, of course, there is the scale of time—yugas and epochs, Kaliyuga and the Quaternary. And yet—mind this!—in both, these vast durations are telescoped in such a way to permit the telling of a story. (192)

Nirmal's awareness of how textual forms reflect the physical earth sharpens his commitment to the political uprising at Marijamphi and shapes his own narrative, even as it constitutes a kind of translation between discourses. This is not necessarily to say that the novel either succeeds or fails in reconciling "epochal, geological [or mythic] time" with the temporality of the individual life. Rather, we see the consequences of Nirmal's efforts to think and even teach this orientation toward the "massive, imperceptible, and dispersed qualities" of the Anthropocene from a situated perspective. Yes, his desire to think this way is partly a utopian fantasy, but it also constitutes an attempt to grapple with environmental conditions in the indirect terms of translation. Meanwhile, he encounters numerous versions of the local, syncretic Bon Bibi legend. Many of the inhabitants of the Sundarbans of the novel, Cheah suggests, make sense of their precarity through myth that "figures time's otherness as the power of gods and deities." The myth shapes indigenous ecological sensibilities that are meant to complement, or perhaps *translate* to, the evolutionary epistemology advocated by Piya and reflected in her GPS record (yet another of the novel's interwoven texts). By constellating multiple epistemologies of population through deep time, the novel may not suggest that any one is adequate, yet it asks how they gain from encounter with one another.

Kanai emulates his uncle when writing a final message to Piya, with whom he has fallen in love despite her preference for Fokir. Reluctantly, Kanai presents her with his own translation of the Bon Bibi myth as Fokir has sung it aloud. He follows it with yet more Rilke:

> Look, we don't love like flowers
> With only one season behind us; when we love
> A sap older than memory arises in our arms. O girl,
> It's like this: inside us we haven't loved just some one
> In the future, but a fermenting tribe; not just one
> Child, but fathers, cradled inside us like ruins
> Of mountains, the dry riverbed
> Of former mothers, yes, and all that
> Soundless landscape under its clouded
> or clear destiny—girl, all this came before you. (298)

The novel embeds within its own *récit* an ancient myth, local history, a lengthy rhyming ballad, and a poem eroticizing the *longue durée*. *The Hungry Tide* compiles many epistemic strategies, reckoning in an explicitly literary mode with being the lived experience of being a species under threat.

The novel's denouement involves a storm that threatens the lives of its diverse cast of characters, including its animals, like the tiger Piya sees clinging to a tree, and emphasizing common vulnerability without erasing distinction. Yet to focus on the event as such would be to deemphasize the fate of the texts that offered multiple epistemic orientations. Nirmal's diary is ultimately washed away in the crisis of a fatal storm. A precious object, it floats away and sinks in the space of a few lines. This comes even after the effects of time have worn it away even before it reaches Kanai's hands: "In places there was much crossing out and filling in, and the words often spilled into the thin margin. Despite the many layers of plastic, the paper was covered with damp spots. In some places the ink had begun to fade" (72). The destruction of both texts in the storm suggests the material fragility of the human voices that can bring perspective to life at species scale. Human narratives are only written and only endure under certain material, environmentally determined conditions, which can too easily not be met. And yet, by calling particular attention to the efforts of cosmopolitan figures like Nirmal, and in the next generation, Kanai and Piya, to navigate this threatening and threatened space through these fragile, translated narratives, the novel highlights the enriched perspective on multispecies living offered by a literary refraction of population science.

3. THE SENTIENT CITY

A fox streaks through London's National Theatre in *Happiness*, as if encapsulating the need for high art to accommodate animal activity. But rather like Ghosh, Aminatta Forna has downplayed her own novel's ecological intervention. In an essay titled "On *Happiness*," Forna identifies her central concern as a critique of the eurocentrism of the concept of trauma. Her novel, she argues, uses "the allegorical significance of the natural world" to depict human capacities for resilience.[60] It is a brief comment suggesting that the novel's interest in the cultural construction of human experience is illuminated by its depiction of the natural world's animal populations as manipulated by culturally exclusionary human values. Forna makes it sound like the novel's interest in the plight of urban foxes in an increasingly xenophobic London has a straightforwardly diagnostic function, heightening the novel's political intervention by using human-animal relationships to index differential levels of political inclusion across categories of race. Indeed, the politicization of liminal animals cuts both ways, with wildlife biologists describing the prevalence of red foxes in Britain in terms of "immigration" and "colonization."[61] The novel's representation of multispecies London, as well as zooming among spaces from Ghana to Iraq to Sarajevo to New England, seems clearly to show Forna's commitment to what Mukoma wa Ngugi terms her "rooted transnationalism."[62] This commitment comes through most clearly though the novel's concluding emphasis on the value of resilience, which evokes a humanistic, optimistic neoliberalism.

But metonymy is at least as apt as allegory as an account of the novel's style, as Molly MacVeagh argues.[63] *Happiness* makes animals participants in city life; they do not live in a separate representational plane. As O'Key notes, the novel's vision of a rewilded London affirms an "internationalism" that becomes "a wider ethics of co-existence."[64] Forna is invested in demonstrating the value of the keen attention an attuned human might pay to the animals themselves.

Cities may be what humans make, with the kind of freedom in species-being Marx associates with animal functions (eating, drinking, dwelling).[65] But they are never exclusively human. In a 2018 essay, "Wilder Things: Modern Life Among the Foxes and Coyotes," Forna argues for approaching the liminal animals who live on the margins of cities and suburbs with a certain degree of anthropocentrism. "Those of us who find beauty in urban foxes do so for the same reason their presence provokes anger in so many, we admire and envy the foxes for their defiance, for choosing freedom over safety," she writes. Or, "Whenever I see the vixen or her cubs I stop whatever I am doing and I watch. I think unabashedly of love. I love them for their gift of wildness and for bringing it to the city, to me in my garden, for the determination with which they face the challenge of survival. For their beauty. I like the way they ruffle the surface of life in the city. A plastic bag floating on a still lake is the sullying fingerprint of man on nature. A fox in the city is nature's act of resistance."[66] For all that the foxes' "value" is rendered in human terms, their prevalence presages a total human extinction Forna is content to romanticize. If these statements risk rendering foxes as exemplary political subjects, they also demonstrate relative indifference to human exceptionalism. This indifference reflects the curiously reticent stance of Forna's self-presentation in the essay. Not much of her is revealed except a commitment to patient observation over time.

Both the essay and *Happiness* demonstrate, in Ernest Dominic Cole's words, an interest in "repositioning animals to a state of coexistence with humans." MacVeagh, building on such a reading, shows that Forna reworks coexistence through her style, prioritizing description over plot to highlight "shifting relations of material objects generally rendered subordinate to character psychology," and reversing the value attached to these categories in order to highlight the "uncertainties of everyday life."[67] I argue that animals' milieus are central to this project; Forna's novel is fascinated by what it is like for humans to endorse this decentering viewpoint, ultimately generating ambivalence toward the very markers of human world-makings on which careful perception, tracking, and advocacy of animal populations depends. Throughout, a non-exclusionary understanding of sentience serves as a model for narrative form even though the novel remains invested in human activities. Rather than attempt to enter the "bubble" of an animal's experience, the novel assumes the coherence of London's multispecies milieu—where *Umwelten* interact—as the condition of its narrative possibility.

Happiness maps a multiethnic, multispecies London by tracking the pathways or territories of two humans who represent distinct disciplines and epistemologies. Jean Turane, a white American wildlife biologist, tracks urban foxes. She also occasionally and ineffectively enters the public sphere to defend their right to exist in the city. She is deeply committed to seeing not only foxes but humans as members of populations. Attila Asare, a Black Ghanaian psychiatrist who trained in England, specializes in "trauma in civilian populations" (117). He occasionally speaks publicly to contest a eurocentric concept of trauma that pathologizes people of color. He also represents a more cosmopolitan lifestyle, which loosely links the arts to the project of psychiatry: he attends theater performances, adores classical and world music, reads literature, and ardently consumes a diverse range of cuisines.[68] What the two characters share, initially, is that both are more concerned with collective dynamics than with individual case studies; she tracks fox populations, and he tracks how the pathologization of groups affects individuals, especially those caught up in the legal system. Despite the narrative's substantial respect for the disciplinary knowledge produced by these two professionals, however, neither of them can produce a total image of the city, either alone or even together. That limit is not presented as a failure or signal of alienation. Rather, it creates a productively overlapping set of maps that build upon one another because they emerge from within different cognitive and affective competencies. Moreover, human species-being is central to the novel's approach to mapping London, initially following the appetitive Attila from one meal to another as he takes intermittent breaks from an exhausting range of personal and professional obligations. Nonhuman species-being is equally important. Attila and Jean collide on the Waterloo Bridge—a coincidence Jean recasts as a "low-probability event" in a "disorderly world" (61)—because Jean is recording the behavior of foxes who move about the city according to feeding and mating patterns. If Forna's London is unknowable in its totality, it becomes narratable through a fox's map first. "The fox wended its way through the pedestrians" begins the novel's portrayal of London; at the same time, this particular fox earns its definite article only because the narrator happens to track its path.

The study of animal territories in cities is itself scientifically multidisciplinary, informing several branches of animal science—wildlife ecology as well as comparative cognition.[69] As told in narrative form, it is the work of "an interested amateur," as Forna calls herself in an essay on assisting a vet in Freetown,

Sierra Leone.[70] Forna likes amateurism for its multidisciplinarity: *Happiness* maps the city in part through the movement of animals as well as by the humans who track them using various kinds of what Donna Haraway has called situated knowledge: overlapping but nonequivalent, and partial but effective. In *Staying with the Trouble*, Haraway evokes an image of entanglement that suits Forna's vision of city life as generating surprising attunements:

> Including human people, critters are in each other's presence, or better, inside each other's tubes, folds, and crevices, insides and outsides, and not quite either. The decisions and transformations so urgent in our times for learning . . . how to become less deadly, more response-able, more attuned, more capable of surprise, more able to practice the arts of living and dying well in multispecies symbiosis . . . must be made without guarantees or the expectation of harmony with those who are no oneself—and not safely other, either.[71]

Forna's kindred comfort with a simultaneously physical and cognitive notion of presence, unburdened from deconstructive concerns with metaphysics, allows her to present low-probability or "surprising" city encounters as if in direct contradiction to Jameson's concept of cognitive mapping, in which the way an individual situates themself in relation to a totality resembles "the alienated city is above all a space in which people are unable to map (in their minds) either their own positions or the urban totality in which they find themselves."[72] Forna, in contrast, presents multiple, interdependent frameworks of cognitive competency in navigating London. Much like the Dickensian city novel, *Happiness* is riven with seeming coincidence because of its focus on a network of strangers, yoked by law, food, war, urban development, gentrification, immigration, and other factors. Levine terms this the "nonhomologous" quality of urban networks in literary realism, which can present "social relationships not as static structures but as constantly superimposed, conflicting, and overlapping relational webs."[73] In a novel like *Happiness*, in which many of the network's nodes are nonhuman, a networked image of totality risks a kind of Latourian abstraction in which all things and even all concepts are material actants.[74] But Forna is resolutely specific that it is *animals' perception* within their milieu that prompts this aesthetic possibility, as when she focalizes her narration through another fox:

> The vixen stopped, raised her head and sniffed, as though she discerned some shift in the molecules of the air; the next moment she slipped sideways from the wall into the overgrown buddleia and was lost from view. (16)

The subjunctive "as though" gives rise to the imagined molecular basis of London life; the view of the vixen's *Umwelt* that prompts this narrative speculation is grounded in behavioral analysis but is not narrowly behavioristic. The coherence of the fox's worldview has primacy, shaping how subsequent, contingent events and non-events garner narrative attention.

And when the novel *does* concern events, Forna subordinates questions of international politics to consideration of interspecies collaboration. One of the novel's several subplots concerns the value of animal knowledge for tracking Attila's young nephew Tano, who has run away after immigration services erroneously displaces his family, which actually has a legal right to residency. As the characters track the child from the household into the street, the novel neither idealizes nor critiques either space as inherently safe or unsafe, perhaps because it is also uninterested in critiquing the institutions that delimit and control those spaces. Hence the *erroneous* immigration intervention; Forna avoids representing and thus having to protest a situation where immigration intervention would have been legal, just as Jean avoids any sustained engagement with police indifference to her report of violence against urban foxes. Biopolitical governance that maintains certain ecological and reproductive conditions works badly—for Forna, it fails to manage populations it purports to. The novel is far more interested, therefore, in representing the effort of making populations known or knowable than in critiquing institutional mismanagement.

Jean, a recent transplant to London who knows only an idiosyncratically fox-centric map of the city, creates another map of the runaway child's region based on her knowledge of the foxes' routes and extrapolating from fox behavior. Jean predicts that Tano will "stay close by and not just because of his mother. These'—and she indicated the markings on the map—'are all fox territories. Foxes stake out an area and then they stay in it. Why? Because that's how they sustain themselves, they know where to hunt, where to find food, water, shelter, where they feel safe from predators. The boy is no different, he's going to stay where he feels most secure. I'm guessing an area roughly this size,' and she drew a loose circle around the X where she had marked the position of the flat, overlapping several fox territories and where the streets were so tightly drawn many of the street names were abbreviated. 'This is where we start'" (84). Her approach, rooted in her disciplinary methods, is then combined with the input of a wide circle of immigrant workers from Nigeria, Ghana, and Sierra Leone, whom she's talked into spotting foxes during their night labor. The foxes' own knowledge of the city intersects productively with the humans' various approaches to collecting information. Attila is skeptical: "He had a city of eight million people, he had a lost boy and he had a team of doormen and dustmen" (104). The anaphora here suggests Attila's dismay at the city's total unmappability. But while they may be minor characters, these Dickensian "doormen and dustmen" are named, sketched with specificity, and accorded authority; their work on the periphery of the streets, at doorways, in hotels, and on the sidewalks, means that they surveil their nodes in the map, which earns them expertise. This collective work is explicitly provisional—Jean marks her map with a "loose circle" and declares "this is where we start"—an obvious indicator of an unknown but promising avenue for political reorganization. The knowledge the team possesses is much more a practice than a theory, perhaps aligned with the foxes' own territory-based approach to navigating their London. The practice is effective. Jean may fail to communicate effectively about the need for interspecies coexistence when she participates in a call-in radio show to advocate against culling urban foxes, but the crew finds the boy.

The novel's fascination with urban patterns—with seeing the city as a milieu—means that its longer plot arcs like finding Tano or Jean's short-lived career in fox PR are outweighed by fleeting interspecies incidents, which are more representative of the novel's overall narrative structure. Many chapters in *Happiness* begin with or include incidents on the Waterloo Bridge, for example, creating a sense of pattern and repetition rather than a series of coincidences. Although the novel has a vast geographical span, it grounds itself in a hyperlocal London milieu and sees where the incidents that happen there take things. This episodic form creates a series of what animal behavior science terms "incident reports." In animal behavior field research, finding the right form to document events remains a question: incident reports are a way of accounting for regular interaction between animals and informed humans, a "careful and unbiased recording of unanticipated and rare events, followed by collation and an attempt at systematic analysis."[75] This form responds to long-standing complaints that field researchers privilege anecdotal, naïve, or biased observations. In *Happiness*, these incident reports are the novel's formalization of the idea of milieu. Many of these interspecies incidents are narrated not through Jean's perspective (though she is the author of many incident reports) but Attila's. Admittedly, Attila has no professional interest in animals and in fact often in his professional life propounds an anthropocentric theory of "what it is to be human"

(260) that suggests a distinctive dignity and self-awareness. Still, he is a habitual and generous observer of animals: over the course of the novel he notices many dogs, squirrels, several kinds of bird (one poops on him), a seal, a ladybug, a gecko, ants, and some disappointing megafauna at the London Zoo. Sometimes they might notice him back: "in the road, the opalescent eye shine of an animal" (64). Other incident reports forgo a human focalizer and are organized around unwittingly shared food sources; it is the rise of fast food that (Jean explains to Attila) makes the postmodern city such a sustaining place for some species. The narrator implements this tenet of liminal animal population biology:

> Three miles distant a dog fox crossed Waterloo Bridge. In its jaws it carried the bone of a Berkshire pork chop, the remainder of which rested, along with a side order of sauteed mushrooms, the Dorset crab starter and a quantity of decent claret, in the belly of a fund manager now headed due west in the back of a cab. The fox climbed the stairs to the open terraces of the National Theatre until it reached the third level where it jumped onto one of the raised flower beds, sniffed at the earth and dug a shallow hole into which it dropped the bone. (96)

In this dispersed assemblage of relations, none of the major human characters "three miles distant" serves as witness. Instead, animal behavior dictates narrative attention, creating a descriptive dilation that, as in similar moments throughout, serves formally to validate Jean's explanation for how urban wildlife came to have its liminal status.

Despite their status as "evidence" for an explicit argument, these incidents contribute to the novel's determination to decenter human characters and remap London according to an animal's priorities. The most striking example is prompted by a small child—who is not a named character—observing a falcon from inside an upper-story restaurant in the Shard: "Once or twice a wing dipped as if the bird was a tightrope walker who had momentarily lost and regained balance.... The child blinked and watched. She did not try to tell her parents. She stood as still as the hovering bird. Then the bird was gone" (86). Another moment of static fascination, this scene refuses a sublime or allegorical recuperation, perhaps because this child is even more ephemeral a character than the falcon is. But the appearance of the subjunctive also grants an artistic quality to the animal's navigation of the wind. It turns out that the falcon (now worthy of the definite article) is not gone, because the narrative follows it for several pages before using its path to gradually track back down its main characters. Not unlike the far shorter, fox-centered narrative incidents, this one more extensively concerns the way an animal's milieu re-territorializes the city. As it does so, its dilation of narrative time gives priority to the animal's own behavioral rhythm as it inhabits its perceptual world:

> Six hundred feet below a pigeon departed the world. The pigeon, which had been pecking at the discarded crust of a pasty from the West Cornwall Pasty Company booth by platform six in the station, was flying away with a piece of pastry in its beak when it was hit at two hundred miles an hour by the falcon and promptly fell to earth to be snatched back up in the raptor's claws a split second later.
>
> The falcon carried the pigeon eastwards, parallel to the riverbank, over the city's municipal buildings in the direction off Tower Bridge, where it turned south. Somewhere in this first twenty seconds of flight the heart of the pigeon stopped beating. A drop of dark blood fell to earth from the pigeon's breast, down it went, the drop of liquid pushed into new shapes by the rush of air. The falcon flew until it arrived at the abandoned gasworks on the Old Kent Road where it perched on a metal strut and with its beak tore open the pigeon's heart.
>
> Attila looked down. A drop hit the pavement. He tilted his face to the sky but he felt nothing. (87)

Fast food on the wing maps London; even as it offers spatial markers from a conventionally human-centered cartography, the passage is fascinated with the novelty and uncertainty of this assemblage of birds, a crust, wind, and blood—the refusal to specify when in a twenty-second span the heart stopped beating, and the "new shapes" of anonymous pigeon blood pushed through the air suggest that something rather unpredictable and perhaps beautiful has come into being—a Deleuzian moment, perhaps. The narrator's descriptive vagueness alongside its precision at least partly counteracts the possibility of reading allegorically (as index of capitalist entanglement and exploitation in the neoliberal world city) the drop that catches Attila's notice, and the beak that tears the heart.

This passage functions primarily as a description of actions, a brief parataxis accelerating the connective descent ("down it went"). The narrative refuses subjectivizing depictions of animal consciousness except via the subjunctive and often casts animal minds in biologistic terms. Starting a chapter on Waterloo Bridge yet again, the narrator reports, "The fox was headed south in the direction of its den, but the fox would not return to its den this night, or the night after, or the night after that. The human shouts and cries in the early evening had disturbed a fragile sense of safety, triggering a survival impulse in the animal's amygdala in the recesses of the temporal lobe" (214). And it is not only animal minds that are neurologized: nearby, a little later, "On the far side of the bridge, out of nowhere, [Attila] tripped and fell. One moment he was upright, the next he was on his hands and knees. A bolt of pain shot through his body as his knee hit the pavement. He remained on all fours in the moments it took his brain to reconfigure what had happened to his body" (235). This moment of being suddenly and briefly a quadruped also calls attention (in a rather vague way) to Attila's neurological makeup.

This orientation toward behavior affirms Attila's orientation to psychiatric practice, which does not overemphasize subjective experience. He is known as a direct speaker, and he offers numerous reflections on the value of humans' ability to adapt to conditions of vulnerability, and on change rather than damage as the result of trauma. Toward the end of the novel when he gives a speech to the British Psychiatric Association, he insists that "people owned the narrative of their own lives, it did not belong to the professionals" (290); to be human, in his view, is to be resilient, an avowed value that, as MacVeagh keenly observes, is partly undercut by the novel's own lack of emphasis on consciousness as a particularly privileged category for accounting for how bodies occupy space. After all, it is only shortly before having this thought that Attila contends with the impending death of his former colleague Rosie from Alzheimer's. Even as he thinks of the burden of self-awareness about the inevitability of suffering as something "all humans possessed, not only in the moment of it happening but for every day of their lives," he admits that "Rosie's condition at least spared her that" (278). Even if, in his public speech, Attila both avows and exhibits an individual capacity for self-reflection, the novel's form suggests ambivalence toward that virtue as only one facet of human worldedness.

Attila trails off at the end of his speech, letting the tacitness of the given world take over from the explicitness of polemic: "all of the weakness is not in them, those who live through the agony, who survive and transform into something else, but in others too. Here....' He swept out an arm, to take in the room, the building, the city, and what lay beyond. The whole of it" (305). Rewriting the finitude of "resilience" as vulnerability, he seems to shift what "others" he includes, coming closer to Jean's populationist and non-individualist awe for "nature's immeasurable adaptability" (100). Not only, then, is it important that he is nonprofessionally attuned to the animals he comes across, but it also matters that he is associated with a kind of anti-psychologism that embraces the characterization of humans as "herd animals" (193). By valuing the potential for change and resilience, he rejects the deep pain, inaccessible truth of the self, and need for narrative excavation ascribed to human survivors of trauma and productively dehumanizes his defense of the cohesive worldview even of those (human or animal) who have suffered.

4. CONCLUSION

If the idea of the "Anthropocene" obscures multispecies interactions, these novels suggest that the Anthropocene only becomes mentionable when a multispecies milieu—a world that coordinates many overlapping *Umwelten*, territories, and local histories—is made imaginable. By the end of *Happiness*, Jean "is considering a study of some sort, the form of which is yet to come to her, maybe some record just for herself" (308); it is the question of form that remains unanswered for Jean, and where Forna's novel makes a clear commitment to the integrity of animals' milieu as a foundation for perceiving a shared world. In *The Hungry Tide*, too, Piya is in the process of developing a new project: founding a trust in Fokir's memory that will sponsor scientific research grounded in multispecies justice (a project that figures in the novel's quasi-sequel, *Gun Island*). For both scientists, their work demands that they understand the spatial, temporal, and historical complexity of a region shaped by the animal-centered logic of territory. For Jean and Piya, encountering humanistic frameworks that emphasize both the situated contingencies of human consciousness and the complexity of human population renews their commitment to studying animal lives. In neither case does the project undertaken constitute radical environmental activism; at most it perpetuates a shift in perception that motivates further daily labors of observation. Committing their lives to the study of animals constitutes, for them, a necessary if all too preliminary move in clarifying that the world may be shaped by human demands, but it is known, felt, and experienced as milieu by many species.

In both novels, realism does not turn away from the givenness of the world, the concern that has driven so much resistance to this form's liberal and neoliberal predilections. If it is quite literally human world-making that the very idea of the "Anthropocene" evokes, realism can make animal milieus appear as intersecting, integrated, multiple, and rich. What mind science seeks to explain, here, finds a narrative answer. Realist narrative proposes a common world. These contemporary explorations of third-person realism's traditional strengths redistribute not only the sensible but sentience itself.

Coda

Milieu: A Creaturely Theory of the Contemporary Novel offers a comparative approach to contemporary fiction, documenting narrative patterns that reflect some highly specific cultural predicaments for zoo tigers, pet dogs, American mountain lions, and London foxes. This book also, more basically, acknowledges that global fiction now simply features "*more* dogs and frogs and bears and chickens and . . . whatever!" (to quote the Muppets) than ever before.[1] And finally, this book claims that fiction's undeniably proliferating animals prompt a broader reckoning with the creatureliness of our own reading.

Sigrid Nunez uses the phrase "a book you read with your skin" to describe her narrator's repulsion at the euthanasia of dogs in *Disgrace*, dogs kept in state-sponsored captivity and put to death. The phrase also accounts for how she bristles at *Disgrace*'s own willing treatment of dogs' lives as expendable.[2] For the sensitive reader, many novels featuring animals can prompt visceral reactions of grief and disgust at pervasive violence toward abjected bodies. While acknowledging the negative force of these images, which often have an allegorical thrust, I have tried to showcase the far wider range of affective orientations afforded by contemporary fiction's efforts to recognize and instantiate a multispecies milieu. I have emphasized that allegory is a key strategy in contemporary fiction because it so neatly captures the logic of biopolitics, itself a logic of capture. But as a robustly conceptual frame, it often struggles to register how embodied creaturely lives are not fully constituted by that system; it tends to reproduce the subsumption of bodies it sets out to analyze. Moreover, as a tool of literary criticism, allegory tends ultimately to emphasize the distinctive knowingness, moral authority, and even salvific intervention of the critic, which comes to resemble a little too strongly the epistemic authority of Foucault's pastoral sovereign. How can we reopen allegoresis to a creaturely milieu? I suggest that contemporary fiction's aesthetics of milieu avoids the conceptual aporias that underwrite the melancholic form of allegory, which insists on a rift between humans and other animals, between systems and bodies.

In contrast, milieu in its ethological origins aligns with affect; as such, noticing it often means deferring the indexical rhythm of critique and reframing what we understand perception to be. Milieu emerges through narrative voice, from metalepsis, to lyricism, to repetition, to the subjunctive: the affective dimensions of these formal techniques emphasize the interdependence of human creatureliness with that of other living beings. In other words, *because* milieu is a theory of immanent, emergent, and relational embodied perception, it is best discerned through and as style. Milieu is ultimately a formal concept that demonstrates the value of formalism even in a postcolonial and globalized context—form not as fragmentation, but rather, form as world-making.

"A book you read with your skin": Nunez's phrase emphasizes that reading is an embodied experience, with phenomenological effects that may or may not rise to the level of decisive moral evaluation or real-world action. Reading in this way is also not equivalent to sympathizing with a nonhuman sufferer—not equivalent to feeling on behalf. I have sought to account rigorously for what the novel can (and cannot) contribute to questions about multispecies justice and interspecies care in a period of ecological catastrophe. Reading a novel is not environmental activism, and many critics have expressed skepticism that "the novel"—especially when it is an individualistic form—has any capacity to foster collective political engagement.[3] But reframing what individuality is like for a human animal might, I would propose, be a step toward thinking at species scale—how it feels to be a product of convergent processes that are simultaneously biological and social, generating experiences that might look individual but are also, in certain ways, collective.[4] This reframing, in other words, might be a step toward disavowing self-sovereignty and the damage that frame has done. Such a step is not sufficient—hence my cautious language—but I would argue that it is necessary, and that literary criticism offers some crucial tools.

By recognizing that sentience is a widely distributed property in the living world, fiction reimagines its own ability to constitute a world and to offer a *theory* of a world. The narratives I have examined redistribute what counts as, in Jacques Rancière's words, "the perceptible, the thinkable, the feasible."[5] As milieus in themselves, novels may be understood to resonate as well as refer, soliciting the creatureliness of human sentience, reframing readers' awareness of their own environmental embeddedness—redirecting attention and perhaps also doing what we conventionally call raising awareness. The period that clinched the cultural prestige of the novel coincided with the rise of cognitive science and comparative cognition; demonstrations of how fictional worlds model real-life human cognition and develop the feeling of realness by critics like Elaine Scarry, Elaine Auyoung, Suzanne Keen, and Blakey Vermeule (among many others) are a path noticed, though not taken, in this book. For these critics, when a novel models embodied knowing, its worldedness emerges relationally through the embodied process of being read. Nathan Snaza enumerates the many possible sensory modalities and affective pathways of response in the situation of reading: "Readers are not simply responding to a text via a sense of themselves as instances of identity categories: they also respond to an entire affective scene of contact among their body, a material and semiotic text, and the ensemble of human and nonhuman agencies affecting them at every moment, even if those touchings do not appear to their consciousness."[6] From the tactile to the olfactory to matters of mood, these modes of reading are at once sociocultural and, at the same time, materially embodied; while these phenomenal states cannot be fully dissociated from or be considered *prior* to the cultural and political conditions that give rise to these identity categories, they are also not equivalent to feeling like that kind of self.

I remain convinced that literary representations of animal sentience should matter to any reader invested how novels work because recognizing intimacies among species prompts these writers to reconfigure the character spaces and the environments of the human. As contemporary fiction grapples with humans as emergent organisms that participate socially in a biotic context with other living creatures, it centers the creatureliness of literary style. Throughout, I have emphasized the impersonal possibilities of first-person narration, the multispecies imaginary of collective narration, and the valuably evasive epistemology of free indirect discourse. I have also noted the prevalence in animal novels of metalepsis, which permits narratives to slip among these modes. Each voice or movement among voices affords distinctive sense-methods for grasping a milieu through their relationships to tone, distribution of attention, and other markers of style. At the same time, I have suggested that anyone interested in animal sentience might find it worthwhile to consider narrative techniques. Through this approach, narrative offers a theoretically significant answer to a question at the intersections of ecocriticism, animal studies, feminist studies, critical race studies, and comparative cognition: What does it mean to recognize, know about, and care about what remain in some ways "other" worlds?

"A book you read with your skin": now in a more neutral, intimate, yet impersonal key. Perhaps the most significant consequence of reimagining the novel as milieu is the decentering of human protagonists, even in first-person fiction. While other critics have documented the precipitous rise of first-person narration in contemporary fiction by the end of the twentieth century, I stress that the formal complexity of texts narrated by *creatures* means that they resist the self-absorption we might assume underpins the first person.[7] This observation reinflects David Herman's provocative claim that narrative operates at the "meso-scale," which is "optimally calibrated for person-level, that is, human-scale, events."[8] Even as these texts do not refuse the phenomenological scale of personhood, they deflate the distinctiveness of being a human individual by reframing our capacities for perception in species terms, returning to what, for Catherine Gallagher, the eighteenth-century novel already endorsed: that "the human referent of the text was a generalization about . . . a 'species.'"[9]

With limited faith in the significance of *any* individual of any species in an era of incipient climate emergency, these novels nonetheless embrace the textured specificity, finitude, and sometimes even agency of a localized but no longer "individual" sentience. Indeed, their approaches to narration experiment with rendering sentience *impersonal* by reframing the centeredness of inhabiting a particular sensorium. The milieu affords a responsive zone for feeling, thinking, and doing, with less of the human self-regard the novel has often been taking to affirm. Put differently, this distinctively literary vision recognizes how sentience shapes, and is shaped by, our multispecies world.

NOTES

Introduction

1. Cusk, *Outline*, 201. On Cusk's rejection of the characterological center as the site of "thought"—on character as itself an obstruction—see Bewes, *Free Indirect*, 1–2.

2. On caring affection, see Puig de la Bellacasa, *Matters of Care*, especially her discussion of Donna Haraway's grounding commitments (90). For Haraway's important term "companion species," see *The Companion Species Manifesto*, which complicates claims that present human-animal domestic alliances in terms of domination.

3. Canguilhem, "The Living and Its Milieu," 8. In Amanda Jo Goldstein's summation, the concept "instantiates a view from and toward a living center for whom *this* set of factors, among the 'anonymity of elements and universal movements,' impose this milieu" (*Sweet Science*, 61). On being in the middle, see Stengers, Massumi, and Manning, "History Through the Middle." Philosopher Alva Noë writes, "Consciousness is not something that happens inside of us ... but something we do or make, and achievement of the whole animal in its environmental context" (*Out of Our Heads*, 10). On literary form as such an environment for thought, see Kramnick, *Paper Minds*, esp. 4–11.

4. In historian of science Evan Thompson's words, "Mental life is also bodily life and is situated in the world (*Biology, Phenomenology, and the Sciences of Mind*, viii). In environmental psychology, this cluster of values is termed 4EA: embedded, extended, enactive, and affective; see Newen, de Bruin, and Gallagher, *The Oxford Handbook of 4E Cognition*. On the integrative dimensionality of "situated" or "involved" knowledge, see Haraway, *When Species Meet*, 16, 289 and Puig de la Bellacasa, *Matters of Care*, 93. "Sentience" can potentially be construed as an anthropocentric measure of animal

significance; for instance, see Holland, *an/other*, 94. I address this issue by further examining the formal structure of the term "world"—glossed as milieu—as an inherently aesthetic approach to sentience.

5. See Brilmyer, *The Science of Character*, 2, pointing out that John Stuart Mill proposed a science of ethology centered on the idea of human character as emerging in a milieu, even though this idea did not develop further in the nineteenth-century sciences. I am indebted to Brilmyer's book for galvanizing my thinking about these issues at a pivotal moment.

6. Schuller, *The Biopolitics of Feeling*, 11. In Schuller's account, an obsession with the idea of different organisms as having different levels of impressibility by their environment was what made milieu an enabling concept for scientific racism.

7. Armstrong, *How Novels Think*, 7. For a view similar to Armstrong's of how novels consolidate individuality, see also Ho, *Nation and Citizenship*, 3.

8. See Hale, *The Novel and the New Ethics*: encounters with otherness are "made possible through the reader's phenomenological experience with modes of ontological otherness that is credited to narrative form," including "otherness within . . . the felt struggle between rational modes of knowledge and affective states of being" (5, 6). Where Hale sees a "return to character" in contemporary fiction along phenomenological lines, I would emphasize something Hale notes rather briefly—that "character" comes to mean something different in animal-led fictions.

9. See Kramnick, *Paper Minds*, 12.

10. Beer, *Darwin's Plots*, 233, 224.

11. Eliot, *Middlemarch*, 194.

12. For other multispecies readings of this passage, see Brilmyer, *Science of Character*, 75; and Kreilkamp, *Minor Creatures*, 26–27, 96.

13. Nancy Yousef argues that the tone of this posthuman gesture enacts the very distractions it laments: "The image of the unsensed world—grass growing, small animal hearts beating, etc.—is indeed extraordinary, but both the temptation to be dazzled by the narrator's picture of epistemological constraint and the resources to recognize it as such and return to the more commonplace inadequacies from which it distracts are given in the structure of the novel as a whole" (*Aesthetic Commonplace*, 108).

14. Not dissimilarly, recent work on modernism's least character-driven texts, like Virginia Woolf's *The Waves* (1931), contests the notion that it makes a decisively inward turn by examining how writers explored phenomenological modes resistant to depth-psychological revelation. See Weil, "Afterword," in *Beastly Modernisms*, for a compelling discussion of Virginia Woolf's engagement with phenomenology, especially in *The Waves*, as a project that "is of and about the animality that feels and sees and smells and hears and desires, and without which there would be no expression, even as it may have no singular face or image that we recognise as animal" (289).

15. As Amy M. King argues (in the relevantly titled volume *Narrative Middles*), realist fiction often "lingers and dilates" in the "reverent attention" evoked by the "stillness of descriptive pause" that unites the practice of nineteenth-century natural history to

the novel form ("Dilatory Description and the Pleasures of Accumulation," 163). Extending the descriptive rhythms of the village novels that interest King, McGregor's novel is almost all reverent pause.

16. Anna Kornbluh argues that metalepsis signals the epistemic freefall of omnicrisis; see Kornbluh, "Us Too." My approach ultimately finds metalepsis more productive despite this instability because it highlights how voice is an environment for sentience.

17. Genette, *Narrative Discourse*, 236.

18. McGregor, *Reservoir 13*, 110. Nicholas Dames, calling *Reservoir 13* "one of the century's very few perfect novels," points out that its ultimate interest is in not in character but in "care systems: their procedures and rules, their impersonality, their mundanity and their slow tempi, their fragility when their inhabitants start to withdraw their consent to them, or even their attention" ("Review of John McGregor"). I am grateful to Andrew H. Miller for calling my attention to this novel; clearly this novel presents special attractions for Victorianists trained on novels written at village scale.

19. As Heather Houser argues, contemporary fiction often depicts multispecies entanglements as perceptible through felt experience rather than scientific and institutionally embedded knowledge practices; see *Ecosickness*, 1–15. On the novel's enduring ethical vision of the form itself as oriented toward otherness, see Hale: postmodernist accounts of the novel, she argues, "conceiv[e] of the otherness of narrative as an impersonal location for the communication of ethical value" (*The Novel and the New Ethics*, 6).

20. In Katherine McKittrick's words, figurative language tends to deemphasize the "material, concrete, grounded" qualities of "physical-material space" and "removes social actors from the production of space and other infrastructures" (*Dear Science*, 10).

21. This does not mean that fiction elevates the biological over the political. Milieus can be deeply and politically "unhealthy," as Stengers points out (*Another Science Is Possible*, 140).

22. For particularly influential accounts of petkeeping, see Haraway, *The Companion Species Manifesto*, 33, and *When Species Meet*; as well as more historical pieces including Tuan, *Dominance and Affection*; Ritvo, *Animal Estate*; and Shell, "The Family Pet."

23. See Lamarck, *Philosophia Zoologique*, esp. 144.

24. See Comte, *Positive Philosophy*; Comte's work brought the term to Anglophone audiences, including George Eliot.

25. See especially Herman's discussion of multiple disciplinary approaches to registering animal minds in *Narratology Beyond the Human*, 206–8.

26. von Uexküll, "A Theory of Meaning," in *Foray into the Worlds*, 144.

27. Elizabeth Grosz offers a particularly pointed defense of the ways von Uexküll's approach shows how biological life predicates artistic making: "What is perhaps . . . most significant about Uexküll's claims is his understanding that the most basic problem of biology is fundamentally a problem of design, the design of organisms" (*Becoming Undone*, 173).

28. Noë, *Out of Our Heads*, 49. See also Wolfe, *Before the Law*, 70.

29. Fleissner, *Maladies of the Will*, 145.

30. Andrews, *How to Study Animal Minds*, 11.

31. Powell, *Contingency and Convergence*, 189, 188. I am grateful to Powell for meeting with me to discuss her approach. Powell's use of von Uexküll's term answers a call from Marc Bekoff and Dale Jamison in the mid-1990s for more evolutionarily oriented accounts of comparative cognition in their brief history of the field; see Bekoff and Jamison, "On Aims and Methods of Cognitive Ethology."

32. Cheah, *What Is a World?*, 97.

33. See Agamben's discussion of bare life immediately before he introduces von Uexküll's work in *The Open*, 38. See also the "absolutely nonanthropocentric" valuation of von Uexküll in Deleuze and Guattari, *A Thousand Plateaus*, 39–40; and Grosz, *Becoming Undone*, 173–86.

34. Agamben, *The Open*, 39.

35. See Derrida, *Aporias*, 35. I further discuss this dimension of Heidegger's argument, and Derrida's response, in Chapter 2. Cheah uses Heidegger's understanding of humans' unique comprehension of temporality to defend worlding as "the opening of a world, our propulsion into a world by the giving and coming of time—is that which is inhuman." He argues that "it is from this vantage point that we can better understand the relations between different living and non-living forms . . . without privileging one over the other," an effort he marks as challenging to sustain ("Worlding Literature," 108). Cheah remains committed to the representation of a transcendental or spiritual register for relation.

36. Traisnel, *Capture*, 195.

37. Canguilhem, "The Living and Its Milieu," 19.

38. For a treatment of the two terms as equivalent, see Traisnel, *Capture*, 156–57.

39. Oliver, *Earth & World*, 4.

40. Canguilhem, "The Living and Its Milieu," 120.

41. See Wynter, "Towards the Sociogenic Principle."

42. Felski, *The Limits of Critique*, 23; and Snaza, *Animate Literacies*, 99. I am thinking, like Snaza prepares to do here, of Eve Kosofsky Sedgwick's phrase "the ecology of knowing" in *Touching Feeling*, 145. See also Kramnick, *Criticism and Truth*: "Method is the steady ground for a worldliness that has no limits at all" (29).

43. Nagel, "What Is It Like to Be a Bat?," 440.

44. Nagel, "What Is It Like to Be a Bat?," 440. On moving beyond privative models of animal cognition, see Mikhalevich, "Simplicity and Cognitive Models"; and Fitzpatrick, "Against Morgan's Canon." These philosophers of science endorse a curative principle: in Andrews's words, "when ignoring sentience hinders the ability to generate new knowledge of animal mind and behavior, and there is potential to generate new knowledge by premising sentience, scientists ought to do so" (*How to Study Animal Minds*, 19).

45. See Wynter, "Towards the Sociogenic Principle."

46. "If the mind is what the brain does, what the brain does, is itself culturally determined through the mediation of the socialized sense of self, as well as of the 'social' situation in which this self is placed" (Wynter, "Towards the Sociogenic Principle," 37).

McKittrick uses Wynter's interest in the sociogenic principle to argue for an affective revision of Black consciousness as an "intimate, psychic, affective way of being that informs and unfolds into practical and cooperative modes of making liberation" (*Dear Science*, 69).

47. As Herman argues, "narrative affords an environment for *Umwelt* exploration by means of story-enabled attributions of mental states and dispositions to intelligent agents inhabiting fundamentally other worlds" (*Narratology Beyond the Human*, 42).

48. This quotation is taken from Susan Bernofsky's translation of an excerpt from von Uexküll's *Environment and Inner World of the Animals* that was included in her translation of Kafka, *Metamorphosis*, 96–97.

49. On narrative as a decolonial method for questions of materiality, including for Wynter, see McKittrick, *Dear Science*.

50. Rancière, "What Medium Can Mean," 35.

51. Rancière, *The Politics of Aesthetics*, 13.

52. Deleuze and Guattari, *A Thousand Plateaus*, 313.

53. Deleuze and Guattari, *A Thousand Plateaus*, 315. Caroline Levine's *Forms* poses the question of how rhythms might "organize and dis-organize the social institutions that surround them" (*Forms*, 74).

54. See Grosz, *Becoming Undone*, 183–85; and Deleuze and Guattari, *What Is Philosophy?*, 97, on animal homes as the first artworks. On the importance of their casting of *Umwelt* as immanent for resisting the potentially totalitarian uses of von Uexküll's concept, see Feiten, Holland, and Chemero, "Worlds Apart," 14.

55. Deleuze and Guattari bring together von Uexküll with Spinoza, writing that we should define a body not by its functions but by "what its affects are"—how it is influenced by and influences other bodies (*A Thousand Plateaus*, 257).

56. Wynter here addresses "Nagel's question with respect to how 'objective processes can give rise to subjective states,' as well as validates Fanon's identification of the socio-cultural objective processes that leads to the 'aberrations of affect,' of both White, non-white / non-black, anti-Black racism and Black autophobia: with these aberrations therefore common to all subjects culturally Westernized in the ethno-class terms of 'Man'" ("Towards the Sociogenic Principle").

57. Snaza, *Animate Literacies*, 95.

58. See Bradley and da Silva, "Four Theses on Aesthetics": "The world, as the totalizing onto-epistemology that is modernity's genesis, limit, and horizon, is a thoroughly aesthetic conceit. To toil within or rail against the field of representation is already to be enmeshed in the aesthetic, for it is by way of the aesthetic that the ontological ground on which we are said to stand becomes experience. In this register, Man—the *transparent I*, the universal subject who would make the world, if not just as he pleases—appears, apropos Sylvia Wynter, as none other than *homo aestheticus*."

59. Boisseron, *Afro-Dog*, 26.

60. See Smith, "Exceeding Beringia." I am grateful to Juliana Hu Pegues for this reference.

61. Million, "Epistemology," 340.

62. Glissant, *Poetics of Relation*, 28.

63. On touch as an exemplary sense for the framework of care, see Puig de la Bellacasa, *Matters of Care*, 93.

64. Stengers, *Another Science Is Possible*, 45.

65. On the exclusion of embodiment and animality in the human rights model of political belonging, see Anker, *Fictions of Dignity*.

66. For some arguments that have particularly impacted my thinking on how difficult alliances demand "suspending damage," in Eve Tuck's words ("Suspending Damage"), see Byrd, *Transit of Empire*, xv–xxxix; and Nash, *Birthing Black Mothers*.

67. Derrida, *Animal That Therefore I Am*, 25. This passage is formative for Sinha's use of the term "milieu."

68. Deleuze, *Spinoza*, 125.

69. See Wadiwel, *War Against the Animals*; and O'Key, *Creaturely Forms*, 1–2.

70. On attention to humans' phenomenal lifeworlds as contributing to critiques of cognitivism from the 1980s onward, and von Uexküll's influence, see Thompson, *Biology, Phenomenology, and the Sciences of Mind*, 15–36, 59.

71. See, for instance, Phillip Brian Harper's claim that "the African American novel itself" takes a "fundamentally allegorical form" in the twentieth century to amplify its political impact ("'Lusting After Relevance,'" 476).

72. Haraway, *Modest_Witness*, 11; Ortiz-Robles, *Literature and Animal Studies*, 1; and Vizenor, *Fugitive Poses*, 133. For Haraway, "figuration" resists capture: like milieu, it is located between things, in a middle zone, opening the human to impersonal cosmic forces, sensations, and becomings that are arguably also part of what we share with other forms of animal life. Heather Keenleyside defends figurative language like the analogy and the simile as a literary means of depicting animals, claiming that the device's core insistence on nonequivalence constitutes an animating "response to the motions of another" that reflects common, mutually responsive creaturely embodiment (*Animals and Other People*, 81).

73. Benjamin, *Origin of the German Trauerspiel*, 174.

74. Tesky, *Allegory and Violence*, 19.

75. Weheliye, *Habeus Viscus*, 1–2; Holland, *an/other*, 5.

76. Foucault, *Security, Territory, Population*, 20.

77. Foucault, *Security, Territory, Population*, 22. As DeCaroli points out, "power comes to be understood as a type of milieu: something one simultaneously inhabits and constitutes" ("Foucault's Milieu," 127).

78. DeCaroli suggests nonetheless that "it is perhaps possible, through the biological dimension of his work, to see in his writings a posthumanist inclination that resituates human social praxis within a broadened conception of the biological domain—a domain that includes the semantic milieu ("Foucault's Milieu," 138).

79. Foucault, *Security, Territory, Population*, 17, 127.

80. Foucault, *Security, Territory, Population*, 242–43.

81. Foucault, *Security, Territory, Population*, 130; Traisnel, *Capture*, 5.
82. Anker and Felski, "Introduction," in *Critique and Postcritique*, 6. See also James, *Discrepant Solace*, 36.
83. Traisnel, *Capture*, 195–96; for a similar view, though not routed through ethology, see also Davé, *Indifference*, 1–5.
84. Brilmyer argues that nineteenth-century novels that engage with ethology similarly "place[] human and nonhuman organisms on the same plane as a strategy to describe human behavior as not more rational or intentional than that of other organisms" (*The Science of Character*, 87).
85. Boxall, *Value of the Novel*, 11. This approach makes stylistic analysis core to literary critical method. See also James, *Discrepant Solace*, 34–36.
86. Hayot, *On Literary Worlds*, 30.
87. Alexander Beecroft frames this scaling as an "ecology," a term that resonates with milieu but remains mostly a metaphor that does not necessitate centering embodied relations (*Ecology of World Literature*). See, in contrast, Stengers's discussion of ecology as practice: "The problem for each practice is how to foster its own force, make present what causes practitioners to think and feel and act. But it is a problem which may also produce an experimental togetherness among practices, a dynamics of pragmatic learning of what works and how. This is the kind of active, fostering 'milieu' that practices need in order to be able to answer challenges and experiment changes, that is, to unfold their own force" ("Introductory Notes on an Ecology of Practices," 196).
88. Boxall, *Value of the Novel*, 11, 96.
89. Ganguly, *This Thing Called the World*, 218; Cheah, *What Is a World*, 2.
90. Kramnick, *Paper Minds*, 6; Levine, *Forms*, esp. 24.
91. Hayot, *On Literary Worlds*, 24, 44–45.
92. See Driscoll, "(A) Is for Animal," especially his connection between the sonic dimensions of voice to Roland Barthes's *The Rustle of Language*, where "the 'rustle' of language necessarily suspends all narrative, because it is radically synchronous and thus disrupts the diachronic, sequential nature of the sentence" (188).
93. In contrast, Anna Kornbluh's *Immediacy* laments the rise of first-person narrative in the late twentieth century as allergic to mediation. I share Kornbluh's investment in identifying literary techniques that produce these valuable categories, but admittedly my approach, routed through close reading, often focuses on the tactics of immediacy.
94. Armstrong, *How Novels Think*, 5.
95. See Raymond Williams's essential "Structures of Feeling" in *Marxism and Literature*.
96. Rancière, *Politics of Aesthetics*, 13.
97. See Woloch, *One Vs. the Many*, esp. 30. Kreilkamp goes as far as to suggest that "any animal that is individuated ... in a novel is thereby domesticated, brought into the realm of the human, a status somewhat resembling that of a pet" (*Minor Creatures*, 186).
98. Jameson, *Allegory and Ideology*, 320. Despite critical reactions against this claim for its profound flattening of aesthetic innovation across non-eurowestern cultures, we

can still see its influence; for example, Ulka Anjaria valorizes a postcolonial realism that turns against allegory and self-reflexivity as a "gesture of incipience and futurity in the face of postcolonial literature's long obsession with the past" (Anjaria, "The Realist Impulse and the Future of Postcoloniality," 278 n.1).

99. Watt, *The Rise of the Novel*, 32. The anthropocentrism of such an individualism is perfectly obvious, as illustrated by Édouard Glissant's essential formulation: we "renounce" depth psychology for its "certainty that there is a universal model, a sort of archetype of humanity, difficult to circumscribe or define, or course, but one that would simultaneously ensure our knowledge in the matter and be its ultimate aim" (*Poetics of Relation*, 24).

100. Figlerowicz, *Flat Protagonists*, 12; Rosenberg, *Scale, Crisis, and the Modern Novel*, 3; Kornbluh, "Ecocide and Objectivity," 265.

101. Figlerowicz, *Flat Protagonists*, 12.

102. Gallagher, "Rise of Fictionality," 341. Deidre Lynch argues that "novel writing's claim to a singular distinction among the disciplines would be founded on the promise that it was this type of writing that tendered the deepest, truest knowledge of character," even as she shows persuasively that character's association with individual human psychological depth was not inevitable but a reflection of economic imperatives (*Economy of Character*, 28).

103. For Armstrong, their production of individuality is no less seductive for its coerciveness: the association between novels and individuality is strong even though the form found it continually "necessary to invalidate competing notions of the subject . . . as idiosyncratic, less than fully human, fantastic, or dangerous" (*How Novels Think*, 5). On nineteenth-century realist form as indexing scientized understandings of population, see especially Steinlight, *Populating the Novel*; Kreilkamp, *Minor Creatures*; and Stout, *Corporate Romanticism*. On novels as demonstrating the objectlike or networked qualities of human characters even in the most traditionally "character-driven" of realist fiction, see Levine, *Forms*; Figlerowicz, *Flat Protagonists*; and Brilmyer, *Science of Character*.

104. See Kreilkamp, *Minor Creatures*, 37.

105. Gallagher, "Rise of Fictionality," 358, 350.

106. Jameson, *Allegory and Ideology*, 53.

107. On pragmatically accepting that literary scholars deal primarily with creative work by humans, see Brown, *The Counterhuman Imaginary*, 1–10.

108. Heidegger, *Being and Time*, 138.

109. Felski and Fraiman, "Introduction [to *In The Mood*]," vi.

110. Narratively, mood and tone are usually taken less to attach to specific elements than to offer a diffuse sensibility that is, in Sianne Ngai's words, not "value- or meaning-based" (*Ugly Feelings*, 7).

111. Song, *Climate Lyricism*, 5; in some contrast, Menely argues that lyric is a "definitive genre of the early Anthropocene" because of its impulse of retreat from an industrialized and "reified world" (*Climate and the Making of Worlds*, 32). On reading for lyricism in fiction, see Cohn, *Still Life*, 18–25. On mood and tone as significant contri-

butions to narrative style that thematize and reflect formally on the functions of consciousness, see also Kramnick, *Paper Minds*, 128–29.

112. Heller-Roazen, *The Inner Touch*, 15; Rosa, *Resonance*; Freeman, *Beside You in Time*, 9. On resonance as a method of literary comparison, see also Dimock, "Theory of Resonance."

113. See Wenzel, *Disposition of Nature*, esp. 10; Houser, *Ecosickness*, 3–4; and Song, *Climate Lyricism*, esp. 14.

114. Haraway, *Staying with the Trouble*, 13. Citing this passage, Cheah offers an especially sharp critique of the ecological valorization of "entanglement" (talk at Cornell University, 20 March 2024). See also Kornbluh, *Immediacy*; and Song, *Climate Lyricism*, 11.

115. Nersessian, *Calamity Form*, 8–9. On an ambivalent relation to method, see also Freeman, *Beside You in Time*, 11.

116. Kornbluh, "Extinct Critique," 775.

117. With this emphasis, Kornbluh's urgent recommendation reminds me particularly of Stengers's point that "being capable of situating oneself—situating what one knows, and actively linking it to questions that one brings in and to ways of working that respond to it—implies being indebted to the existence of others who ask different questions, importing them into the situation differently, relating to the situation in a way that resists appropriation in the name of any kind of abstract ideal" (*Another Science Is Possible*, 45). For a similar response to Kornbluh's injunction, see Song, *Climate Lyricism*, 14.

118. In Cohn, *Still Life*, I argue for tensions within the *Bildungsroman*, prompted by physiological psychology, that disrupt individualistic models of subjectivity.

119. The phrase comes from Haraway, *When Species Meet*, 77.

120. In *The Force of Nonviolence*, Judith Butler's discussion of "grievable lives" suggests that this idea is premised on interdependence: "We have to think not only about persons, but animals; and not only about living creatures, but living processes, the systems and forms of life" (43).

121. Lupton, *Thinking with Shakespeare*, 1; Boggs, *Animalia Americana*, 161. See Santner, for whom the creaturely in twentieth-century contexts marks "the peculiar proximity of the human to the animal at the very point of their radical difference" (*On Creaturely Life*, 12).

122. Pick, *Creaturely Poetics*, 4–5. See Thompson, *Novel Creatures*, 3; and O'Key, *Creaturely Forms*. See Herman, *Narratology Beyond the Human*, 5–6, for an intentionally broad use of the term to signal trans-species commonality, and Rosa's persistent use of the term "creature" throughout *Resonance*. On Lupton vs. Pick, see Anna West's assessment of my discussion of the creaturely in my essay "No Insignificant Creature" in her *Thomas Hardy and Animals*, 11. West sides with Pick against Lupton, highlighting the universalizing appeal of Simone Weil's framework, which I discuss further in Chapter 3 because Weil is an important touchstone for Sigrid Nunez. It is helpful, I think, to hold both meanings of the creaturely together because different literary forms

afford distinct vantages on the embodied vulnerability that applies to each of the two senses of the term.

123. Rosa, *Resonance*, 36. See Weil, "The Animal Novel That Therefore This Is Not?," 120–121.

124. Sinha, *Entangled Fictions*, 4.

125. Herman, *Narratology Beyond the Human*, 5.

126. Despret, *What Would Animals Say*, 162.

127. Boxall, *Value of the Novel*, 15.

128. Boisseron, *Afro-Dog*, 26.

129. McHugh, *Animal Stories*, 219. See also Freeman's contention that "sense methods" show that "engroupment is a sensory matter" (*Beside You in Time*, 12).

130. Joshua Bennett positions *Umwelt* as enabling "open" rather than "normative" or proprietary relations between species (*Being Property Once Myself*, 145); see also Holland, *an/other*, 7. "World" is a particularly loaded signifier of value for Holland throughout.

131. In this sense, my project aligns with Houser's emphasis on affective impact in *Ecosickness*.

132. Bartoszyńska, *Estranging the Novel*, 127. See also Dimock, "Theory of Resonance," 1062.

133. Shlovsky, "From *Art as Technique*," 219.

134. See Song, *Climate Lyricism*, 4–5.

135. Puig de la Bellacasa, *Matters of Care*, 113. In Puig de la Bellacasa's defense of care, "Worlds seen through care accentuate a sense of interdependency and involvement" (*Matters of Care*, 17). Reversing this emphasis, I observe finally that an affirmative commitment to interdependency entails an examination of how those worlds become perceptible.

Chapter 1

This chapter draws on material published as Cohn, Elisha, "Paperback Tigers: Breaking the Zoo." *Contemporary Literature*, vol. 56, no. 4 (2015): pp. 568–600 © 2015 by the Board of Regents of the University of Wisconsin System. Reprinted courtesy of the University of Wisconsin Press.

1. Ortiz-Robles, *Literature and Animal Studies*, 1.

2. Derrida, *Animal That Therefore I Am*, 6, 9.

3. On the durability of the lion as a figure for sovereignty from the medieval into the economic modernity, see La Berge, *Marx for Cats*, esp. 3; 17; 117.

4. On the rise and demise of the "tyger" as a figure for revolution and especially Black Jacobinism, see La Berge, *Marx for Cats*, 127–28, 171. On the popularity of the tiger narrative now, see Martyris, "Exit, Pursued by a Tiger." In Fiona McFarlane's *The Night Guest* (2014), when the aging protagonist loses consciousness in the embrace of a dream-tiger, the novel stresses the incapacity of institutions (government care agencies but also banks, shops, and even families) to fully confront the physical and mental experiences of aging. In Lucy Ellmann's *Ducks, Newburyport* (2019), which I discuss at

length in Chapter 4, the narrator reflects on the escape of many animals from an abusive private zoo in Zanesville, Ohio, in 2011, where she emphasizes the police shooting of the tiger. Recent award-winning books for children also use escaped zoo animals and/or tigers to more affirmingly refuse human social regulation; see Peter Brown's *Mr. Tiger Goes Wild* (2013)—dedicated "To Tigers Everywhere"—and Ariel Cohn and Aron Steinke's *The Zoo Box* (2014).

5. On the global fate of tigers under threat, see Quammen, *Monster of God*. The conservation of species might be said to work according to what Lauren Berlant calls the logic of slow death, whereby a population is defined by its deterioration under capitalist governmentalism. See Berlant, *Cruel Optimism*, 95–96. Ghosh's *The Hungry Tide*, which I discuss in Chapter 5, shows the paradoxical coupling of the preservation of life with death, when the creation of a protected zone for tigers led to the 1979 massacre of refugees living in a preserve at Marichjhanpi.

6. Freeman, *Beside You in Time*, 7.

7. See Taylor, "Beasts of Burden," 200. On the centrality of care ethics to debates about intersections between disability and animal studies, see Oliver, "Service Dogs," 241–58.

8. On the need for innovative literary forms to convey intimacy with other animals, see McHugh, *Animal Stories*, 219, 217.

9. Jameson, *Antinomies of Realism*, 96.

10. Ahuja, "Postcolonial Critique," 567. See Wenzel, *Disposition of Nature*; and Song, *Climate Lyricism*.

11. Haraway, *When Species Meet*, 1.

12. For an essential account of the dynamics of capture, which I discuss further shortly, see Traisnel, *Capture*. On the novel as zoo, see De Boever, *Narrative Care*, 67–72, and *States of Exception*, 24; and Thompson, *Novel Creatures*, 14.

13. Zoobreak texts would thus be variations of what Elizabeth Anker calls "human rights bestsellers," novels that exoticize tragic postcolonial human dilemmas (*Fictions of Dignity*, 35–36).

14. Massumi, *What Animals Teach Us*, 68.

15. Braverman, *Zooland*, 126, 27.

16. On zoo technologies, see Braverman, *Zooland*, 72–74; and Rothfels, "Immersed with Animals," 217–18.

17. By way of contrast, in Arvind Adiga's *The White Tiger*, "There is a sign in the National Zoo in New Delhi, near the cage with the white tiger, which says: Imagine yourself in the cage" (150).

18. Braverman, *Zooland*, 90. These techniques include elevated exhibit spaces that create a sense of awe, vanishing mesh, glass panels, wraparound views, and partial views that rarefy glimpses of the animals.

19. Chrulew, "Abnormal Animals," 735. See also Chrulew's "Managing Love and Death at the Zoo," which includes one photograph of "A Siberian Tiger (*Panthera tigris altaica*) behind bars," seemingly as a provocation to the reader to consider the real meaning of interspecies love in a zoo context.

20. Berger, "Why Look at Animals?," 26.

21. Ritvo points out the symbolic mastery implied by zoos' partial organization: Beginning in 1840, animals were displayed according to the standard taxonomic categories for vertebrates, demonstrating "nature not only confined and restrained, but interpreted and ordered" (*Animal Estate*, 218). This taxonomy would elicit from zoogoers what Robert Young calls "colonial desire," a desire associated with political power that has its roots in the idea of classifying humans as part of the animal kingdom on the hierarchical scale of the Great Chain of Being (*Colonial Desire*, 6). The broken zoo trope has a long twentieth-century history. In David Garnett's *A Man in the Zoo* (1924), a man signs up to be displayed in the Ape House. While living in the zoo, the protagonist has a nightmare about being prevented from voting because he bears "the Mark of the Beast" (96). In Angus Wilson's *The Old Men at the Zoo* (1961), an England at war with Europe sacrifices political prisoners to zoo animals in a revival of gladiatorial combat.

22. See Roscher, "Curating the Body Politic."

23. Salih, "The Animal You See," 300, 307, 303. I will discuss a similar critique of animal-centered reporting on Hurricane Katrina in Chapter 3. See also Ahuja, "Animal Death as National Debility." In my article "Paperback Tigers," I discuss two works that treat the 2003 bombing of the Baghdad Zoo that use first-person animal speakers, experimenting with anthropomorphism in genres that emphasize dialogue and visual effects. Rajiv Joseph's play *Bengal Tiger at the Baghdad Zoo* (2010) and Brian K. Vaughn and Nico Henrichon's 2006 graphic novel *Pride of Baghdad* feature talking animals to suggest that the criterion for conceiving of humans and animals as part of one community is a shared capacity for feeling, agency, and dignity that can too easily be infringed upon. As Alison Howell and Andrew W. Neal point out (drawing on many news sources), the Baghdad Zoo "was vested with high aspirations, as a space that could work: first, to discipline Iraqis, second, to reform and educate Iraqis and make them humane, and third, to win hearts and minds while also being profitable for inter- national speculators and corporations seeking to turn the zoo into a theme park" ("Human Interest," 215).

24. See Ball, "Primal Revenge," 544. Zoos and animal subjects often serve primarily to lament that human populations have been reduced to the animalized life that hovers outside the state-drawn boundaries of the human person. From such a perspective, zoo animals become vehicles for marginalization and self-exoticization. For instance, in Daljit Nagra's poem "Tippoo Sultan's Incredible White-Man-Eating Tiger Toy-Machine!!!" (2011): "To flesh a career / in poems you rifle / through your stash / of coolly imperial / diction." Facing down poetry's "rifle," the poem's audience becomes a tiger—"You're awfully / scary once in your stripes!" This line offers a tempting invitation to a powerful sense of agency, but it remains framed in imperialism's iconography that renders the colonial or postcolonial subject as animal. Stripes are at once the tiger's skin and the prisoner's garb; if it's in a cage, it must have been scary before it was subdued. The poem's conceit turns on the nineteenth-century hierarchy that assigned "primitive animal vitality and emotionalism [to] the lower races" while reserving ratio-

nality for the empire's agents" (Young, *Colonial Desire*, 49). The poem engages in what Ball terms "melancholic anthropomorphism," which "adumbrates a sense of shared doom, coddles 'imperialist nostalgia' for a state of nature, and arouses a dream of imminent revenge by our current victims" ("Primal Revenge," 537). But the tiger, a creature of mythic strength and violence against humans, is merely a "toy-machine."

25. I am grateful to the Cornell English faculty working group for discussion of this phrasing. Wolfe claims that species difference has been "fundamental . . . to the formation of Western subjectivity and sociality as such, an institution that relies on the tacit agreement that the full transcendence of the 'human' requires the sacrifice of the 'animal' and the animalistic" (*Animal Rites*, 6).

26. On biopolitical fables of human subjectivity, see Armstrong, "The Affective Turn," 463.

27. Evan Maina Mwangi points out that interspecies intimacies in this novel are strictly carceral; see his *Postcolonial Animal*, 134. See also Fryer, "Rewriting Abject Spaces"; and Stobie, "Dystopian Dreams from South Africa." Critics including Wendy Woodward, Madeline Wilson, and Jason D. Price argue that Beukes's novel should be read as more than an allegory; Woodward, for instance, argues that animals "also embody intermediaries between traditional indigenous knowledges and a violent modernity" ("'The Only Facts Are Supernatural Ones,'" 231), while for Wilson, Beukes highlights the violence of the state's tendency to partition humans from animals rather than solely condemn state violence against humans ("Breaking Down Borders"). See also Price, *Animals and Desire in South African Fiction*, arguing that, across numerous novels, "the biopower of populations, material bodies, and affect can resist the state's exercise of biopolitics and its complicity with the capitalist machine" (15).

28. Slaughter, *Human Rights, Inc.*, 4.

29. Another example, less focused on political institutions per se, is Eka Kurniawan's *Man Tiger*: A young man rebels against the constraints of his Indonesian village life, his abusive father, and his mother's exploitative seducer by letting loose the female white tiger contained within him. Kurniawan writes, "The tiger was there, a part of him, the two of them inseparable until death. He leaned against the wall, rubbed his navel, below which he sensed the tigress now resided. She wasn't tame after all" (45). Resisting a compulsory heteronormativity and humanity, Margio's becoming-tiger is presented factually in the text; as a tiger, he rips open his enemy's throat. The novel combines social realism with a more enchanted vision of familial and cultural identity, as Margio inherits his dream-visions of the tiger from his grandfather, referencing early Indonesian weretiger folktales. In its mixing of realism with tropes from oral tradition, this novel allegorizes not only an individual but cultural resistance to an impoverished vision of identity.

30. Adiga, *White Tiger*, 150, 237.

31. Walther, *Multispecies Modernity*, 27.

32. Johnston, "'A Nother World,'" 127; see also Nixon, *Slow Violence*, 46.

33. Bennett, *Being Property Once Myself*, 7.

34. Singh, *Unthinking Mastery*, 122; for similar views, see also O'Key, *Creaturely Forms*, 165; and Thompson, *Novel Creatures*, 125. As Singh acknowledges, postcolonial movements have at times avoided animal identifications, remaining "bound to a masterful formulation of an emergent postcolonial subjectivity" (121). Moreover, to map speciesism and racism directly onto one another obscures specific, contextual alliances and also diminishes recognition of even the possibility of conflict between humans' and animals' oppression. Graham Huggan and Helen Tiffin warn that "serious consideration of the status of the animal seems to be fundamentally compromised by humans' deployment of animals and the animalistic to destroy or marginalize other human societies" (*Postcolonial Ecocriticism*, 135). See also Heise's critique of a strong alignment of speciesism with racism in *Imagining Extinction*, where she points out that "suggesting that racism and speciesism are systematically connected in the cultural logic of colonialism does not in and of itself answer the question of what to do when moral obligations toward oppressed humans conflict with moral obligations toward nonhumans, or what to do when the solutions that would theoretically satisfy both sets of obligations are not available in practice. Nor is it self-evident that such answers could be provided in the abstract, by way of general principles" (166). I will discuss the narrative treatment of these conflicts in Chapter 5.

35. Philip Armstrong in his *What Animals Mean in the Fiction of Modernity* also observes that the "modern disposition that regards living things as abstractions" makes them into "commodities, capital, raw material, objects of study" (186). What even abstract animals index need not necessarily be blandly humanist, though; for example, animals can signal "the unsteadiness of categorical hierarchies and the legitimacy afforded to some of their leakages," and "the persistent ways in which animals are overdetermined within human imaginaries," in Mel Y. Chen's words (*Animacies*, 90). Similarly, Boggs (*Animalia Americana*, 12) and Ortiz-Robles (*Literature and Animal Studies*, 145–46) acknowledge the prevalence of the analogy, parable, and allegory but advocate moving beyond their limitations; Vizenor advocates the totemic cultural heritage among the Anishinaabe and in Indigenous writing more broadly, of metaphors involving animals, distinguishing them from mere "generic," anthropocentric similes (*Fugitive Poses*, 130–40).

36. Mbembe, *Necropolitics*, 24. On some rhetorical strategies of racist animalization, see Chen, *Animacies*, 98.

37. Anker, *Fictions of Dignity*, 22.

38. Anna Kornbluh lauds this novel precisely for its allegorical commitment to abstraction and refusal of to center character; see her "Ecocide and Objectivity," 265. However, insofar as the novel aligns with the pervasive trope of the broken zoo and the sublime animal encounter, I suggest that allegory is only one possible way of divesting from an excessive investment in human agency. I discuss the sublime tiger encounter, and alternatives, further in Chapter 5.

39. Millet, *How the Dead Dream*, 136, 137.

40. Heise, *Imagining Extinction*, 48, 57.

41. Davé, *Indifference*, 6–7.
42. Martel, *Life of Pi*, 16. Hereafter cited parenthetically by page number.
43. Foucault, *Security, Territory, Population*, 17, 127.
44. Derrida, *Animal That Therefore I Am*, 399.
45. Esposito, *Third Person*, 11.
46. Anker, *Fictions of Dignity*, 33.
47. Thompson, *Novel Creatures*, 18.
48. For a similar reading of "aesthetic preference" at the end of *Life of Pi*, see Thompson, *Novel Creatures*, 30–31.
49. Derrida, *Animal That Therefore I Am*, 405.
50. Agamben, *The Open*, 92. See Haraway, *When Species Meet*: "Abstractions, which require our best calculations, mathematics, reasons, are built in order to be able to break down so that richer and more responsive invention, speculation, and proposing—worlding—can go on" (93).
51. McHugh, *Animal Stories*, 8. See Keenleyside, *Animals and Other People*, 17; Armstrong, *What Animals Mean*, 3; Thompson, *Novel Creatures*, 9; and Walther, *Multispecies Modernity*, 5. As Colleen Glenney Boggs notes, the ease with which animality can be detached from actual animals proves problematic (*Animalia Americana*, 14).
52. See Fletcher, "Allegory Without Ideas," 13–14, 20. See DeLoughrey's *Allegories of the Anthropocene*, where the recent prevalence of allegorical texts about climate crisis allows scholars to "periodize a break in the human relation to the planet, a perceived rupture between people and place" (14); or, similarly, Menely, *Climate and the Making of Worlds*. However, the status of the body, the given, or the common remains manipulable. For Theresa Kelley, allegory not only transforms particularity into abstraction but allows abstraction to be "checked by feeling and particulars." Although she acknowledges that allegory itself appears to allegorize the process of reification, it is never more so than when "it does so openly by wearing its factitiousness on its sleeve (so to speak) whereas the symbol presents itself as an organic form that is indivisible from its transcendent ground" (*Reinventing Allegory*, 24). I want to put special emphasis on her "feeling and particulars" to observe the unique status of feeling, affect, and/or perception in the defense of allegory as rupture between levels that is never fully resolvable, which for Kelley renders it more expansive than reductive, requiring a "stereoscopic" rather than hierarchic reading that invites mobile, "transversal" identifications that highlight the difficulty of ideologizing the sentient body.
53. Shukin, *Animal Capital*, 42.
54. Anker and Felski, "Introduction," 7, 8.
55. Galloway, *Interface Effect*, 27.
56. Agamben, *The Open*, 28; Esposito, *Third Person*, 11.
57. Wolfe, *Animal Rites*, 6. On the move from "rights to lives," see Pick, *Creaturely Poetics*, 11; and Boggs, *Animalia Americana*, 10.
58. Benjamin, *Origin of the German Trauerspiel*, 177. Our very tendency to "freight indirection with the melancholy air of dissemblance," in Anahid Nersessian's words,

makes allegory productive for biopolitically informed scholars of the Anthropocene, where the figure productively indexes a historically conditioned crisis of meaning (*Calamity Form*, 12).

59. See Santner, *On Creaturely Life*: "We sense early on ... that something has gone amiss in this project, that it bears a certain *symptomatic* weight" (56). For O'Key, in Sebald "the zoological garden testifies to a rupture in human-animal relations" but "also creates an opportunity for a new, melancholic connection between human and nonhuman" (*Creaturely Forms*, 74).

60. Tesky, *Allegory and Violence*, 19.

61. DeLoughrey, *Allegories of the Anthropocene*, 13.

62. Traisnel, *Capture*, 30.

63. Jameson, *Political Unconscious*, 27.

64. As I noted in the introduction, Traisnel also turns to von Uexküll as an alternative at the end of *Capture*; see 194–96.

65. Jameson, *Allegory and Ideology*, 320.

66. Jameson, *Allegory and Ideology*, 82.

67. Foucault, *Security, Territory, Population*, 128.

68. Woloch, *One vs. the Many*, 19.

69. Jameson, *Allegory and Ideology*, 9; Jameson, *Antinomies of Realism*, 37.

70. Jameson, *Antinomies of Realism*, 153.

71. Jameson, *Allegory and Ideology*, 2.

72. Jameson, *Allegory and Ideology*, 34. I find this and other uses of metaphors rather ironic given that he ascribes an entirely different rhythm to metaphor itself.

73. Kornbluh, *Order of Forms*, 49; my emphasis.

74. Wadiwel, "Restriction, Norm, *Umwelt*," 761.

75. Song, *Climate Lyricism*, 4, 118; see also Cohn, *Still Life*.

76. Perhaps Murakami's choice reflects the historical record that a major figure in the development of the zoo, Takasaki Tatsunosuke, favored the Siberian tiger Pino. See Itoh, *Japanese Wartime Zoo Policy*, 116.

77. Malamud, *Reading Zoos*, 210, 211.

78. Shillinger, "Mythic Novel of the Balkan Wars."

79. Obreht, *The Tiger's Wife*, 278. Hereafter cited parenthetically by page number.

80. Debating the mutual relevance of animal and disability studies, see *New Literary History*'s special issue, *Animality/Posthumanism/Disability*.

81. On collective narration, see chapter 2. The speculative quality of these statements connects it to the prevalence of the subjunctive when describing animal states of mind in more firmly realist novels, as I discuss in chapter 5.

82. Nersessian, *Calamity Form*, 19.

Chapter 2

1. See Kohn, *How Forests Think*, 131. In Kohn's trans-species anthropology of lived connections among species, the "trans-species pidgin" accounts for efforts to speak

across species lines. "It is not enough," he writes," to imagine how animals speak or attribute human speech to them. We are also confronted by, and forced to respond to, the constraints imposed by the particular characteristics of the semiotic modalities animals use to communicate among themselves" (147). Jameson allows that allegory struggles to represent bodies, desires, and affects—which perhaps explains the function of humor around unruly bear bodies throughout Tawada, *Memoirs of a Polar Bear*.

2. Tawada, *Memoirs of a Polar Bear*, 24. Hereafter cited parenthetically by page number.

3. Kuzniar, *Melancholia's Dog*, 29, 56.

4. Cary Wolfe asks, "What can it mean to imagine a language we cannot understand, spoken by a being who cannot speak?" ("In the Shadow of Wittgenstein's Lion," 31). Kari Weil warns, "Such questions have deliberate echoes of the title of Gayatri Chakravorty Spivak's seminal essay in postcolonial theory, 'Can the Subaltern Speak?,' where ... the critical establishment's attempt to give voice to dispossessed peoples will only result in their speaking the language of Western intellectuals or being further dependent upon Western intellectuals to speak for them" (Weil, *Thinking Animals*, 3).

5. Bennett, *Vibrant Matter*, 104. For an important critique of Bennett's work as (despite the sentence I have quoted) inadequately attuned to representational or propositional content as it equalizes human and nonhuman agency, see Kohn, *How Forests Think*, 40–41. Kohn argues for animals' capacities to represent using signs, albeit not through symbolic reference. I am not alone, however, in seeing consonance between Bennett's interest in the object-world and Arendt's depiction of the *oikos*; see Lupton, *Thinking with Shakespeare*, 15. On the problem of representing animal consciousness in language, see, among many others, Beer, "Animal Presences." Lars Bernaerts, Marco Caracciolo, Luc Herman, and Bart Vervaeck identify animal narrators as paradoxical, and suggest that successful nonhuman narrators work through a balance of empathy and de-familiarization ("Storied Lives of Non-Human Narrators"). When, as William Nelles puts it, the "narrating self's knowledge exceeds that of the experiencing self ... in its command of human language," the results can be "awkward" ("Beyond the Bird's Eye," 189). Nelles argues that heterodiegetic narration has more potential to successfully represent animals' perspectives, whereas "homodiegetic narration, constrained to attribute the implausible capability of human language directly to a nonhuman narrator, compromises the verisimilitude required for a convincing illusion of representation" (Nelles, "Beyond the Bird's Eye," 192), though explanatory narrative frames or other narrators—in other words, shifts of narrative level—can mitigate the problem.

6. In the novels I examined in the previous chapter, animals were minor characters in human dramas and not protagonists of their own stories, allowing these texts to avoid outright anthropomorphism, even when allegorical structures maintained an anthropocentric logic of capture.

7. Anderson, Felski, and Moi, "Introduction," in *Character*, 13. They point out that an interest in "character" that feels real and has social impacts does not preclude an investment in posthumanism.

8. See Kreilkamp, *Minor Creatures*, 127. Bruce Boehrer argues that before the Cartesian and biopolitical moment of the modern period, when character became conflated with a distinctively human exercise of rational individuality, pre-modern writers treated character as a set of dispositions and affects that does not preclude animals from counting as characters (*Animal Characters*, 16).

9. Donovan, *Aesthetics of Care*, 61.

10. Fludernik, *Toward a Natural Narratology*, 26; see also Bal, *Narratology*, 112–13.

11. Herman, *Narratology Beyond the Human*, 6. For a discussion of a relatively rare case of a realistic and historically situated animal-narrated narrative, Verlyn Klinkenborg's *Timothy, or Notes of an Abject Reptile* (2006), see MacVeagh, "Reptilian Scales," esp. 405–6.

12. Middelhoff, "(Not) Speaking for Animals and the Environment," 342, 347.

13. See Anker's account of the limits of paradox as a tool of critique that often reinforces the norms it sets out to dismantle in *On Paradox*.

14. Boxall, *Value of the Novel*, 28, 29.

15. Gerald Prince identifies collective narration as well as metalepsis as productive foci for what he calls postcolonial narratology, where the question of narrative authority's alignment with political citizenship and sovereignty is in question ("On a Postcolonial Narratology," 377–78).

16. See de Bruyn, "Anthropocene Audio."

17. Mwangi, *Postcolonial Animal*, 82.

18. Aristotle, *Politics*, 40; Steiner, *Animals and the Limits of Postmodernism*, 196. Aristotle does allow that animals living in groups, such as bees, have a kind of political organization in his *History of Animals*. On the historical importance accorded to the capacity for speech in excluding animals from political consideration, see Donaldson and Kymlicka, "Animals in Political Theory." On according animals legal standing, their lack of language notwithstanding, in pre-Cartesian contexts, see Shannon, *Accommodated Animal*, 15. On the nineteenth-century use of language as a criterion for exclusively human personhood in a period when comparative zoology had begun to inform the *dispositif* of the person, see Esposito, *Third Person*, 40.

19. Arendt, *Human Condition*, 36.

20. Tobias Menely points out that the late eighteenth- and early nineteenth-century framework of sensibility privileged being sensitive to sensations and feelings, rather than rationality and the making of linguistic meaning, as markers of a creature's political significance. This framework's emphasis on "a communicativity that begins in the passivity of the passions and stands always in excess of conventional meaning" (*Animal Claim*, 9) makes humans and animals more alike than different: both make vocal as well as gestural and sonic expressions to communicate their experiences.

21. Derrida, *Aporias*, 35. Kári Driscoll emphasizes that in Derrida's own work, the sonic qualities of voice elude *logos*; see Driscoll, "(A) Is for Animal," 187.

22. Arendt, *Human Condition*, 9. See Cheah: "Arendt's move away from radical finitude in her centering of human existence in beginning and its repetitions and the

recalling of past birth rather than ending and the anticipation of future death" (*What Is a World?*, 137).

23. Oliver, *Earth & World*, 74; see also 79.
24. Arendt, *Human Condition*, 9.
25. Arendt, *Human Condition*, 176.
26. Arendt, *Human Condition*, 178.
27. Oliver, *Earth & World*, 81. See also Esposito, *Origin of the Political*, 29–35.
28. Keenleyside, *Animals and Other People*, 88.
29. Wynter, "Towards the Sociogenic Principle," 30.
30. The emphasis on transnational identity is understandable given Tawada's previous and later novels that center on Japanese women living in Europe. For animal-centered criticism, see, for example, Baker, *Writing Animals*; and Hoffmann, "Queering the Interspecies Encounter."
31. Walkowitz, "On Not Knowing," 340.
32. See Jameson, *Allegory and Ideology*, 41–42.
33. De Man, *Allegories of Reading*, 17.
34. Douglas Slaymaker points out that the Japanese title, which translates to *The Snow Apprentice*, reflects the deferral of recognition that the narrator is a polar bear and renders identity "a non-question for many pages" that is "only apparent, forced, or required in the languages of translation" ("The Hands of Bears," 247).
35. Knott, "Transmigration and Cultural Memory," 217.
36. Tawada plays with this story without mentioning it by name in a 2004 lecture, "Tawada Yoko Does Not Exist," in which she opens by announcing "I intend, today, to present an academic paper on the nonexistence of the writer Tawada Yoko" (23).
37. See Weil, *Thinking Animals*, 10. On Kafka's story, see also Coetzee, *Elizabeth Costello*, in which the fictional novelist discusses the story at some length. See also Margot Norris, "Kafka's Hybrids," 17; and Naama Harel, "De-Allegorizing Kafka's Ape," 54. Bernaerts, Caracciolo, Herman, and Vervaeck argue that Kafka innovates defamiliarizing modes of narration to create an imaginary phenomenological world that, despite its strangeness, affords empathy. Their analysis, however, focuses on his less allegorically charged, more enigmatic story "The Burrow" ("Storied Lives of Non-Human Narrators").
38. Totten and Tawada, "Writing in Two Languages," 96. Many of these scenes resonate for critics who read Tawada's oeuvre in Japanese and German as resisting identity politics and embracing a "being foreign" that also becomes a depersonalized "absence from herself": see, for example, Banoun, "Words and Roots," 153.
39. Apter, *Against World Literature*, 4.
40. Totten and Tawada, "Writing in Two Languages," 95.
41. See my discussion of the suspended quality of narrative daydreams in Cohn, *Still Life*.
42. Tawada, *Memoirs of a Polar Bear*.
43. The grandmother bear, concluding with an unsituated description of a horizon,

balances on a melting ice floe; Tosca and her human trainer Barbara share a hot kiss that reminds them of polar snow; and Knut leaves the world in a spaceship of a snowstorm.

44. In "Tawada Yoko Does Not Exist," Tawada associates impersonal, atemporal dream states with animals, describing a writing process in which she accidentally introduced the word "animals" in likely recollection of Benjamin's association of buried memories with animals in Kafka: "while writing those words I was possessed by one of the changelings and lost consciousness" (27). Regarding the depiction of the "Inuk" in this passage, I would argue that it is not reducible to a fetishization of indigeneity; rather that conversation, depicted in affectively neutral terms, appears simply one instance of interspecies communication that gestures in a nondeterministic way to the potential of an Indigenous cosmology to foster interspecies intimacy. On Tawada's critique of the anthropological display of polar cultures, see Knott, "Transmigration and Cultural Memory."

45. Lupton, *Thinking with Shakespeare*, 9.

46. This is one of Catherine Gallagher's criteria for the historical novel in *Telling It Like It Wasn't*.

47. Miriam Neirick explains, "Animal trainers were themselves among the individual circus performers who were feted in the post-Stalinist press, and their success was often attributed to the individuality of their animals" (*When Pigs Could Fly*, 197); moreover, "animal trainers most often presented themselves as gentle teachers or loving friends to their animals. Trainers and their admirers in the press commonly offered the example of Soviet training methods, which were based on kindness, understanding, and Pavlovian conditioning rather than the more violent practices that were purportedly employed in the west, as further evidence that working conditions were more human under socialism than capitalism" (*When Pigs Could Fly*, 21).

48. Though they are certainly not talking about circuses, Haraway and Hearne do present training as potentially a collaboration, an approach which at most applies to the second section of *Memoirs of a Polar Bear*, "The Kiss of Death."

49. On many-gendered mothers, see Maggie Nelson's *The Argonauts* (2015), which evokes the importance of interspecies relations but does not dwell on it.

50. Kreilkamp, *Minor Creatures*, 146.

51. On the balance between queer interspecies eroticism and biopolitical critique in the novel, see Reid, "Queer Desires and Sugary Kisses," and Hoffman, "Queering the Interspecies Encounter."

52. See Ngai, *Our Aesthetic Categories*.

53. Lupton, *Thinking with Shakespeare*, 37.

54. Glory is an important term for Arendt; for Peg Birmingham, who points out Arendt's engagement with the primacy of glory in Thomas Hobbes's political allegory *Leviathan*, she is invested in "rethinking glory and immortality as the political task of bearing an enduring world" that does not privilege glorious sacrifice in the form of sovereign power to kill ("Arendt and Hobbes," 4).

55. Bulawayo does not use this word in response to questions about the "allegori-

cal" status of her text. Or, in the words of Alice in Lewis Carroll's looking-glass world, "glory doesn't mean 'a nice knock-down argument.'"

56. Bulawayo made this remark in a reading given at Cornell University on 17 April 2023. Mwangi points out that innovations around animal narration might gesture to traditional forms of orature, as if to counter Walter Benjamin's claims that the novel eclipses oral literatures. Still, he argues that in African fiction orature itself may rarely include animal narrators; see Mwangi, *Postcolonial Animal*, 82. Mukoma wa Ngugi cautions against overdetermining readings of transnational African novels through the concept of orality in *The Rise of the African Novel*. On the idea that orality should not be a determining category for understanding "the African novel," see also Jeanne Marie Jackson, *African Novel of Ideas*, 17.

57. Ngugi, *Rise of the African Novel*, 15.

58. Ngugi, *Rise of the African Novel*, 108.

59. Cline, "In 'Glory.'" Kevin Okoth, writing in the *London Review of Books*, likewise de-emphasizes the animal content of the novel, though he rightly identifies tone and voice as key to the novel's post-allegorical structure ("Serious Battle and Slay").

60. See Boehrer, *Animal Characters*, 1–2; Boehrer positions Orwell's novel as properly understood in the tradition of the beast fable.

61. McHugh, *Animal Stories*, 182; Ortiz-Robles, *Literature and Animal Studies*, 175–76.

62. Bennett, *Being Property Once Myself*, 11. Mwangi's explicitly vegan advocacy falls slightly differently, for he notes that African allegories can serve as "call[s] for unity" in national struggles for self-determination, but "although we might be vulnerable as colonized subjects, compared to animals we are privileged and should not abuse that privilege" (*Postcolonial Animal*, 181).

63. I am grateful to Kali Handelman for pointing this out.

64. Goat farming is economically important in Zimbabwe; see, for instance, https://www.sundaynews.co.zw/demand-for-goat-meat-spikes.

65. For a certain kind of reader, Destiny's appearance as a protagonist midway through the novel is orienting; moreover, unlike in Tawada's text where significant effort goes into emphasizing the way a bear sensibility pervades anthropomorphized bear consciousness, there is little sense that Destiny exists in a goat *Umwelt*; her goat qualities are nominal. See, for example, Violet Kupersmith's review, where she admits, "When a goat named Destiny and her mother, Simiso, enter the story almost a third of the way in, there is a palpable sense of relief, of everything clicking into place around them. Both bear physical and psychological scars, their bodies reflections of their traumatized land, offering a shattering lesson about the power in speaking the name of wounds, and what the cost of breaking this silence is. They are the human heart in a parable of greed and corruption, not revolution, making beasts of men" ("NoViolet Bulawayo").

66. McHugh, *Animal Stories*, 168.

67. See Mwangi, *Postcolonial Animal*, 103. The only exception is the crocodile who roams the countryside, functioning hyper-allegorically as an index of government cor-

ruption that is already abundantly apparent to all Jidadans, as their Twitter activity shows. He claims he is "not a real crocodile" (317), which is on the one hand patently true even in the world of *Glory*, but on the other hand this claim turns out to be a deception to cover up his capacity for violence.

68. For a similar message, see South African poet Katleho Kano Shoro's poem, "Animals of Color," in *Serurubele*, 8, which offers a rejoinder to Oswald Mtshali's "Pigeons in Oppenheimer Park" in *Sounds of a Cowhide Drum*. "Pigeons" imagines animals' vitality as a counter to the apartheid-era police state.

69. Very occasional references to historically "real" events and people feel all the more pointed in this context, such as the mention that there is a "Rhodes Road for white animals, and Independence Road for Black animals" (Bulawayo, *Glory*, 252). Hereafter cited parenthetically by page number. As always in *Glory*, the possibilities of speech and perspective for world-making are foregrounded.

70. See Diabate, *Naked Agency*, 87, where she discusses Zimbabwe during the Liberation War, though overall her project demonstrates that "naked agency" is a strategy that has been used in many national contexts.

71. Diabate, *Naked Agency*, 23.

72. Esposito, *Third Person*, 19.

73. In Bulawayo's own rendition of the word when reading the text aloud, it does not carry a particular tone or emphasis.

74. On we-voices as witnesses, see Bekhta, "We-Narratives."

75. Bekhta, "We-Narratives," 167. See also Margolin, "Telling in the Plural," 591.

76. On we-narration as epistemically limited, see Richardson, *Unnatural Voices*, 40.

77. As Bulawayo puts it, "things are spontaneous, things are random" (Cornell University, 17 April 2023).

78. Novelistic "voice itself," Joelle Mann argues, "critiques the expressions of our mediated, hyper-informational culture while, at the same time, recuperating vocal agency in the face of our mass media" (*Mixed Media*, 5, 3).

79. Garrett Stewart makes the point that silent reading (the kind of reading we usually do when we read novels), "is the place where what is called up is voice but only under suspension" (*Reading Voices*, 2).

80. A similar sense of inescapability (and anger) appears in another set of repetitions concerned with the Savior's government's corruption (see Bulawayo, *Glory*, 249).

81. Mann, *Mixed Media*, 7.

82. Mbyuha Nehanda's conflict with the British revolved in part around the availability of meat.

83. Cheah, *What Is a World?*, 152.

84. See Ngugi, *Rise of the African Novel*, 125.

85. Of second-person narration, Richardson comments, "Its very essence is to eschew a fixed essence" (*Unnatural Voices*, 19). On free indirect discourse, see Chapter 4.

86. I am grateful to Christina Fogarasi for insights into narrative strategies in contemporary anti-trauma fiction.

Chapter 3

1. Haushofer, *The Wall*, 30. *The Wall* bears similarities to both texts discussed in this chapter—the reticence of Nunez's narrator, and the emphasis on birth as a source of optimism and connection in *Salvage the Bones*. Reckoning with the devastating losses of some of these beloved animals, the narrator recognizes her reliance upon new birth for their mutual survival. I am grateful to Ayelet Ben-Yishai for pointing out to me the resonances between this novel and *The Friend*.

2. Haushofer, *The Wall*, 26, 108.

3. Temple Grandin's work, such as *Animals in Translation*, famously advocates for humane approaches to slaughter by attending to the phenomenology of the slaughterhouse.

4. On *Elizabeth Costello*'s narrative strategies as a compelling refusal of human mastery, see Singh, *Unthinking Mastery*, 121–48.

5. Even when Elizabeth turns from the problem of slaughter to consider the biophilia of Ted Hughes's jaguar poems, she focuses on the observation of wild and captive animals, rather than domesticated ones. I am indebted to Haraway's conception of companion species in this chapter. In her acknowledgments, she evokes "the lively knottings that tie together the *world* I inhabit," human and nonhuman both (*Companion Species Manifesto*, vii; my emphasis).

6. Donovan, *Aesthetics of Care*, 182. Kuzniar finds Derrida more accepting of pet love than other theorists, whereas Haraway does not. Haraway observes critically that Derrida refuses to try an "alternative form of engagement" that could serve as a "possible introduction to other-worlding"—a point that has been underlined explicitly or implicitly by many feminist thinkers (Haraway, *When Species Meet*, 20). Haraway is likewise critical of the work of Gilles Deleuze and Félix Guattari, which she argues is dismissive of actual practices of living with animals and has an implicitly sexist bias against alliances between women and animals. See, as a recent example of the impact of Derrida vs. Haraway, Parry, *Other Animals*, 4. See also Fraiman, "Pussy Panic," 91. Fraiman sharply questions the preeminence of Derrida's approach in the light of work by women theorists and scientists that emphasize more positive affective relations with animals. Wolfe's overview of the field, "Human, All Too Human," and Calarco's *Zoographies*, for instance, identify Derrida's account as foundational. For an effort to smooth over the gender divide, see Michael Lundblad, "Introduction: The End of the Animal," 8–9.

7. Derrida, "The Politics of Friendship," 664. On this moment in Derrida as grounding the possibilities of a "cynical friendship," see Wallen, *Whose Dog Are You?*, 120.

8. Derrida, *Animal That Therefore I Am*, 28. On the force of *Elizabeth Costello*'s biopolitical resonance for question of race and political belonging, see Boisseron, *Afro-Dog*, 98.

9. For another take that implicitly questions the dominance of this text for animal studies, see Slicer, "Joy."

10. Kendall-Morwick, *Canis Modernis*, 11; Armbruster, "Good Dog," 354; and McHugh, *Animal Stories*, 9.

11. A forceful message to this effect appears in a range of cynomorphic narratives,

from John Berger's *King: A Street Story* (1999), to Paul Auster's *Timbuktu* (1999), to Patrice Nganang's *Dog Days: An Animal Chronicle* (2001, trans. 2006). These novels, all published within a short time frame, allegorize both subjectivity and citizenship by making "public dogs" an index of the crowd—an unmanageable group that implies the possibility of political control. Their canine narrators underscore a gap between imaginative and politically motivated responses to state-sponsored abjection. Moradewun Adenjunmobi argues that *Dog Days* is thus representative of a larger trend in contemporary African novels that explore "the conditions under which subordinated individuals and communities exhibit a clear eyed understanding of the mechanics of subordination, but do not seek to undermine the power structures dictating their subordination" ("The Infrapolitics of Subordination," 439).

12. André Alexis's *Fifteen Dogs* (2015) is explicitly framed as a moral fable about the pressures of human self-awareness. *Fifteen Dogs* imagines the gods of ancient Greece meddling with a group of dogs in present-day Toronto by granting them "human" intelligence. The novel dramatizes the miseries and pleasures of consciousness, but mostly the former as the dogs contend with their newfound insight. While their leader declares, "We will have no masters," most of the dogs long to be members of a companion species. Yet they end up as unhappy strays, vulnerable to human whim and pleasure: "*This* was humanity, this unpredictability, this cruel behavior and bullying" (Alexis, *Fifteen Dogs*, 33, 46). By constantly turning the dogs out of doors, the novel refuses to "privatize the dog" (Howell, *At Home and Astray*, 20)—refuses to imagine a more inclusive human-based community even as it also resists imagining a truly cynocentric world. Thus, rather than blur species boundaries, the novel imagines being "adrift between species" as painful (Alexis, *Fifteen Dogs*, 47). Still, the novel grants particular power to the human literary imagination; the dogs who come closest to appreciating human language and canonical literature survive longest, while Prince, who becomes a poet, is granted the "happiest" death and immortality. Thus, *Fifteen Dogs* serves primarily to think through the advantages and disadvantages of human self-awareness. Alexis's novel, however, represents a particularly limited approach and retains a highly distanced narrative voice, loftily looking down on its animal characters from Mount Olympus. Complicating the novel's aim of critiquing the casual cruelties of the human world, the dogs also suffer because of the uniquely detached vindictiveness of the gods, underlined by Alexis's detached omniscient narration.

13. Dayan, *With Dogs at the Edge of Life*, 10. A few other novels narrated in the first person by a human are worth mentioning in this context: Jamil Jan Kochai's *99 Nights in Logar* (2019) offers a coming-of-age narrative in which a young Afghani boy living in the United States returns to his family's village and goes on a search for a fearsome, nearly mythical guard dog and at the same time, in search of himself; Chetna Maroo's *Western Lane* (2023) includes a scene in which girls who have recently lost their mother encounter a frightening but somehow familiar homeless dog when out alone, as if signaling their own new alienation from home. There are likely many, many more examples of dogs' presence in recent trauma narratives. Likewise, children's literature is full

NOTES TO CHAPTER 3

of "public dogs." See, for an inventive example, Dave Eggers's *The Eyes and the Impossible*, a 2024 Newbery Medal Winner.

14. Herman, *Narratology Beyond the Human*, 34.

15. Nunez, *The Friend*, 68. Hereafter cited parenthetically by page number. In both cases, the issue of power is heightened, only to be defused, by the fact that the dogs in question are purebred, their bodies shaped by long and often violent "situated histories" of dog breeding (and I'll have more to say about pit bulls). Yet the novels are not hamstrung by that past but rather, as in Donna Haraway's account of dog breeding, "deepen responsibility to get on together without the dream of past, present, or future peace" (*When Species Meet*, 106). On "purebreds" as particularly raising the specter of human projection, see Wallen, *Whose Dog Are You?*

16. Bennett, *Being Property Once Myself*, 16.

17. Oliver, *Earth & World*, 76. Oliver makes a carefully plotted case for the areas in which Arendt's thought is applicable in multispecies contexts, concluding that while many of her formulations are anthropocentric, the promising "notion of shared cohabitation must be stretched to nonhuman animals, other living beings, and to the earth itself" (*Earth & World*, 213).

18. Arendt, *Human Condition*, 9.

19. Cheah, *What Is a World?*, 147; Lupton, *Thinking with Shakespeare*, 9.

20. Holland, *an/other*, 8. Holland observes the relevance of Nash's understanding of relation in *an/other*, 263 n.3; she also suggestively creates an imaginative alliance with "our dead Hannah Arendt" (13) as offering a subversive intimacy with Heidegger.

21. See David Herman's comments on Virginia Woolf's *Flush*, which he argues "replaces the evaluative hierarchy that underwrites Heidegger's account with an ecological approach foregrounding the plurality and diversity of ways of world making—across a swell as within species" (*Narratology Beyond the Human*, 167).

22. Lupton, *Thinking with Shakespeare*, 9. Here I would align my argument strongly with Jennifer C. Nash's account of Black motherhood, which I discuss shortly.

23. On the value of Simone Weil's thought, especially in her proposal of attention as the answer to corporeal suffering, in an animal studies context, see Anat Pick: "As Weil put it: 'to be a created thing is not necessarily to be afflicted, but it is necessarily to be exposed to affliction.' My use of vulnerability belongs to the ethicoreligious exploration of creaturely exposure." Pick continues, in summary, "Attentiveness to vulnerability is produced in the state Weil calls 'perfect detachment,'" a mode that resonates with the reticence of many of Sigrid Nunez's narrators (*Creaturely Poetics*, 15). Such a combination of reticence and attentiveness is also evident in Haushofer's *The Wall*.

24. Nunez, *What Are You Going Through*, 71, 75, 78, 80.

25. See Guyer, "Critical Anthropomorphism," which offers *The Friend* as a defense of anthropomorphism.

26. See Christina Fogarasi's "Everyday Trauma as Open Secret," esp. 120. I am so grateful to Christina for many conversations about this mutually involving novel, and for her comments on an early version of this chapter in conversation with Molly MacVeagh.

27. Kuzniar, *Melancholia's Dog*, 88.

28. On suffering's inevitability, and the incapacity of positive feeling or "affect" to counter its intransigence in Weil's work, see Cameron, *Impersonality*, 113–14.

29. On cats: I'm writing this sentence with a cat draped over half my lap, and note the comparative absence of novels centered around dyadic cat-love relationships. Rather, cats in fiction—particularly Japanese fiction—go missing. In the novels of Haruki Murakami, such as *The Wind-Up Bird Chronicle* (trans. 1997) and *1Q84* (trans. 2011), a cat's disappearance can provoke unworldly investigations of the conditions of existence that never reaffirm the real. In *1Q84*, Murakami explicitly builds upon but distorts the fable form. He writes that for his protagonist Tengo, reading a novel means plunging into "a deep, magical forest"; we see Tengo reading a German fable called "The Town of Cats." The story depicts a man stranded in a town inhabited only by larger-than-life cats: Tengo understands from the story that "the young man knows that he is irretrievably lost. This is no town of cats, he finally realizes. It is the place where he is meant to be lost. It is another world, which has been prepared especially for him" (Murakami, *1Q84*, 222, 478). Ortiz-Robles writes that for Murakami, "the cat story seems to operate as something of an allegory or parable in the context of the novel as a whole, offering a way to understand the condition of being 'lost,' a state of being shared by several of the novel's characters" (*Literature and Animal Studies*, 121). The cat appears to stand for a hermeneutic orientation itself, yet for a character to attend to a cat's presence or absence is also to attend to his own embodiment in richer ways than are usually permitted. Takahashi Hiraide's *The Guest Cat* (trans. 2014) likewise positions animal affinities against industrial development and urbanization; it depicts a young couple's cautious yet joyful intimacy with a neighborhood cat. Imagining the cat as a "guest" underlines the way in which the novel presents the cat as an enigmatic yet respectable stranger. The larger significance of the relationship emerges when the cat's death is framed in relation to a real estate boom in 1980s Tokyo, which reshapes and anonymizes communities. Ultimately, however, the novel does not amount to a fable about uncertainty, as in Murakami, but probes the value of lucidly encountering a particular feline life, but even so, the focus is on the evanescence of the cat rather than the possibility of sustained, mutual relation. I would also note that I do not think Derrida's famous essay, given its interest in human epistemological humility in the face of a particular animal's enigmatic presence, could have as compellingly depicted an encounter with a dog (unlike in the work of Emmanuel Levinas; see Boisseron, *Afro-Dog*, 166). As I discuss in Chapter 4, depictions of wild cats retain this evasiveness.

30. Coetzee, *Disgrace*, 214.

31. That Lurie fetishizes the fact that he has had sex with Bev Shaw, the director of the animal shelter, despite her reported unattractiveness strikes me as fairly damning.

32. Attridge, *J. M. Coetzee and the Ethics of Reading*, 203 n.16; Anker, *Fictions of Dignity*, 180, 181. Taking the logic of association further, Paul Patton applies a Deleuzian conception of "life" to argue that Lurie becomes-dog. See Patton, "Becoming-animal," 101–119.

33. On the evasive location of thought in *Elizabeth Costello*, see Bewes, *Free Indirect*, 5. According to Pick, *Elizabeth Costello* is "a text about the state of being confounded" and thus "not properly philosophical at all" (*Creaturely Poetics*, 9).

34. Coetzee, *Disgrace*, 215. I agree with Herman's brief assessment: "Instead of reconfiguring his self-narrative to move beyond a diagnosis of the identificatory acts as irrational or insane in the context of Lurie's prior story of self. . . . Lurie seeks to block the threat of self-destabilization presented by his engagements with the dogs" (*Narratology Beyond the Human*, 63).

35. Donovan, *Aesthetics of Care*, 166.

36. On the canine as narrative prosthesis, see Chez, *Victorian Dogs*, 3.

37. While Attridge sees *Disgrace* as totally eschewing a portable "model" (*J. M. Coetzee and the Ethics of Reading*, 190), Anker suggests that anti-instrumentality itself might constitute a "posture that might better aid South African recovery" (*Fictions of Dignity*, 151). Despite the valid question of whether even in this conclusion the supposedly power-disencumbered Lurie still remains associated with political coercion, *Disgrace* has invited fewer explicitly biopolitical readings than his *The Life and Times of Michael K*.

38. Pick, *Creaturely Poetics*, 65.

39. Nunez gives the counterfictional (or counter-counterfictional) pet the name of the pampered dog in Charles Dickens's *David Copperfield*, suggesting a counterpoint to the banally extravagant but emotionally compensatory care Dora heaps upon her dog.

40. von Uexküll, *Foray into the Worlds*, 222; Kendall-Morwick, *Canis Modernis*, 81.

41. Kuzniar, *Melancholia's Dog*, 11.

42. Wallen, *Whose Dog Are You?*, 107.

43. On the canine associations of cynicism, see Cohn, "Dickens's Talking Dogs," 552.

44. Heidegger, *Fundamental Concepts*, 210. See Boisseron, *Afro-Dog*, 171, for a discussion of this passage as highlighting the disconcerting ability for the dog to perceive the human sharing the space.

45. Derrida, *Animal That Therefore I Am*, 160.

46. Heidegger, quoted in Derrida, *Animal That Therefore I Am*, 176.

47. According to Derrida, Heidegger claims that despite the apparent implications of deprivation there is no "evaluative ranking" of levels of being, a claim consistent with von Uexküll's rejection of what he takes to be Darwinism's claim that complex animals are more "perfect." Derrida registers what he calls Heidegger's "keen[ness]" to avoid hierarchy while acknowledging the difficulty of accepting his account of his own theory (*Animal That Therefore I Am*, 155).

48. Von Uexküll's framework remains useful for the study of comparative cognition; for instance, his discussion of dogs' use of domestic interiors is admiringly cited in Alexandra Horowitz's bestselling *Inside of a Dog*.

49. von Uexküll, *Foray into the Worlds*, 94.

50. See Kendall-Morwick, *Canis Modernis*, 81.

51. Von Uexküll, *Foray into the Worlds*, 96, 96.

52. Although she recognizes the role of sexism in her own work as a writer, she highlights that there is nothing in her own mourning to rival that intensity. Though she deplores exploitation, the narrator recognizes and does not try to excuse her social privileges.

53. According to Sianne Ngai, tone, more than other features of literary language, can function as an "operational negation" of a text's thematic concerns, because tone is not "value- or meaning-based" and "is never entirely reducible to a reader's emotional response to a text or reducible to the text's internal representation of feeling" (*Ugly Feelings*, 11–12, 28–29). Though the German word *Ton* has less of an association with sound than the English word, it features these same ambiguities.

54. In the introduction to the recent English translation of von Uexküll's *Foray into the Worlds*, Dorion Sagan notes the ethologist's interest in animals' capacity to understand signs, particularly those "of its own continued being and thus contrarily its own potential demise," and he confirms death's centrality to worldedness by making the "fear of death" specially significant in raising the profile of the concept of *Umwelt* (von Uexküll, *Foray into the Worlds*, 27). He thus contrasts von Uexküll's emphasis on animals' potential attunement toward death with Heidegger's understanding of being-toward-death as distinctive to the human perceptual world and a reason for the elevation of humans' existential *Dasein* over animals' more immediate and merely perceptual *Umwelt*. The novel suggests a similar connection by portraying the shared mourning of the dog and his new human in sensory terms.

55. The narrator gives no sign of echoing the "squirrel's heartbeat" passage of *Middlemarch*, but as in George Eliot's rendering, "the point of the passage seems to be that to hear this insignificant (nonsignifying, noninterpretable) being's heartbeat would be akin to madness"—yet it also "opens it up for consideration" (Kreilkamp, *Minor Creatures*, 27).

56. See Fogarasi, "Everyday Trauma as Open Secret."

57. Rilke, to whose *Letters to a Young Poet* the narrator alludes, praised dogs: "Can you imagine with me how glorious it is . . . to see into a dog, in passing—*into* him—to ease oneself into the dog exactly at his center, the place out of which he exists as a dog, that place in him where God would, so to speak, have sat down for a moment when the dog was complete" (quoted in Kuzniar, *Melancholia's Dog*, 23). Still, Rilke's work often suggests an aporia between animals and human worlds that privileges animal perception over the human mind: as in the eighth *Duino Elegy*, where he writes, "With all its eyes the animal world / beholds the Open. Only our eyes / are as if inverted and set all around it / like traps at its portals to freedom. / What's outside we only know from the animal's countenance" (47); see Kuzniar, *Melancholia's Dog*, 65, and Weil, *Thinking Animals*, 119–120. Nunez's narrator repurposes the epistemological caution in Rilke by diminishing differences without erasing them.

58. Horowitz, *Inside of a Dog*, 97, 104.

59. Menely, *Animal Claim*, 14.

60. A situation at the heart of a forthcoming novel by Emily Fridlund.

61. Coetzee, *Disgrace*, 210. Attridge argues that the connection between dogs and song particularly emphasizes the novel's anti-instrumentalism; see "Age of Iron," 109.

62. See Rohman, "No Higher Life." See de Bruyn, "Anthropocene Audio," on the limitations of this perspective.

63. McHugh, *Animal Stories*, 132. See also Herman, *Narratology Beyond the Human*, 55.

64. Song, *Climate Lyricism*, 110.

65. Bennett, *Being Property Once Myself*, 161. See Boisseron, *Afro-Dog*, and Holland, *an/other*.

66. Dayan, *With Dogs at the Edge of Life*, 9. See also Weaver, "Becoming in Kind," where Weaver turns a critical eye on an implicitly racist dog-rescue culture that emphasizes the dogs' "salvation" (698).

67. Boisseron, *Afro-Dog*, xxv.

68. *Salvage the Bones* is the novel that Kornbluh's *Immediacy* discusses most substantively (110–111), indicting its lyricism as leaning into the immediacy of suffering. The perspectives of Black critics on this novel and on animal alliance more broadly, I would argue, point in a more affirming direction that also accords the novel's lyricism a more pointed significance as a formally complex use of first-person narrative.

69. Lloyd, "Creaturely, Throwaway Life," 246.

70. Sheldon, *Child to Come*, 158.

71. Boisseron, *Afro-Dog*, xx, 36.

72. Nash, *Birthing Black Mothers*, 106, 121. Nash advocates for institution-building, and admittedly there is little of that in this novel, perhaps reflecting the failures of national institutions in the aftermath of Katrina, though I do find it notable that the ending sees the characters able to live with friends in houses that are still standing; they express a commitment to seeking routine medical care and imagine alternative kinship structures that offer support beyond the nuclear family.

73. Norwood, *Made from This Earth*, 190. See also Armbruster, "'What There Was Before Language.'"

74. Interspecies love, in this context, might be understood as promoting a kind of cruel optimism. The cover of Lauren Berlant's *Cruel Optimism* features a painting, Rita Lehrer's *If Body: Rive and Zora in Middle Age*, depicting a half-blind, post-operative, and yet happy dog alongside a woman in formal gloves who has collapsed in some kind of despair. Berlant comments about her choice of this image, "What we do have together, in the middle of this thing, is a brush with solidarity, and that's real . . . The painting is an aspirational concept. Disability, vulnerability, queerness, femininity, companion species solidarity—there is so much experimental suturing to be tried and so much confidence to be maintained, but because there is so much there is optimism that sitting in the situation will allow more of a flourishing" (*Cruel Optimism*, 266, 267).

75. Fielder, "Animal Humanism," 488, 489. See also Boisseron's similar orientation in her comments on attention to pets during Katrina (*Afro-Dog*, xv).

76. Lloyd, "Creaturely, Throwaway Life," 252–53.

77. See Kuzniar, *Melancholia's Dog*, 38. For a reading that emphasizes the compensatory nature of the children's attachment to China, see Marotte, "Pregnancies, Storms, and Legacies of Loss."

78. Dickey, *Pit Bull*, 192.

79. Dayan, *With Dogs at the Edge of Life*, 96.

80. In contrast, when Esch describes them as "one," she preserves power relations: "I wonder if he has trained her to do this, to stand at his side, to not dirty even her haunches with sitting so that they gleam. China is white as the sand that will become a pearl, Skeetah black as an oyster, but they stand as one before these boys who do not know what it means to love a dog that way that Skeetah does" (Ward, *Salvage the Bones*, 162).

81. Arendt, *Human Condition*, 30.

82. Dayan, *With Dogs at the Edge of Life*, 96. See also Weaver, "Becoming in Kind."

83. Stockton, *The Queer Child*, 90. On the queerness of petkeeping, see also Flegel, *Pets and Domesticity*.

84. An "antinormative, distinctly wild kinship," in Bennett's words (*Being Property Once Myself*, 151).

85. Relatedly, she depicts the dogs' mating as a violent rather than loving act, resonating with the notion raised by Ackerley in *My Dog Tulip* that breeding can be construed as rape.

86. Sheldon, *Child to Come*, 158.

87. Bennett, *Being Property Once Myself*, 167.

88. Bennett, *Being Property Once Myself*, 156.

89. Keenleyside, *Animals and Other People*, 2.

90. Keenleyside, *Animals and Other People*, 7. Keenleyside's defense of figurative language involves distinguishing animals from objects. While I am somewhat sympathetic to discussions of animacy that reach beyond the animal to the physical world more broadly, I would certainly underscore Keenleyside's insight that personification, simile, and other figurative techniques especially distinguish the representation of animals in literary history.

91. For Lloyd, similarly, in this passage, "The ingestion of animal flesh is a transformative act, at least figuratively, turning Esch into the creature she's eating. Imaginatively, external animal becomes internal self, and thus the links between outside and inside, human and creaturely are collapsed" ("Creaturely, Throwaway Life," 250).

92. Lloyd, "Creaturely, Throwaway Life," 247.

93. Ward, quoted in Bakare and Harmon, "National Book Awards," *The Guardian*, 17 November 2017 https://www.theguardian.com/books/2017/nov/16/national-book-awards-jesmyn-ward-wins-major-prize-for-sing-unburied-sing

94. English, *Economy of Prestige*, 243.

Chapter 4

1. Ellmann, *Ducks, Newburyport*, 584. Hereafter cited parenthetically by page number. On the mythical Mishipeshu's distinctively dangerous water power, see Nelson, "Hydromythology," 221–22; Ellmann's narrator moves toward that mythos after imagining an endangered animal's existence in more secular terms.

2. Rose, *Wild Dog Dreaming*, 3–4.

3. Heise, *Imagining Extinction*, 35; see also 165. On Linda Hogan and the anti-apocalyptic, see Hardin, "Standing Naked Before the Storm," 147.

4. Especially when this love depends on the rubric of the cute, as I discussed in relation to Sianne Ngai's account of the category in Chapter 2.

5. See especially Haraway, *Staying with the Trouble*. I discuss this issue further in Chapter 5.

6. See Adamson's defense of contemporary fiction—"often written by women and 'bursting with originality, passion, insight and beauty' " *as* theory ("Why Bears Are Good to Think With," 30).

7. Crist, "Ecocide and the Extinction of Animal Minds," 59. See also Chrulew and De Vos, "Extinction"; Smith, "Ecological Community"; and Buchanan, "Precarious Communities."

8. In defense of Hogan's choice to write about contexts other than her Chickasaw community and its history, see Stromberg, "Circles Within Circles," 100–101. See also McHugh, *Love in a Time of Slaughters*, 34.

9. See Stromberg, "Circles Within Circles," 102.

10. Berlant, *Cruel Optimism*, 102.

11. Ricoeur, *Time and Narrative*, 2.10.

12. According to McLauchlan, "Heroic visions of conservation and anti-extinction action shift focus away from the multispecies reality of life, overlooking the ways in which a forest, to return to Bouffier's work, is always a multispecies happening, a (never-entirely harmonious) collaboration of soils, bacteria, fungi, water, sunlight and more. . . . tragic heroic modes not only reduce complexity, but require that ecologies be reduced to reductive battle scenarios" ("Multispecies Collective," 136).

13. Felski, "Identifying with Characters," in Anderson, Felski, and Moi, *Character*, 110; Felski defends commonsense responses to character while emphasizing their social contingency.

14. Anderson, "Thinking with Character," in Anderson, Felski, and Moi, *Character* 131, 135. Anderson identifies rumination as a particular achievement of third-person narration; first-person narration, I would argue, condenses the modeling of rumination as a potential for the kind of readerly alignments potentiated by first-person narratives, as articulated by Felski.

15. Anderson, "Thinking with Character," 134.

16. Anderson, "Thinking with Character," 135.

17. McHugh, *Love in a Time of Slaughters*, 2.

18. Banfield, *Unspeakable Sentences*, 274.

19. Bartoszyńska, "The Voice of Experience."
20. Justice, *Our Fire Survives the Storm*, 28.
21. On the need for multidisciplinarity and particularly the privileging of Indigenous perspectives in decolonizing animal studies, see McHugh, *Love in a Time of Slaughters*, 6–9.
22. Byrd, *Transit of Empire*, 38.
23. Colebrook, "We Have Always Been Post-Anthropocene," 4.
24. Justice, *Our Fire Survives the Storm*, 28.
25. Byrd, *Transit of Empire*, ixxvii.
26. von Uexküll, *Foray into the Worlds*, 54.
27. Hogan, *Radiant Lives*, 40. See also her discussion of Indigenous and Aboriginal entomology (86–88).
28. TallBear, "Why Interspecies Thinking Needs Indigenous Standpoints." On TallBear's comparison between knowledges, see Byrd, "Beast of America," 602. Zoe Todd likewise points out that the recent revelation of multispecies ontologies in eurowestern academic contexts could be better framed as indebted to Indigenous philosophy, whereas the jump to the abstraction of the concept of the Anthropocene obscures the potential for cross-disciplinary connection rooted in Indigenous knowledge-practices. For Vine Deloria, "the Indian knowledge of the natural world, of the human world . . . far surpasses anything devised by Western civilization" (*Power and Place*, 2). In "Relativity, Relatedness, and Reality," Deloria offers examples of animals as practitioners of ecological knowledge. On the importance of "living in relation" as a guiding cross-cultural value, see also Smith, *Decolonial Methodologies*, 193. TallBear more pointedly goes on to emphasize that multispecies thinking is only part of the picture, in which unsettling the life/nonlife divide is essential to a project more fully aligned with new materialism's debt to Indigenous thought. See also Paula Gunn Allen's comments on eurowestern science as playing catchup in *The Sacred Hoop*, xiv.
29. Justice, *Why Indigenous Literatures Matter*, 38, 92. See also Winona LaDuke, "Return of the Sturgeon," especially her claim that "Sturgeon are people" (36), the kind of claim Justice is summarizing. See also Tallbear, "Beyond the Life/Not-Life Binary."
30. For another example of this belated relation to Indigenous critique (in addition to this book chapter), see Braidotti, *Posthuman Feminism*, 91–97.
31. For an alternative use of "milieu" as representing a pervasive atmosphere of eurowestern ideology, see Smith, *Decolonial Methodologies*, 128.
32. For Omishto in *Power*, enumeration is paralyzing: she dislikes thinking about "the number of Taiga Indians still in this world" because its smallness is "too large for me" (85). Hereafter cited parenthetically by page number.
33. Smith, "Exceeding Beringia," 162, 160.
34. Heather Houser, likewise, argues "Environmental understanding does not emerge from a vacuum of quantification but out of a cauldron mixing information, imagination, speculation, feeling, and even unknowing" (*Infowhelm*, 7).
35. Rose and van Dooren, "Extinctions."

36. For Haraway in *When Species Meet*, "To knot companion and species together in encounter, in regard and respect, is to enter the world of becoming with," a "world" of "species interdependence." "Worlding" appears far more prominently, however, in *Staying with the Trouble*, where Haraway's centering of Indigenous practices through "relays of patterning" yields a vastly more emphatic picture of interspecies relations *as* world-making. In turn, Justice remarks that Haraway's work is "very much in keeping with a wide range of Indigenous practices and the literary works that consider them" (Justice, *Why Indigenous Literatures Matter*, 75).

37. Hogan, *Radiant Lives*, 7.

38. Hogan, *Radiant Lives*, 18, 133, 137.

39. Hogan, *Radiant Lives*, 117.

40. Hogan, *Radiant Lives*, 112.

41. Helen Makhdoumian, "Rewriting *Billie*," 89. See also Piatote, "Native Women's Writing and the Law."

42. See, for example, Womack, *Red on Red*.

43. On the biopolitical dimension of the novel, see Thompson, *Novel Creatures*, 40–41.

44. McHugh, *Love in a Time of Slaughters*, 37.

45. See Lee Chancy Olsen, "Troubling Sovereignty" on the novel's anti-biopolitical viewpoint.

46. Cooper, "Woman Chasing Her God," 155.

47. McHugh, *Love in a Time of Slaughters*, 35. See also Cooper, "Woman Chasing Her God," and Olsen, "Troubling Sovereignty."

48. See Cooper, "Woman Chasing Her God": "*Power* insists that violent religious symbolism must be revised in order to provide a sacred rhetoric better able to describe the human relationship with the natural world in a way that realistically reflects the current environmental crisis. In particular, Hogan's novel explores the capacity of narrative to reorient readers away from pernicious religious rhetoric and toward forms of spirituality that are ecologically responsible" (154).

49. On the novel as a "coming-of-age" tale, see Baria, "Linda Hogan's Two Worlds," 70.

50. As I discuss in Chapter 5, the subjunctive offers significant resources for representing animal bodyminds.

51. Braidotti, "Four Theses," 37.

52. Yusoff, "Politics of the Anthropocene," 6. See also Ginn, Bastian, Farrier, and Kidwell, "Introduction: Unexpected Encounters with Deep Time."

53. Charles Dickens's *Bleak House* (1853) opens by evoking the deep time of London: "London. Michaelmas term lately over, and the Lord Chancellor sitting in Lincoln's Inn Hall. Implacable November weather. As much mud in the streets as if the waters had but newly retired from the face of the earth, and it would not be wonderful to meet a Megalosaurus, forty feet long or so, waddling like an elephantine lizard up Holborn Hill. Smoke lowering down from chimney-pots, making a soft black drizzle, with flakes

of soot in it as big as full-grown snowflakes—gone into mourning, one might imagine, for the death of the sun" (1).

54. See Astrov on the role of repetition in Indigenous writing: "This drive that forces man to express himself in rhythmic patterns has its ultimate source in psychic needs, for example the need of spiritual ingestion and proper organization of the multiform perceptions and impressions rushing forever upon the individual from without and within.... Furthermore, repetition, verbal and otherwise, means accumulation of power" (quoted in Allen, *The Sacred Hoop*, 63).

55. Anderson, "Thinking with Character," 133.

56. Bowen-Mercer, "Dancing the Chronotopes of Power," 61.

57. Hogan, *Radiant Lives*, 48.

58. Hogan, *Radiant Lives*, 117.

59. McHugh, *Love in a Time of Slaughters*, 71.

60. On Sisa as character, see Olsen, "Troubling Sovereignty," 29, and McHugh, *Love in a Time of Slaughters*, 42; on Omishto's imagination as a counter-ecocidal power in itself, see McHugh, *Love in a Time of Slaughters*, 35; and Cooper, "Woman Chasing Her God," 44. On imagination as a value more broadly, see Justice, *Why Indigenous Literatures Matter*, 96.

61. Genette, *Narrative Discourse*, 236.

62. Ferguson, "Jane Austen, *Emma*, and the Impact of Form," 166.

63. Reading more thematically, Hilary Thompson argues that "it is left to Omishto's rendering of [the panther's] voice to first express planetary laments—Omishto thinks of her narrative recreations not as clear intimations of guaranteed renewal or of an afterlife, but as but as the aftermath" (*Novel Creatures*, 49).

64. Byrd, *Transit of Empire*, 222.

65. Kornbluh indicts the symptomatic functions of the list aesthetic in contemporary realism; see *Immediacy*, esp. 68, 103.

66. This rhythm resonates with Canon Schmitt's defense of narrative description, where "It's a case of parataxis—*and* this *and* this *and* this—eventuating in hypotaxis—*and* this, *therefore* that"—even as any eventual conclusion is not guaranteed ("Interpret or Describe?," 115).

67. Together the two characters read a '70s-era self-defense manual for women that offers tips on defense not only against men but also against women who attack "'tigress-style,'" lest the novel lose an opportunity to connect sexism with speciesism.

68. Her response to factory-farmed chicken is especially strong and recurring; she compares processing plants to Auschwitz—precisely the comparison that generates so much debate in *Elizabeth Costello*. The associative logic Ellmann assigns to her narrator prevents this idea from being owned as an argument and avoids having to evaluate the consequences of the comparison.

69. McLauchlan, "Multispecies Collective," 147.

70. Vinciane Despret expresses dissatisfaction with scientific applications of the

NOTES TO CHAPTER 4   239

term *Umwelt*, which she considers too narrowly construed to constitute a meaningful evaluation of the term's potential; see Despret, *What Would Animals Say*, 163–65.

71. The dog follows the mountain lion and is eventually taken in by the "Cherokee tracker"; the mom recognizes him on the news but refuses to claim him, suspecting he is happier there. Here Ellmann seems to short-circuit the sacrificial plot common to dog stories that I discuss in Chapter 3.

72. The similarity of physical experience is not limited to mothering; the mountain lion is also called a cougar, and it is perhaps worth noting that both the mom (in her early forties) and the mountain lion each express pleasure in sex.

73. Ricoeur, *Time and Narrative*, 2.90.

74. This possibility struck me in part because I listened to the novel (twice!) as an audiobook read by a single narrator—a surprisingly wonderful, immersive, lengthy experience.

75. I am indebted to Molly MacVeagh for her observations about "recoil and leap" as itself ruminative.

76. Ferguson, "Jane Austen, *Emma*, and the Impact of Form," 165.

77. De Bruyn, "The Mom and the Many," 284.

78. Hogan, *Radiant Lives*, 106.

79. De Bruyn, "The Mom and the Many," 282; Bennett, *Vibrant Matter*, 50.

80. Vizenor, *Fugitive Poses*, 15.

81. Byrd, *Transit of Empire*, xv.

82. Her views on human migration seem to fit a classic liberal model—for instance, she is both bemused and grateful to be saved from the snowstorm by Jesus—specifically, "Jesus Pérez López of New Philadelphia," a moniker that seems meant as a recentering of national identity (hence "New" Philadelphia) around immigration and cultural inclusion.

83. Byrd, *Transit of Empire*, xx.

84. For instance, she does not seem to know about or offer her kids Louise Erdrich's Birchbark House series, marketed and frequently touted in "mommy" social media as an anti–*Little House* and centered on an Ojibwa community in the late 1840s.

85. Fraiman, "Gendered Narratives in Animal Studies," 293.

86. Smith, "Exceeding Beringia," 159, 166. See also Vizenor, *Fugitive Poses*, 126.

87. Schmitt, "Interpret or Describe?," 111.

88. Bennett, *Vibrant Matter*, x.

89. Byrd, "Beast of America," 613.

90. On the novel's interest in the molecular, see MacVeagh, "All Together Now."

91. See Poovey, *A History of the Modern Fact*.

92. Freedgood, *Worlds Enough*, 45.

93. Jameson, *Antinomies of Realism*, 153.

94. For a juxtaposition of heroic conversation efforts with the more ordinary work of environmental caretaking, see McLauchlan, "Multispecies Collective." On a femi-

nist ethic of care for animals in literature, see especially Donovan, *Aesthetics of Care*; I would emphasize that this framework would benefit from reading a more diverse range of authors to achieve more formal specificity.

95. Colebrook, "We Have Always Been Post-Anthropocene," 1, 7.

96. Colebrook, "We Have Always Been Post-Anthropocene," 19. On Indigenous fiction's attunement to the silencing of Indigenous women by colonial violence that at times includes white feminism, see Huhndorf, "Mapping the Future."

97. Braidotti, "Four Theses," 38.

Chapter 5

1. Walther, *Multispecies Modernity*, 24. Perhaps the consummate expression of this logic appears in the conclusion of Indra Sinha's *Animal's People*, where Sinha's protagonist, who rewrites as animality his disability (caused by an explosion at a pesticide factory, a fictionalization of the 1984 Bhopal Disaster) experiences a sublime vision as part of his self-discovery. Cheon Myeong-Kwan's *Whale* (trans. 2023) makes similar use of sublime whale visions.

2. Stoekl, "After the Apocalypse," 44.

3. On tiger tropes, see Chapter 1 of this book and La Berge, *Marx for Cats*.

4. Mathur, *Crooked Cats*, 6.

5. See Rosenberg, *Scale, Crisis, and the Modern Novel*, esp. 7.

6. On the centrality of scale for framing issues of recent literary responses to ecological crisis, see, for instance, Wenzel, *Disposition of Nature*, esp. 1–2; and Whitmarsh, *Writing Our Extinction*, esp. 20–26.

7. Morris, "Making the Case for Metonymic Realism," 15.

8. Anjaria, "The Realist Impulse," 280. As Alex Woloch and Emily Steinlight in particular have demonstrated, transparency and opacity have long been unevenly distributed across realist character systems: the nineteenth-century realist novel has long been a complex tool for theorizing how populations converge—for Steinlight, realist fiction's Malthusian imagination "does not separate humanity or the city from the larger realm of creaturely life" (*Populating the Novel*, 26).

9. See Howell, "The Trouble with Liminanimals."

10. It is notable that the animals in these novels are *not* megafauna (butterflies and birds) and are not potentially encountered or mapped as individuals, another reason I have chosen to focus on novels in which the animals can be grouped at different scales depending on the context. See also Richard Powers's *The Overstory*, which accords sentience to trees; on the relevance of Powers's project to animal studies, see O'Key, *Creaturely Forms*, 175.

11. On comedy as an alternative to nostalgia, see Heise, *Imagining Extinction*, 15. Not a gambit these rather solemn novels undertake!

12. Foucault, *Security, Territory, Population*, 127.

13. See Todd, "Indigenizing the Anthropocene," where she cites Hartigan, "Multispecies vs Anthropocene."

14. On how specifically literary/narrative frameworks make climate crisis affecting for readers, see Houser, *Ecosickness*, 19.

15. See DeWitt, *Moral Authority*, 1–12.

16. Andrews, *How to Study Animal Minds*, 63.

17. Powell, *Contingency and Convergence*, 197.

18. Spivak, "Three Women's Texts," esp. n.1. On the relevance of Spivak's work to animal studies, see Weil, "The Animal Novel That Therefore This Is Not," 125. On disentangling Spivak's use of the term from philosophical and phenomenological traditions, see Cheah, *What Is a World?*, 8; and Ganguly, *This Thing Called the World*, 82.

19. Goodlad, "Introduction: Worlding Realisms Now."

20. Esty, "Realism Wars," 337, 319.

21. Ghosh, *Great Derangement*, 63, 17. In making this argument, Ghosh leans on the idea that realism depends on what he terms "filler," the narration of extraneous detail that presents the feel of the real, as in Roland Barthes's "The Reality Effect" or Fredric Jameson's "The Realist Floorplan." "The very gestures by which [the realist novel] conjures up reality," Ghosh writes, "are actually a concealment of the real" (Ghosh, *Great Derangement*, 23). We could also perhaps see him responding to something like Ian Duncan's claim that there is a "customary" dimension to realist fiction, involving "repetition and habituation," as that which "produces the effects of continuity and consistency that knit together an intelligible, familiar world and our identity in it" (*Human Forms*, 119)—reinforcing and reinventing a received version of reality.

22. See Heise's review of *The Great Derangement*, "Climate Stories," where she argues that Ghosh significantly undervalues the contributions of sci-fi.

23. Ghosh, *Great Derangement*, 59, 61.

24. See Song, *Climate Lyricism*, 11, on *Gun Island*'s Cinta, who offers a didactic endorsement of reframing human attention as a mode of climate action.

25. As Wenzel puts it, "Reading for the planet is after something more: to attend to subtle aspects of environmental imagining that are occluded when one reads thematically—for the nature bits" (*Disposition of Nature*, 12); see also Whitmarsh, *Writing Our Extinction*, 21.

26. See also Levine, *Forms*, 19.

27. See Lukács, *The Meaning of Contemporary Realism*, where he argues that "allegory is that aesthetic genre which lends itself par excellence to a description of man's alienation form objective reality" (40).

28. Anderson, *Bleak Liberalism*, 48.

29. Anderson, *Bleak Liberalism*, 78.

30. Boxall, *Value of the Novel*, 68.

31. This meta-reflection on the process of appraisal is what makes fiction "feel real," in Elaine Auyoung's terms: novels both invoke in their readers and model in their characters "mundane physical experiences that ... become a means by which they can come to know, in deep and durable ways, a vibrant, expansive world that has no real existence. This small miracle is a major source of the surprise and delight that novels uniquely

afford" (*When Fiction Feels Real*, 14). Auyoung argues that the techniques of literary realism prepare us for the perceptual challenges of the real world as documented by cognitive science, where the integration of sensation tends to prevail. Auyoung distinguishes her argument from Jameson's recent contention that novels train readers in "forming new habits of perception" (*Antinomies of Realism*, 59) accessible *only* within the aesthetic realm, but for my purposes, we may not need to choose a direction of fit between fiction and reality; it is the association of narrative form with the possibility of integrative perception that I hope to highlight.

32. Shaw, *Narrating Reality*, xii.
33. See Ben-Yishai, "Walking the Boundaries."
34. Powell, *Contingency and Convergence*, 211, 190, 205, 212. Powell rebuts key objections to von Uexküll's original concept of *Umwelt* by stressing its overall "elegance and utility" (189) while applying it in an evolutionary context that von Uexküll himself rejected.
35. Powell, *Contingency and Convergence*, 210.
36. Wenzel, *Disposition of Nature*, 11; see also Fornoff, *Subjunctive Aesthetics*, 1–10.
37. Hayot, *On Literary Worlds*, 44.
38. Hayot, *On Literary Worlds*, 78.
39. See Levine, *Forms*, 130.
40. Ghosh, *Great Derangement*, 9, 11.
41. Heise, *Imagining Extinction*, 7. On the dialoguing of multiple orientations toward knowledge-making in the novel, see Kaur, "'Home Is Where the Orcaella Are.'"
42. Ghosh, *Hungry Tide*, 73. Hereafter cited parenthetically by page number.
43. Mathur, *Crooked Cats*, 31.
44. Mathur, *Crooked Cats*, 43.
45. Walther, *Multispecies Modernity*, 60.
46. Heise, *Imagining Extinction*, 244.
47. See Buell, *Contesting Environmental Imaginaries*, 108.
48. Cheah, *What Is a World?*, 246–47.
49. See Ahuja, "Posthuman New York."
50. Whether Nirmal correctly grasps Rilke's texts is another question; Driscoll compellingly demonstrates that an anthropocentric reading of Rilke misrepresents the poet's profound interest in how "worlds are the product of a multiperspectival co-shaping" ("Second Glance," 45). See also Weil, *Thinking Animals*, 119.
51. See Santner, *On Creaturely Life*, 1–5.
52. See Huggan and Tiffin, *Postcolonial Ecocriticism*; Walther, *Multispecies Modernity*, 57–61; and O'Key, *Creaturely Forms*.
53. On the idealization and sacrificial death of Fokir, see Li, "Necroidealism," 288–291. Tellingly, Piya describes Fokir as demonstrating "incredible instinct" (289) in his knowledge of the river, a term that has a long history in the othering of working-class humans through animalization. From its nineteenth-century origins in evolutionary psychology, the term "instinct" is a biopolitical tool; it marks an "anti-experiential

epistemology" that "does not permit the consciousness that produces the reasonable, consistent self that could ground liberal political philosophy," therefore allowing entire working populations to be understood as "primitive, class-marked...types at the core," fixed and aggregated rather than associated with individual personality and progressive modernity (Frederickson, *The Ploy of Instinct*, 13, 64). Even though when Piya first meets Fokir she tells herself that *he* sees *her* as an individual "and not, as it were, a representation of a species" (*Hungry Tide*, 76), this is a thought that needs to be worked through rather than assumed, for her; "muteness" or language difference leads to the possibility of configuring social difference as species difference. Despite Kanai's takedown of Piya's projection onto Fokir, the novel's own romanticization of Fokir's subaltern orientation toward the natural world remains a widely acknowledged problem.

54. On Bon Bibi, see Jalais, *Forest of Tigers*, 203–4; Cheah, *What Is a World?*, 25.
55. Rilke, *Duino Elegies*, 49.
56. Driscoll, "Second Glance," 45.
57. Driscoll, "Second Glance," 45.
58. Tsai, "Animality, Biopolitics, and Umwelt," 158.
59. Cheah, *What Is a World?*, 269.
60. Forna, "On *Happiness*," 419.
61. Soulsbury, "Red Foxes," 68.
62. Ngugi, *Rise of the African Novel*, 184.
63. See MacVeagh, "Metabolic Description," 1.
64. O'Key, *Creaturely Forms*, 166. On city novels, see also Steinlight, *Populating the Novel*, 26.
65. See Karl Marx: "Man only feels himself freely active in his animal functions—eating, drinking, procreating, or at most in his dwelling and in dressing-up, etc.; and in his human functions he no longer feels himself to be anything but an animal. What is animal becomes human and what is human becomes animal" (*Economic and Philosophic Manuscripts*, 66).
66. Forna, "Wilder Things," in *The Window Seat*, 234.
67. Cole, "Decentering Anthropocentrism," 288; MacVeagh, "Metabolic Description," 3.
68. His omnivorousness even extends to sentimental love of Robert Louis Stevenson's *A Child's Garden of Verses*.
69. See Andrews, *How to Study Animal Minds*, 1.
70. Forna, "The Last Vet," in *The Window Seat*, 144.
71. Haraway, *Staying with the Trouble*, 98.
72. Jameson, *Postmodernism*, 51.
73. Levine, "Narrative Networks," 518.
74. See Latour, *Reassembling the Social*, 54–55; and Levine, "Narrative Networks," 19.
75. Richard Byrne, quoted in Andrews, *How to Study Animal Minds*, 53.

Coda

1. *Muppets Take Manhattan*, 1:23:05–1:23:20.
2. Nunez, *The Friend*, 45. I am grateful to Kari Weil for highlighting this phrase.
3. For somewhat equivocal accounts that, like mine, emphasize not only the value but the limitations of reframing attention, see Wenzel, *Disposition of Nature*; and Song, *Climate Lyricism*.
4. For a provocative recent incarnation of this argument, see especially Levine, "Literary Studies and Collective Life," where traditional novels have a limited capacity to grapple with collective life because "the scale of a few persons is also ... the register best suited to political powerlessness—the separation of individuals and families from larger collectives" (698).
5. Rancière, *The Emancipated Spectator*, 72–73.
6. Snaza, *Animate Literacies*, 113.
7. See Kornbluh, *Immediacy*, 72–84; and McGurl, *The Program Era*, 227–70, on the "Find Your Voice" model of fiction-writing.
8. Herman, *Narratology Beyond the Human*, 254.
9. Gallagher, "Rise of Fictionality," 342.

BIBLIOGRAPHY

Ackerley, J. R. *My Dog Tulip*. New York: Fleet, 1965.
Adamson, Joni. "Why Bears Are Good to Think With and Theory Doesn't Have to Be Murder: Transformation and Oral Tradition in Louise Erdrich's *Tracks*." *Studies in American Indian Literatures*, Series 2, 4.1 (1992): 28–48.
Adenjunmobi, Moradewun. "The Infrapolitics of Subordination in Patrice Nganang's *Dog Days*." *Journal of Contemporary African Studies* 32.4 (2014): 438–52.
Adiga, Arvind. *The White Tiger*. New York: Free Press, 2008.
Agamben, Giorgio. *The Open*. Trans. Kevin Attell. Stanford, CA: Stanford University Press, 2004.
Ahuja, Neel. "Animal Death as National Debility: Climate, Agriculture, and Syrian War Narrative." *New Literary History* 51.4 (2020): 855–74.
———. "Postcolonial Critique in a Multispecies World." *PMLA* 124.2 (2009): 556–63.
———. "Posthuman New York: Ground Zero of the Anthropocene." In *Animalities: Literary and Cultural Studies Beyond the Human*. Ed. Michael Lundblad. Edinburgh: Edinburgh University Press, 2017.
Alexis, André. *Fifteen Dogs*. Toronto: Coach House Books, 2015.
Allen, Paula Gunn. *The Sacred Hoop: Recovering the Feminine in American Indian Traditions*. Boston: Beacon Press, 1992.
Anderson, Amanda. *Bleak Liberalism*. Chicago: University of Chicago Press, 2016.
Anderson, Amanda, Rita Felski, and Toil Moi. *Character: Three Inquiries in Literary Studies*. Chicago: University of Chicago Press, 2019.
Andrews, Kristen. *How to Study Animal Minds*. Cambridge, UK: Cambridge University Press, 2020.

Anjaria, Ulka. "The Realist Impulse and the Future of Postcoloniality," *Novel* 49.2 (2016): 278–94.

Anker, Elizabeth S. *Fictions of Dignity: Embodying Human Rights in World Literature.* Ithaca, NY: Cornell University Press, 2012.

———. *On Paradox: The Claims of Theory.* Durham, NC: Duke University Press, 2022.

Anker, Elizabeth S., and Rita Felski. "Introduction." In *Critique and Postcritique.* Ed. Elizabeth S. Anker and Rita Felski. Durham, NC: Duke University Press, 2017.

Apter, Emily. *Against World Literature: On the Politics of Untranslatability.* London: Verso, 2013.

Arendt, Hannah. *The Human Condition.* Chicago: University of Chicago Press, 1958.

Aristotle. *Aristotle's Politics.* Trans. Carnes Lord. 2nd ed. Chicago: University of Chicago Press, 2013.

Armbruster, Karla. "Good Dog: The Stories We Tell About Our Canine Companions and What They Mean for Humans and Other Animals." *Papers on Language and Literature* 38.5 (Fall 2002): 351–76.

———. "'What There Was Before Language': Animals and the Challenges of Being Human in the Novels of Toni Morrison." *Comparative Critical Studies* 2.3 (2005): 363–80.

Armstrong, Nancy. "The Affective Turn in Contemporary Fiction." *Contemporary Literature* 55.3 (2014): 441–65.

———. *How Novels Think.* New York: Columbia University Press, 2005.

Armstrong, Philip. *What Animals Mean in the Fiction of Modernity.* London: Routledge, 2008.

Attridge, Derrick. "Age of Iron, State of Grace: Music and Dogs in Coetzee's *Disgrace*." *Novel* (2000): 98–121.

———. *J. M. Coetzee and the Ethics of Reading: Literature in the Event.* Chicago: University of Chicago Press, 2004.

Auster, Paul. *Timbuktu.* New York: Henry Holt, 1999.

Auyoung, Elaine. *When Fiction Feels Real: Representation and the Reading Mind.* New York: Oxford University Press, 2018.

Bakare, Lanre, and Steph Harmon, "National Book Awards." *The Guardian*, 17 November 2017. https://www.theguardian.com/books/2017/nov/16/national-book-awards-jesmyn-ward-wins-major-prize-for-sing-unburied-sing

Baker, Timothy C. *Writing Animals: Language, Suffering, and Animality in Twenty-First-Century Fiction.* London: Palgrave Macmillan, 2019.

Bal, Mieke. *Narratology: An Introduction to the Theory of Narrative*, 3rd ed. Toronto: University of Toronto Press, 2003.

Ball, Karyn. "Primal Revenge and Other Anthropomorphic Projections for Literary History." *New Literary History* 39.3 (2008): 533–63.

Banfield, Ann. *Unspeakable Sentences: Narration and Representation in the Language of Fiction.* London: Routledge & Kegan Paul, 1984.

Banoun, Bernard. "Words and Roots: The Loss of the Familiar in the Works of Yoko

Tawada." Trans. Joshua Humphreys. In *Yoko Tawada: Voices from Everywhere*. Ed. Douglas Slaymaker. Lanham, MD: Lexington Books, 2007.

Baria, Amy Greenwood. "Linda Hogan's Two Worlds." *Studies in American Indian Literatures* 10.4 (1998): 67–73.

Bartoszyńska, Katarzyna. *Estranging the Novel: Poland, Ireland, and Theories of World Literature*. Baltimore: Johns Hopkins University Press, 2021.

———. "The Voice of Experience." Unpublished presentation, 2023.

Beecroft, Alexander. *An Ecology of World Literature: From Antiquity to the Present Day*. London: Verso, 2015.

Beer, Gillian. "Animal Presences: Tussles with Anthropomorphism." *Comparative Critical Studies* 2.3 (2005): 311–22.

———. *Darwin's Plots: Evolutionary Narrative in Darwin, George Eliot, and Nineteenth-Century Fiction*, 2nd ed. Cambridge, UK: Cambridge University Press, 2000.

Bekhta, Natalya. "We-Narratives: The Distinctiveness of Collective Narration." *Narrative* 25.2 (2017): 164–81.

Bekoff, Marc, and Dale Jamison. "On Aims and Methods of Cognitive Ethology." In *Readings in Animal Cognition*. Ed. Marc Bekoff and Dale Jamison. Boston: MIT Press, 1996.

Ben-Yishai, Ayelet. "Walking the Boundaries in Victorian Fiction: Realism as Communal Epistemology." *Nineteenth-Century Contexts* 37.3 (2015): 197–214.

Benjamin, Walter. *Origin of the German Trauerspiel*. Trans. Howard Eiland. Cambridge, MA: Harvard University Press, 2019.

Bennett, Jane. *Vibrant Matter: A Political Ecology of Things*. Durham, NC: Duke University Press, 2010.

Bennett, Joshua. *Being Property Once Myself: Blackness and the End of Man*. Cambridge, MA: Harvard University Press, 2020.

Berger, John. *King: A Street Story*. New York: Pantheon Books, 1999.

———. "Why Look at Animals?" In *About Looking*. New York: Vintage, 1986.

Berlant, Lauren. *Cruel Optimism*. Durham, NC: Duke University Press, 2011.

Bernaerts, Lars, Marco Caracciolo, Luc Herman, and Bart Vervaeck. "The Storied Lives of Non-Human Narrators." *Narrative* 22.1 (2014): 68–93.

Bewes, Timothy. *Free Indirect: The Novel in a Postfictional Age*. New York: Columbia University Press, 2022.

Birch, Carol. *Jamrach's Menagerie*. Edinburgh: Canongate, 2011.

Birmingham, Peg. "Arendt and Hobbes: Glory, Sacrificial Violence, and the Political Imagination." *Research in Phenomenology* 41 (2011): 1–22.

Boehrer, Bruce. *Animal Characters: Nonhuman Beings in Early Modern Literature*. Philadelphia: University of Pennsylvania Press, 2010.

Boggs, Colleen Glenney. *Animalia Americana: Animal Representations and Biopolitical Subjectivity*. New York: Columbia University Press, 2013.

Boisseron, Bénédicte. *Afro-Dog: Blackness and the Animal Question*. New York: Columbia University Press, 2018.

Bowen-Mercer, Carrie. "Dancing the Chronotopes of Power: The Road to Survival in Linda Hogan's *Power*." In *From the Center of Tradition: Critical Perspectives on Linda Hogan*. Boulder: University of Colorado Press, 2003.

Boxall, Peter. *The Value of the Novel*. Cambridge: Cambridge University Press, 2015.

Bradley, Rizvana, and Denise Ferreira da Silva. "Four Theses on Aesthetics." *E-Flux Journal* 120 (September 2021). https://www.e-flux.com/journal/120/416146/four-theses-on-aesthetics/

Braidotti, Rosi. "Four Theses on Posthuman Feminism." In *Anthropocene Feminism*. Ed. Richard Grusin. Minneapolis: University of Minnesota Press, 2017.

———. *Posthuman Feminism*. Cambridge, UK: Polity, 2022.

Braverman, Irus. *Zooland: The Institution of Captivity*. Stanford, CA: Stanford Law Books, 2013.

Brilmyer, S. Pearl. *The Science of Character*. Chicago: University of Chicago Press, 2021.

Brown, Laura. *The Counterhuman Imaginary: Earthquakes, Lapdogs, and Traveling Coinage in Eighteenth-Century Literature*. Ithaca, NY: Cornell University Press, 2023.

Brown, Peter. *Mr. Tiger Goes Wild*. New York: Little, Brown, 2013.

Buchanan, Brett. "Precarious Communities: Towards a Phenomenology of Extinction." In *Ontologies of Nature: Continental Perspectives and Environmental Reorientations*. Ed. Gerard Kuperus and Marjolein Oele. Cham, Switzerland: Springer, 2017.

Buell, Lawrence. *Contesting Environmental Imaginaries: Nature and Counternature in a Time of Global Change*. Leiden, Netherlands: Brill, 2017.

Bulawayo, NoViolet. *Glory*. New York: Viking Press, 2022.

Butler, Judith. *The Force of Nonviolence: An Ethico-Political Bind*. London: Verso, 2020.

Byrd, Jodi. "Beast of America: Sovereignty and the Wildness of Objects." *South Atlantic Quarterly* 117.3 (July 2018): 599–615.

———. *The Transit of Empire: Indigenous Critiques of Colonialism*. Minneapolis: University of Minnesota Press, 2011.

Calarco, Matthew. *Zoographies: The Question of the Animal from Heidegger to Derrida*. New York: Columbia University Press, 2008.

Cameron, Sharon. *Impersonality: Seven Essays*. Chicago: University of Chicago Press, 2007.

Canguilhem, Georges. "The Living and Its Milieu." Trans. John Savage. *Grey Room* 3 (Spring 2001): 6–31.

Carroll, Lewis. *Alice in Wonderland*. New York: Norton, 1971.

Cheah, Pheng. *What Is a World? On Postcolonial Literature as World Literature*. Durham, NC: Duke University Press, 2016.

———. "Worlding Literature: Living with Tiger Spirits." *Diacritics* 45.2 (2017): 86–114.

Chen, Mel Y. *Animacies: Biopolitics, Racial Mattering, and Queer Affect*. Durham, NC: Duke University Press, 2011.

Chez, Keridiana. *Victorian Dogs, Victorian Men: Affect and Animals in Nineteenth-Century Literature and Culture*. Columbus: Ohio State University Press, 2017.

Chrulew, Matthew. "Abnormal Animals." *New Literary History* 51.4 (2020): 729–50.

———. "Managing Love and Death at the Zoo: The Biopolitics of Endangered Species Preservation." *Australian Humanities Review* 50 (2010): 137–57.
Chrulew, Matthew, and Rick De Vos, "Extinction: Stories of Unravelling and Reworlding." *Cultural Studies Review* 25.1 (2019): 23–28.
Cline, Jake. "In 'Glory,' Talking Animals Bear Resemblance to Real-Life Tyrants." 6 March 2022. https://www.washingtonpost.com/books/2022/03/06/glory-novioletbulawayo-book-review/
Coetzee, J. M. *Disgrace*. London: Penguin, 1999.
———. *Elizabeth Costello*. London: Penguin, 2003.
Cohn, Ariel, and Aron Nels Steinke. *The Zoo Box*. New York: First Second, 2014.
Cohn, Elisha. "Dickens's Talking Dogs: Allegories of Animal Voice in the Victorian Novel." *Victorian Literature and Culture* 47.3 (2018): 541–74.
———. "Paperback Tigers: Breaking the Zoo." *Contemporary Literature* 56.4 (2015): 568–600.
———. *Still Life: Suspended Development in the Victorian Novel*. New York: Oxford University Press, 2016.
Cole, Ernest Dominic. "Decentering Anthropocentrism: Human-Animal Relations in Aminatta Forna's *Happiness*." *Journal of the African Literature Association* 12.3 (2018): 287–305.
Colebrook, Claire. "We Have Always Been Post-Anthropocene: The Anthropocene Counterfactual." In *Anthropocene Feminism*. Ed. Richard Grusin. Minneapolis: University of Minnesota Press, 2017.
Comte, Auguste. *The Positive Philosophy of Auguste Comte*. Trans. Harriet Martineau. London: Trübner, 1853.
Cooper, Lydia R. "Woman Chasing Her God: Ritual, Renewal, and Violence in Linda Hogan's *Power*." *ISLE: Interdisciplinary Studies in Literature and the Environment* 18.1 (2011): 143–59.
Crist, Eileen. "Ecocide and the Extinction of Animal Minds." In *Ignoring Nature No More: The Case for Compassionate Conservation*. Ed. Marc Bekoff. Chicago: University of Chicago Press, 2013.
Cusk, Rachel. *Outline*. New York: Picador, 2014.
Dames, Nicholas. Review of John McGregor, *Lean Fall Stand*. In "On Our Nightstands, May 2022." *Public Books*. https://www.publicbooks.org/on-our-nightstandsmay-2022
Davé, Naisargi N. *Indifference: On the Praxis of Interspecies Being*. Durham, NC: Duke University Press, 2023.
Dayan, Colin. *With Dogs at the Edge of Life*. New York: Columbia University Press, 2018.
De Boever, Arne. *Narrative Care: Biopolitics and the Novel*. London: Bloomsbury, 2014.
———. *States of Exception in the Contemporary Novel*. London: Bloomsbury, 2012.
De Bruyn, Ben. "Anthropocene Audio: The Animal Soundtrack of the Contemporary Novel." *Critique: Studies in Contemporary Fiction* 57.2 (2016): 151–65.

———. "The Mom and the Many: Animal Subplots and Vulnerable Characters in *Ducks, Newburyport.*" *Genre* 54.2 (2021): 265–92.
DeCaroli, Steven. "Foucault's Milieu." *Ex-position* 45 (2021): 117–40.
Deleuze, Gilles. *Spinoza: Practical Philosophy.* Trans. Robert Hurley. San Francisco: City Lights Books, 1988.
Deleuze, Gilles, and Félix Guattari, *A Thousand Plateaus.* Trans. Brian Massumi. London: Continuum, 1980.
———. *What Is Philosophy?* Trans. Hugh Tomlinson and Graham Burchill. New York: Columbia University Press, 1996.
Deloria Jr., Vine. *Power and Place: Indian Education in America.* Golden, CO: Fulcrum, 2001.
———. "Relativity, Relatedness, and Reality." *Winds of Change* (Autumn 1992): 34–40.
DeLoughrey, Elizabeth M. *Allegories of the Anthropocene.* Durham, NC: Duke University Press, 2019.
De Man, Paul. *Allegories of Reading: Figural Language in Rousseau, Nietzsche, Rilke, and Proust.* New Haven, CT: Yale University Press, 1979.
Derrida, Jacques. *The Animal That Therefore I Am.* Trans. David Wills. New York: Fordham University Press, 2008.
———. *Aporias.* Trans. Thomas Dutoit. Stanford, CA: Stanford University Press, 1993.
———. *The Politics of Friendship.* Trans. George Collins. London: Verso, 1997.
Despret, Vinciane. *What Would Animals Say If We Asked the Right Questions.* Minneapolis: University of Minnesota Press, 2012.
DeWitt, Anne. *Moral Authority, Men of Science, and the Victorian Novel.* Cambridge: Cambridge University Press, 2013.
Diabate, Naminata. *Naked Agency: Genital Cursing and Biopolitics in Africa.* Durham, NC: Duke University Press, 2020.
Dickens, Charles. *Bleak House.* Ed. Nichola Bradbury. London: Penguin, 2003.
Dickey, Bronwyn. *Pit Bull: The Battle over an American Icon.* New York: Knopf, 2016.
Dimock, Wai Chee. "A Theory of Resonance." *PMLA* 112.5 (1997): 1060–71.
Donaldson, Sue, and Will Kymlicka, "Animals in Political Theory." In *Oxford Handbook of Animal Studies.* Ed. Linda Kalof. Oxford: Oxford University Press, 2017.
Donovan, Josephine. *The Aesthetics of Care: On the Literary Treatment of Animals.* London: Bloomsbury Academic, 2016.
Driscoll, Kári. "(A) Is for Animal: Speech and Voice in Ovid and Kafka." In Franz Kafka, *The Metamorphosis.* Trans. Susan Bernofsky. Ed. Mark M. Anderson. New York: Norton, 2014.
———. "Second Glance at the Panther, or, What Does It Mean to Read Zoopoetically?" *Frame* 31.1 (2018): 29–47.
Duncan, Ian. *Human Forms: The Novel in the Age of Evolution.* Princeton, NJ: Princeton University Press, 2019.
Eggers, Dave. *The Eyes and the Impossible.* New York: Knopf, 2023.
Eliot, George. *Middlemarch.* Ed. Rosemary Ashton. London: Penguin, 2003.

Ellmann, Lucy. *Ducks, Newburyport*. Norwich, UK: Galley Beggar Press, 2019.
English, James. *The Economy of Prestige: Prizes, Awards, and the Circulation of Cultural Value*. Cambridge: Harvard University Press, 2005.
Esposito, Roberto. *The Origin of the Political: Hannah Arendt or Simone Weil?* Trans. Vincento Binetti and Gareth Williams. New York: Fordham University Press, 2017.
———. *The Third Person: Politics of Life and Philosophy of the Impersonal*. Trans. Zakiya Hanafi. London: Polity, 2012.
Esty, Jed. "Realism Wars." *Novel* 49.2 (2016): 316–42.
Feiten, Tim Elmo, Kristopher Holland, and Anthony Chemero. "Worlds Apart? Reassessing von Uexküll's Umwelt in Embodied Cognition with Canguilhem, Merleau-Ponty, and Deleuze." *Journal of French and Francophone Philosophy* 28.1 (2020): 1–26.
Felski, Rita. *The Limits of Critique*. Chicago: University of Chicago Press, 2015.
Felski, Rita, and Susan Fraiman. "Introduction." *New Literary History* 43.3 (*In The Mood* special issue) (2012): v–xii.
Ferguson, Frances. "Jane Austen, *Emma*, and the Impact of Form." *Modern Language Quarterly* 61.1 (2000): 157–80.
Fielder, Brigitte. "Animal Humanism: Race, Species, and Affective Kinship in Nineteenth-Century Abolition." *American Quarterly* 65.3 (September 2013): 487–514.
Figlerowicz, Marta. *Flat Protagonists: A Novel Theory of Character*. New York: Oxford University Press, 2016.
Fitzpatrick, Simon. "Against Morgan's Canon." In *The Routledge Handbook on the Philosophy of Animal Minds*. Ed. Kristin Andrews. London: Routledge, 2019.
Flegel, Monica. *Pets and Domesticity in Victorian Literature and Culture: Animality, Queer Relations, and the Victorian Family*. New York: Routledge, 2015.
Fleissner, Jennifer L. *Maladies of the Will: The American Novel and the Modernity Problem*. Chicago: University of Chicago Press, 2022.
Fletcher, Angus. "Allegory Without Ideas." In *Thinking Allegory Otherwise*. Ed. Brenda Machosky. Stanford, CA: Stanford University Press, 2010.
Fludernik, Monika. *Toward a Natural Narratology*. Berlin: De Gruyter, 2011.
Fogarasi, Christina. "Everyday Trauma as Open Secret: Narrative Reticence in *The Friend*." *Studies in American Fiction* 49.1 (2022): 119–41.
Forna, Aminatta. *Happiness*. London: Bloomsbury, 2018.
———. "On *Happiness*." *Cambridge Journal of Postcolonial Literary Enquiry* 6.3 (2019): 418–422.
———. *The Window Seat: Notes from a Life in Motion*. New York: Grove Press, 2021.
Fornoff, Carolyn. *Subjunctive Aesthetics: Mexican Cultural Production in the Era of Climate Change*. Nashville, TN: Vanderbilt University Press, 2024.
Foucault, Michel. *Security, Territory, Population: Lectures at the Collège de France 1977–78*. Trans. Graham Burchell. New York: Palgrave Macmillan, 2007.
Fraiman, Susan. "Gendered Narratives in Animal Studies." In *Narrative Theory Un-*

bound: Queer and Feminist Interventions. Ed. Susan Lanser and Robyn Warhol. Columbus: Ohio State University Press, 2015.

———. "Pussy Panic Versus Liking Animals: Tracking Gender in Animal Studies." *Critical Inquiry* 39.1 (2012): 89–115.

Frederickson, Kathleen. *The Ploy of Instinct: Victorian Sciences of Nature and Sexuality in Liberal Governance*. New York: Fordham University Press, 2014.

Freedgood, Elaine. *Worlds Enough: The Invention of Realism in the Victorian Novel*. Princeton, NJ: Princeton University Press, 2019.

Freeman, Elizabeth. *Beside You in Time: Sense Methods and Queer Sensibilities*. Durham, NC: Duke University Press, 2019.

Fryer, Jocelyn. "Rewriting Abject Spaces and Subjectivities in Lauren Beukes's 'Zoo City.'" *English in Africa* 43.2 (2016): 111–29.

Gallagher, Catherine. "The Rise of Fictionality." In *The Novel*, Vol. 1. Ed. Franco Moretti. Princeton, NJ: Princeton University Press, 2006.

———. *Telling It Like It Wasn't: The Counterfactual Imagination in Literature and History*. Chicago: University of Chicago Press, 2018.

Galloway, Alexander. *The Interface Effect*. London: Polity, 2012.

Ganguly, Debjani. *This Thing Called the World: The Contemporary Novel as Global Form*. Durham, NC: Duke University Press, 2018.

Garnett, David. *A Man in the Zoo*. New York: Knopf, 1924.

Genette, Jean. *Narrative Discourse: An Essay in Method*. Trans. Jane E. Lewin. Ithaca, NY: Cornell University Press, 1983.

Ghosh, Amitav. *The Great Derangement: Climate Change and the Unthinkable*. Chicago: University of Chicago Press, 2016.

———. *Gun Island*. New York: Farrar, Straus and Giroux, 2019.

———. *The Hungry Tide*. Boston: Houghton Mifflin, 2005.

Ginn, Franklin, Michelle Bastian, David Farrier, and Jeremy Kidwell. "Introduction: Unexpected Encounters with Deep Time." *Environmental Humanities* 10.1 (2018): 213–25.

Glissant, Edouàrd. *The Poetics of Relation*. Trans. Betty Wing. Ann Arbor: University of Michigan Press, 1990.

Goldstein, Amanda Jo. *Sweet Science: Romantic Materialism and the New Logics of Life*. Chicago: University of Chicago Press, 2017.

Goodlad, Lauren. "Introduction: Worlding Realisms Now." *Novel* 49.2 (2016): 183–201.

Grandin, Temple. *Animals in Translation: Using the Mysteries of Autism to Decode Animal Behavior*. New York: Scribner, 2005.

Grosz, Elizabeth. *Becoming Undone: Darwinian Reflection on Life, Politics, and Art*. Durham, NC: Duke University Press, 2011.

Guyer, Sara. "Critical Anthropomorphism After #MeToo: Reading *The Friend*." *Diacritics* 48.1 (2020): 30–50.

Hale, Dorothy. *The Novel and the New Ethics*. Stanford, CA: Stanford University Press, 2020.

Haraway, Donna. *The Companion Species Manifesto*. Chicago: Prickly Paradigm Press, 2003.
———. *Modest_Witness@Second_Millennium. FemaleMan_Meets_OncoMouse: Feminism and Technoscience*. London: Routledge, 2016.
———. *Staying with the Trouble: Making Kin in the Cthulucene*. Durham, NC: Duke University Press, 2016.
———. *When Species Meet*. Minneapolis: University of Minnesota Press, 2008.
Hardin, Michael. "Standing Naked Before the Storm: Linda Hogan's Power and the Critique of Apocalyptic Narrative." In *From the Center of Tradition: Critical Perspectives on Linda Hogan*. Ed. Barbara J. Cook. Boulder: University of Colorado Press, 2003.
Harel, Naama. "De-Allegorizing Kafka's Ape: Two Animalistic Contexts." In *Kafka's Creatures: Animals, Hybrids, and Other Fantastic Beings*. Ed. Marc Lucht and Donna Yarri. Lanham, MD: Lexington Books, 53–67.
Harney, Stefano and Fred Moten. *The Undercommons: Fugitive Planning & Black Study*. Wivenhoe, UK: Minor Compositions, 2013.
Harper, Phillip Brian. "'Lusting After Relevance': The Allegorical Import of the African American Novel." *Novel* 55.3 (2022): 464–79.
Hartigan, John. "Multispecies vs Anthropocene." *Somatosphere*, 13 December 2014, www.somatosphere.net/2014/12/multispecies-vs-anthropocene.html
Haushofer, Marlen. *The Wall*. Trans. Shaun Whiteside. New York: New Directions, 2022.
Hayot, Eric. *On Literary Worlds*. New York: Oxford University Press, 2012.
Heidegger, Martin. *Being and Time*. Trans. J. Macquarrie and E. Robinson. New York: HarperCollins, 1962.
———. *The Fundamental Concepts of Metaphysics: World, Finitude, Solitude*. Trans. William McNeill and Nicholas Walker. Bloomington: Indiana University Press, 1995.
Heise, Ursula. "Climate Stories: Review of Amitav Ghosh's *The Great Derangement*." *b2o: An Online Journal*, February 19, 2018. https://www.boundary2.org/2018/02/ursula-k-heise-climate-stories-review-of-amitav-ghoshs-the-great-derangement/
———. *Imagining Extinction: The Cultural Meanings of Endangered Species*. Chicago: University of Chicago Press, 2016.
Heller-Roazen, Daniel. *The Inner Touch: An Archaeology of Sensation*. Princeton, NJ: Princeton University Press, 2005.
Herman, David. *Narratology Beyond the Human: Storytelling and Animal Life*. Oxford: Oxford University Press, 2018.
Hiraide, Takahashi. *The Guest Cat*. Trans. Eric Selland. New York: New Directions, 2014.
Ho, Janice. *Nation and Citizenship in the Twentieth-Century British Novel*. Cambridge: Cambridge University Press, 2015.
Hoffmann, Eva. "Queering the Interspecies Encounter: Yoko Tawada's *Memoirs of a Polar Bear*." In *What Is Zoopoetics? Texts, Bodies, Entanglement*. Ed. Kári Driscoll and Eva Hoffmann. London: Palgrave Macmillan, 2018.

Hogan, Linda. *Power.* New York: Norton, 1998.
———. *The Radiant Lives of Animals.* New York: Beacon Press, 2020.
Holland, Sharon Patricia. *an/other: A Black Feminist Consideration of Animal Life.* Durham, NC: Duke University Press, 2023.
Horowitz, Alexandra. *Inside of a Dog: What Dogs See, Smell, and Know.* New York: Simon and Schuster, 2010.
Houser, Heather. *Ecosickness in Contemporary U.S. Fiction: Environment and Affect.* New York: Columbia University Press, 2016.
———. *Infowhelm: Environmental Art and Literature in an Age of Data.* New York: Columbia University Press, 2020.
Howell, Alison, and Andrew W. Neal. "Human Interest and Human Governance in Iraq: Humanitarian War and the Baghdad Zoo." *Journal of Intervention and Statebuilding* 6.2 (2012): 213–322.
Howell, Philip. *At Home and Astray: The Domestic Dog in Victorian Britain.* Charlottesville: University of Virginia Press, 2015.
———. "The Trouble with Liminanimals." *Parallax* 25.4 (2019): 395–411.
Huggan, Graham, and Helen Tiffin. *Postcolonial Ecocriticism: Literature, Animals, Environment.* London: Routledge, 2010.
Huhndorf, Shari M. "Mapping the Future: Indigenous Feminism." In *Cambridge History of Indigenous Literature.* Ed. Melanie Benson Taylor. Cambridge: Cambridge University Press, 2020.
Itoh, Mayumi. *Japanese Wartime Zoo Policy: The Silent Victims of World War II.* London: Palgrave Macmillan, 2010.
Jackson, Jeanne-Marie. *The African Novel of Ideas: Philosophy and Individualism in the Age of Global Writing.* Princeton, NJ: Princeton University Press, 2021.
Jalais, Annu. *Forest of Tigers: People, Politics, and Environment in the Sundarbans.* London: Routledge, 2010.
James, David. *Discrepant Solace: Contemporary Literature and the Work of Consolation.* Oxford: Oxford University Press, 2019.
Jameson, Fredric. *Allegory and Ideology.* London: Verso, 2020.
———. *The Antinomies of Realism.* London: Verso, 2013.
———. *The Political Unconscious: Narrative as a Socially Symbolic Act.* Ithaca, NY: Cornell University Press, 1981.
———. *Postmodernism, or The Cultural Logic of Late Capitalism.* Durham, NC: Duke University Press, 1991.
Johnston, Justin Omar. "'A Nother World' in Sinha's *Animal's People.*" *Twentieth Century Literature* 62.2 (2016): 119–44.
Justice, Daniel Heath. *Our Fire Survives the Storm: A Cherokee Literary History.* Minneapolis: University of Minnesota Press, 2006.
———. *Why Indigenous Literatures Matter.* Waterloo, ON: Wilfred Laurier University Press, 2018.
Kafka, Franz. *The Metamorphosis.* Trans. Susan Bernofsky. New York: Norton, 2016.

Kaur, Rajender. "'Home Is Where the Orcaella Are': Toward a New Paradigm of Transcultural Ecocritical Engagement in Amitav Ghosh's 'The Hungry Tide.'" *Interdisciplinary Studies in Literature and Environment* 14.1 (Winter 2007): 125–41.

Keenleyside, Heather. *Animals and Other People: Literary Forms and Living Beings in the Long Eighteenth Century*. Philadelphia: University of Pennsylvania Press, 2016.

Kendall-Morwick, Karalyn. *Canis Modernis: Human/Dog Coevolution in Modernist Literature*. Pittsburgh, PA: Penn State University Press, 2020.

Kelley, Theresa M. *Reinventing Allegory*. Cambridge, UK: Cambridge University Press, 1997.

King, Amy S. "Dilatory Description and the Pleasures of Accumulation: Toward a History of Novelistic Length." In *Narrative Middles: Navigating the Nineteenth-Century Novel*. Ed. Caroline Levine and Mario Ortiz-Robles. Columbus: Ohio State University Press, 2015.

Kingsolver, Barbara. *Flight Behavior*. New York: HarperPerennial, 2012.

Klinkenborg, Verlyn. *Timothy, or Notes of an Abject Reptile*. New York: Knopf, 2006.

Knott, Suzuko Mausel. "Transmigration and Cultural Memory in Yoko Tawada's *Etüden im Schnee*." In *Yoko Tawada: On Writing and Rewriting*. Ed. Douglas Slaymaker. Lanham, MD: Lexington Books, 2020.

Kochai, Jamil Jan. *99 Nights in Logar*. New York: Viking Press, 2019.

Kohn, Eduardo. *How Forests Think: Toward an Anthropology Beyond the Human*. Berkeley: University of California Press, 2013.

Kornbluh, Anna. "Ecocide and Objectivity: Literary Thinking in *How the Dead Dream*." In *The Work of Reading: Literary Criticism in the 21st Century*. Ed. Anirudh Sridhar, Mir Ali Hosseini, and Derrick Attridge. London: Palgrave Macmillan, 2021.

———. "Extinct Critique." *South Atlantic Quarterly* 119.4 (2020): 767–77.

———. *Immediacy*. London: Polity, 2024.

———. *The Order of Forms: Realism, Formalism, and Social Space*. Chicago: University of Chicago Press, 2019.

———. "Us Too: Ecocide and Metalepsis in Susan Choi's Crisis-Form." *Polygraph* 29 (2024): 147–61.

Kramnick, Jonathan. *Criticism and Truth: On Method in Literary Studies*. Chicago: University of Chicago Press, 2023.

———. *Paper Minds: Literature and the Ecology of Consciousness*. Chicago: University of Chicago Press, 2018.

Kreilkamp, Ivan. *Minor Creatures: Persons, Animals, and the Victorian Novel*. Chicago: University of Chicago Press, 2018.

Kupersmith, Violet. "NoViolet Bulawayo Allegorizes the Aftermath of Robert Mugabe." *New York Times*, 6 March 2022. https://www.nytimes.com/2022/03/06/books/review/noviolet-bulawayo-glory.html)

Kurniawan, Eka. *Man Tiger*. Trans. Labodalih Sembiring. London: Verso, 2015.

Kuzniar, Alice A. *Melancholia's Dog*. Chicago: University of Chicago Press, 2006.

La Berge, Leigh Claire. *Marx for Cats: A Radical Bestiary*. Durham, NC: Duke University Press, 2023.

LaDuke, Winona. "Return of the Sturgeon: Namewag Bi-azhegiiwewaad." In *The Winona LaDuke Reader*. McGregor, MN: Voyageur Press, 2002.

Lamarck, Jean-Baptiste. *Philosophie Zoologique*. Paris: Dentu et l'Auteur, 1809.

Latour, Bruno. *Reassembling the Social: An Introduction to Actor-Network Theory*. Oxford: Oxford University Press, 2005.

Levine, Caroline. *Forms: Whole, Rhythm, Hierarchy, Network*. Princeton, NJ: Princeton University Press, 2015.

———. "Literary Studies and Collective Life." *New Literary History* 53.4 (2022)/54.1 (2023): 693–720.

———. "Narrative Networks: *Bleak House* and the Affordances of Form." *Novel* 42.3 (2009): 517–23.

Li, Victor. "Necroidealism, or the Subaltern's Sacrificial Death." *Interventions: International Journal of Postcolonial Studies* 11.3 (2009): 275–92.

Lloyd, Christopher. "Creaturely, Throwaway Life After Katrina: *Salvage the Bones* and *Beasts of the Southern Wild*." *South: A Scholarly Journal* 42.2 (2016): 246–64.

Lukács, Georg. *The Meaning of Contemporary Realism*. Trans. John Mander and Necke Mander. London: Merlin Press, 1963.

Lundblad, Michael. "Introduction: The End of the Animal—Literary and Cultural Animalities." In *Animalities: Literary and Cultural Studies Beyond the Human*. Ed. Michael Lundblad. Edinburgh: Edinburgh University Press, 2018.

Lupton, Julia Reinhard. *Thinking with Shakespeare: Essays on Politics and Life*. Chicago: University of Chicago Press, 2011.

Lynch, Deidre. *The Economy of Character: Novels, Market Culture, and the Business of Inner Meaning*. Chicago: University of Chicago Press, 1998.

MacVeagh, Molly. "All Together Now: *Ducks, Newburyport* and Climate Anxiety's Molecular Form." *ISLE: Interdisciplinary Studies in Literature and Environment* (2023): 1–20.

———. "Metabolic Description in Aminatta Forna's *Happiness*." *ARIEL: A Review of International English Literature* 52.3–4 (2021): 1–23.

———. "Reptilian Scales: Verlyn Klinkenborg's *Timothy* and Thin Description." *Contemporary Literature* 60.3 (2019): 402–26.

Makhdoumian, Helen. "Rewriting *Billie* and Asserting Rhetorical Sovereignty in Linda Hogan's *Power*." *Studies in American Indian Literatures* 28 (Winter 2016): 80–110.

Malamud, Randy. *Reading Zoos: Representations of Animals and Captivity*. New York: New York University Press, 1998.

Mann, Joelle. *Mixed Media in Contemporary Literature: Voices Gone Viral*. London: Routledge, 2021.

Margolin, Uri. "Telling in the Plural: From Grammar to Ideology." *Poetics Today* 21.3 (2000): 591–618.

Maroo, Chetna. *Western Lane*. New York: Farrar, Straus and Giroux, 2023.

Marotte, Mary Ruth. "Pregnancies, Storms, and Legacies of Loss in Jesmyn Ward's *Salvage the Bones*." In *Ten Years After Katrina: Critical Perspectives of the Storm's Effect on American Culture and Identity*. Ed. Mary Ruth Marotte and Glenn Jellenik. Lanham, MD: Lexington Books, 2014.

Martel, Yann. *Life of Pi*. New York: Harcourt, 2001.

Martyris, Nina. "Exit, Pursued by a Tiger." *The Millions*. 25 April 2012. https://themillions.com/2012/04/exit-pursued-by-a-tiger.html

Marx, Karl. *Economic and Philosophic Manuscripts of 1844*. Trans. M. Milligan. Moscow: Progress, 1959.

Massumi, Brian. *What Animals Teach Us About Politics*. Durham, NC: Duke University Press, 2014.

Mathur, Nayanika. *Crooked Cats: Beastly Encounters in the Anthropocene*. Chicago: University of Chicago Press, 2021.

Mbembe, Achille. *Necropolitics*. Durham, NC: Duke University Press, 2009.

McFarlane, Fiona. *The Night Guest*. New York: Farrar, Straus and Giroux, 2014.

McGregor, John. *Reservoir 13*. London: Catapult, 2017.

McGurl, Mark. *The Program Era: Postwar Fiction and the Rise of Creative Writing*. Cambridge, MA: Harvard University Press, 2009.

McHugh, Susan. *Animal Stories: Narrating Across Species Lines*. Minneapolis: University of Minnesota Press, 2011.

———. *Love in a Time of Slaughters: Human-Animal Stories Against Genocide and Extinction*. Pittsburgh: Penn State University Press, 2019.

McKittrick, Katherine. *Dear Science and Other Stories*. Durham, NC: Duke University Press, 2021.

McLauchlan, Laura. "A Multispecies Collective Planting Trees: Tending to Life and Making Meaning Outside of the Conservation Heroic." *Cultural Studies Review* 25.1 (2019): 135–53.

Menely, Tobias. *The Animal Claim: Sensibility and the Creaturely Voice*. Chicago: University of Chicago Press, 2015.

———. *Climate and the Making of Worlds: Toward a Geohistorical Poetics*. Chicago: Chicago University Press, 2021.

Myeong-Kwan, Cheong. *Whale*. Trans. Chi-Young Kim. New York: Archipelago, 2023.

Middelhoff, Frederike. "(Not) Speaking for Animals and the Environment: Zoopoetics and Ecopoetics in *Memoirs of a Polar Bear*." In *Texts, Animals, Environments: Zoopoetics and Ecopoetics*. Freiberg, Germany: Rombach, 2019.

Mikhalevich, Irina. "Simplicity and Cognitive Models: Avoiding Old Mistakes in New Experimental Contexts." In *The Routledge Handbook on the Philosophy of Animal Minds*. Ed. Kristin Andrews and Jacob Beck. London: Routledge, 2018.

Millet, Lydia. *How the Dead Dream*. New York: Mariner, 2008.

Million, Dian. "Epistemology." In *Native Studies Keywords*. Ed. Stephanie Nohelani Teves, Andrea B. Smith, and Michelle H. Rajeha. Phoenix: University of Arizona Press, 2015.

Morris, Pam. "Making the Case for Metonymic Realism." In *Realisms in Contemporary Culture: Theories, Politics, and Medial Configurations*. Berlin: De Gruyter, 2013.

Mtshali, Oswald. *Sounds of a Cowhide Drum*. Cape Town: Renoster Books, 1971.

Murakami, Haruki. *1Q84*. Trans. Jay Rubin. New York: Vintage, 2011.

———. *The Wind-Up Bird Chronicle*. Trans. Jay Rubin. New York: Vintage, 1997.

Mwangi, Evan Maina. *The Postcolonial Animal: African Literature and Posthuman Ethics*. Lansing: University of Michigan Press, 2019.

Nagel, Thomas. "What Is It Like to Be a Bat?" *Philosophical Review* 83.4 (1974): 435–50.

Nagra, Daljit. "Tippoo Sultan's Incredible White-Man-Eating Tiger Toy-Machine!!!" London: Faber and Faber, 2011.

Nash, Jennifer C. *Birthing Black Mothers*. Durham, NC: Duke University Press, 2021.

Neirick, Miriam. *When Pigs Could Fly and Bears Could Dance: A History of the Soviet Circus*. Madison: University of Wisconsin Press, 2012.

Nelles, William. "Beyond the Bird's Eye: Animal Focalization." *Narrative* 9.2 (2001): 188–94.

Nelson, Maggie. *The Argonauts*. Minneapolis, MN: Greywolf Press, 2015.

Nelson, Melissa K. "The Hydromythology of the Anishinaabeg: Will Misipizhu Survive Climate Change, or Is He Creating It?" In *Centering Anishinaabeg Studies: Understanding the World Through Stories*. Ed. Jill Doerfler, Niigaanwewidam James Sinclair, and Heidi Kiiwetinepinesiik Stark. Winnipeg: University of Manitoba Press, 2013.

Nersessian, Anahid. *Calamity Form: On Poetry and Social Life*. Chicago: University of Chicago Press, 2020.

Newen, Albert, Leon de Bruin, and Shaun Gallagher. *The Oxford Handbook of 4E Cognition*. Oxford: Oxford University Press, 2018.

Ngai, Sianne. *Our Aesthetic Categories: Zany, Cute, Interesting*. Cambridge, MA: Harvard University Press, 2012.

———. *Ugly Feelings*. Cambridge, MA: Harvard University Press, 2005.

Nganang, Patrice. *Dog Days: An Animal Chronicle*. Trans. Amy Reed. Charlottesville: University of Virginia Press, 2006.

wa Ngugi, Mukoma. *The Rise of the African Novel: Politics of Language, Identity, and Ownership*. Ann Arbor: University of Michigan Press, 2018.

Nixon, Rob. *Slow Violence: The Environmentalism of the Poor*. Cambridge, MA: Harvard University Press, 2013.

Noë, Alva. *Out of Our Heads: Why You Are Not Your Brain and Other Lessons from the Biology of Consciousness*. New York: Hill and Wang, 2009.

Norris, Margot. "Kafka's Hybrids: Thinking Animals and Mirrored Humans." In *Kafka's Creatures: Animals, Hybrids, and Other Fantastic Beings*. Ed. Marc Lucht and Donna Yarri. Lanham, MD: Lexington Books. 17–32.

Norwood, Vera. *Made from This Earth: American Women and Nature*. Chapel Hill: University of North Carolina Press, 1993.

Nunez, Sigrid. *The Friend*. New York: Riverhead Books, 2018.

———. *What Are You Going Through*. New York: Riverhead Books, 2020.
Obreht, Téa. *The Tiger's Wife*. New York: Random House, 2011.
O'Key, Dominic. *Creaturely Forms in Contemporary Literature: Narrating the War Against the Animals*. London: Bloomsbury Academic, 2022.
Okoth, Kevin. "Serious Battle and Slay." 18 August 2022. https://www.lrb.co.uk/the-paper/v44/n16/kevin-okoth/serious-battle-and-slay
Oliver, Kelly. *Earth & World: Philosophy After the Apollo Missions*. New York: Columbia University Press, 2015.
———. "Service Dogs: Between Animal Studies and Disability Studies." *philoSOPHIA* 6.2 (2016): 241–58.
Olsen, Lee Chancey. "Troubling Sovereignty, Grounding Ecological Ethics: Reading Resistance and Resilience in Linda Hogan's *Power*." *Resilience: A Journal of the Environmental Humanities* 8.2 (2021): 24–43.
Ortiz-Robles, Mario. *Literature and Animal Studies*. London: Routledge, 2016.
Oz, Frank, dir. *The Muppets Take Manhattan*. Los Angeles, Tristar Pictures, 1984. DVD.
Parry, Catherine. *Other Animals in Twenty-First Century Fiction*. London: Palgrave, 2017.
Patton, Paul. "Becoming-animal and Pure Life in Coetzee's *Disgrace*." *ARIEL: A Review of International English Literature* 35.1–2 (2004): 101–19.
Piatote, Beth. "Native Women's Writing and the Law." In *The Cambridge History of Native American Literature*. Ed. Melanie Benson Taylor. Cambridge: Cambridge University Press, 2020.
Pick, Anat. *Creaturely Poetics: Animality and Vulnerability in Literature and Film*. New York: Columbia University Press, 2011.
Poovey, Mary. *A History of the Modern Fact*. Chicago: University of Chicago Press, 1998.
Powell, Rachell. *Contingency and Convergence: Toward a Cosmic Biology of Body and Mind*. Cambridge, MA: MIT Press, 2020.
Powers, Richard. *The Echo Maker*. New York: Farrar, Straus and Giroux, 2006.
———. *The Overstory*. New York: Norton, 2018.
Price, Jason D. *Animals and Desire in South African Fiction: Biopolitics and the Resistance to Colonization*. London: Palgrave Macmillan, 2017.
Prince, Gerald. "On a Postcolonial Narratology." In *A Companion to Narrative Theory*. Ed. James Phelan and Peter J. Rabinowitz. London: Blackwell, 2005.
Puig de la Bellacasa, María. *Matters of Care: Speculative Ethics in More Than Human Worlds*. Minneapolis: University of Minnesota Press, 2017.
Quammen, David. *Monster of God*. New York: Norton, 2004.
Quintana, Pilar. *The Bitch*. Trans. Lisa Dillman. New York: World Editions, 2020.
Rancière, Jacques. *The Emancipated Spectator*. London: Verso, 2009.
———. *The Politics of Aesthetics*. London: Continuum, 2004.
———. "What Medium Can Mean." Trans. Steven Corcoran. *Parrhesia* 11 (2011): 35–43.

Reid, Daisy. "Queer Desires and Sugary Kisses: The Sweetness of Interspecies Encounters in *Memoirs of a Polar Bear*." *Green Letters: Studies in Ecocriticism* 26.1 (2022): 116–30.

Richardson, Brian. *Unnatural Voices: Extreme Narration in Modern and Contemporary Fiction*. Columbus: Ohio State University Press, 2006.

Ricoeur, Paul. *Time and Narrative*. Vol. 2. Chicago: University of Chicago Press, 1984.

Rilke, Rainer Maria. *Duino Elegies*. Trans. Edward Snow. Berkeley: University of California Press, 2000.

Ritvo, Harriet. *The Animal Estate: The English and Other Creatures in the Victorian Age*. Cambridge, MA: Harvard University Press, 1987.

Rohman, Carrie. "No Higher Life: Bio-aesthetics in J. M. Coetzee's *Disgrace*." *Modern Fiction Studies* 60.3 (2014): 562–78.

Rosa, Harmut. *Resonance: A Sociology of Our Relation to the World*. Trans. James Wagner. London: Polity, 2021.

Roscher, Mieke. "Curating the Body Politic: The Spatiality of the Zoo and the Symbolic Construction of German Nationhood (Berlin 1933–1961)." In *Animal Places: Lively Cartographies of Human-Animal Relations*. Ed. Jacob Bull, Tora Holmberg, and Cecilia Åsberg. London: Routledge, 2016.

Rose, Deborah Bird. *Wild Dog Dreaming: Love and Extinction*. Charlottesville: University of Virginia Press, 2011.

Rose, Deborah Bird, and T. van Dooren. "Extinctions." In *Encyclopedia of Geography*. London: Sage Publications, 2010. http://www.sage-ereference.com/geography/Article_n410.html

Rosenberg, Aaron. *Scale, Crisis, and the Modern Novel: Extreme Measures*. Cambridge: Cambridge University Press, 2023.

Rothfels, Nigel. "Immersed with Animals." In *Representing Animals*, ed. Nigel Rothfels. Indianapolis: Indiana University Press, 2002.

Salih, Sara. "The Animal You See." *Interventions: International Journal of Postcolonial Studies* 16.3 (2014): 299–324.

Santner, Eric. *On Creaturely Life: Rilke, Benjamin, Sebald*. Chicago: University of Chicago Press, 2006.

Schlovsky, Viktor. "From *Art as Technique*." In *Modernism: An Anthology of Sources and Documents*. Ed. Vassiliki Kolocotroni, Jane Goldman, and Olga Taxidou. Chicago: University of Chicago Press, 1998.

Schmitt, Canon. "Interpret or Describe?" *Representations* 135 (2016): 102–118.

Schuller, Kyla. *The Biopolitics of Feeling: Race, Sex, and Science in the Nineteenth Century*. Durham, NC: Duke University Press, 2017.

Sebald, W. G. *Austerlitz*. Trans. Anthea Bell. New York: Random House, 2001.

Sedgwick, Eve Kosofsky. *Touching Feeling: Affect, Pedagogy, Performativity*. Durham, NC: Duke University Press, 2003.

Shannon, Laurie. *The Accommodated Animal: Cosmopolity in Shakespearean Locales*. Chicago: University of Chicago Press, 2013.

Shaw, Harry. *Narrating Reality: Austen, Scott, Eliot.* Ithaca, NY: Cornell University Press, 1999.
Sheldon, Rebekah. *The Child to Come: Life After the Human Catastrophe.* Minneapolis: University of Minnesota Press, 2016.
Shell, Marc. "The Family Pet." *Representations* 15 (1986): 121–53.
Shillinger, Liesl. "A Mythic Novel of the Balkan Wars." *New York Times Sunday Book Review*, 13 March 2011, BR1.
Shoro, Katleho Kano. *Serurubele.* Cape Town: Modjaji Books, 2017.
Shukin, Nicole. *Animal Capital: Rendering Life in Biopolitical Times.* Minneapolis: University of Minnesota Press, 2009.
Singh, Julietta. *Unthinking Mastery: Dehumanism and Decolonial Entanglements.* Durham, NC: Duke University Press, 2017.
Sinha, Indra. *Animal's People.* New York: Simon and Schuster, 2009.
Sinha, Suvadip. *Entangled Fictions: Nonhuman Animals in an Indian World.* London: Routledge, 2023.
Slaughter, Joseph R. *Human Rights, Inc.* New York: Fordham University Press, 2007.
Slaymaker, Douglas. "The Hands of Bears, the Hands of Men: Animal Writing in Tawada Yoko's *Yuki no reshusei.*" In *Yoko Tawada: On Writing and Rewriting.* Ed. Douglas Slaymaker. Lanham, MD: Lexington Books, 2019.
Slicer, Deborah. "Joy." In *Ecofeminism: Feminist Intersections with Other Animals and the Earth.* Ed. Carol J. Adams and Lori Gruen, 2nd ed. London: Bloomsbury, 2022.
Smith, Jen Rose. "Exceeding Beringia: Upending Universal Human Events and Wayward Transits in Arctic Spaces." *Environment and Planning: Society and Space* 39.1 (2021): 158–75.
Smith, Linda Tuhiwai. *Decolonial Methodologies: Research and Indigenous Peoples.* London: Bloomsbury, 2021.
Smith, Mick. "Ecological Community, the Sense of the World, and Senseless Extinction." *Environmental Humanities* 2 (2013): 21–41.
Snaza, Nathan. *Animate Literacies: Literature, Affect, and the Politics of Humanism.* Durham, NC: Duke University Press, 2019.
Song, Min Hyoung. *Climate Lyricism.* Durham, NC: Duke University Press, 2022.
Soulsbury, Carl D. "Red Foxes." In *Urban Carnivores: Ecology, Conflict, and Conservation.* Ed. Stanley D. Gehrt, Seth P. D. Riley, and Brian L. Cypher. Baltimore: Johns Hopkins University Press, 2010.
Spivak, Gayatri Chakravorty. "Three Women's Texts and a Critique of Imperialism." *Critical Inquiry* 12 (1985): 243–61.
Steiner, Gary. *Animals and the Limits of Postmodernism.* New York: Columbia University Press, 2013.
Steinlight, Emily. *Populating the Novel: Literary Form and the Politics of Surplus.* Ithaca, NY: Cornell University Press, 2018.
Stengers, Isabelle. *Another Science Is Possible: A Manifesto for Slow Science.* London: Blackwell, 2017.

———. "Introductory Notes on an Ecology of Practices." *Cultural Studies Review* 11.1 (2005): 196.

Stengers, Isabelle, Brian Massumi, and Erin Manning. "History Through the Middle: Between Macro and Mesopolitics—an Interview with Isabelle Stengers." *Inflexions*, 25 November 2008. https://www.inflexions.org/n3_stengershtml.html

Stewart, Garrett. *Reading Voices: Literature and the Phonotext*. Berkeley: University of California Press, 1990.

Stobie, Cheryl. "Dystopian Dreams from South Africa: Lauren Beukes's *Moxyland* and *Zoo City*." *African Identities* 10.4 (2012): 367–80.

Stockton, Katherine Bond. *The Queer Child, or, Growing Sideways in the Twentieth Century*. Durham, NC: Duke University Press, 2009.

Stoekl, Allan. "After the Apocalypse: Two Versions of the Sustainability in Light of Climate Change." *Diacritics* 41.3 (2013): 40–57.

Stout, Daniel. *Corporate Romanticism: Liberalism, Justice, and the Novel*. New York: Fordham University Press, 2017.

Stromberg, Ernest. "Circles Within Circles: Linda Hogan's Rhetoric of Indigenism." In *From the Center of Tradition: Critical Perspectives on Linda Hogan*. Boulder: University of Colorado Press, 2003.

TallBear, Kim. "Beyond the Life/Not-Life Binary: A Feminist Indigenous Reading of Cryopreservation, Interspecies Thinking, and the New Materialisms." In *Cryopolitics: Frozen Life in a Melting World*. Ed. Joanna Radin and Emma Kowal. Cambridge, MA: MIT Press, 2017.

———. "Why Interspecies Thinking Needs Indigenous Standpoints." https://culanth.org/fieldsights/why-interspecies-thinking-needs-indigenous-standpoints

Tawada, Yoko. *Memoirs of a Polar Bear*. Trans. Susan Bernofsky. New York: New Directions, 2016.

———. "Tawada Yoko Does Not Exist." Trans. Douglas Slaymaker. In *Yoko Tawada: Voices from Everywhere*. Ed. Douglas Slaymaker. Lanham, MD: Lexington Books, 2007.

Taylor, Sunaura. *Beasts of Burden: Animal and Disability Liberation*. New York: New Press, 2017.

Tesky, Gordon. *Allegory and Violence*. Ithaca, NY: Cornell University Press, 1995.

Thompson, Evan. *Biology, Phenomenology, and the Sciences of Mind*. Cambridge, MA: Belknap Press, 2007.

Thompson, Hilary. *Novel Creatures: Animal Life in the New Millennium*. London: Routledge, 2018.

Todd, Zoe. "Indigenizing the Anthropocene." In *Art in the Anthropocene: Encounters Among Aesthetics, Politics, Environments and Epistemologies*. Ed. Heather Davis and Etienne Turpin. London: Open Humanities Press, 2015.

Totten, Monika, and Yoko Tawada. "Writing in Two Languages: A Conversation with Yoko Tawada." *Harvard Review* 17 (1999): 93–100.

Traisnel, Antoine. *Capture: American Pursuits and the Making of a New Animal Condition*. Minneapolis: University of Minnesota Press, 2020.

Tsai, Robin Chen-Hsing. "Animality, Biopolitics, and Umwelt in Amitav Ghosh's *The Hungry Tide*." In *Animalities: Literary and Cultural Studies Beyond the Human*. Ed. Michael Lundblad. Edinburgh: Edinburgh University Press, 2018.

Tuan, Yi-Fu. *Dominance and Affection: The Making of Pets*. New Haven, CT: Yale University Press, 1984.

Tuck, Eve. "Suspending Damage: A Letter to Communities." *Harvard Educational Review* 79.3 (2009): 407–27.

Vizenor, Gerald. *Fugitive Poses: Native American Indian Scenes of Absence and Presence*. Lincoln: University of Nebraska Press, 1998.

von Uexküll, Jacob. *A Foray into the Worlds of Animals and Humans*. Trans. Joseph D. O'Neil. Minneapolis: University of Minnesota Press, 2010.

Wadiwel, Dinesh. "Restriction, Norm, *Umwelt*: A Response." *New Literary History* 51.4 (2020): 751–63.

———. *The War Against the Animals*. Leiden, Netherlands: Brill, 2015.

Walkowitz, Rebecca. "On Not Knowing: Lahiri, Tawada, Ishiguro." *New Literary History* 51.2 (2020): 323–46.

Wallen, Martin. *Whose Dog Are You? The Technology of Dog Breeds and the Aesthetics of Modern Human-Canine Relations*. East Lansing: Michigan State University Press, 2017.

Walther, Sundhya. *Multispecies Modernity: Disorderly Life in Postcolonial Literature*. Waterloo, ON: Wilfred Laurier University Press, 2021.

Ward, Jesmyn. *Salvage the Bones*. New York: Bloomsbury, 2011.

Watt, Ian. *The Rise of the Novel*. Berkeley, CA: University of California Press, 1957.

Weaver, Harlan. "Becoming in Kind: Race, Class, Gender and Nation in Cultures of Dog Rescue and Dogfighting." *American Quarterly* 65.3 (2013): 689–709.

Weheliye, Alexander G. *Habeus Viscus: Racializing Assemblages, Biopolitics, and Black Feminist Theories of the Human*. Durham, NC: Duke University Press, 2014.

Weil, Kari. "Afterword: The Animal in the Mirror." In *Beastly Modernisms: The Figure of the Animal in Modernist Literature and Culture*. Ed. Saskia McCracken and Alex Goody. Edinburgh: Edinburgh University Press, 2023.

———. "The Animal Novel That Therefore This Is Not." In *New Approaches to the Twentieth-Century Anglophone Novel*. Ed. Syblie Baumbach and Birgit Neumann. London: Palgrave Macmillan, 2019.

———. *Thinking Animals: Why Animal Studies Now?* New York: Columbia University Press, 2012.

Wenzel, Jennifer. *The Disposition of Nature: Environmental Crisis and World Literature*. New York: Columbia University Press, 2019.

West, Anna. *Thomas Hardy and Animals*. Cambridge: Cambridge University Press, 2017.

Whitmarsh, Patrick. *Writing Our Extinction: Anthropocene Fiction and Vertical Science*. Stanford, CA: Stanford University Press, 2023.

Williams, Raymond. *Marxism and Literature*. Oxford: Oxford University Press, 1977.

Wilson, Angus. *The Old Men at the Zoo*. New York: Viking Press, 1961.

Wilson, Madeline. "Breaking Down Borders: Animal Bodies in Lauren Beukes's *Moxyland* and *Zoo City*." In *Postcolonial Animalities*. Ed. Suvadip Sinha and Amit R. Baishya. London: Routledge, 2019.

Wolfe, Cary. *Animal Rites: American Culture, the Discourse of Species, and Posthumanist Theory*. Chicago: University of Chicago Press, 2003.

———. *Before the Law: Humans and Other Animals in a Biopolitical Frame*. Chicago: University of Chicago Press, 2013.

———. "Human, All Too Human: 'Animal Studies' and the Humanities." *PMLA* 124.2 (2009): 564–75.

———. "In the Shadow of Wittgenstein's Lion: Language, Ethics, and the Question of the Animal." In *Zoontologies: The Question of the Animal*. Ed. Cary Wolfe. Minneapolis: University of Minnesota Press, 2003.

Woloch, Alex. *The One vs. the Many*. Princeton, NJ: Princeton University Press, 2003.

Womack, Craig. *Red on Red: Native American Literary Separatism*. Minneapolis: University of Minnesota Press, 1999.

Woodward, Wendy. "'The Only Facts Are Supernatural Ones': Dreaming Animals and Trauma in Some Contemporary Southern African Texts." In *Indigenous Creatures, Native Knowledges, and the Arts*. Ed. Wendy Woodward and Susan McHugh. London: Palgrave Macmillan, 2017.

Wynter, Sylvia. "Towards the Sociogenic Principle: Fanon, the Puzzle Conscious Experience, of 'Identity' and What It's Like to Be 'Black.'" In *National Identity and Sociopolitical Change: Latin America Between Marginalization and Integration*. Ed. Mercedes Durán-Cogan and Antonio Gómez-Moriana. Minneapolis: University of Minnesota Press, 1999.

Young, Robert. *Colonial Desire: Hybridity in Theory, Culture, and Race*. London: Routledge, 1995.

Yousef, Nancy. *The Aesthetic Commonplace: Wordsworth, Eliot, Wittgenstein, and the Language of Every Day*. Oxford: Oxford University Press, 2022.

Yusoff, Kathryn. "Politics of the Anthropocene: Formation of the Commons as a Geologic Process." *Antipode* 50.1 (2017): 55–76.

INDEX

abstraction: allegory and, 18, 91, 219n50, 219n52; animals as, 47; Anthropocene and, 169, 218n38, 326n28; appropriation and, 213n117; conceptual, 116; example of, 21; function of, 6; living things as, 218n35; resistance to, 15–16
Ackerley, J. R., 114
Adenjunmobi, Moradewun, 228n11
Adiga, Aravind, 41, 166
affect, in theory, 2, 13, 16, 64, 162, 200–201; in *Antinomies of Realism*, 24, 51, 164, 173; in comparative cognition, 24–25, 107, 174; and literary style, 30, 131–134, 170; use of in zoos, 38–39. *See also specific novels*
affective flatness, 23–24
affordances, 6, 8, 11, 22, 34
African Americans, 115, 116, 117, 126
Agamben, Giorgio, 9, 47, 48
Ahuja, Neel, 37
Alexis, André, 228n12
allegiances, 13–14, 115

allegory: affect and, 24; African, 225n62; animal, 5, 8, 38–46; animal novels after, 28–34; biopolitical, 20, 36, 42, 48, 95–96, 201; capture and, 17, 49; as challenge, 47; characteristics of, 17–18; in character systems, 25; contemporary, 16; counter, 124; critique of, 48, 50; defined, 65; effectiveness of, 5–6; form of, 49; function of, 16, 201, 218n38; human soul and, 17; in *Life of Pi* (Martel), 36; limitations of, 16; management need and, 47; to milieu, 15–20, 43; national, 23; political authoritarianism, 47; realism and, 51–52; sacrificial, 96, 102–3; significance of, 40; skepticism regarding, 125; strategy of, 200–201; style as complicating, 32; as trope, 71; in zoobreak novels, 35; zoos and, 38–46. *See also specific novels*
Allegory and Ideology (Jameson), 51
Allen, Paula Gunn, 144–45

265

INDEX

analogy, 12, 19, 57, 117, 210n72, 218n35
Anderson, Amanda, 134, 173
Andrews, Kristen, 8, 170
animal allegories, 5, 8, 38–46. *See also* allegory; specific novels
Animal Capital (Shukin), 47–48
Animal Farm (Orwell), 82, 83
animal fiction, cultural shifts and, 6. *See also specific novels*
animality, 42, 45
animalization, 47, 48–49, 242n53
animal narration/narratives, 62, 63–64, 66–69. *See also specific novels*
animals: affinities of, 40; allegorical role of, 23; alliances with, 30; autonomy and, 16; biopolitics and, 20, 40, 95; bodily responsiveness of, 29; capacities of, 66–67, 81–82, 221n5; centrality of, 2, 24; characteristics of, 84, 125; collaboration by, 107; communication of, 81–82; companionate relationships with, 24, 94–95; comparative cognition and, 7–8, 174; consciousness of, 174–75, 196; conservation of, 215n5; as creaturely, 28–29; cross-species relationships of, 57–58; death of, 9, 28, 67, 95; differentiation of, 48; eating of, 84; ecological devastation and, 131; endangered, 130–31; environmental world of, 106–7; as experiencing, agential subjects, 29–30; as fiction figures, 45–46; as formal innovations, 1; functions of, 190; grief toward, 168; human agency and, 150; human response to, 179–80; human responsibility toward, 43, 93–94, 168; incident reports and, 194; individualization of, 211n97; kinship of, 164; knowing, in the subjunctive, 176–89; knowledge of, 193; legal recognition of, 66–67; liminal, 189, 190; as literary characters, historically, 23; marginalization

of, 216n24; melancholic connection with, 49; as mirrors, 44; mixed communities of, 164; mood and, 25; mourning for, 146; pain and, 54; perception of, 174, 192; personhood of, 85; political status of, 84, 95; power relations and, 234n80; racial coding of, 84; sacrifice of, 95; self-exoticization of, 216n24; self-harm of, 56–57; sentience of, 150–51; sound and, 111–12, 113; species differences of, 84; suffering of, 28, 66–67; taxonomy of, 216n21; territories of, in cities, 191–92; as tropes, 47, 48; violence against, 28; vulnerability of, 28, 38; war against, 16; in war zones, 40; way of being of, 106; women's roles regarding, 98; world-formation and, 9. *See also specific novels*
Animal's People (Sinha), 41–42, 47, 240n1
The Animal That Therefore I Am (Derrida), 67, 95
animal trainers, 77, 224n47
Animate Literacies (Snaza), 10
Anjaria, Ulka, 168, 212n98
Anker, Elizabeth, 20, 42, 45, 48, 102
Anthropocene, 124, 167, 168, 171, 198
anthropocentrism, 17, 36, 44, 63, 94, 212n99, 221n6
anthropomorphism, 59, 100
anthropophagy, 36
Antinomies of Realism (Jameson), 51, 173
Aporias (Derrida), 67
Apter, Emily, 73
Arendt, Hannah, 65, 66, 67–68, 75, 89, 98, 224n54
Aristotle, 66, 222n18
Armbruster, Karla, 95
Armstrong, Nancy, 2, 22
Armstrong, Philip, 47, 102, 218n35
Attridge, Derrick, 102

INDEX

Austen, Jane, 153
Auster, Paul, 228n11
Austerlitz (Sebald), 49
authoritarianism, 47–48, 64, 71, 90
Auyoung, Elaine, 202, 241–42n31

Baghdad Zoo, 216n23
Banfield, Ann, 135
Bartoszyńska, Katarzyna, 31, 135
Beecroft, Alexander, 211n87
Beer, Gillian, 2–3
Being and Time (Heidegger), 25
Bekoff, Marc, 208n31
Beloved (Morrison), 117
Bengal Tiger at the Baghdad Zoo (Joseph), 216n23
Benjamin, Walter, 17, 49, 225n56
Bennett, Joshua, 30, 41, 83, 98, 115, 125, 157
Ben-Yishai, Ayelet, 173–74, 227n1
Berger, John, 39, 228n11
Berlant, Lauren, 133, 233n74
Berlin Zoo, 39, 69–82
Bernofsky, Susan, 71
Beukes, Lauren, 40
Bhopal disaster, 41
Bildungsroman, 37, 41, 53, 143
Billie, James E., 140
biopolitical allegories, 20, 95–96, 201. *See also specific novels*
biopolitics, 6, 15, 18, 36, 40–42, 48, 95
biopower, 2, 19, 47
Birch, Carol, 166
birds, 196
birth, 67–68, 98, 99
The Bitch (Quintana), 33, 96
Black Beauty (Sewell), 63
Black consciousness, 209n46
Black maternity, 98
Black studies, 5, 15, 30, 83, 115–17, 138
Blake, William, 36
Bleak House (Dickens), 237–38n53
Boehrer, Bruce, 222n8

Boggs, Colleen Glenney, 28
Boisseron, Bénédicte, 13, 30, 83, 115, 116
Bon Bibi legends, 180, 187
Bond Stockton, Katherine, 121
Bowen-Mercer, Carrie, 145
Boxall, Peter, 20–21, 30, 64, 173
Braidotti, Rosi, 143, 164
Braverman, Irus, 38, 39
Brown, Laura, 29, 96
Bruyn, Ben De, 155–56, 157
Bulawayo, NoViolet, 5, 32, 64, 82–92, 225n56
Butler, Judith, 213n120
Byrd, Jodi, 136, 137, 145, 157, 162

Canguilhem, Georges, 1, 5, 7, 8, 9–10, 12, 18–19, 111
capitalism, 41, 48, 50, 171
Capitalocene, 168
captivity, 39, 49, 78, 106, 179–80
capture: allegory and, 38–39, 49–52; anthropocentric logic of, 221n6; biopolitics and, 5, 15–20; example of, 132; figuration and, 210n72; milieu as, 14, 30, 138; of population, 24
care: ethics of, 4, 20, 43, 61, 111, 164 214n135, 215n7, 239n94; pastoral, 19, 45
Casanova, Pascale, 21
cats, 35–36, 99–100, 230n29. *See also specific novels*
character, 2–3, 23–24, 63, 170
Cheah, Pheng, 8–9, 21, 89, 178, 186–87
Chen-Hsing Tsai, Robin, 183
Cherokee nation, 158–59
Chez, Keridiana, 103
The Child to Come (Sheldon), 124
Chrulew, Matthew, 39
circus, in the Soviet Union, 76–77
citizenship, 45
climate crisis, 29, 33, 138, 161, 167, 171–72, 179. *See also specific novels*

Coetzee, J. M., 94, 95, 101–3, 112–13
cognition: of animals, 5, 7, 8, 11–12, 34, 63; of dogs, 111; of dolphins, 182–83
Cole, Ernest Dominic, 190
Colebrook, Claire, 164
collective narration, 86–88
colonialism, 160, 216n21
coming-of-age narrative, 23, 28, 37, 41, 143
companion species narratives, 37, 95, 96, 97, 105, 129. *See also* petkeeping; specific novels
comparative cognition, 174–76
Comte, Auguste, 7
consciousness: of animals, 174–75; defined, 205n3; of humans, 3, 42; as privileged category, 197; as sentience, 26
contemporary fiction, 3–4, 50, 162. *See also specific novels*
Course on Positive Philosophy (Comte), 7
creature: characteristics of, 8; cognition, 16; defined, 28, 29; environmental collaboration by, 8; operations of, 28; vital norms of, 8
Creaturely Forms (O'Key), 28–29
crisis, 15, 27–29, 133, 172. *See also specific novels*
Crist, Eileen, 131
critique: allegory and, 6, 15–18, 20, 31, 47–48, 168; method of, 2, 10, 23, 25, 27, 41, 136, 201, 222n13. *See also specific novels*
Cruel Optimism (Berlant), 233n74
Cusk, Rachel, 1

Dames, Nicholas, 207n18
Damrosch, David, 21
Darwin, Charles, 2–3
Darwinism, 231n47
Davé, Naisargi, 29
Dayan, Colin, 96, 115, 121
death: of animals, 9, 28, 67, 95; of humans, 9, 95; powerlessness in, 97; as protection, 95; as sacrifice, 101–3; as shared with animals, 95
death allegories, 95, 98. *See also specific novels*
DeCaroli, Steven, 210n77, 210n78
decolonization, 40, 133, 137
defamiliarization, 31
dehumanization, 58–59
DeKoven, Marianne, 102
Deleuze, Gilles, 12, 15–16, 95, 227n6
Deloria, Vine, 236n28
DeLoughrey, Elizabeth M., 49
Derrida, Jacques: on animals, 47; on animal's gaze, 44; *The Animal That Therefore I Am*, 67, 95; *Aporias*, 67; on cats, 35; on death, 67; on fabulation, 46; on Heidegger, 106, 231n47; on milieu, 15; on mortality, 95; on pet love, 227n6; "The Politics of Friendship," 95
description, as narrative mode, 162
Despret, Vinciane, 30
Diabate, Naminata, 84–85
Diamond, Cora, 67
Dickens, Charles, 105, 192, 194, 231n39, 237–38n53
Dickey, Bronwyn, 119
Dimock, Wai Chee, 172
Disgrace (Coetzee), 101–3, 112–13, 200
DJ Euphonik, 86
Dog Days (Nganang), 228n11
dogfighting, 118–19, 123
dog narratives, 95, 96, 97, 105, 129. *See also specific novels*
dogs: birthing by, 123, 125–26; cognition of, 111; communication by, 111–12, 113; cynical friendship with, 105; as emotional supplement, 102–3; environmental world of, 106–7; euthanasia of, 102; as figures for Blackness, 115, 116; as friends, 93; human worlds

and, 232n57; Hurricane Katrina and, 126–27; love for, 118; mourning by, 100–101; pit bulls as, 115, 118–19, 121; power of, 229n15; relationships with, 121; as scapegoat, 102; sensory world of, 108–9; sexuality of, 114, 120–21; in shared milieu of the home, 96; sitting tone of, 107; *Umwelt* of, 107. *See also* companion species narratives; petkeeping; specific novels
dolphins, 181–85
Donaldson, Sue, 65
Donovan, Josephine, 63, 102, 164
Driscoll, Kári, 182
Ducks, Newburyport (Ellmann): decolonization and, 137; as frenetic, 148; milieus in, 33; narrator in, 136; overview of, 130–32, 148–63, 214–15n4; repetition in, 148–49; rhythm in, 154, 163, 164; rumination in, 134, 148–49, 160–61, 164; structure of, 161–62; tragedy in, 133
Duncan, Ian, 241n21

eating, 126
The Echo Maker (Powers), 168
ecocriticism, 27, 34, 124, 164, 169, 203
ecological activism, 6, 27, 80, 201
ecological crisis, 124, 131
ecology: critical method and, 208n4, 211n87; ethology and, 7; milieu and, 20–23, 27, 131, 137, 164; narrative style and, 99, 167; scaling as, 211n87; wildlife, 191
Eliot, George, 3, 232n55
Elizabeth Costello (Coetzee), 94, 95, 102
Ellmann, Lucy, 5, 33, 130, 131, 133–34, 214–15n4. *See also Ducks, Newburyport* (Ellmann)
Endangered Species Act, 140
endangerment, 130–31, 146. *See also* specific novels

English, James, 129
environment, 2–3, 5, 8, 9, 10, 26
epistemophilia, 105
Esposito, Roberto, 45, 48, 86
Esty, Jed, 171
ethology, 137–38
euthanasia, 102
extinction narratives, 132–33. *See also* specific novels
The Eyes and the Impossible (Eggers), 221n13

fables, function of, 45, 46
The Fairie Queene (Spenser), 36
Fanon, Frantz, 11
Felski, Rita, 10, 20, 25, 48, 133
Ferguson, Frances, 135, 153, 154
fiction, theory of the world in, 202. *See also specific novels*
Fielder, Brigitte, 117, 129
Fifteen Dogs (Alexis), 228n12
Figlerowicz, Marta, 23
figurative language, 16, 207n20, 210n72
first-person narrative: by animals, 63 (*See also* animal narration/narratives); characteristics of, 22; in extinction narratives, 133; function of, 133; limitations of, 211n93; rumination and, 134; value of, 11. *See also specific novels*
Flat Protagonists (Figlerowicz), 23
Fleissner, Jennifer, 8
Fletcher, Angus, 47
Flight Behavior (Kingsolver), 168
Floyd, George, 88
Flush (Woolf), 229n21
focalization, 87
Fogarasi, Christina, 100, 226n86, 229n26
A Foray into the Worlds of Animals and Humans (von Uexküll), 183
form, 1–12, 20–28. *See also* allegory; style; specific novels
formalism, 28, 31, 201

Forna, Aminatta, 5, 34, 168–70, 189–98
Fornoff, Carolyn, 175
Foucault, Michel, 18–19, 50–51, 63, 72, 168
foxes, 189, 190. *See also Happiness* (Forna)
Fraiman, Susan, 25, 94
Freedgood, Elaine, 76, 162–63
free indirect discourse, 4, 33–34, 59, 89, 102, 134–35, 147, 152–53, 170, 203
Freeman, Elizabeth, 26, 36–37, 79
The Friend (Nunez), 33, 96–98, 100–101, 103–12, 129
The Fundamental Concepts of Metaphysics (Heidegger), 106

Gallagher, Catherine, 24, 203
Galloway, Alexander, 48
Ganguly, Debjani, 21
Garnett, David, 216n21
Genette, Jean, 5, 147, 153, 163
geologic deep time, 144
Ghosh, Amitav, 5, 34, 166, 168–70, 171–72, 176–89, 198
Gibson, James, 8
Glenney Boggs, Colleen, 28
Gliddon, George, 117
Glissant, Édouard, 14, 212n99
globalization, 41, 71, 82, 201
Glory (Bulawayo), 32, 64–66, 82–92, 226n69
Gnadenhutten Massacre, 159
Goldstein, Amanda Jo, 205n3
Goodlad, Lauren, 171
Great Chain of Being, 216n21
The Great Derangement (Ghosh), 171–72, 176
grief, 146, 168
grievable lives, 213n120
Grosz, Elizabeth, 7, 207n27
Gruen, Lori, 164
Guattari, Félix, 12, 95, 227n6
The Guest Cat (Hiraide), 230n29

Gun Island (Ghosh), 172
Gunn Allen, Paula, 144–45

Hale, Dorothy, 206n8
Hamlet (Shakespeare), 36
Happiness (Forna), 34, 168–70, 189–98
Haraway, Donna: criticism of, 227n6; on dog breeding, 229n15; on figurative language, 16; influence of, 172; on interspecies collaboration, 77; on multispecies existence, 29, 37; on ordinary multispecies living, 94; on situated knowledge, 192; on species, 27; *Staying with the Trouble*, 192
Harney, Stefano, 13
Haushofer, Marlen, 93–94
Hayot, Eric, 21, 22, 26, 175
Hearne, Vicki, 77
Heidegger, Martin, 9, 25, 67, 106, 231n47
Heise, Ursula, 43, 131, 172, 176
Heller-Roazen, Daniel, 26
Henrichon, Nico, 216n23
Herman, David, 7, 29, 63, 96, 97, 203
heterodiegetic narration, 221n5
Hiraide, Takahashi, 230n29
Hobbes, Thomas, 224n54
Hogan, Linda: influence of, 5; mode of attention of, 133–34; on multispecies existence, 29; *The Radiant Lives of Animals*, 137, 139, 145, 157; on world(s), 139. *See also Power* (Hogan)
Holland, Sharon Patricia, 18, 30, 83, 99, 115
homology, 12
Horowitz, Alexandra, 111
household, natural community in, 120–21
Houser, Heather, 26, 207n19, 236n34
Howell, Alison, 216n23
Howell, Philip, 96
How the Dead Dream (Miller), 42–43
Huggan, Graham, 177, 218n34

The Human Condition (Arendt), 67–68
humanism, 6, 36, 40, 51, 189
human rights, 45
humans: animalization of, 48–49; as animal species, 5, 68; anthropocentric theory of, 194–95; behavior of, 154–55; captivity of, 78; consciousness of, 3; death of, 9, 95; decentering viewpoint of, 190; differentiation of, 48; as herd animals, 198; knowledge-production of, 10; linguistic agency of, 66; as political animal, 66; resilience of, 197; response to animals by, 179–80; scale for, 2–3; social and cultural determinants of, 13; soul of, 17; as special kinds of beings, 68; as storytelling species, 11; subtraction of, from the environment, 178–79; thought structure of, 10
humor, 62
The Hungry Tide (Ghosh), 34, 166, 168–70, 176–89, 198
Hurricane Katrina, 114, 116, 117, 124, 126–27

If Body (Lehrer), 233n74
immigration, 193
impersonality, 23, 26, 33, 73–74, 80, 86, 91, 134, 202
incident reports, 194
Indigenous studies/theory: cosmology of, 224n44; importance of, 156–57, 236n27–30; killing animals and, 140; more-than-human milieus and, 136–39; overview of, 13–16; perspectives from, 130–31; relationships and, 164; repetition in, 238n54; silencing in, 240n96
individualism, and character, 20–21, 63, 81, 86; in theory of the novel, 1–6, 23–25, 50–51, 131, 154, 212n103; as western ideology, 17, 45, 212n99

initiation, 69–70, 75–76, 85, 89
institution-building, 233n72
interiority, 109–10, 167–68
internationalism, 189
IQ84 (Murakami), 230n29

Jackson, Michael, 76
Jameson, Fredric: on affect and allegory, 24; on allegory, 47, 48, 50; *Antinomies of Realism*, 51, 173; on humanism, 51; on intelligibility and experience, 163–64; on perception, 242n31; *The Political Unconscious*, 50; on realism, 50, 173; on "Third World" novels, 23, 50; on waning protagonicity, 37
Jamison, Dale, 208n31
Jamrach's Menagerie (Birch), 166
Joseph, Rajiv, 216n23
The Jungle Book (Kipling), 57–58
Justice, Daniel Heath, 135, 137, 138

Kafka, Franz, 73
Keen, Suzanne, 202
Keenleyside, Heather, 16, 29, 47, 68, 125, 210n72
Kendall-Morwick, Karalyn, 95, 107
Killer Kua, 86
King (Berger), 228n11
King, Amy M., 206–7n15
Kingsolver, Barbara, 168
kinship, 98, 115, 127, 130, 136–38, 142, 164
Kipling, Rudyard, 57–58
Knott, Suzuko Mausel, 72
knowledge-production, 14–15
Kochai, Jamil Jan, 228n13
Kornbluh, Anna: on allegory, 218n38; on building worlds, 136; on characterological depth, 23; on first-person narrative, 211n93; on free indirect discourse, 135; on metalepsis, 207n16; on realism, 52; on the world, 27
Kramnick, Jonathan, 22

Kreilkamp, Ivan, 24, 29, 50–51, 79, 211n97
Kupersmith, Violet, 225n65
Kurniawan, Eka, 41, 217n29
Kuzniar, Alice, 62, 100, 102, 105, 133
Kymlicka, Will, 65

Lamarck, Jean-Baptiste, 6–7
language, function of, in writing, 73–74
Lehrer, Rita, 233n74
Leviathan (Hobbes), 224n54
Levine, Caroline, 22, 26, 175
Li, Victor, 177
Liberation War (Zimbabwe), 84
Life of Pi (Martel), 32, 35, 36, 43–46
The Limits of Critique (Felski), 10
The Lion King (film), 36
lions, 36. *See also Ducks, Newburyport* (Ellmann)
literary realism, 22–23, 31, 33, 52, 241–42n31. *See also* realism
"The Living and Its Milieu" (Canguilhem), 7, 9–10
Lloyd, Christopher, 116, 126
London, 191, 194. *See also Happiness* (Forna)
London Zoo, 39
Lukàcs, Georg, 163, 172
Lupton, Julia Reinhard, 28, 98
Lynch, Deidre, 24, 212n102
lyrical style, 26
lyricism, 26, 53, 99, 111, 186, 212n111

MacVeagh, Molly, 189, 190, 197
Makdoumian, Helen, 140
Malamud, Randy, 54
Man, Paul de, 48, 71
A Man in the Zoo (Garnett), 216n21
Mann, Joelle, 88
Man Tiger (Kurniawan), 41, 217n29
Marichijhanpi, 177, 187
Maroo, Chetna, 228–29n13

Martel, Yann, 5, 32, 35, 43–46
Marx, Karl, 243n65
Marxism, 187
Massumi, Brian, 38
Mathur, Nayanika, 167
mating, 38, 160, 191
Mbembe, Achille, 42
McFarlane, Fiona, 166, 214n4
McGregor, Jon, 4–5
McGurl, Mark, 172
McHugh, Susan, 29, 30, 47, 83, 84, 95, 132, 141
McKittrick, Katherine, 207n20, 209n46
Melancholia's Dog (Kuzniar), 100
melancholy, 97, 105, 117–18
Memoirs of a Polar Bear (Tawada): allegory in, 32, 64–65, 91–92; lyricism in, 65, 74; narration in, 62; overview of, 64, 69–82; sense methods in, 79; vocality exploration in, 65–66
Menely, Tobias, 111, 219n52, 222n20
metalepsis, analysis of, 75–76, 86–87, 147–48; definition of, 5; in Genette, 5, 147, 153, 163; political value of 207n16, 222n15; prevalence in animal novels of, 65, 89, 203
method, environment and, 10
microenvironments, 183
Middlehoff, Frederike, 63–64
Middlemarch (Eliot), 3, 4
migrant novel, 71, 72
milieu: accessibility of, 10; affect and, 201; allegiances and, 13–14; allegory to, 15–20, 43; as biopolitical tool, 2; changing of, 12; as coded, 12; as ecological relationship, 19; emergence of, 12, 201; geographic, 116–17; human knowledge-production and, 10; in human thought and behavior, 10; as immanence, 12; individualism and, 2; knowledge production and, 14–15; as multidisciplinary concept, 11; multi-

species, 29, 168, 198; novel as, 20–28; as perceptible, 30; poetics of, 138; as political territory, 18; as problem concept, 14; questions regarding, 15–16; responsive zone in, 203; rhythm of, 12; rivalry of, 1; as sensed, 15; as sentience, 20–21; shared, 45, 96, 97, 111, 115; species relations in, 36; as territorialized, 18; theorizing, 6–15; *Umwelt versus,* 7; uneven possibilities of, 13; as vibratory, 12; as way of thinking about the world, 27–28; as work of art, 12. *See also specific novels*
Mill, John Stuart, 206n5
Miller, Lydia, 42
Million, Dian, 14
mood, 10, 16, 25–26, 109, 148, 202, 212n110. *See also* rumination; subjunctive
Moretti, Franco, 163
Morgan, Benjamin, 172
Morris, Pam, 167–68
Morrison, Toni, 117
mortality. *See* death
Moten, Fred, 13
motherhood, 78, 80, 115, 121, 122–24, 151–52
mountain lioness, 132, 139, 151–59. *See also Ducks, Newburyport* (Ellmann)
mourning, 100–101, 105, 146
Mr. Tiger Goes Wild (Brown), 215n4
Mugabe, Robert, 82, 83
Murakami, Haruki, 5, 32, 35, 36–37, 52–56, 230n29. *See also The Wind-Up Bird Chronicle* (Murakami)
Mwangi, Evan Maina, 28, 65, 83, 84, 217n27
My Dog Tulip (Ackerley), 114

Naess, Arne, 164
Nagel, Thomas, 11, 13, 150, 175, 209n56
Nagra, Dalijt, 216n24
naked agency, 84–85
Nash, Jennifer C., 98, 116
natality, 68–70, 75, 98, 114
National Theatre (London), 189
Nazis, 39
Neal, Andrew W., 216n23
Neirick, Miriam, 76, 224n47
Nelles, William, 221n5
Nersessian, Anahid, 27, 61
Ngai, Sianne, 81, 232n53
Nganang, Patrice, 228n11
The Night Guest (McFarlane), 166, 214n4
99 Nights in Logar (Kochai), 228n13
Noë, Alva, 8, 205n3
Norwood, Vera, 117
Nott, Josiah, 117
novel: affective flatness of, 23–24; capacity of, 201; community-making in, 21; contemporary, 24; function of, 21, 23; as milieu, 20–28; mood in, 25; world as key term for theory of, 21. *See also specific novels*
Novel Creatures (Thompson), 28–29
Nunez, Sigrid, 5, 33, 96–98, 99–100. *See also The Friend* (Nunez)

objective phenomenology, 11
Obreht, Téa, 5, 32, 35, 36–37, 56–60
oikos, 98, 120–21
O'Key, Dominic, 16, 28–29, 189, 243n64
The Old Men at the Zoo (Wilson), 216n21
Oliver, Kelly, 10, 68, 98
On Revolution (Arendt), 65
opaque, 14
Orcaella brevirostris (Irawaddy dolphin), 181–85
Ortiz-Robles, Mario, 16, 29, 35, 47, 83, 230n29
Orwell, George, 82, 84
oscillation, 185
otherness, 206n8
Outline (Cusk), 1

pain, 54
panthers, 131–32, 146–47. *See also Power* (Hogan)
Parry, Catherine, 28
pastoral power, 19, 38, 44, 50–51, 63, 168
perception: in animals, 7–10, 39, 50, 81, 107, 183–84, 192; constituting a milieu, 12–13, 19, 154; in literature, 164, 172–74, 198, 201, 203
personhood, 34, 64, 81, 83, 91, 138, 203
pet culture, 6, 93–99, 115
petkeeping: care in, 111; collaboration in, 107; companionate relationships in, 94–95; in Derrida, 95; human responsibility in, 93–94; intimacies of, 94–95; ontological captivity of, 106; of pit bulls, 115; process of, 106. *See also* companion species narratives
phenomenality, 7, 13, 15, 138
Pick, Anat, 29, 103, 229n23
pit bulls, 115, 118–19, 121. *See also* dogs
poetry, 111, 151, 178–79
The Political Unconscious (Jameson), 50
"The Politics of Friendship" (Derrida), 95
Poovey, Mary, 162
postcolonial studies, 15; example of, 15, 41–42, 69, 82; novel form and, 171, 176, 201, 211–12n24, 211–12n98, 215n13, 218n34, 221n4, 222n15
Powell, Rachell, 8, 12, 170–71, 174
Power (Hogan): decolonization and, 137; milieus in, 33; narrator in, 136; overview of, 131–32, 140–48, 156; rhythm in, 144–46; rumination in, 134, 144, 164; sense methods in, 132, 143–44; tragedy in, 133
Powers, Richard, 168
Pride of Baghdad (Henrichon), 216n23
Prince, Gerald, 222n15
Project Tiger, 177
Puig de la Bellacasa, Maria, 34

Quintana, Pilar, 33, 96

racialization, 2, 14, 18, 42, 157, 159
racial pseudoscience, 117
racism, 218n34
The Radiant Lives of Animals (Hogan), 137, 139, 145, 157
Rancière, Jacques, 12, 23, 202
rationalism, 94, 134
reading, 26–27, 201
realism: aesthetic dislocation and, 173; allegory and, 51–52; animal milieus and, 198–99; creaturely imagination of, 171–76; defined, 23, 173; events in, 172; examples of, 2–3, 22–23; givenness of the world and, 198–99; integration and, 174; interiority and, 167–68; limitations of, 34; modes of, 175–76; overview of, 167; perception in, 173; rejection of, 171–72; as revealing, 50; sensations in, 170; sense-making and, 172; sentience and, 172; structural gap and, 173; tension in, 173; world(s) and, 171. *See also* third-person narrative
realist fiction, 163–64, 168, 206–7n15, 241n21. *See also specific novels*
Reinhard Lupton, Julia, 28
repetition, 144–45, 148–49
"A Report to the Academy" (Kafka), 73
Reservoir 13 (McGregor), 4–5, 207n18
resilience, 197
resonance, 5–6, 26, 29, 31, 54, 113, 169
revenge, 154–55
rhythm: in critical method, 51–52, 173, 201; as a feature of milieu, 12–13; in narrative, 33, 98–99, 133–34, 181, 185, 206–7n15, 209n53, 238n54
Richardson, Samuel, 186
Ricoeur, Paul, 133, 152
Rilke, Rainer Maria, 111, 178–79, 182, 186, 188, 232n57, 242n50

Rohman, Carrie, 112
rooted transnationalism, 189
Rosa, Harmut, 26, 29
Rose, Deborah Bird, 130
Rosenberg, Aaron, 167, 172
rumination, 134, 144, 148–49, 160–61, 164, 235n14

sacrificial allegory, 96, 102–3. *See also* allegory
Sagan, Dorion, 137, 232n54
Salih, Sarah, 40
Salvage the Bones (Ward), 33, 95, 97–98, 111, 114–28
San Diego Zoo, 38–39
Santner, Eric, 28
scale: Anthropocene and, 124, 167, 175; novel form and, 170–75, 244n4; small, 21, 35, 37, 164; species and, 2, 9, 178, 185, 201, 203, 216n2
Scarry, Elaine, 202
Schmitt, Canon, 162
Schuller, Kyla, 2
The Seagull (Chekhov), 62
Sebald, W. G., 49
security, milieu and, 18
Security, Territory, Population (Foucault), 18
self-harm, 56–57
self-refashioning, 167
self-sovereignty, 42
sense, hierarchies of, 54–55
sense methods: defined, 26, 79; examples of, 36–37; function of, 53; in *Power* (Hogan), 132, 143–44; in *The Tiger's Wife* (Obrecht), 59; in *The Wind-Up Bird Chronicle* (Murakami), 54–55
sense of place, 5
sentience: allegory-as-critique and, 49; consciousness as, 26; defined, 205–6n4; as distributed property, 202; experience and, 8; individual's perceptions as, 4; milieu as, 20–21;

realism and, 172; rendering of, 2, 150–51; *Umwelt* as deep structure of, 8
settler colonialism, 160
Sewell, Anna, 63
sexuality, 114, 120–21, 122
Shaw, Harry, 173
sheep, 18–19, 50–51
Sheldon, Rebekah, 116, 124
shepherd, 19, 44, 50–51, 168
Shlovsky, Victor, 31
Shukin, Nicole, 47–48
Sikwane, Mbali, 86
simile, 11, 175
Singh, Julietta, 29, 42
Sinha, Indra, 41–42, 47, 240n1
Sinha, Suvadip, 29
situated knowledge, 192
Slaughter, Joseph R., 23, 41
Slaymaker, Douglas, 223n34
Smith, Jen Rose, 13–14, 138, 161
Snaza, Nathan, 10, 13, 29, 202
social media, 87–88
sociogenic principle, 10
Song, Min Hyoung, 26, 37, 53, 115
sovereignty, 19, 36, 47
Soviet Union, 76–77
speciesism, 218n34, 238n67
speech, 12, 37, 63–70, 98, 220–21n1, 222n18. *See also specific novels*
Spivak, Gayatri Chakravorty, 171
spontaneity, 87
state power, 19
Staying with the Trouble (Haraway), 192
Steinlight, Emily, 50–51, 240n8
Stengers, Isabelle, 14–15
Stewart, Garrett, 87–88
Stockton, Katherine Bond, 121
Stoekl, Allan, 167, 178
structures of feeling, 22–23
style, 2–4, 26–27, 203. *See also specific novels*
subjunctive, 175, 176–89

sublimity, 167
suffering, 19, 28, 67, 101, 146, 229n23, 230n28, 233n68
suicide, 103–4

TallBear, Kim, 137, 138
Tawada, Yoko, 5, 32, 64, 69–82, 91–92
Taylor, Sunaura, 37
territorialization, 12, 18
Tesky, Gordon, 17, 49
theory in the middle, 47–52
Theory of the Novel (Lukàcs), 172
third-person narrative: conflicts in, 168; creaturely milieu in, 170; logic of the "world" in, 172; objectivity of, 11; realism and, 167. *See also* realism; specific novels
"Third World" novels, 23, 50
"Tholukuthi Hey" (song), 86
Thompson, Evan, 205n4
Thompson, Hilary, 28–29, 46, 47, 177, 238n63
Tiffin, Helen, 177, 218n34
tigers: allegorical potential of, 36; anthropophagy and, 36; characteristics of, 36, 45, 180; conservation of, 215n5; distortions of perception regarding, 166–67; population decline of, 36; self-harm of, 56–57; sublimity of, 167; *Umwelt* of, 180–81; in zoobreaks, 35; in zoos, 38–39. *See also* specific novels
The Tiger's Wife (Obreht): affect in, 57–59; allegory in, 32; as alternative to path in animal studies, 61; companionship in, 37; overview of, 35, 36, 56–60; sense methods in, 36–37, 52, 59; value alliances in, 36–37
Timbuktu (Auster), 228n11
Time and Narrative (Ricoeur), 152
"Tippoo Sultan's Incredible White-Man-Eating Tiger Toy Machine!!!" (Nagra), 216–17n24

Todd, Zoe, 168, 236n28
tone, 25–26, 107, 108, 212n110
tracking, 158–59
tragedy, 132–33. *See also* specific novels
Traisnel, Antoine, 9, 17, 19, 29, 49–50
transit/transmotion, 157–58
transnationalism, 189
Trauerspiel (Benjamin), 49
trauma, 56, 88, 100, 108, 116, 133, 142–143, 189
Trexler, Adam, 172
Tsai, Robin Chen-Hsing, 183
Tuck, Eve, 40
Twitter, 87–88
two worlds, function of, 137. *See also* world(s)
"Tyger" (Blake), 36
Tyler, Ann, 151, 153

Umwelt: as behavioral milieu, 9–10; in comparative cognition, 170–71; as deep structure of sentience, 8; defined, 7, 13–14; of dogs, 107; feline, 32; as first-person portal, 12; limitations of, 108; nonreductive alignments and, 52–53; norming, 57; origin of, 50; realism and, 50; as self-organizing, 8; sensory inputs and, 174; of tigers, 180–81; zoos and, 39
Union Carbide plant (India), 41
United States v. James E. Billie, 140

Vaughn, Brian K., 216n23
Vermeule, Blakey, 202
Vizenor, Gerald, 16, 157
voice, 66, 68, 110, 112, 113–14, 124
von Uexküll, Jacob: on animal perfection, 231n47; on biology, 207n27; on dogs, 105; on environment, 106–7; ethology of, 20; *A Foray into the Worlds of Animals and Humans,* 183; influence of, 111; on milieu, 5; on narrative form,

11–12; on perception, 7, 9, 50, 174; on reciprocal genesis of meaning, 7–8; on *Umwelt*, 25, 39; on world, 137
vulnerability, 28, 38, 229n23

Waal, Franz de, 7
Wadiwel, Dinesh, 16, 52–53
Walkowitz, Rebecca, 71, 92
The Wall (Haushofer), 93–94
Wallen, Martin, 105
Walther, Sundya, 29, 41, 47, 167
waning protagonicity, 37
Ward, Jesmyn, 5, 33, 97–98, 114–29
Watt, Ian, 23
The Waves (Woolf), 206n14
Weheliye, Alexander G., 18
Weil, Kari, 29, 221n4
Weil, Simone, 29, 99, 213n122, 229n23
we-narration, 87
Wenzel, Jennifer, 26, 37, 175
Western Lane (Maroo), 228–29n13
What Animals Mean in the Fiction of Modernity (Armstrong), 218n35
What Are You Going Through (Nunez), 99–100
"What Is It Like to Be a Bat?" (Nagel), 11
The White Tiger (Adiga), 41, 166
Williams, Raymond, 22–23
Wilson, Angus, 216n21
The Wind-Up Bird Chronicle (Murakami): on allegory, 32; alliances in, 36–37; companionship in, 37; overview of, 35, 36, 52–56; sense methods in, 36–37, 52, 54–55
With Dogs at the Edge of Life (Dayan), 96
Wittgenstein, Ludwig, 63
Wolfe, Cary, 48, 62, 221n4
Woloch, Alex, 23, 25, 51, 240n8
wolves, 42–43
Woolf, Virginia, 206n14, 229n21
worlding/world-making, 8–9, 136, 138, 171, 173

world(s): aesthetic, 22; as anti-conceptual concept, 145; artwork interaction with, 22; boundaries of, 145; bubble imagery regarding, 183; as form, 22; function of, in the novel, 21, 137; grieving other, 139–48; literary texts as part of encountered, 22; meaning of, 139; as milieu, 13; opacity of, 14; phenomenality of, 138–39; realism and, 171; rifts between, 145; sensing of, 14; separate, 145–46; as temporal openness, 21; theory of the novel and, 21; in third-person realism, 172
World War II, 39, 57
Wynter, Sylvia, 5, 10, 11, 13, 69, 209n46

Yang, K. Wayne, 40
Yong, Ed, 7
Young, Robert, 216n21
Yousef, Nancy, 206n13
Yusoff, Kathryn, 144

Zimbabwe, 82, 84
zoobreak novels: alliances in, 36–37; characteristics of, 35; companionship in, 37; lyricism in, 53; sense methods in, 36–37, 52, 54–55, 59; waning protagonicity in, 37. *See also specific novels*
The Zoo Box (Steinke and Cohn), 215n4
Zoo City (Beukes), 40, 47
Zoological Philosophy (Lamarck), 6–7
zoopoetics, 64
zoos: allegorical, 38–46; Berlin Zoo, 39, 69–82; captivity and, 39–40; caring in, 39; cultural histories of, 39; London Zoo, 39; organization of, 216n21; power relations and, 39–40; recognition in, 42–43; San Diego Zoo, 38–39; tactics of, 38–39; *Umwelt* and, 39; use of space in, 39

The authorized representative in the EU for product safety and compliance is:
Mare Nostrum Group B.V.
Mauritskade 21D
1091 GC Amsterdam
The Netherlands
Email address: gpsr@mare-nostrum.co.uk

KVK chamber of commerce number: 96249943

The authorized representative in the EU for product safety and compliance is:
Mare Nostrum Group
B.V Doelen 72
4831 GR Breda
The Netherlands